Lineberger Memorial

Library

D1599249

Lutheran Theological Southern Seminary   Columbia, S.C.

THE LOEB CLASSICAL LIBRARY

FOUNDED BY JAMES LOEB 1911

EDITED BY

JEFFREY HENDERSON

SENECA

IX

TRAGEDIES

II

LCL 78

SENECA

OEDIPUS · AGAMEMNON · THYESTES

[SENECA]

HERCULES ON OETA · OCTAVIA

EDITED AND TRANSLATED BY

JOHN G. FITCH

HARVARD UNIVERSITY PRESS
CAMBRIDGE, MASSACHUSETTS
LONDON, ENGLAND
2004

⁵⁄₀ M-W ⁶⁄₀₄ 21.50

Copyright © 2004 by the President and Fellows
of Harvard College
All rights reserved

LOEB CLASSICAL LIBRARY® is a registered trademark
of the President and Fellows of Harvard College

Library of Congress Catalog Card Number 2004042428
CIP data available from the Library of Congress

ISBN 0-674-99610-0

Composed in ZephGreek and ZephText by
Technologies 'N Typography, Merrimac, Massachusetts.
Printed and bound by Edwards Brothers, Ann Arbor, Michigan
on acid-free paper made by Glatfelter, Spring Grove, Pennsylvania.

CONTENTS

ACKNOWLEDGMENTS

In addition to the debts acknowledged in Volume 1, my thanks are due to Cedric Littlewood and Marcus Wilson for commenting on my draft material on *Thyestes* and *Octavia* respectively. As someone enjoying the otium of retirement, I appreciate their finding time in busy professional schedules to share their insight and expertise with me, and so with readers of this edition. Rolando Ferri kindly gave me access to the proofs of his edition of *Octavia* while I was preparing this volume. Thanks also to Scott Smith for allowing me to see an early draft of his translation of *Thyestes*.

J.G.F.

Abbreviations in bibliographies and notes are those of *The Oxford Classical Dictionary*, 3rd edn. (Oxford, 1996), xxix–liv.

Senecan Plays:

Ag = Agamemnon

Herc = Hercules

Med = Medea

Oed = Oedipus

Pha = Phaedra

Phoen = Phoenician Women

Thy = Thyestes

Tro = Trojan Women

Probably Not By Seneca:

HO = Hercules on Oeta

Oct = Octavia

OEDIPUS

INTRODUCTION

Background

An oracle came once to Laius, king of Thebes, that he would die at the hands of his own son. Laius and his queen Jocasta therefore handed the infant to Phorbas, their chief shepherd, to be exposed on Mt Cithaeron with a metal rod driven through his ankles. But instead Phorbas passed him to another shepherd in the service of Polybus and Merope, king and queen of Corinth. Being childless, the royal couple raised the infant as their own son, and he was named Oedipus, Swollen-foot, for his injuries.

As a young man, Oedipus received an oracle from Delphi that he was fated to kill his father and marry his mother. He fled from Corinth, believing his parents to be Polybus and Merope. During his travels he was driven violently off the road in a remote area by an old man in a chariot, whom he killed in angry retaliation: the old man, unknown to Oedipus, was Laius. When his travels brought him to Thebes, Oedipus freed the city from the murderous Sphinx by solving the riddle she posed, and the grateful Thebans bestowed on him the vacant throne and the hand of Queen Jocasta in marriage.

Many years have passed since then, and sons and daughters have been born to Oedipus and Jocasta. But now an all-consuming plague has descended on Thebes, as a result of this ongoing, albeit unwitting, incest. Oedipus must find a solution for this new threat to the city. To this end he has sent Creon, the brother of Jocasta, to consult Apollo's oracle at Delphi.

Summary

Act 1
Oedipus expresses his anxieties over his predicted fate and the present plague in Thebes. However, he vigorously rejects Jocasta's charge of spinelesssness.

Ode 1. The chorus describes the plague's deadly effect on the people of Thebes, animals and plants.

Act 2
Creon reports the response of the Delphic Oracle, that Laius' murderer must leave Thebes. Oedipus pronounces a curse on the unknown murderer. Tiresias orders a divinatory sacrifice; his daughter Manto describes to him the omens of the sacrificial fire and the animals' entrails. Unable to name the murderer, Tiresias proposes to summon Laius' ghost.

Ode 2. An ode in honour of Bacchus as a Theban god associated with the vital forces of nature.

Act 3
Creon reluctantly announces the results of the necromancy: Laius' ghost has accused Oedipus himself both of the murder and of incest. Oedipus imprisons Creon on suspicion of conspiracy with Tiresias.

Ode 3. The chorus believes the cause of the plague

is not Oedipus, but the gods' longstanding anger against Thebes.

Act 4
By questioning Jocasta, the old Corinthian who received Oedipus as an infant, and the shepherd Phorbas who handed the infant to the Corinthian, Oedipus realises the truth.

Ode 4. Praise of modest status, as opposed to the perils of high status.

Act 5
Scene 1. A messenger describes Oedipus' self-blinding.
    Choral interval: the power of Fate.
Scene 2. Jocasta speaks to Oedipus and commits suicide. Oedipus takes himself into exile.

Comment

Seneca's play is recognisably based on Sophocles' *Oedipus the King* (whether at first hand or through intermediaries), but also diverges from it in large measure. Stern critics would see these divergences as signs of degeneration from the standards of a renowned ancestor. But it will be more fruitful to inquire what the significance of these divergences might be, granting Seneca an artist's right to shape something new out of inherited material.

Sophocles' Oedipus is initially a benign ruler amidst his people, self-confident and determined. In complete contrast, Seneca's Oedipus at the beginning of his play is isolated and already obsessed with anxiety and guilt. This is in keeping with the inward turn of Seneca's dramas and their concern with mental states (see vol. 1 p. 5). Oedipus' un-ease is due in part to his possession of supreme power, and in part to his awareness of the prophecy that dooms him to kill his father and marry his mother. These two sources of fear reinforce each other: he suspects that as king he is somehow responsible for the plague, and he links that re-sponsibility with the crimes he is fated to commit.

In Sophocles' play there is a thematic contrast between knowledge and ignorance, and a related contrast between sight and blindness. Oedipus, who earlier had sufficient in-sight to solve the Sphinx's riddle, sets himself to solve the new mystery of the plague, and succeeds by unremitting intelligent inquiry; but Tiresias, though blind, has an even sharper insight into the truth. In Seneca, however, Oedi-pus' inquiry is handled in a brief, perfunctory fashion in just a hundred lines (768–867), while Tiresias' blindness has exactly the opposite significance to what it had in Soph-ocles: "For one lacking sight, much of the truth lies hid-den" (295). Indeed Seneca's play emphasises concealment and the "hidden." Kingship itself hides many evils behind its attractive facade (7). Creon finds the Delphic Oracle's response "entangled" and cryptic (212–216), whereas in Sophocles he thinks it clear (96, 106). Potentially revealing omens are concealed in the body and womb of the sacri-ficial heifer, and even when they are brought to light, their significance is hidden from the expert interpreter Tiresias. Truth must therefore be sought from an even remoter hid-ing place, the nether world. Even when plainly stated by the ghost of Laius (who first tries to conceal himself, 621), the truth remains hidden from Oedipus and the chorus (709) because it seems incredible. The chorus' own lan-guage of "unnatural parturition" and sons returned to the mother's bosom (731, 746–747) has a significance hidden from it.

The deep disquiet of Seneca's Oedipus arises not only from his consciousness that much is hidden, but also from his position as king. In Senecan drama kingship is regularly a source of unease for the ruler, because he is a lightning rod for external dangers to the state, and also because he is inevitably oppressive to, and feared by, his subjects. Oedipus automatically assumes that Laius was feared in this way (243). The tree that dominates the Dircaean grove is emblematic of kingship: it both protects lesser trees and at the same time oppresses them with its heavy shade (542–544). Power cannot be shared (as *Thyestes* and *Phoenician Women* attest), so that the ruler is isolated from potential peers as well as from subjects, an isolation that fuels his paranoia. Once Oedipus comes to believe that Creon is plotting against him, he finds grounds for suspicion even in Creon's political inactivity, even indeed in his loyalty (682–686). This is the kind of paranoia depicted in Suetonius' and Tacitus' accounts of several Roman emperors. From Seneca on, tyranny is a recurrent theme in both historical and imaginative literature at Rome. The Nero of the *Octavia* echoes Oedipus verbally[1] as well as in some of his attitudes.

---

[1] *Quidquid excelsum est cadat*, *Oct* 471: *omne quod dubium est cadat*, *Oed* 702. It has been suggested that the Oedipus of Seneca's play was intended as a specific parallel to Nero, who killed his mother as Oedipus does in a sense (*Oed* 1044–1045), and allegedly committed incest with her. But the play was probably written before Nero's reign (see vol. 1 pp. 12–13). The similarity of Nero's actions to mythical precedents reflects the nature of power itself.

In an *Oedipus* play the Oedipal overtones of this view
of power become apparent. As the possessor of political
power both oppresses and fears those below him, so with
the possessor of power in the family. Laius must either kill
his son or be killed by him: it is not difficult to see this as a
metaphor for any dominating father. Laius could not even
share the road with an unknown young man (770). Seneca's
play, then, combines political and psychological issues in a
way that is based in Sophocles but goes beyond him.

The meanings attached to Oedipus' self-blinding are
also very different in Sophocles and Seneca. In Sophocles
Oedipus explains that he could not bear, for shame, to look
upon his family, whether in the world of life or of death;
but his self-blinding also fits the play's thematic association
of blindness with inner sight, that is, knowledge of truth.
In Seneca that thematic association disappears, as we have
seen. His Oedipus fastens on blindness as an *adequate*
self-punishment: death by the sword would be too brief,
whereas blindness is a prolonged death, a death-in-life
(936–949). In fact it places him in a no-man's-land between the world of the living (characterised by light and
sight) and the dead (949–951): this is emotionally accept-
able, since it isolates him from painful contact, and it also
has connotations of ritual appropriateness, namely segre-
gation of deathly pollution from the life-giving cosmos,
rather as Laius said Oedipus should be denied connection
with earth and sky (658; see Mader 1995).

Is Oedipus' self-punishment in any sense admirable?
Responses to such questions necessarily vary according to
the audience, particularly in the unstable world of Seneca's
tragedies. The combination of intense passion with the

grotesque physicality of eyes starting from their sockets seems likely to alienate any possible admiration or even sympathy. Oedipus' vehement insistence on violent self-punishment is no more virtuous than that of Hercules in Act 5 of *Herc*, or than the vehement insistence on punishing *others* which we encounter so often among Seneca's *dramatis personae*.

There is a further aspect also. With the truth revealed, Oedipus seizes eagerly upon an identity as "the iniquity of the age" (875), a unique *monstrum* or prodigy; this identity offers renown, however terrible, and certainty after long doubt. Similarly he seizes on the unique punishment of self-blinding as appropriate to that identity (942–945). "Such vision as this is right for Oedipus" (1003); and in a sense he himself *becomes* Oedipus, the mythic figure of terrible deeds. Here we see that heroic *mis*-identification of the self with externals, with actions (often terrible), which lies at the heart of Senecan tragedy (see vol. 1 p. 7). As Medea achieves an untrammelled but insane selfhood by cutting her relationship to Jason and the children, so Oedipus achieves a kind of absoluteness in the isolation of his no-man's-land. Even as he goes into exile, the thought of relieving Thebes of the plague (1052–1058) is preceded and followed by concern about his own condition in exile. His self-absorption continues in *Phoenician Women*, where he says that while giving up kingship of Thebes, he retains kingship over himself (105)—by which he means not the philosophical self-governance defined in Ode 2 of *Thyestes*, but an intransigent isolation.

A striking difference between Seneca's play and Sophocles' lies in the scenes of animal sacrifice and necromancy,

which are at the heart of Seneca's play but have no counterpart in Sophocles. These Senecan scenes do not advance
the plot, but rather magnify and intensify the horror of the
situation. The sacrifice does so by showing Oedipus' terrible deeds reflected in the natural world. A connection with
the outside world has already been established, of course,
in descriptions of the plague, and even in the play's opening line, where the Titan-sun is as full of doubt as Oedipus himself. But the sacrifice and examination of entrails
brings out fully the monstrosity of what has happened,
thrusting in our face the corruption of the very organs of
life. This scene is based on something much more substantial than the "pathetic fallacy," which imaginatively attributes human feelings to nonhuman nature. The practice of
divination through viscera, especially the liver, was well established at Rome, with a college of 60 accredited diviners
(*haruspices*) as well as many nonofficial practitioners; individual Roman officials and emperors often had a *haruspex*
on their staff. Seneca's scene, then, is based on a religious practice that occurred regularly in the Roman world;
and the notion it implies, of a physical interconnection
between human and nonhuman worlds, would not have
seemed alien to a Roman audience, even if some were in-
tellectually sceptical of its validity.

Between the scenes of sacrifice and necromancy, and in
the sharpest contrast to them, stands the choral hymn to
Bacchus. Bacchus is here associated with nature's vitality,
with all that is lost or polluted in Thebes: heaven's light,
bright colours, vigorous ivy and springtime flowers, an
abundance of water, milk, and wine. He meets the violence
of the pirates not with violence but with the lively energy
of nature, into which they too are drawn by metamorphosis

into dolphins (449–464).[2] The extreme contrast between this hymn and the juxtaposed scenes, then, suggests a dualistic opposition between the force of life and that of death. In this picture death, along with its concomitants such as disease, is not depicted as part of nature's processes, but rather as an opposing force that has its own separate dark world (the underworld) in contrast to the sunlit upper world of creative nature. For cogency's sake we might call these forces Eros and Thanatos, as long as we do not set too much store by the labels.

This dualistic construction of Eros and Thanatos could be explored in many directions. One important connection is with the dualism of comedy and tragedy as dramatic genres. The story that ends the Bacchus ode (487–503) is the archetypal story of countless comic dramas: the handsome, insouciant young man (here a god) rescues the imperilled maiden, falls in love with her and marries her, overcoming the hostility of the threatening father (usually hers, but sometimes his own, as here). This is a story about life processes in human society: the younger generation establishes itself as adult, and marriage allows and encourages procreative sex. Tragic drama, including Seneca's, is often concerned with the opposite story: the marriage bond is broken in some way (*Herc*, *Med*, *Pha*, *Ag*), young people are destroyed (add *Tro*, *Phoen*, *Thy*), the sexual drive is directed outside marriage (Agamemnon, Clytemnestra) or misdirected within the family (Phaedra, Oedipus). If Freud was not completely mistaken, the potential for such misdirection of Eros is present in each family that

2 Some critics, however, find sinister overtones in this episode: see Mastronarde (1970) and Henry and Walker (1983).

has a male child; hence Oedipus' story is in a sense the archetypal tragedy, concerned most directly with the corruption of Eros into Thanatos. Comedy has its own dramatic world, in which Eros is triumphant; tragedy has its separate dramatic world, where Thanatos prevails.

Eros and Thanatos operate not only in society and the world at large but also in the inner world of the psyche, which is where this discussion began. In Senecan drama destructive impulses and desires are often portrayed as arising from the lower mind, as it were. Medea's decision to kill her children is formed in the unconscious mind, and appals her—but also dominates her—when it rises to consciousness (*Med* 917–925). Atreus' revenge cannot be formulated by his conscious mind but swells up within him, accompanied by a roar (real or imagined?) from the depths of the earth (*Thy* 260–265). Clearly there is a correspondence between the lower part of the mind and the lower part of the cosmos, the underworld, where dwell Furies, Crime, and blind self-destructive Rage (e.g. *Herc* 96–98, *Oed* 590–594). Sometimes these worlds can hardly be distinguished. Are the Furies real when seen by the distraught Medea (958–966)? Is the Ghost of Tantalus in *Thyestes* to be understood literally, or as an embodiment of the grandfather's influence, by example and inheritance, on the present generation? In *Oedipus* the minatory Laius arising from the underworld is certainly real within Creon's narrative, yet recognisably similar to the Laius who arises presumably from Oedipus' psyche in *Phoenician Women* 39–44. Similarly there is a sense in which what is "hidden" in this play corresponds to what is hidden in the mind: not necessarily the mind of this Oedipus— though he does seem to have suppressed the memory of killing an old man, and the peril of marrying a woman old enough to be his mother—but in the mind of everyman as Oedipus. The richness of meaning in Seneca's plays depends in part on the interplay in them between subjective and objective, internal and external, microcosm and macrocosm.

Two diverse topics remain to be touched upon: Fate, and stage performance. Towards the end of the play there is a startling brief burst of philosophical teaching from the chorus (980–994): we must conform ourselves to Fate, which comes from on high and proceeds by an inexorable chain of causation. This is that rarity in the tragedies, a piece of orthodox Stoic doctrine. The Stoic duty of submission to Fate presupposes that Fate is purposive and ultimately beneficent, the decree of a single divine purpose that can also be called Providence and Reason. This presupposition is quite alien to the dark worldview of Seneca's tragedies, with its base in the polytheism of myth. The fate to which Oedipus is condemned before birth is purposeless at best, while the spokesman of fate, Phoebus, seems positively malign in not dispelling the young Oedipus' ignorance of his true parentage. The Stoicizing little ode, then, looks like a foreign object lodged in the body of the play. Its presence exemplifies Seneca's practice of using choral odes as vehicles for alternative viewpoints, some of which do not cohere with the dramatic context: instances include Ode 2 of *Trojan Women*, which rejects the possibility of existence after death, and Ode 2 of *Medea*, which ends with a "modern" viewpoint on the subjugation of the sea. Stoicizing critics, however, have naturally accorded the passage greater interpretative significance for the play as a whole.

13

In the debate whether Seneca intended his plays to be staged (vol. 1 pp. 19–21), the animal sacrifice of *Oedipus* has often been taken as evidence against staging, because of its technical difficulties: after being struck twice, the bull rushes around; the carcasses are opened for extispicy, and then rise up to attack the officiants. Some critics have tried to evade these difficulties by proposing that all that actually happens onstage is Manto's description of what she sees taking place offstage. This neat solution will not work, however, since the animals must be onstage for Manto to examine the viscera in their carcasses with her own hands (lines 354 and 380). Undoubtedly Roman technicians, well versed in producing spectacular animal shows, *could* have staged such a scene: Pliny records having watched bulls which were trained for shows to fall and get up again, to lie down and be lifted up (*Natural History* 8.70.182). The question becomes, then, whether Seneca would have thought such show-like effects appropriate to tragedy. More probably he intended the scene's impact to come from his powerfully descriptive verse, not from spectacle. It follows that the scene was designed for recitation, not performance. But this conclusion need not apply to all of Seneca's dramas, particularly if *Oedipus* was among the first to be composed.

Sources

Examination of the evidence,[3] meagre though it is, for Aeschylus' and Euripides' Oedipus plays, and for nondra-

---

[3] Collected and discussed in Töcherle's edition pp. 9–15, and in T. Gantz, *Early Greek Myth* pp. 492–502.

matic versions of the myth, leaves no doubt that Seneca's play derives from Sophocles' *Oedipus the King*. The chief differences between Seneca and Sophocles have been discussed above. Clearly Seneca saw Sophocles' play within the context of a rich and varied literary tradition. His descriptions of the plague (36–70, 133–201), for example, stand in a series of plague accounts including Thucydides Book 2, Lucretius Book 6, Vergil's *Georgics* 3, and Ovid's *Metamorphoses* 7: Seneca's account evokes particularly Vergil and Ovid. The hymn to Bacchus likewise stands in a long tradition of hymns used in tragedy to contrast with the atmosphere of the surrounding scenes: a famous example is the hymn to Bacchus in Sophocles' *Antigone* (1115–1154), but there were numerous examples of odes to Bacchus or other gods in later drama. As always, Ovid is a strong presence in Seneca's writing, for example in ode 3 where the treatment of Theban mythical history is heavily indebted to *Metamorphoses* 3. Töchterle's commentary gives a detailed account of Seneca's sources and his interaction with them.

BIBLIOGRAPHY

Commentary

K. Töchterle, *Lucius Annaeus Seneca, Oedipus: Kommentar mit Einleitung, Text und Übersetzung* (Heidelberg, 1994).

Criticism

D. Henry and B. Walker, "The *Oedipus* of Seneca: an Imperial Tragedy," in Boyle (ed.), *Seneca Tragicus: Ramus*

Essays on Senecan Drama (Victoria, Australia, 1983), 128–139.

G. Mader, "*Nec Sepultis Mixtus et Vivis Tamen/Exemptus*: Rationale and Aesthetics of the "Fitting Punishment" in Seneca's *Oedipus*," *Hermes* 123 (1995), 303–319.

D. J. Mastronarde, "Seneca's *Oedipus*: the Drama in the Word," *TAPA* 101 (1970), 291–315.

J. P. Poe, "The Sinful Nature of the Protagonist of Seneca's *Oedipus*," in Boyle (1983), 140–158.

DRAMATIS PERSONAE

OEDIPUS, *king of Thebes*
JOCASTA, *queen of Thebes and wife to Oedipus*
CREON, *brother of Jocasta*
TIRESIAS, *the blind prophet of Thebes*
MANTO, *daughter of Tiresias*
OLD MAN, *messenger from Corinth*
PHORBAS, *shepherd of the royal flocks*
MESSENGER, *a palace servant*
CHORUS *of Thebans*

Scene

The scene is set at the royal palace of Thebes, in front of which stands an altar.

OEDIPUS

Iam nocte Titan dubius expulsa redit
et nube maestus squalida exoritur iubar,
lumenque flamma triste luctifica gerens
prospiciet avida peste solatas domos,
5 stragemque quam nox fecit ostendet dies.
      Quisquamne regno gaudet? o fallax bonum,
quantum malorum fronte quam blanda tegis!
ut alta ventos semper excipiunt iuga
rupemque saxis vasta dirimentem freta
10 quamvis quieti verberant fluctus maris,
imperia sic excelsa Fortunae obiacent.
quam bene parentis sceptra Polybi fugeram!
curis solutus exul, intrepidus vagans
(caelum deosque testor) in regnum incidi.
15 infanda timeo, ne mea genitor manu
perimatur; hoc me Delphicae laurus monent,
aliudque nobis maius indicunt scelus.
est maius aliquod patre mactato nefas?
pro misera pietas! eloqui fatum pudet:
20 thalamos parentis Phoebus et diros toros
nato minatur impia incestos face.

---

13 vagans *A*: vacans *E*

18

OEDIPUS

ACT 1

OEDIPUS

Now darkness is driven off, and the Titan returns hesitantly, his beams made gloomy by filthy clouds. As his cheerless fire delivers a sombre light, he will look forth on homes left desolate by the greedy plague, and day will reveal the havoc that night has wrought.

Does anyone find joy in kingship? So deceptive a good, hiding so many evils behind its seductive appearance! As the high ridges always catch the winds, and as a rocky crag that cleaves the vast deep is battered by waves however calm the sea, so supreme power lies open to Fortune's blows. How good it was to have fled the sceptre of my father Polybus! But while wandering in exile without a care, free of fears, I stumbled accidentally (gods in heaven be my witness) into kingship. What I fear is unspeakable: that I may kill my father with my own hand. The Delphic laurels warn me of this, and decree another, greater crime for me. Is any iniquity greater than a father's murder? Unhappy ties of kinship! I am ashamed to utter my fate. Phoebus threatens the son with his parent's bed, a monstrous marriage, an unnatural, incestuous union. This fear

19

hic me paternis expulit regnis timor,
hoc ego penates profugus excessi meos;
parum ipse fidens mihimet in tuto tua,
25   Natura, posui iura. cum magna horreas,
quod posse fieri non putes metuas tamen.
cuncta expavesco meque non credo mihi.
    Iam iam aliquid in nos fata moliri parant.
nam quid rear quod ista Cadmeae lues
30   infesta genti strage tam late edita
mihi parcit uni? cui reservamur malo?
inter ruinas urbis et semper novis
deflenda lacrimis funera ac populi struem
incolumis asto—scilicet Phoebi reus.
35   sperare poteras sceleribus tantis dari
regnum salubre? fecimus caelum nocens.
    Non aura gelido lenis afflatu fovet
anhela flammis corda, non Zephyri leves
spirant, sed ignes auget aestiferi canis
40   Titan, leonis terga Nemeaei premens.
deseruit amnes umor atque herbas color
aretque Dirce, tenuis Ismenos fluit
et tinguit inopi nuda vix unda vada.
obscura caelo labitur Phoebi soror,
45   tristisque mundus nubilo pallet die.
nullum serenis noctibus sidus micat,
sed gravis et ater incubat terris vapor;
obtexit arces caelitum ac summas domos
inferna facies. denegat fructum Ceres
50   adulta, et altis flava cum spicis tremat,
arente culmo sterilis emoritur seges.

²³ hoc *Bentley*: non *A*: nunc *E*   ⁴⁵ die *E*: novo *A*

drove me from my father's kingdom, it was on this account that I left my hearth for exile. Distrusting myself, I safeguarded the laws of Nature. When you dread some great evil, you must fear even what you think impossible. I take fright at everything, and do not place my trust even in myself.

At this very moment fate is preparing some device against me. What else am I to think, when this pestilence destroys the race of Cadmus with such widespread havoc, but spares me alone? What evil am I being saved for? Amidst the city's ruins, amidst deaths constantly demanding new tears, amidst the nation's piles of bodies *I* stand unscathed—the man accused by Phoebus! Could you expect that a healthy kingdom would be accorded to such crimes? I have made the heavens baneful.

No gentle breeze with its cooling breath soothes our hearts that pant with heat, no light westerlies breathe, but the Titan, hard by the back of the Nemean lion, augments the fires of the scorching dog star. Rivers are devoid of moisture, grasses of colour; the Dirce is dry; Ismenos' meagre flow scarcely wets the bare channel with its scanty water. Phoebus' sister glides obscured through the heavens, and the overcast daylight discolours the gloomy sky. There are no stars glittering in clear night skies: a heavy black vapour blankets the earth. The citadels of the heavenly gods, their high homes, are concealed behind a hellish vista. The mature grain refuses its harvest: though the golden field trembles with tall ears, the crop is barren, and dies on its parched stalks.

Nec ulla pars immunis exitio vacat,
sed omnis aetas pariter et sexus ruit,
iuvenesque senibus iungit et natis patres
55 funesta pestis. una fax thalamos cremat,
fletuque acerbo funera et questu carent.
quin ipsa tanti pervicax clades mali
siccavit oculos, quodque in extremis solet,
periere lacrimae. portat hunc aeger parens
60 supremum ad ignem, mater hunc amens gerit
properatque ut alium repetat in eundem rogum.
quin luctu in ipso luctus exoritur novus,
suaeque circa funus exequiae cadunt.
tum propria flammis corpora alienis cremant;
65 diripitur ignis, nullus est miseris pudor.
non ossa tumuli sancta discreti tegunt:
arsisse satis est—pars quota in cineres abit!
dest terra tumulis, iam rogos silvae negant.
non vota, non ars ulla correptos levant:
70 cadunt medentes, morbus auxilium trahit.
    Adfusus aris supplices tendo manus
matura poscens fata, praecurram ut prior
patriam ruentem, neve post omnes cadam
fiamque regni funus extremum mei.
75 o saeva nimium numina, o fatum grave!
negatur uni nempe in hoc populo mihi
mors tam parata! sperne letali manu
contacta regna, linque lacrimas, funera,
tabifica caeli vitia quae tecum invehis
80 infaustus hospes, profuge iamdudum ocius—
vel ad parentes.

No quarter is immune or exempt from destruction. Each age and sex perishes equally; the young are joined to the old, fathers to sons by the deadly plague. A single torch cremates married couples, and funerals are unaccompanied by bitter tears and laments. Indeed, this great disaster's unremitting carnage has dried people's eyes: as happens in extremes of misery, their very tears have died. One son is carried to the final fire by an ailing father, another is brought by a crazed mother, who then hurries to fetch yet another son to the same pyre. Even in the midst of grief new grief arises, and mourners fall around the corpse they are following. Then people cremate the bodies of their kin on flames belonging to strangers; fire is stolen—the wretched have no shame. There are no individual grave mounds covering revered bones: no, to have burnt the body is enough—yet how small a portion is turned to ash! There is no land for graves, the forests no longer yield pyres. No prayer, no skill relieves those stricken; healers fall, the disease drags down all succour.

Prostrate at the altar, stretching out hands in supplication, I demand an early fate, so as to anticipate the fatherland's collapse, not fall after everyone and become the last death in my own kingdom. The gods are too cruel, fate too harsh! Death, so readily available, is denied me alone out of the whole nation! Spurn the kingdom infected by your deadly hand, leave behind the tears, the deaths, the corruptive maladies in the sky which you bring with you as a fateful stranger. Quickly, make your belated escape—even to your parents!

SENECA

IOCASTA

Quid iuvat, coniunx, mala
gravare questu? regium hoc ipsum reor,
adversa capere, quoque sit dubius magis
status et cadentis imperi moles labet,
85 hoc stare certo pressius fortem gradu.
haud est virile terga Fortunae dare.

OEDIPUS

Abest pavoris crimen ac probrum procul,
virtusque nostra nescit ignavos metus.
si tela contra stricta, si vis horrida
90 Mavortis in me rueret, adversus feros
audax Gigantas obvias ferrem manus.
nec Sphinga caecis verba nectentem modis
fugi: cruentos vatis infandae tuli
rictus et albens ossibus sparsis solum;
95 cumque e superna rupe iam praedae imminens
aptaret alas, verbera et caudae movens
saevi leonis more conciperet minas,
carmen poposci. sonuit horrendum insuper,
crepuere malae, saxaque impatiens morae
100 revulsit unguis viscera expectans mea.
nodosa sortis verba et implexos dolos
ac triste carmen alitis solvi ferae.

96 alas . . . caudae *E*: ales . . . cauda *A*
97 conciperet *E*: concuteret *A*

---

[1] The riddle (as first attested by Asclepiades, who perhaps took it from a Greek tragedy now lost) ran as follows:

OEDIPUS

JOCASTA

How does it help, my husband, to make troubles heavier by bemoaning them? The quality of a king lies, I think, in the very ability to take on adversities. The more unsure his situation, the more the balance of supreme power tilts toward falling, so much more firmly should he stand, resolute and unbudging. It is not manly to retreat before Fortune.

OEDIPUS

The charge and stigma of cowardice is foreign to me, my manhood knows no fainthearted fears. If weapons were drawn against me, if war's dread violence were sweeping down on me, I would be boldly advancing even against the savage Giants. I did not bolt from the Sphinx when she wove her words in dark measures; I braved the bloody gaping jaws of that unspeakable sibyl, and the ground white with scattered bones. And as from her high crag, already poised over her prey, she flexed her wings and developed her menace, lashing her tail like a savage lion, I asked for her riddle. Up above me she shrieked fearfully, her jaws snapped, and impatient with delay her talons tore the rocks, anticipating my flesh. But I untied the knotted oracular words, the entwined device, the grim riddle of the winged beast.[1]

A manifold thing lives on earth, two-footed and also four-footed,
    Three-footed too; it changes its form alone of all creatures
    Moving on land or up in the sky or down in the sea.
    But when the number of feet on which it travels is greatest,
    Then the speed of its limbs is slowest and feeblest of all.
The answer: a human, who crawls as an infant, walks as an adult, and uses a stick in old age.

SENECA

　　Quid sera mortis vota nunc demens facis?
　　licuit perire. laudis hoc pretium tibi
105　sceptrum et peremptae Sphingis haec merces datur.
　　ille, ille dirus callidi monstri cinis
　　in nos rebellat, illa nunc Thebas lues
　　perempta perdit. una iam superest salus,
　　si quam salutis Phoebus ostendat viam.

CHORUS

110　Occidis, Cadmi generosa proles,
　　urbe cum tota; viduas colonis
　　respicis terras, miseranda Thebe.
　　carpitur leto tuus ille, Bacche,
　　miles, extremos comes usque ad Indos,
115　ausus Eois equitare campis,
　　figere et mundo tua signa primo.
　　cinnami silvis Arabas beatos
　　vidit et versas equitis sagittas,
　　terga fallacis metuenda Parthi;
120　litus intravit pelagi rubentis:
　　promit hinc ortus aperitque lucem
　　Phoebus et flamma propiore nudos
　　　　inficit Indos.
　　Stirpis invictae genus interimus,
125　labimur saevo rapiente fato.
　　ducitur semper nova pompa Morti;

103–105 attributed to Oedipus by E, to Jocasta by A

---

　2 After affirming his courage in the encounter with the Sphinx, Oedipus recognises its adverse consequences. Since he now finds himself praying for death (cf. line 72), it would have been better to die then; his "reward" for his courage is the kingship, a dubious

[*To himself*] Why now, too late, make senseless prayers
for death? You *had* the chance to perish. This is the prize
of your glory, your wage for dispatching the Sphinx—the
royal sceptre. Yes, it is that cunning monster's cursed dust
that is renewing war against us; that scourge I dispatched is
now destroying Thebes.[2] There is one deliverance left: the
chance that Phoebus may show some path to deliverance.[3]

CHORUS

You are falling, noble offspring of Cadmus,
with the whole city. You behold your lands
widowed of farmers, pitiful Thebes.
Death picks off that soldiery,
your companions, Bacchus, to farthest India,
who dared to ride on eastern plains
and plant your standards in the dawning world.
They saw the Arabs, rich in their groves
of cinnamon, and the horsemen with arrows reversed,
the dangerous backs of the cunning Parthians;[4]
they stepped on the shore of the crimson sea,
where Phoebus begins his rise and unfolds
the light, and colours the naked Indians
      with his closer flame.
In us an unconquered lineage is dying;
we sink in the grasp of relentless fate.
Always a new group files toward Death,

boon (cf. line 6); and it appears to him that the Sphinx, far from
being defeated, is renewing its attack on Thebes.

[3] Through his oracle at Delphi, which Creon has been sent to
consult.

[4] A reference to the proverbial "Parthian shot," delivered
while in flight or pretended flight.

longus ad manes properatur ordo
agminis maesti, seriesque tristis
haeret et turbae tumulos petenti
130   non satis septem patuere portae;
stat gravis strages, premiturque iuncto
    funere funus.
Prima vis tardas tetigit bidentes.
laniger pingues male carpsit herbas;
135   colla tacturus steterat sacerdos:
dum manus certum parat alta vulnus,
aureo taurus rutilante cornu
labitur segnis. patuit sub ictu
ponderis vasti resoluta cervix:
140   nec cruor, ferrum maculavit atra
turpis e plaga sanies profusa.
segnior cursu sonipes in ipso
concidit gyro, dominumque prono
    prodidit armo.
145   Incubant agris pecudes relictae;
taurus armento pereunte marcet;
deficit pastor grege deminuto,
tabidos inter moriens iuvencos.
non lupos cervi metuunt rapaces,
150   cessat irati fremitus leonis,
nulla villosis feritas in ursis;
perdidit pestem latebrosa serpens,
aret et sicco moritur veneno.
    Non silva sua decorata coma
155   fundit opacis montibus umbras,
non rura virent ubere glebae,

a long, sad column hastening in sequence
to the shades; but the gloomy line is delayed,
since the seven gates do not open wide
enough for the crowd seeking graves; the heavy
carnage is clogged, a funeral is crowded
      by a funeral close by.
First touched by the scourge were the slow sacrificial
sheep, which could scarcely graze the lush grass.
A priest took his stand to smite a victim,
but while his raised hand aimed the stroke,
the bull, with his horns gleaming gold-red,[5]
sank down limply. His drooping neck
was opened under the weighty blow:
no blood, but a foul gore poured
from the dark gash and stained the blade.
A steed slowed in his running and fell
on the very track, throwing his master
      over his sinking shoulder.
Livestock lie abandoned in the fields;
the bull weakens as the cattle perish;
the herdsman fails, his herd diminished,
dying among the wasting bullocks.
Deer do not fear predatory wolves,
the angry lion's roar ceases,
there is no savagery in shaggy bears;
the lurking snake has lost his poison,
he dies parched, his venom dried up.
    No forests graced by their own foliage
    cast shadows on the shaded hills,
    no fields grow green through the soil's richness,

[5] The horns of bulls destined for sacrifice were gilded.

29

non plena suo vitis Iaccho
bracchia curvat:
omnia nostrum sensere malum.

160   Rupere Erebi claustra profundi
turba sororum face Tartarea,
Phlegethonque sua motam ripa
miscuit undis Styga Sidoniis.
Mors atra avidos oris hiatus

165 pandit et omnes explicat alas;
quique capaci turbida cumba
flumina servat
durus senio navita crudo,
vix assiduo bracchia conto
lassata refert,

170 fessus turbam vectare novam.
quin Taenarii vincula ferri
rupisse canem
fama et nostris errare locis,
mugisse solum,
vaga per lucos ⟨volitasse sacros⟩

175 simulacra virum maiora viris,
bis Cadmeum
nive discussa tremuisse nemus,
bis turbatam sanguine Dircen,
nocte silenti
⟨bis per muros⟩ Amphionios
ululasse canes.

180   O dira novi facies leti

174 *lacuna identified, and supplement proposed, by Zwierlein*
179 *lacuna identified by Leo; supplement proposed by Fitch*

no vines, filled with their own Iacchus,
bend their branches.
All things have felt our bane.
    The throng of sisters[6] with Tartarean torches
has burst the barriers of deep Erebus.
Phlegethon has shifted the Styx from its banks
and mingled it with Sidonian[7] streams.
Dark Death opens his greedy jaws
agape, and unfurls his wings to the full.
And the ferryman who keeps the turbid river
with his roomy skiff,
though tough in his vigorous old age,[8]
can scarcely raise his arms, wearied
with constant poling,
tired of ferrying each new throng.
Yet more, the hound[9] has burst his chains
of Taenarian iron,
some say, and roams at large in our land;
the earth has groaned;
through the ⟨sacred⟩ groves ⟨have flitted⟩ errant
images of men, larger than men;
Cadmus' woodland has trembled twice,
shaking off its snow;
twice the Dirce has clouded with blood;
in the silent night
⟨twice among⟩ Amphion's ⟨walls⟩
came the howling of dogs.
    O strange and dreadful form of death,

---

6 The Furies.   7 I.e. Theban; the adjective is transferred
from Cadmus, Thebes' founder.   8 Charon.
    9 Cerberus.

	gravior leto!
	piger ignavos alligat artus
	languor, et aegro rubor in vultu,
	maculaeque cutem sparsere leves.
185	tum vapor ipsam corporis arcem
	flammeus urit
186	multoque genas sanguine tendit,
187ᵃ	oculique rigent,
188ᵇ	resonant aures
189	stillatque niger naris aduncae
190	cruor et venas rumpit hiantes;
	intima creber viscera quassat
	gemitus stridens,
187ᵇ,188ᵃ	et sacer ignis pascitur artus.
	iamque amplexu frigida presso
	saxa fatigant;
	quos liberior domus elato
	custode sinit,
195	petitis fontes
	aliturque sitis latice ingesto.
	prostrata iacet turba per aras
	oratque mori:
	solum hoc faciles tribuere dei.
	delubra petunt,
200	haud ut voto numina placent,
	sed iuvat ipsos satiare deos.

Quisnam ille propero regiam gressu petit?

184 cutem *M. Müller*: caput *EA*
186 tendit *E*: tinguit* *A*
187ᵇ, 188ᵃ *transposed after* 192 *by Richter*

32

more grievous than death!
Heavy languor binds the torpid limbs,
a flush appears on the sick face,
and small spots spread across the skin.
Then a fiery heat burns in the very
zenith of the body,
and distends the eyes with copious blood;
the gaze is fixed, the ears ring,
dark blood drips from the curving nostrils
and breaks out of the gaping veins;
strident groans
repeatedly shake the body to its core,
and a cursed fire feeds on the limbs.
Now they burden cooling rocks
with a tight embrace;
those whose homes, emptied of guardians,
allow them freedom, seek out springs,
and feed their thirst as they gulp down water.
Crowds lie prostrate among the altars
and pray to die—
the one thing granted readily by the gods.
They head for the shrines,
not to appease the deities with vows,
but from pleasure at sating the very gods.

ACT 2

Who is this, making for the palace with hurried steps? Is

202–205 *attributed to Chorus by* A: 202–204 *to Oedipus,* 205 *to Chorus by* E

adestne clarus sanguine ac factis Creo
an aeger animus falsa pro veris videt?
205   adest petitus omnibus votis Creo.

OEDIPUS

Horrore quatior, fata quo vergant timens,
trepidumque gemino pectus affectu labat:
ubi laeta duris mixta in ambiguo iacent,
incertus animus scire cum cupiat timet.
210   Germane nostrae coniugis, fessis opem
si quam reportas, voce properata edoce.

CREO

Responsa dubia sorte perplexa iacent.

OEDIPUS

Dubiam salutem qui dat afflictis negat.

CREO

Ambage flexa Delphico mos est deo
215   arcana tegere.

OEDIPUS

Fare, sit dubium licet:
ambigua soli noscere Oedipodae datur.

CREO

Caedem expiari regiam exilio deus
et interemptum Laium ulcisci iubet:
non ante caelo lucidus curret dies
220   haustusque tutos aetheris puri dabit.

207 affectu *Heinsius*: afflictu *E*: eventu *A*
212 iacent *E*: latent *A*

34

OEDIPUS

Creon here, famed in descent and deeds, or does my sick
mind see false for true? Creon *is* here, sought by all our
prayers.

OEDIPUS

[*Aside*] I am trembling with fear, apprehensive about fate's
direction. My anxious heart wavers between two feelings:
when joy is mixed ambiguously with distress, the unsure
mind both desires and fears to know.

Brother of my wife, if you bring some help in our trouble, declare your news quickly!

CREON

The oracle's response is entangled, inconclusive.

OEDIPUS

To give inconclusive deliverance to sufferers is to refuse it.

CREON

It is the Delphic god's custom to conceal secrets in twisted
ambiguities.

OEDIPUS

Tell it, however inconclusive: to know the meaning of ambiguities is Oedipus' gift alone.[10]

CREON

The god bids us to expiate the king's murder with exile—
to avenge the killing of Laius. Not until then will the sun
ride brightly through the heavens, or give us wholesome
draughts of pure air.

---

10 The first half of Oedipus' name in Greek suggests not only
"swelling" (note on 813) but also "knowing" (οἶδα).

SENECA

OEDIPUS

Et quis peremptor incliti regis fuit?
quem memoret ede Phoebus, ut poenas luat.

CREO

Sit, precor, dixisse tutum visu et auditu horrida;
torpor insedit per artus, frigidus sanguis coit.
225 ut sacrata templa Phoebi supplici intravi pede
et pias numen precatus rite summisi manus,
gemina Parnasi nivalis arx trucem fremitum dedit;
imminens Phoebea laurus tremuit et movit domum,
ac repente sancta fontis lympha Castalii stetit.
230 incipit Letoa vates spargere horrentes comas
et pati commota Phoebum; contigit nondum specum,
emicat vasto fragore maior humano sonus:
"Mitia Cadmeis remeabunt sidera Thebis,
si profugus Dircen Ismenida liquerit hospes
235 regis caede nocens, Phoebo iam notus et infans.
nec tibi longa manent sceleratae gaudia caedis:

234 liquerit *E*: liqueris *A*

---

11 Lines 223–232 of the Latin are in a more solemn metre (trochaic tetrameter) than that of regular dialogue; lines 233–238 are in dactylic hexameter, the standard metre for oracles.

OEDIPUS

And who was the murderer of that renowned king? Say
whom Phoebus means, so that he can be punished.

CREON[11]

I pray it be safe to speak of things fearful to see and
    hear!
Numbness settles upon my limbs, my blood congeals
    like ice.
When I entered Phoebus' hallowed shrine, treading with
    suppliant steps,
and reached my hands in the ritual way, in reverent
    prayer to the god,
snowy Parnassus' twofold peaks gave a harsh rumbling
    sound,
Phoebus' impending laurel tree trembled and shook the
    shrine,
and the holy water suddenly stopped in the Castalian
    spring.
Then the Letoan seer began to toss her bristling hair,
frenzied, suffering Phoebus' power; she had not yet
    reached the cave,
when a superhuman voice burst forth, a mighty
    clamorous roar:
"Kindly stars will return to Thebes, the city of Cadmus,
If only the stranger leaves Ismenian Dirce for exile,
Guilty of killing a king, known from an infant to
    Phoebus.
Fleetingly you will enjoy the rewards of your lawless
    murder;

tecum bella geres, natis quoque bella relinquens,
turpis maternos iterum revolutus in ortus."

OEDIPUS

Quod facere monitu caelitum iussus paro,
240 functi cineribus regis hoc decuit dari,
ne sancta quisquam sceptra violaret dolo.
regi tuenda maxime regum est salus;
quaerit peremptum nemo quem incolumem timet.

CREO

Curam perempti maior excussit timor.

OEDIPUS

245 Pium prohibuit ullus officium metus?

CREO

Prohibent nefandi carminis tristes minae.

OEDIPUS

Nunc expietur numinum imperio scelus.
Quisquis deorum regna placatus vides:
tu, tu penes quem iura praecipitis poli,
250 tuque, o sereni maximum mundi decus,
bis sena cursu signa qui vario legis,
qui tarda celeri saecula evolvis rota,
sororque fratri semper occurrens tuo,
noctivaga Phoebe, quique ventorum potens
255 aequor per altum caerulos currus agis,
et qui carentes luce disponis domos,

---

237 relinquens *E*: relinques *A*   246 prohibent *A*: spinx
et *E*   251 legis *M. Müller*: regis *EA*

---

[12] Jupiter.   [13] The sun.

War you will wage with yourself, leaving war to your sons
    in addition,
You who have foully returned once more to your source
    in the mother."

OEDIPUS

What I am preparing to do on the gods' advice should have
been accorded to the dead king's ashes, so that no one
should violate the sanctity of sceptered power through
treachery. A king particularly must ensure the safety of
kings; no subject investigates the murder of one who in-
timidated him when alive.

CREON

Concern for his murder was expelled by a greater fear.

OEDIPUS

Could any fear prevent that loyal duty?

CREON

It was prevented by the grim threat of the unspeakable
riddle.

OEDIPUS

Now the crime must be expiated at the divine command. All you gods who look with favour on kingship: you
first, in whose hands are the laws of the racing heavens;[12]
and you, greatest glory of the cloudless sky, who thread the
twelve signs in your varying course and roll out the slow
ages with your swift wheel;[13] and you, the sister always
moving contrary to your brother, night-roaming Phoebe;
and you, lord of the winds, who drive your cerulean chariot
across the levels of the deep;[14] and you who govern the

---

[14] Neptune.

adeste! cuius Laius dextra occidit,
hunc non quieta tecta, non fidi lares,
non hospitalis exulem tellus ferat;
260 thalamis pudendis doleat et prole impia;
hic et parentem dextera perimat sua,
faciatque (num quid gravius optari potest?)
quidquid ego fugi. non erit veniae locus.
per regna iuro quaeque nunc hospes gero
265 et quae reliqui, perque penetrales deos,
per te, pater Neptune, qui fluctu brevi
utrimque nostro geminus alludis solo;
et ipse nostris vocibus testis veni,
fatidica vatis ora Cirrhaeae movens.
270 ita molle senium ducat et summum diem
securus alto reddat in solio parens,
solasque Merope noverit Polybi faces,
ut nulla sontem gratia eripiet mihi.
      Sed quo nefandum facinus admissum loco est?
275 memorate: aperto marte an insidiis iacet?

CREO

Frondifera sanctae nemora Castaliae petens
calcavit artis obsitum dumis iter,
trigemina qua se spargit in campos via.
secat una gratum Phocidos Baccho solum,
280 unde altus arva deserit, caelum petens,
clementer acto colle Parnasos biceps;
at una bimares Sisyphi terras adit;
Olenia in arva tertius trames cava
convalle serpens tangit errantes aquas
285 gelidumque dirimit amnis Eveni vadum.

285 Eveni *Madvig*: elei *E*: elidis* *A*

40

halls devoid of light:[15] bear witness. The man whose hand
killed Laius—may no peaceful home support him, no dependable hearth, no hospitable land in his exile. May he
find grief in a shameful wedlock and unnatural offspring;
may he even kill his parent with his own hand, and may he
do (surely no heavier curse exists) all that I fled from.
There will be no room for pardon. I swear by the kingship
I now hold and by that I left, by the gods of my hearth,
and by you, father Neptune, who play with shallow waves
against my land on both its shores;[16] you yourself,[17] who
guide the prophetic lips of the Cirrhaean sibyl, must also
come as witness to my words. So may my father pass an
agreeable old age and end his days secure on his high
throne, so may Merope know union only with Polybus, as
surely as no influence will wrest the guilty man from me.

[*To all present*] But where was the monstrous crime
committed? Tell me: did he die in open battle or by a trap?

CREON

As he journeyed towards holy Castalia's leafy woods, he
trod a path hedged in by dense brush, where three roads
branch out across open country. One cuts through the land
of Phocis, dear to Bacchus, where high Parnassus leaves
behind the farmland and with gently climbing foothills lifts
his twin peaks towards heaven. One leads to Sisyphus' land
with its two seas.[18] Heading for the lands of Olenos, the
third track, winding through a hollow valley, reaches the
wandering waters and cuts across the chill shallows of

15 Dis.
16 He believes that Corinth with its Isthmus is his native land.
17 Apollo.
18 I.e. Corinth and its Isthmus.

41

SENECA

hic pace fretum subita praedonum manus
aggressa ferro facinus occultum tulit.
     In tempore ipso sorte Phoebea excitus
Tiresia tremulo tardus accelerat genu
290 comesque Manto luce viduatum trahens.

OEDIPUS

Sacrate divis, proximum Phoebo caput,
responsa solve; fare, quem poenae petant.

TIRESIA

Quod tarda fatu est lingua, quod quaerit moras,
haud te quidem, magnanime, mirari addecet:
295 visu carenti magna pars veri latet.
sed quo vocat me patria, quo Phoebus, sequar:
fata eruantur; si foret viridis mihi
calidusque sanguis, pectore exciperem deum.
     Appellite aris candidum tergo bovem
300 curvoque numquam colla depressam iugo.
Tu lucis inopem, nata, genitorem regens
manifesta sacri signa fatidici refer.

MANTO

Opima sanctas victima ante aras stetit.

TIRESIA

In vota superos voce sollemni voca,
305 arasque dono turis Eoi extrue.

---

300 depressam *Bentley*: depressum *EA*

42

the river Evenus. Here, as he counted on peacetime, a band of brigands suddenly attacked him with the sword, and performed the crime unwitnessed.

But just in time, summoned by Phoebus' prophecy, Tiresias hurries here, though slowed by palsied limbs, and with him Manto, haling her father bereft of sight.

OEDIPUS

You who are consecrated to the gods, and stand nearest to Apollo, resolve the oracle, say whom it targets for punishment.

TIRESIAS

That my tongue is slow to speak, that it seeks delay, should surely not surprise you, great-souled king. For one lacking sight, much of the truth lies hidden. But where my country and where Phoebus call me, I shall follow; we must root out what fate has decreed. If my blood were hot and vigorous, I would receive the god into my breast.[19]

[*To attendants*] Drive to the altar a bull whose hide is white, and a heifer whose neck was never burdened with the curved yoke. You, daughter, who guide your father, light-deprived, must recount the visible signs given by the ritual of divination.

MANTO

A choice victim is stationed before the holy altar.

TIRESIAS

Summon the gods to our offerings with the ritual words, and heap up the altar with a gift of eastern incense.

---

[19] I.e. he would seek the truth through prophetic inspiration rather than through divination.

MANTO

Iam tura sacris caelitum ingessi focis.

TIRESIA

Quid flamma? largas iamne comprendit dapes?

MANTO

Subito refulsit lumine et subito occidit.

TIRESIA

Utrumne clarus ignis et nitidus stetit
310 rectusque purum verticem caelo tulit
et summam in auras fusus explicuit comam?
an latera circa serpit incertus viae
et fluctuante turbidus fumo labat?

MANTO

Non una facies mobilis flammae fuit:
315 imbrifera qualis implicat varios sibi
Iris colores, parte quae magna poli
curvata picto nuntiat nimbos sinu
(quis desit illi quive sit dubites color),
caerulea fulvis mixta oberravit notis,
320 sanguinea rursus; ultima in tenebras abît.
sed ecce pugnax ignis in partes duas
discedit, et se scindit unius sacri
discors favilla. genitor, horresco intuens:
libata Bacchi dona permutat cruor,
325 ambitque densus regium fumus caput
ipsosque circa spissior vultus sedet
et nube densa sordidam lucem abdidit.
quid sit, parens, effare.

44

MANTO

Now I have piled the incense on the gods' sacred hearth.

TIRESIAS

What of the flame? Is it already catching hold of the plentiful nourishment?

MANTO

It suddenly shone out, and suddenly died down.

TIRESIAS

Did the fire rise bright and clear? Did it lift a pure peak straight towards the sky, and extend tall plumes into the air? Or creep around the sides without direction, and falter with murky colour and billowing smoke?

MANTO

The flame was changeable, with more than one appearance. As Iris the shower-bringer weaves various colours into herself, when she spans a great section of sky and heralds storm clouds with her variegated bow (you would hesitate to say what colour is or is not there), so it shimmered, its bluish colour mottled with yellow, and then blood red; at the end it trailed into blackness.

But oh! The combative flame is separating into two halves, the embers of a single ritual dividing in hostility. Father, I shudder to watch! The libation of wine changes into blood; dense smoke surrounds the king's head, and settles even thicker around his very eyes, blocking the light in the murk of a dense cloud. What is it, father? Tell us.

TIRESIA

Quid fari queam
inter tumultus mentis attonitae vagus?
330 quidnam loquar? sunt dira, sed in alto mala.
solet ira certis numinum ostendi notis;
quid istud est quod esse prolatum volunt
iterumque nolunt et truces iras tegunt?
pudet deos nescioquid. Huc propere admove
335 et sparge salsa colla taurorum mola.
placidone vultu sacra et admotas manus
patiuntur?

MANTO

Altum taurus attollens caput
primos ad ortus positus expavit diem
trepidusque vultum obliquat et radios fugit.

TIRESIA

340 Unone terram vulnere afflicti petunt?

MANTO

Iuvenca ferro semet opposito induit
et vulnere uno cecidit; at taurus duos
perpessus ictus huc et huc dubius ruit
animamque fessus vix reluctantem exprimit.

TIRESIA

345 Utrum citatus vulnere angusto micat
an lentus altas irrigat plagas cruor?

MANTO

Huius per ipsam qua patet pectus viam
effusus amnis, huius exiguo graves

339 obliquat *A*: solis *E*

46

TIRESIAS

What could I tell, lost in a turmoil of amazement? What
am I to say? Terrible evils are here, but deeply hidden.
Divine anger is usually shown by unmistakable signs. What
is this that they both want and do not want disclosed,
disguising their fierce anger? The gods find something
shameful. Quickly, bring the cattle here and sprinkle
their necks with the salted meal. Do they bear the ritual
handling with calm expressions?

MANTO

The bull raised his head high; when stationed to face the
East, he flinched from the sunlight and shunned its rays,
averting his gaze in fright.

TIRESIAS

Was a single wound sufficient to fell each of them?

MANTO

When the blade was held out, the heifer thrust herself
against it and fell from a single wound. But the bull, after
suffering two blows, plunges erratically here and there,
and though weakened can scarcely yield up his struggling
life.[20]

TIRESIAS

Does the blood spurt out quickly from a narrow wound, or
well up gradually in deep gashes?

MANTO

This one's pours in a flood through the path opened in her
chest, but that one's heavy wounds are stained with just

[20] Ideally the sacrificial animal should die easily and with
apparent willingness.

maculantur ictus imbre; sed versus retro
350   per ora multus sanguis atque oculos redit.

TIRESIA

Infausta magnos sacra terrores cient.
sed ede certas viscerum nobis notas.

MANTO

Genitor, quid hoc est? non levi motu, ut solent,
agitata trepidant exta, sed totas manus
355   quatiunt, novusque prosilit venis cruor.
cor marcet aegrum penitus ac mersum latet,
liventque venae. magna pars fibris abest
et felle nigro tabidum spumat iecur,
ac (semper omen unico imperio grave)
360   en capita paribus bina consurgunt toris;
sed utrumque caesum tenuis abscondit caput
membrana, latebram rebus occultis negans.
hostile valido robore insurgit latus
septemque venas tendit; has omnes retro
365   prohibens reverti limes obliquus secat.
mutatus ordo est, sede nil propria iacet,
sed acta retro cuncta: non animae capax
in parte dextra pulmo sanguineus iacet,
non laeva cordi regio, non molli ambitu
370   omenta pingues visceri obtendunt sinus.
natura versa est; nulla lex utero manet.
scrutemur, unde tantus hic extis rigor.
quod hoc nefas? conceptus innuptae bovis!

---

[21] This detail foreshadows Oedipus' self-blinding. The blood
of a well-omened sacrifice would spurt out onto the altar.
[22] The liver was regarded as particularly informative in divina-

scanty drops. However, much blood turns back and flows over the eyes and face.[21]

TIRESIAS

This ill-omened sacrifice arouses great fears. But tell me the signs of the entrails, which are dependable.

MANTO

Father, what is this? The organs are not trembling with slight movements as usual, but making my whole hand shake, and abnormal blood is spurting from the veins. The heart is diseased and wasted throughout, and deeply hidden; the veins are discoloured; a great part of the entrails is missing. The liver is rotten and oozing with black bile, and just here are two protruding heads of equal size—always a grievous omen for undivided supreme power. Each cloven head is covered by a thin membrane, which gives no concealment for secrets. The hostile side extends with sturdy strength, and has seven spreading veins; a border cutting across all of them prevents their return.[22] The whole order is changed, nothing lies in its proper place, everything is turned around: the lungs lie on the right side, with no room for breath and clogged with blood; the region of the heart is not on the left; the caul does not extend its fatty folds in a soft coating over the entrails. Nature is inverted, no lawfulness remains in the womb. I must examine what causes such stiffness in the innards. What is this monstrosity? A foetus in an unmated heifer! And not positioned as usual,

tion, one side bespeaking hostile influences, the other friendly. The two heads (in place of the usual one) portend the strife of Oedipus' sons over the kingship of Thebes, and the seven veins on the hostile side foreshadow the "Seven against Thebes."

nec more solito positus alieno in loco
375 implet parentem. membra cum gemitu movet,
rigore tremulo debiles artus micant.
—infecit atras lividus fibras cruor
temptantque turpes mobilem trunci gradum,
et inane surgit corpus ac sacros petit
380 cornu ministros; viscera effugiunt manum.
neque ista, quae te pepulit, armenti gravis
vox est nec usquam territi resonant greges:
immugit aris ignis et trepidant foci.

OEDIPUS

Quid ista sacri signa terrifici ferant
385 exprome; voces aure non timida hauriam:
solent suprema facere securos mala.

TIRESIA

His invidebis quibus opem quaeris malis.

OEDIPUS

Memora quod unum scire caelicolae volunt,
contaminarit rege quis caeso manus.

TIRESIA

390 Nec alta caeli quae levi pinna secant
nec fibra vivis rapta pectoribus potest
ciere nomen. alia temptanda est via:
ipse evocandus noctis aeternae plagis,
emissus Erebo ut caedis auctorem indicet.
395 reseranda tellus, Ditis implacabile
numen precandum, populus infernae Stygis
huc extrahendus. ede cui mandes sacrum;

---

386 suprema *Avantius*: extrema *EA*: *the line deleted by Peiper.*

but filling its mother in an unnatural place. It groans as it moves; its weak limbs quiver, stiff and trembling. —Livid blood has stained the dark organs; the disfigured torsos make vigorous attempts to walk; one of the gaping bodies rises and attacks the priests with its horns; the entrails escape from my hands. That is not the deep call of cattle that strikes your ears, no herds are lowing anywhere in fear: it is the moaning of the fire on the altar, the shuddering of the sacrificial hearth.

OEDIPUS
[*To Tiresias*] Interpret these signs from the ominous ritual. I shall mark your words without flinching; extreme troubles are apt to make people calm.

TIRESIAS
You will envy these troubles for which you are seeking help.

OEDIPUS
Tell us the one thing the gods want known: who polluted his hands with the murder of the king?

TIRESIAS
Neither birds that cut through heaven's heights on light wings,[23] nor organs torn from living bodies, can call up the name. Another path must be tried. He himself must be summoned from the regions of eternal night, so that once released from Erebus he can identify his murderer. We must open the earth, make prayers to Dis the implacable, and draw out here the throngs of infernal Styx. Say whom you entrust with this ritual, since it is taboo for you, who

23 A reference to divination by the flight of birds (*auspicium*).

nam te, penes quem summa regnorum, nefas
invisere umbras.

OEDIPUS

Te, Creo, hic poscit labor,
400   ad quem secundum regna respiciunt mea.

TIRESIA

Dum nos profundae claustra laxamus Stygis,
populare Bacchi laudibus carmen sonet.

CHORUS

Effusam redimite comam nutante corymbo,
mollia Nysaeis armatus bracchia thyrsis,
405   lucidum caeli decus, huc ades
      votis, quae tibi nobiles
        Thebae, Bacche, tuae
      palmis supplicibus ferunt.
huc adverte favens virgineum caput,
vultu sidereo discute nubila
410   et tristes Erebi minas
      avidumque fatum.
Te decet cingi comam floribus vernis,
  te caput Tyria cohibere mitra
    hederave mollem
415   bacifera religare frontem,
spargere effusos sine lege crines,
rursus adducto revocare nodo:
qualis iratam metuens novercam

---

[24] Parts of this ode (405–415, 472–502) and the next (709–737)
are polymetric, i.e. the metre varies from line to line. Such virtu-
osity cannot be conveyed in translation; the indentations used in

hold the highest power of the kingdom, to look upon the shades.

OEDIPUS

This task calls for you, Creon, whom my kingdom regards as next after myself.

TIRESIAS

While we are loosing the barriers of the deep Stygian world, let a hymn sound out from the people in praise of Bacchus.

CHORUS[24]

You whose flowing hair is wreathed with nodding ivy,
and who bear the thyrsus of Nysa as a weapon in your
　　soft hands,
　　shining glory of heaven, attend
　　　　the prayers that your famous city
　　　　　　of Thebes offers you, Bacchus,
　　　　with palms lifted in supplication.
Turn here your girlish face in favour;
with your star-bright countenance dispel the clouds,
　　　　the grim threats of Erebus,
　　　　　　　and greedy fate.
It suits you to circle your hair with springtime flowers,
　　to bind your head with a Tyrian turban,
　　　　　　or fasten berried
　　ivy around your soft forehead,
　　to toss your flowing locks in disarray,
　　to arrange them again with a firm knot;
　　just as, in fear of your angry stepmother,[25]

---

the text represent it only partially. *Oed* and *Ag* are the only plays of the corpus with polymetric odes. 　　　　[25] Juno.

creveras falsos imitatus artus,
420 crine flaventi simulata virgo,
lutea vestem retinente zona.
inde tam molles placuere cultus
et sinus laxi fluidumque syrma.
Vidit aurato residere curru,
425 veste cum longa regeres leones,
omnis Eoae plaga vasta terrae,
qui bibit Gangen niveumque quisquis
frangit Araxen.

Te senior turpi sequitur Silenus asello,
430 turgida pampineis redimitus tempora sertis;
condita lascivi deducunt orgia mystae.
te Bassaridum comitata cohors
nunc Edono pede pulsavit
sola Pangaeo,
435 nunc Threicio vertice Pindi.
439 tibi commotae pectora matres
440 fudere comam.
436 nunc Cadmeas inter matres
impia maenas
comes Ogygio venit Iaccho,
nebride sacra praecincta latus
441 thyrsumque levem vibrante manu.
iam post laceros Pentheos artus
Thyades oestro membra remissae
velut ignotum videre nefas.

434 Pangaeo *Leo*: -i *E (A omits 430–471)*
439–440 *transposed after* 435 *by Fitch*

you grew up assuming a false form,
a pretended girl with golden hair,
with a yellow girdle fastening your dress.
Hence your liking for such soft garments,
clothes in loose folds, a flowing robe.
 Seated on your gilded chariot
in a long robe, guiding your lions
you were seen by the whole vast region of the East,
those who drink the Ganges and break the ice
  on the snowy Araxes.

You are followed by old Silenus on his unseemly donkey,
with garlands woven from ivy festooning his swollen
 temples.
Your wanton initiates conduct your secret cultic rites.
 Your attendant troop of Bassarids
 have pounded the earth in dances,
 now on Edonian Pangaeum,
 now on the Thracian summit of Pindus.
 Mothers with hearts enraptured by you
 have loosened their hair.
 Now amidst Cadmean mothers
 an unnatural maenad
 has come in the company of Ogygian Iacchus,
 her body girt in the sacred fawnskin,
 her hand brandishing the light thyrsus.[26]
 Then after the rending of Pentheus' limbs
 the Thyads, their bodies relieved of frenzy,
 looked on the atrocity as something unknown.

[26] The maenad is Agave, mother of Pentheus.

445 Ponti regna tenet nitidi matertera Bacchi,
Nereidumque choris Cadmeia cingitur Ino;
ius habet in fluctus magni puer advena ponti,
cognatus Bacchi, numen non vile Palaemon.
    Te Tyrrhena, puer, rapuit manus,
450   et tumidum Nereus posuit mare,
    caerula cum pratis mutat freta.
    hinc verno platanus folio viret
    et Phoebo laurus carum nemus;
    garrula per ramos avis obstrepit;
455   vivaces hederas remus tenet,
    summa ligat vitis carchesia;
    Idaeus prora fremuit leo,
    tigris puppe sedet Gangetica.
    tum pirata freto pavidus natat,
460   et nova demersos facies habet:
    bracchia prima cadunt praedonibus
    inlisumque utero pectus coit,
    parvula dependet lateri manus,
    et dorso fluctum curvo subit,
465   lunata scindit cauda mare:
    et sequitur curvus fugientia
        carbasa delphin.

Divite Pactolus vexit te Lydius unda,
aurea torrenti deducens flumina ripa;
laxavit victos arcus Geticasque sagittas
470 lactea Massagetes qui pocula sanguine miscet;

The realm of the sea is held by the aunt of shining
    Bacchus,
Ino daughter of Cadmus, with Nereid choruses round
    her;
and a boy, newcomer, sways the waves of the mighty sea,
kin to Bacchus, a godhead of no slight power, Palaemon.
    [*To Bacchus*] You were seized as a boy by a Tyrrhene
        crew.
    Nereus calmed the swollen seas,
    and changed the deep-blue waters to meadows;
    so there were plane trees verdant with spring foliage,
    and laurels whose groves are dear to Phoebus;
    birds vied in chattering among the branches,
    the oars were covered with vigorous ivy,
    grapevines twined at the mastheads;
    a lion from Ida roared at the prow,
    a tiger from Ganges sat in the stern.
    Then the frightened pirates swim in the sea,
    and as they sink take on new forms:
    first the robbers' arms fall away,
    their chests are squashed to join their bellies,
    little hands hang down at their sides,
    they dive in the waves with curving backs,
    cut through the sea with crescent tails:
    and the sails of the fleeing ship are chased
        by humpbacked dolphins.

The Lydian river Pactolus bore you on its rich waves,
carrying golden currents down its swirling stream.
The Massagetan, who mingles blood with cups of milk,
unstrung his bow in defeat, set down his Getic arrows.

regna securigeri Bacchum sensere Lycurgi,
  sensere terrae Zalacum feroces
    et quos vicinus Boreas ferit
    arva mutantes, quasque Maeotis
475   alluit gentes frigido fluctu,
      quasque despectat vertice e summo
  sidus Arcadium geminumque plaustrum.
  ille dispersos domuit Gelonos,
  arma detraxit trucibus puellis:
480 ore deiecto petiere terram
      Thermodontiacae catervae,
    positisque tandem levibus sagittis
        Maenades factae.
  sacer Cithaeron sanguine undavit
485   Ophioniaque caede;
    Proetides silvas petiere, et Argos
    praesente Baccho coluit noverca.
  Naxos Aegaeo redimita ponto
tradidit thalamis virginem relictam,
490   meliore pensans damna marito.
        pumice ex sicco
      fluxit Nyctelius latex;
    garruli gramen secuere rivi,
    conbibit dulces humus alta sucos

---

[27] Respectively the Great and Lesser Bear, both near the northern pole.

[28] Lines 484–485 refer to Pentheus' death. The Proetides, daughters of King Proetus of Argos, resisted Bacchus' rites, and were driven mad; the city then acknowledged his godhead. The presence of Juno, a preeminent divinity in Argos, probably indi-

The power of Bacchus was felt by the axman Lycurgus'
 realm;
  the fierce lands of the Zalaces felt it too,
   and those whom Boreas smites at close range,
   nomadic peoples, and the tribes against whom
   Maeotis washes with its cold waves,
   and those on whom the Arcadian constellation
  and the twin Wain[27] look down from the high pole.
  He tamed the scattered Geloni
  and wrested arms from the warrior girls:
  they fell to the ground with faces bowed,
   those squadrons from Thermodon,
  at last laid aside their light arrows,
    and became maenads.
  Sacred Cithaeron streamed with blood
    from Ophionian slaughter;
  the Proetides fled to the woods, and Argos
  paid homage to Bacchus in his stepmother's
   presence.[28]
  Naxos ringed by the Aegean sea
gave in marriage a deserted maiden,[29]
  requiting her loss with a better husband.
    From its dry pumice
   flowed Nyctelian liquor;
  chattering streams cut through the grass;
  the earth drank deep of the sweet fluids,

cates that she approved the new worship of Bacchus, suppressing
her stepmotherly jealousy: in some versions the Proetides had
insulted her.

 29 Ariadne, deserted by Theseus: she became the bride of
Bacchus.

495 niveique lactis candidos fontes
et mixta odoro Lesbia cum thymo.
ducitur magno nova nupta caelo;
    sollemne Phoebus
carmen infusis humero capillis
500   cantat et geminus Cupido
      concutit taedas;
telum deposuit Iuppiter igneum
oditque Baccho veniente fulmen.

Lucida dum current annosi sidera mundi,
Oceanus clausum dum fluctibus ambiet orbem,
505 Lunaque dimissos dum plena recolliget ignes,
dum matutinos praedicet Lucifer ortus,
altaque caeruleum dum Nerea nesciet Arctos,
candida formosi venerabimur ora Lyaei.

OEDIPUS

Etsi ipse vultus flebiles praefert notas,
510 exprome cuius capite placemus deos.

CREO

Fari iubes tacere quae suadet metus.

---

[30] Because it had been fatal to Bacchus' mother Semele.

white springs of snowy milk
and Lesbian wine blended with scented thyme.
The new bride was escorted to the vast heavens;
        Phoebus, with hair
flowing down to his shoulders, sang
    the ceremonial hymn, while twin Cupids
        swung their torches.
Jove laid aside his fiery weapon,
  and abhorred the thunderbolt at Bacchus' coming.[30]

As long as the shining stars of the age-old heavens run
  on,
as long as Ocean circles the encompassed earth with its
  waves
and as long as the Moon at the full recovers its fires that
  waned,
as long as the Daystar heralds the dawn each early
  morning
and as long as the lofty Bear knows nothing of sea-blue
  Nereus,
so long we shall worship the radiant face of comely
  Lyaeus.

ACT 3

OEDIPUS

Though your very face signifies sorrow, tell us: whose life
must we take to appease the gods?

CREON

You bid me say what fear urges me to keep silent.

OEDIPUS

Si te ruentes non satis Thebae movent,
at sceptra moveant lapsa cognatae domus.

CREO

Nescisse cupies nosse quae nimium expetis.

OEDIPUS

515 Iners malorum remedium ignorantia est.
itane et salutis publicae indicium obrues?

CREO

Ubi turpis est medicina, sanari piget.

OEDIPUS

Audita fare, vel malo domitus gravi
quid arma possint regis irati scies.

CREO

520 Odere reges dicta quae dici iubent.

OEDIPUS

Mitteris Erebo vile pro cunctis caput,
arcana sacri voce ni retegis tua.

CREO

Tacere liceat. ulla libertas minor
a rege petitur?

OEDIPUS

Saepe vel lingua magis
525 regi atque regno muta libertas obest.

---

[31] This dialogue from 511 is adapted in Chapman, *Byron's Conspiracy* III.3.55–69, beginning so:
La Brosse You bid me speak what fear bids me conceal.
Byron   You have no cause for fear, and therefore speak.

OEDIPUS

If the collapse of Thebes is not enough to move you, the fallen sceptre of your kinsman's house should move you.

CREON

You will wish you had not learned what you so demand to know.

OEDIPUS

Ignorance is a feeble remedy for troubles.[31] Will you really bury information about the people's wellbeing?

CREON

When the cure is foul, being healed is repugnant.

OEDIPUS

Tell us what you have heard, or you will learn, broken by suffering, what an angry king's might can perform.

CREON

Kings hate the very words they bid be spoken.

OEDIPUS

You will be sent to Erebus as a scapegoat for all, unless your words reveal the secrets from the ritual.

CREON

Allow me silence. Can any smaller freedom be requested from a king?

OEDIPUS

Often the freedom of silence is more dangerous than speech to king and kingdom.

La Brosse	You'll rather wish you had been ignorant
	Than be instructed in a thing so ill.
Byron	Ignorance is an idle salve for ill.

CREO

Ubi non licet tacere, quid cuiquam licet?

OEDIPUS

Imperia solvit qui tacet iussus loqui.

CREO

Coacta verba placidus accipias precor.

OEDIPUS

Ulline poena vocis expressae fuit?

CREO

530 Est procul ab urbe lucus ilicibus niger
Dircaea circa vallis inriguae loca.
cupressus altis exerens silvis caput
virente semper alligat trunco nemus,
curvosque tendit quercus et putres situ
535 annosa ramos: huius abrupit latus
edax vetustas; illa, iam fessa cadens
radice, fulta pendet aliena trabe.
amara bacas laurus et tiliae leves
et Paphia myrtus et per immensum mare
540 motura remos alnus et Phoebo obvia
enode Zephyris pinus opponens latus.
medio stat ingens arbor atque umbra gravi
silvas minores urget et magno ambitu
diffusa ramos una defendit nemus.
545 tristis sub illa, lucis et Phoebi inscius,
restagnat umor frigore aeterno rigens;
limosa pigrum circumit fontem palus.

CREON

If silence is not allowed, what is anyone allowed?

OEDIPUS

One who is silent when bidden to speak undermines authority.

CREON

Since my words are coerced, I pray you receive them kindly.

OEDIPUS

Was anyone yet punished for speech wrung from him?

CREON

There lies at a distance from the city a grove dark with holm oaks, on the sides of the well-watered Vale of Dirce. Cypresses thrust their heads above the high trees and encircle the wood with their evergreen trunks; ancient oaks stretch out bent branches, rotten and crumbling. One of these has its side torn away by devouring time, while a second, already tilting with weakened roots, hangs propped on another tree's trunk. The bitter-berried laurel is there, slight linden trees, the Paphian myrtle, the alder destined to drive oars[32] through the boundless sea, and the pine fronting the sun, setting its straight-grained bole against the westerlies. In the midst stands a massive tree that crowds lesser trees with its heavy shade, and with its great circle of spreading branches serves by itself as protector of the woodland. In gloom beneath it, untouched by Phoebus' light, lies a pool chilled by perpetual cold; a muddy swamp surrounds the sluggish spring.

---

[32] I.e. alder is fashioned into ships, whose rowers drive oars . . .

Huc ut sacerdos intulit senior gradum,
haud est moratus: praestitit noctem locus.
550 tum effossa tellus, et super rapti rogis
iaciuntur ignes. ipse funesto integit
vates amictu corpus et frondem quatit;
554 squalente cultu maestus ingreditur senex,
553 lugubris imos palla perfundit pedes,
555 mortifera canam taxus astringit comam.
nigro bidentes vellere atque atrae boves
antro trahuntur. flamma praedatur dapes,
vivumque trepidat igne ferali pecus.

Vocat inde manes teque qui manes regis
560 et obsidentem claustra letalis lacus,
carmenque magicum volvit et rabido minax
decantat ore quidquid aut placat leves
aut cogit umbras; sanguinem libat focis
solidasque pecudes urit et multo specum
565 saturat cruore; libat et niveum insuper
lactis liquorem, fundit et Bacchum manu
laeva, canitque rursus ac terram intuens
graviore manes voce et attonita citat.
latravit Hecates turba; ter valles cavae
570 sonuere maestum, tota succusso solo
pulsata tellus. "Audior," vates ait,
"rata verba fudi: rumpitur caecum chaos,
iterque populis Ditis ad superos datur."

549 *Zwierlein suggests a lacuna after* moratus *or* locus.
553 *transposed after* 554 *by Weber*

33 This ritual is dramatised in the *Oedipus* of John Dryden and
Nathaniel Lee (1679), e.g. (Tiresias speaking) "Is the sacrifice

When the aged priest arrived here, he made no delay:
the place afforded darkness. Then a pit was dug in the
earth, and over it were tossed firebrands snatched from
pyres. The seer clothes his body in funereal garments, and
waves a branch. The old man steps forward in the squalid
clothes of mourning: a gloomy robe sweeps down over his
feet, the deathly yew binds his grey hair. Dark-fleeced
sheep and black cattle are dragged to the hole; flames
plunder the feast, and the still-living flesh quivers in the
fire of the dead.[33]

Next he summons the shades, and you who rule the
shades, and the one who holds access to the lake of the
dead;[34] he reels off a magic chant, and in a threatening,
frenzied tone he recites whatever placates or else coerces
the insubstantial ghosts. He pours a libation of blood on
the altar, burns the carcasses whole, and drenches the pit
in copious blood. In addition he makes a libation of snowy
milk, and pours wine with his left hand, chants once more,
and gazing at the earth summons the shades in a deeper,
inspired voice. Howling came from the pack of Hecate;
thrice the hollow chasms groaned, the ground was jolted
from below and the whole earth shook. "I have been
heard," said the priest, "the spells I uttered were valid:
blind chaos bursts open, and the throngs of Dis are granted
a path to the upper world." Every tree cringed, with its

made fit? / Draw her backward to the pit: / Draw the barren Heifer
back; / Barren let her be and black. / Cut the curled hair that grows
/ Full betwixt her horns and brows: / And turn your faces from the
Sun: / Answer me, if this be done?"

[34] Charon.

SENECA

        subsedit omnis silva et erexit comas,
575   duxere rimas robora et totum nemus
        concussit horror; terra se retro dedit
        gemuitque penitus, sive temptari abditum
        Acheron profundum mente non aequa tulit,
        sive ipsa tellus, ut daret functis viam,
580   compage rupta sonuit, aut ira furens
        triceps catenas Cerberus movit graves.
        Subito dehiscit terra et immenso sinu
        laxata patuit. ipse pallentes deos
        vidi inter umbras, ipse torpentes lacus
585   noctemque veram: gelidus in venis stetit
        haesitque sanguis. saeva prosiluit cohors
        et stetit in armis omne vipereum genus,
588   fratrum catervae dente Dircaeo satae.
590   tum torva Erinys sonuit et caecus Furor
        Horrorque et una quidquid aeternae creant
        celantque tenebrae: Luctus avellens comam
        aegreque lassum sustinens Morbus caput,
        gravis Senectus sibimet et pendens Metus
589   avidumque populi Pestis Ogygii malum.
595   nos liquit animus; ipsa quae ritus senis
        artesque norat stupuit. intrepidus parens
        audaxque damno convocat Ditis feri
        exsangue vulgus. ilico, ut nebulae leves,
        volitant et auras libero caelo trahunt.
600   non tot caducas educat frondes Eryx,
        nec vere flores Hybla tot medio creat
        cum examen arto nectitur densum globo,
        fluctusque non tot frangit Ionium mare,
        nec tanta gelidi Strymonis fugiens minas

68

leaves bristling; hard treetrunks split open, and the entire woodland shuddered. The ground shrank back and groaned deep within: either Acheron was displeased at the assault on its hidden depths, or Earth herself cracked apart her structure to give passage to the dead, or else Cerberus the three-headed shook his heavy chains in furious anger.

Suddenly the earth gaped and split apart into a vast cavity. With my own eyes I saw the pallid gods among the shades, I saw the stagnant lakes and authentic night. My blood stopped still, cold in my veins. Out leapt a fierce squadron and stood under arms—the whole snaky brood, the ranks of brothers sown from Dircean teeth.[35] Then came the sound of grim Erinys and blind Rage and Horror, and with them all that the everlasting darkness spawns and shrouds: Grief tearing away its hair, Disease barely supporting its weary head, Old Age burdensome to itself, edgy Fear, and the evil of Plague, hungry for the Ogygian people. Our courage left us; even she who knew the old man's rituals and arts was awestruck. But fearlessly, emboldened by his blindness, her father summoned the bloodless multitude of cruel Dis. Straightway, like swirling mists, they flitted about, breathing the air of the open sky. Not so many are the leaves that grow on Mt Eryx to fall there, not so many the flowers that Hybla produces in midspring, when the dense swarm clusters in a tight ball, not so many the breaking waves on the Ionian sea, not so large the winged flocks that flee chill Strymon's threats and migrate

---

[35] See footnote on line 730.

---

589 *transposed after* 594 *by Leo*
602 arto *Richter*: alto *EA*

605 permutat hiemes ales et caelum secans
tepente Nilo pensat Arctoas nives,
quot ille populos vatis eduxit sonus.
pavide latebras nemoris umbrosi petunt
animae trementes. primus emergit solo,
610 dextra ferocem cornibus taurum premens,
Zethus, manuque sustinet laeva chelyn
qui saxa dulci traxit Amphion sono,
interque natos Tantalis tandem suos
tuto superba fert caput fastu grave
615 et numerat umbras. peior hac genetrix adest
furibunda Agave, tota quam sequitur manus
partita regem; sequitur et Bacchas lacer
Pentheus tenetque saevus etiamnunc minas.

    Tandem vocatus saepe pudibundum extulit
620 caput atque ab omni dissidet turba procul
celatque semet. instat et Stygias preces
geminat sacerdos, donec in apertum efferat
vultus opertos Laius—fari horreo.
stetit per artus sanguine effuso horridus,
625 paedore foedo squalidam obtentus comam,
et ore rabido fatur: "O Cadmi effera,
cruore semper laeta cognato domus,
vibrate thyrsos, enthea natos manu
lacerate potius! maximum Thebis scelus
630 maternus amor est. patria, non ira deum,
sed scelere raperis: non gravi flatu tibi
luctificus Auster nec parum pluvio aethere
satiata tellus halitu sicco nocet
sed rex cruentus, pretia qui saevae necis
635 sceptra et nefandos occupat thalamos patris,

from winter, crossing the skies to exchange Arctic snows for the warm Nile, as were the throngs brought forth by the seer's utterance. In panic the timid spirits seek out hiding places in the shadowed grove. First to emerge from the ground is Zethus, his right hand restraining a fierce bull by the horns, and Amphion, holding in his left hand the lyre whose sweet sound once shifted stones. Amongst her children the Tantalid, at last safe in her pride, carries her head high in insufferable arrogance and counts her ghosts. Here is a worse mother than she, frenzied Agave, followed by the whole troop that sundered the king; the Bacchae are followed by the torn Pentheus, still fiercely continuing his threats.

The one repeatedly summoned at last raises his head, sullied as it is, but stays concealed far from the main crowd. Insistently the priest redoubles his Stygian prayers, until Laius reveals his hidden face. I shudder to speak of it. He stands caked in the blood that poured over his body, with his hair covered in squalid filth, and speaks in rage: "O savage house of Cadmus, always delighting in kindred blood: shake the thyrsus, rend your sons with god-driven hands, rather than this![36] In Thebes the greatest crime is the love of a mother. O fatherland, you are not ravaged by the gods' anger, but by a crime. It is not the unwholesome breath of the scourging south wind that harms you, nor the dry exhalations of a land too little watered by heaven's rains, but a bloodstained king, who as the prize for his cruel murder claimed his father's sceptre and taboo mar-

---

[36] I.e. even the murder of Pentheus by his own mother and aunts was less terrible than Oedipus' deeds.

[invisa proles: sed tamen peior parens
quam natus, utero rursus infausto gravis]
egitque in ortus semet et matri impios
fetus regessit, quique vix mos est feris,
640   fratres sibi ipse genuit—implicitum malum,
magisque monstrum Sphinge perplexum sua.
Te, te cruenta sceptra qui dextra geris,
te pater inultus urbe cum tota petam
et mecum Erinyn pronubam thalami traham,
645   traham sonantes verbera, incestam domum
vertam et penates impio marte obteram.
    "Proinde pulsum finibus regem ocius
agite exulem. quodcumque funesto gradu
solum relinquet, vere florifero virens
650   reparabit herbas; spiritus puros dabit
vitalis aura, veniet et silvis decor;
Letum Luesque, Mors Labor Tabes Dolor,
comitatus illo dignus, excedent simul.
et ipse rapidis gressibus sedes volet
655   effugere nostras, sed graves pedibus moras
addam et tenebo: repet incertus viae,
baculo senili triste praetemptans iter.
eripite terras, auferam caelum pater."

OEDIPUS

Et ossa et artus gelidus invasit tremor:
660   quidquid timebam facere fecisse arguor.
—tori iugalis abnuit Merope nefas
sociata Polybo; sospes absolvit manus

636–637 *deleted by Zwierlein*
656 repet *recc.*: repetet *E*: reptet *A*

riage bed.[37] He has pushed to his very source, forced unnatural procreation back on his mother, and as scarcely happens even among wild beasts, he has sired brothers for himself—an entangled evil, a monstrosity more enigmatic than his own Sphinx. You who hold the sceptre in your bloodied hand, I shall seek you out, your unavenged father, along with the whole city; with me I shall bring the Erinys who attended your bride chamber, bring those whose whips resound;[38] I shall overthrow this incestuous house, and wipe out its lineage in unnatural warfare.

"So then, expel the king quickly from your borders, drive him into exile. Each piece of ground that he forsakes with his fatal steps will bloom in a springtime flowering and regain its verdure; the life-giving air will be pure to breathe, and beauty will appear in the woodlands. Carnage and Plague, Death, Distress, Decay and Pain will depart with him, a worthy retinue. He himself will want to move swiftly to escape our abodes, but I shall put cumbersome delays before his feet and hold him back. He will creep unsure of his path, testing his dismal way with an old man's stick. You must dispossess him of the earth; I his father will deprive him of the sky."

OEDIPUS

A cold shiver pierces my body to its bones. All that I feared doing I am accused of having done. But Merope is married to Polybus, disproving any defilement of the marriage bed,

---

[37] 636–637 (deleted) may mean "detested offspring—yet worse as a father than as a son, burdening that ill-fated womb a second time."

[38] The Furies.

Polybus meas: uterque defendit parens
caedem stuprumque. quis locus culpae est super?
665 multo ante Thebae Laium amissum gemunt,
Boeota gressu quam meo tetigi loca.
falsusne senior an deus Thebis gravis?
—iam iam tenemus callidi socios doli:
mentitur ista praeferens fraudi deos
670 vates, tibique sceptra despondet mea.

CREO

Egone ut sororem regia expelli velim?
si me fides sacrata cognati laris
non contineret in meo certum statu,
tamen ipsa me fortuna terreret nimis
675 sollicita semper. liceat hoc tuto tibi
exuere pondus nec recedentem opprimat;
iam te minore tutior pones loco.

OEDIPUS

Hortaris etiam, sponte deponam ut mea
tam gravia regna?

CREO

Suadeam hoc illis ego,
680 in utrumque quîs est liber etiamnunc status:
tibi iam necesse est ferre fortunam tuam.

OEDIPUS

Certissima est regnare cupienti via
laudare modica et otium ac somnum loqui;
ab inquieto saepe simulatur quies.

CREO

685 Parumne me tam longa defendit fides?

and Polybus is alive, declaring my hands innocent. Each
parent refutes the charges, murder and incest. What room
is left for guilt? Thebes mourned the loss of Laius long before I set foot on Boeotian soil. Is the old man lying, or is
the god ill-disposed to Thebes? *Now* I grasp the accompli-
ces in this clever scheme: the seer makes up these fictions,
using the gods to cloak his treachery, and promises my
sceptre to you.

CREON

Would *I* want my sister driven from the palace? If I were
not kept firmly in my own position by my vowed allegiance
to a kindred house, I would still be deterred by the very nature of such a fortune, always too full of anxiety. May it be
granted you to put aside this burden safely, without its
crushing you as you withdraw. You will set yourself more
safely now in a humbler position.

OEDIPUS

Are you actually prompting me to lay down such a heavy
kingship of my own free will?

CREON

I would urge this on people who still have freedom to move
in either direction. You have no choice now but to bear
your fortune.

OEDIPUS

The surest path for someone desiring a throne is to praise a
modest life and talk of leisure and sleep. Quiet is often
feigned by unquiet spirits.

CREON

Is my long loyalty not a sufficient defence?

OEDIPUS

Aditum nocendi perfido praestat fides.

CREO

Solutus onere regio regni bonis
fruor, domusque civium coetu viget;
nec ulla vicibus surgit alternis dies
690 qua non propinqui munera ad nostros lares
sceptri redundent: cultus, opulentae dapes,
donata multis gratia nostra salus.
quid tam beatae desse fortunae rear?

OEDIPUS

Quod dest: secunda non habent umquam modum.

CREO

695 Incognita igitur ut nocens causa cadam?

OEDIPUS

Num ratio vobis reddita est vitae meae?
num audita causa est nostra Tiresiae? tamen
sontes videmur. facitis exemplum: sequor.

CREO

Quid si innocens sum?

OEDIPUS

Dubia pro certis solent
700 timere reges.

CREO

Qui pavet vanos metus,
veros meretur.

OEDIPUS

Quisquis in culpa fuit,
dimissus odit: omne quod dubium est ruat.

OEDIPUS

OEDIPUS

Loyalty provides the disloyal man with access to do harm.

CREON

Free of a king's burdens, I enjoy the benefits of kingship.
My house thrives as citizens gather there, and as each day
follows night the bounty of the nearby throne flows into my
home: elegant living, rich feasts, security granted to many
through my influence. What could I think missing from
such a well-blessed fortune?

OEDIPUS

What *is* missing! Prosperity never accepts any limitation.

CREON

Must I fall as guilty, then, without investigation of my case?

OEDIPUS

Did you two give consideration to my life? Was my case
heard by Tiresias? Yet I am held guilty. You made the precedent, I follow it.

CREON

What if I am innocent?

OEDIPUS

Kings regularly take unproven fears for certainties.

CREON

He who indulges empty fears earns himself real fears.

OEDIPUS

Anyone faulted feels hatred, even if let off; let all that is
suspect fall!

---

702 dubium est ruat *Enk*: obvium est eat *E*: dubium putat *A*

77

CREO

Sic odia fiunt.

OEDIPUS

Odia qui nimium timet
regnare nescit: regna custodit metus.

CREO

705 Qui sceptra duro saevus imperio gerit,
timet timentes: metus in auctorem redit.

OEDIPUS

Servate sontem saxeo inclusum specu.
ipse ad penates regios referam gradum.

CHORUS

Non tu tantis causa periclis,
710 non haec Labdacidas petunt
fata, sed veteres deum
irae sequuntur. Castalium nemus
umbram Sidonio praebuit hospiti
lavitque Dirce Tyrios colonos,
715 ut primum magni natus Agenoris,
fessus per orbem furta sequi Iovis,
sub nostra pavidus constitit arbore
praedonem venerans suum,
monituque Phoebi
iussus erranti comes ire vaccae,
720 quam non flexerat
vomer aut tardi iuga curva plaustri,

[705] gerit *Cornelissen*: regit *EA*

78

CREON

This is how hatred arises.

OEDIPUS

One unduly afraid of being hated is incapable of ruling; a throne is safeguarded by fear.

CREON

One who wields the sceptre with tyrannical harshness fears those who fear him; terror rebounds on its author.

OEDIPUS

[*To attendants*] Keep the guilty man shut up in a rocky cave. I shall return to the royal palace.

CHORUS

You are not the cause of these great hazards,
    not such is the fate that attacks
    the Labdacids: no, the ancient anger
of the gods is pursuing us. The Castalian grove
offered its shade to the stranger from Sidon,
    and Dirce bathed the settlers from Tyre,
when first the son of great Agenor,
    tired of tracking Jove's thefts through the world,
halted afraid beneath our trees,
    doing homage to his plunderer.[39]
            By Phoebus' command
    bidden to follow a straying cow
            that had never been governed
    by the plough or the curving yoke of a lumbering
    cart,

---

[39] Cadmus' sister Europa had been kidnapped by Jove (hence "his plunderer"). Cadmus was "afraid" to return to his father Agenor without finding her.

deseruit fugas nomenque genti
inauspicata de bove tradidit.

Tempore ex illo nova monstra semper
protulit tellus.
aut anguis imis vallibus editus
annosa circa robora sibilat,
supraque pinus,
supra Chaonias celsior arbores
erexit caeruleum caput,
cum maiore sui parte recumberet;
aut feta tellus impio partu
effudit arma:
sonuit reflexo classicum cornu
lituusque adunco stridulos cantus
elisit aere

    *   *   *   *

non ante linguas agiles et ora
vocis ignotae clamore primum
hostico experti.
agmina campos cognata tenent,
dignaque iacto semine proles,
uno aetatem permensa die,
post Luciferi nata meatus
ante Hesperios occidit ortus.
horret tantis advena monstris

725 (line 725)
730 (line 730)
735 (line 735)
740 (line 740)

---

727 circa *Reeve*: supra *EA*   727bis supraque *A*: superat-
que *E*   734 *lacuna identified by Leo*

---

40 "Boeotians," supposedly from βοῦς, 'cow' (Latin *bos*, used here).

he gave up roaming and passed on to his people
a name[40] from that ill-omened animal.

Ever since that time the land has brought forth
       new monsters.
A serpent rose from the valley's depths
hissing around the ancient tree trunks;
       above the pines,
high above the Chaonian trees
      it raised its blue-green head,
while the bulk of its body lay on the ground.[41]
   Or else the earth, in unnatural parturition,
       poured forth weapons;
the battle call sounded from the winding horn,
and the trumpet blared out strident notes
       from its curved brass

         *   *   *   *   *

who first tested their tongues, never quickened
   before,
and mouths in the battle cries
       of their unknown voices.
Ranks of kinsmen took the field,
a progeny worthy of the flung seed;
they measured their lifespan in one day,
born after the Morning Star emerged,
fallen before the Evening Star rose.
The stranger shuddered at these portents,

[41] Cadmus proceeded to slay this serpent, which was sacred to
Mars. He then sowed its teeth (the "flung seed" of 739); from
them sprang up armed men, who fought each other as the following lines recount.

populique timet bella recentis,
745 donec cecidit saeva iuventus
genetrixque suo reddi gremio
modo productos vidit alumnos.
hac transierit civile nefas!
illa Herculeae norint Thebae
750 proelia fratrum.
      Quid Cadmei fata nepotis,
cum vivacis cornua cervi
frontem ramis texere novis
dominumque canes egere suum?
755 praeceps silvas montesque fugit
citus Actaeon,
agilique magis
pede per saltus ac saxa vagus
metuit motas zephyris plumas
et quae posuit retia vitat—
760 donec placidi fontis in unda
cornua vidit vultusque feros:
ibi virgineos foverat artus
nimium saevi diva pudoris.

OEDIPUS

Curas revolvit animus et repetit metus.
765 obisse nostro Laium scelere autumant
superi inferique, sed animus contra innocens
sibique melius quam deis notus negat.

---

[42] The stranger is Cadmus; the mother is Earth.
[43] This wish draws attention to its own fruitlessness: later Theban generations such as Hercules' will actually know that there was a second civil war, viz. that between Oedipus' sons.

dismayed at the warfare of the newborn folk,
until the savage warriors fell
and their mother saw returned to her bosom
the sons she had just brought forth.[42]
With this may civil war's horrors have passed!
May Hercules' Thebes know only of that one
battle of brothers.[43]

What of the fate of Cadmus' grandson
when the horns of a long-lived stag
covered his forehead with strange branches
and his hounds hunted their master!
Swift Actaeon
fled headlong amidst forests and hills;
through brush, over rocks,
he wandered on more agile feet,
fearing the feathers moving in the breeze
and avoiding the nets he himself had set—
until in the water of the placid pool
he saw his horns and animal face.
There she had bathed her virgin limbs,
the goddess of chastity too fierce.[44]

ACT 4

OEDIPUS

My mind turns over its cares and revisits its fears. The
powers above and below declare that Laius died through a
crime of mine, but on the other hand my mind, which is innocent and better known to itself than to the gods, denies

[44] Diana.

redit memoria tenue per vestigium,
cecidisse nostri stipitis pulsu obvium
770 datumque Diti, cum prior iuvenem senex
curru superbus pelleret, Thebis procul
Phocaea trifidas regio qua scindit vias.

    Unanima coniunx, explica errores, precor:
quae spatia moriens Laius vitae tulit?
775 primone in aevo viridis an fracto occidit?

IOCASTA

Inter senem iuvenemque, sed propior seni.

OEDIPUS

Frequensne turba regium cinxit latus?

IOCASTA

Plures fefellit error ancipitis viae,
paucos fideles curribus iunxit labor.

OEDIPUS

780 Aliquisne cecidit regio fato comes?

IOCASTA

Unum fides virtusque consortem addidit.

OEDIPUS

Teneo nocentem: convenit numerus, locus—
sed tempus adde.

IOCASTA

       Decima iam metitur seges.

OEDIPUS

it. Yet a memory returns along a faint track, of someone
felled by a blow from my staff when he blocked my way,
and sent to Dis—an old man, who first forced me arro-
gantly aside with his chariot when I was young—at a distance from Thebes, where the region of Phocis splits the
road three ways.

[*To Jocasta*] Wife, you share my thoughts: straighten
out my confusion, I beg you. What span of life had Laius
when he died? Did he fall when flourishing in his early
prime, or in broken age?

JOCASTA

Between old age and youth, but closer to old age.

OEDIPUS

Was there a large retinue surrounding the king?

JOCASTA

Most went astray, confused by the unclear path, but a few
stayed by his chariot in loyal service.

OEDIPUS

Did anyone fall beside the dying king?

JOCASTA

One loyal and courageous man shared his fate.

OEDIPUS

I have the guilty man: the number and place match. And
what of the time?

JOCASTA

Now is the tenth harvest.

[*Old man from Corinth enters*]

SENECA

SENEX CORINTHIUS

Corinthius te populus in regnum vocat
785   patrium: quietem Polybus aeternam obtinet.

OEDIPUS

Ut undique in me saeva Fortuna irruit!
edissere agedum, quo cadat fato parens.

SENEX

Animam senilem mollis exsolvit sopor.

OEDIPUS

Genitor sine ulla caede defunctus iacet.
790   testor, licet iam tollere ad caelum pie
puras nec ulla scelera metuentes manus.
sed pars magis metuenda fatorum manet.

SENEX

Omnem paterna regna discutient metum.

OEDIPUS

Repetam paterna regna; sed matrem horreo.

SENEX

795   Metuis parentem, quae tuum reditum expetens
sollicita pendet?

OEDIPUS

Ipsa me pietas fugat.

SENEX

Viduam relinques?

OEDIPUS

Tangis en ipsos metus.

OLD MAN

The people of Corinth call you to your father's throne:
Polybus has reached his eternal rest.

OEDIPUS

How cruel Fortune attacks me on every side! Come now,
explain how the old man met his fate.

OLD MAN

A gentle sleep released his aged spirit.

OEDIPUS

My father lies dead without a hint of bloodshed! I testify
that now in good conscience I can lift my hands to heaven,
hands that are pure and fear no crimes. Yet the more fearful portion of my destiny remains.

OLD MAN

Your father's throne will dispel any fears.

OEDIPUS

I would claim my father's throne, but I am in dread of my
mother.

OLD MAN

You fear your mother, who is longing for your return in
anxious suspense?

OEDIPUS

My very affection keeps me away.

OLD MAN

You will leave her widowed?

OEDIPUS

Ah, you touch exactly on my fear.

SENECA

SENEX

Effare mersus quis premat mentem timor;
praestare tacitam regibus soleo fidem.

OEDIPUS

800 Conubia matris Delphico monitu tremo.

SENEX

Timere vana desine et turpes metus
depone. Merope vera non fuerat parens.

OEDIPUS

Quod subditivi praemium nati petit?

SENEX

Regum superbam liberi astringunt fidem.

OEDIPUS

805 Secreta thalami fare quo excipias modo.

SENEX

Hae te parenti parvulum tradunt manus.

OEDIPUS

Tu me parenti tradis; at quis me tibi?

SENEX

Pastor nivoso sub Cithaeronis iugo.

OEDIPUS

In illa temet nemora quis casus tulit?

SENEX

810 Illo sequebar monte cornigeros greges.

OEDIPUS

Nunc adice certas corporis nostri notas.

SENEX

Forata ferro gesseras vestigia,

88

OEDIPUS

OLD MAN

Spell out this hidden fear that burdens your mind. I am a
man who keeps loyal silence for kings.

OEDIPUS

Warned by Delphi, I dread marriage with my mother.

OLD MAN

Put aside these monstrous and empty fears. Merope was
not your true mother.

OEDIPUS

What did she seek to gain by smuggling in a son?

OLD MAN

Children secure the loyalty of haughty kings.

OEDIPUS

Tell me how you know the secrets of her bedchamber.

OLD MAN

These hands passed you as a baby to your mother.

OEDIPUS

You passed me to my mother: who passed me to you?

OLD MAN

A herdsman, under the snowy ridge of Cithaeron.

OEDIPUS

What chance took you to those woodlands?

OLD MAN

I was herding flocks of horned animals on that mountain.

OEDIPUS

Now tell me also the unmistakable marks on my body.

OLD MAN

Your ankles had been pierced with iron, and you took your

tumore nactus nomen ac vitio pedum.

OEDIPUS

Quis fuerit ille qui meum dono dedit
815   corpus requiro.

SENEX

Regios pavit greges;
minor sub illo turba pastorum fuit.

OEDIPUS

Eloquere nomen.

SENEX

Prima languescit senum
memoria, longo lassa sublabens situ.

OEDIPUS

Potesne facie noscere ac vultu virum?

SENEX

820   Fortasse noscam: saepe iam spatio obrutam
levis exoletam memoriam revocat nota.

OEDIPUS

Ad sacra et aras omne compulsum pecus
duces sequuntur: ite, propere accersite,
famuli, penes quem summa consistit gregum.

IOCASTA

825   Sive ista ratio sive fortuna occulit,
latere semper patere quod latuit diu:
saepe eruentis veritas patuit malo.

824 quem *Zwierlein*: quos *EA*
825–827, 829–832, 835–836 *attributed to Jocasta by Weil, to Old Man by EA*

90

name from the misshapen swelling of your feet.[45]

OEDIPUS

I need to know who handed over my body.

OLD MAN

He tended the royal flocks: under him was a subordinate group of herdsmen.

OEDIPUS

Tell me his name.

OLD MAN

Old men's first weakness is their memory, tired and ebbing away in slow decay.

OEDIPUS

Could you recognise the man by the features of his face?

OLD MAN

Perhaps so: even a memory that is faint and obscured by time can be recalled by a small token.

OEDIPUS

All the flocks were driven to the rites at the altar, and their leaders are with them: go, servants, quickly summon the man who has chief control of the herds.

JOCASTA

Whether chance or rational purpose has concealed these facts, let things long hidden stay hidden forever: truth when exposed often harms the one that unearths it.

---

[45] Oedipus supposedly means "swollen-footed" (Οἰδί-πους).

SENECA

OEDIPUS
Malum timeri maius his aliquod potest?

IOCASTA
Magnum esse magna mole quod petitur scias.
830 concurrit illinc publica, hinc regis salus,
utrimque paria; contine medias manus.
nihil lacessas, ipsa se fata explicent.

OEDIPUS
Non expedit concutere felicem statum:
tuto movetur quidquid extremo in loco est.

IOCASTA
835 Nobilius aliquid genere regali appetis?
ne te parentis pigeat inventi vide.

OEDIPUS
Vel paenitendi sanguinis quaeram fidem:
sic nosse certum est. —Ecce grandaevus senex,
arbitria sub quo regii fuerant gregis,
840 Phorbas. refersne nomen aut vultum senis?

SENEX
Adridet animo forma; nec notus satis,
nec rursus iste vultus ignotus mihi.

OEDIPUS
Regnum obtinente Laio famulus greges
agitasti opimos sub Cithaeronis plaga?

PHORBAS
845 Laetus Cithaeron pabulo semper novo
aestiva nostro prata summittit gregi.

---

832 *The text printed is E's:* A *has* ut nil accersas*, ipsa te fata
explicent   838 sic *Leo:* si E: sed A
843–844 *attributed to Oedipus by Gronovius, to Old Man by EA*

92

OEDIPUS

Can we fear any greater harm than this we see?

JOCASTA

A thing is great if sought with great effort, be sure of it. The people's wellbeing on one side is pitted against the king's wellbeing on the other—a well-matched pair: keep your hands clear of it. Do not provoke matters, let destiny unfold itself.

OEDIPUS

There is no advantage in shaking up a happy state of affairs, but there is safety in changing a desperate situation.

JOCASTA

Do you aspire to something nobler than royal birth? Take care: you may be displeased with the father you discover.

OEDIPUS

I shall look for certainty, even about shameful blood ties; these are the terms on which I am resolved to know.

See here, the old man full of years who had command of the royal herds, Phorbas. [*To old Corinthian*] Do you recall the old man's name or face?

OLD MAN

His appearance tallies with my mind; that face is not really familiar, yet again not unfamiliar to me.

OEDIPUS

[*To Phorbas*] When Laius held the throne, did you drive fattening flocks in his service on the slopes of Cithaeron?

PHORBAS

Cithaeron is always rich in fresh pasture, and produces summer grazing for our flock.

SENEX

Noscisne memet?

PHORBAS

Dubitat anceps memoria.

OEDIPUS

Huic aliquis a te traditur quondam puer?
effare. dubitas? cur genas mutat color?
850　quid verba quaeris? veritas odit moras.

PHORBAS

Obducta longo temporum tractu moves.

OEDIPUS

Fatere, ne te cogat ad verum dolor.

PHORBAS

Inutile isti munus infantem dedi:
non potuit ille luce, non caelo frui.

SENEX

855　Procul sit omen! vivit et vivat precor.

OEDIPUS

Superesse quare traditum infantem negas?

PHORBAS

Ferrum per ambos tenue transactum pedes
ligabat artus; vulneri innatus tumor
puerile foeda corpus urebat lue.

OEDIPUS

860　Quid quaeris ultra? fata iam accedent prope. —
quis fuerit infans edoce.

OEDIPUS

OLD MAN
Do you recognise me?

PHORBAS
My memory is hesitant and uncertain.

OEDIPUS
Was a boy once handed to this man by you? Speak! You hesitate? Why do your cheeks change colour? Why are you searching for words? Truth hates delay.

PHORBAS
You are raising matters obscured by a long stretch of time.

OEDIPUS
Acknowledge it, or pain will force you to the truth.

PHORBAS
I gave him a worthless gift of a baby: it could not have enjoyed heaven's light.

OLD MAN
May the omen come to nothing! He lives, and I pray he will live.

OEDIPUS
Why do you say the baby you handed him does not survive?

PHORBAS
There was a metal rod driven through both its feet, pinning its legs together; the swelling caused by the wound was inflaming the child's body with a foul infection.

OEDIPUS
[*Aside*] Why search further? Now destiny comes close. [*To Phorbas*] Tell me fully, who was the baby?

SENECA

PHORBAS
Prohibet fides.

OEDIPUS
Huc aliquis ignem! flamma iam excutiet fidem.

PHORBAS
Per tam cruentas vera quaerentur vias?
ignosce quaeso.

OEDIPUS
Si ferus videor tibi
865   et impotens, parata vindicta in manu est:
dic vera. quisnam, quove generatus patre,
qua matre genitus?

PHORBAS
Coniuge est genitus tua.

OEDIPUS
Dehisce, tellus, tuque, tenebrarum potens,
in Tartara ima, rector umbrarum, rape
870   retro reversas generis ac stirpis vices!
congerite, cives, saxa in infandum caput,
mactate telis: me petat ferro parens,
me natus, in me coniuges arment manus
fratresque, et aeger populus ereptos rogis
875   iaculetur ignes. saeculi crimen vagor,
odium deorum, iuris exitium sacri,
qua luce primum spiritus hausi rudes
iam morte dignus. redde nunc animos pares,
nunc aliquid aude sceleribus dignum tuis.
880   i, perge, propero regiam gressu pete:
gratare matri liberis auctam domum!

96

OEDIPUS

PHORBAS

My loyalty forbids.

OEDIPUS

Bring fire, one of you! Flames will soon drive out loyalty.

PHORBAS

Is truth to be sought by such bloody means? Forgive me, I beg you.

OEDIPUS

If you think me cruel and ruthless, you have vengeance ready to hand: tell me the truth! Who was he? Sired by what father, born of what mother?

PHORBAS

He was born of your wife.

OEDIPUS

Split open, Earth! And you who govern the darkness, ruler of the shades, carry off to the depths of Tartarus this inversion of the roles of stock and offspring. Citizens, hurl stones at this unspeakable body, slay me with your spears. Let father and son attack me with the sword, let husbands and brothers take arms against me, let the people in their sickness seize firebrands from the pyres to hurl at me. I am at large, the iniquity of the age, abomination of the gods, violation of holy law, already deserving death on the day I drew my first childish breaths. [*To himself*] Now respond with matching courage, now show some daring worthy of your crimes. Go ahead, speed your steps into the palace: congratulate your mother on enhancing our house with children!

CHORUS

Fata si liceat mihi
fingere arbitrio meo,
temperem Zephyro levi
885 vela, ne pressae gravi
spiritu antennae tremant.
lenis et modice fluens
aura nec vergens latus
ducat intrepidam ratem;
890 tuta me media vehat
vita decurrens via.

Cnosium regem timens
astra dum demens petit,
artibus fisus novis,
895 certat et veras aves
vincere ac falsis nimis
imperat pinnis puer,
nomen eripuit freto.
callidus medium senex
900 Daedalus librans iter
nube sub media stetit
alitem expectans suum
(qualis accipitris minas
fugit et sparsos metu
905 colligit fetus avis),
donec in ponto manus
movit implicitas puer
compede audacis viae.

902 suum *Ascensius*: suam *EA*
908 compede *Bücheler*: comes *EA, unmetrically: the line deleted by Goebel*

98

OEDIPUS

CHORUS

If I were allowed to fashion
fate to my own desire,
I would trim my sails to the light
westerly wind, lest the sailyards
shake in a heavy gale.
A gentle, moderate breeze
that does not heel the side
would guide my untroubled boat.
Running a middle course,
my life would carry me safe.

    As he madly sought the stars
in flight from the Cnossian king,
confident in new skills,
and struggled to rise above
real birds, demanding too much
of his false wings, a boy
robbed a sea of its name.[46]
Balancing a middle path
shrewd old Daedalus rested
midway beneath the clouds
awaiting his fledgling son
(as a bird will escape a threatening
hawk, and then regather
its young ones scattered in flight),
until in the sea the boy
moved his hands enmeshed
in the bonds of that bold journey.

---

[46] The boy was Icarus, after whom the sea was renamed
Icarian; the king of Cnossus was Minos.

quidquid excessit modum
910   pendet instabili loco.

Sed quid hoc? postes sonant,
maestus et famulus manu
regius quassat caput. —
Ede quid portes novi.

NUNTIUS

915   Praedicta postquam fata et infandum genus
deprendit ac se scelere convictum Oedipus
damnavit ipse, regiam infestus petens
invisa propero tecta penetravit gradu,
qualis per arva Libycus insanit leo,
920   fulvam minaci fronte concutiens iubam.
vultus furore torvus atque oculi truces,
gemitus et altum murmur, et gelidus volat
sudor per artus, spumat et volvit minas
ac mersus alte magnus exundat dolor.
925   secum ipse saevus grande nescioquid parat
suisque fatis simile. "Quid poenas moror?"
ait "hoc scelestum pectus aut ferro petat
aut fervido aliquis igne vel saxo domet.
quae tigris aut quae saeva visceribus meis
930   incurret ales? ipse tu scelerum capax,
sacer Cithaeron, vel feras in me tuis
emitte silvis, mitte vel rabidos canes—
nunc redde Agaven. anime, quid mortem times?
mors innocentem sola Fortunae eripit."

922 volat *A*: fluit *E*

All that strays from the mean
is poised in an unsteady place.
    What is this? A sound from the doors:
see, a slave from the palace
pounds his head in sorrow.
Tell us the news you bring.

ACT 5

MESSENGER

After Oedipus had grasped the fate foretold for him and
his unspeakable parentage, and condemned himself as one
convicted of crime, he headed threateningly to the palace
and pressed with hurried steps into the odious rooms, as a
Libyan lion rages through the countryside with a menacing
glare, shaking its tawny mane. His face was wild with fury,
his eyes savage, there were groans and deep mutterings,
cold sweat ran over his limbs, he spilled threats from his
foaming mouth, as his great pain poured from deep within
him. In his mind he fiercely planned some mighty deed to
match his destiny. "Why delay punishment?" he said, "Let
someone assail this guilty breast with the sword, or subdue
it with stones or blazing fire. What tigress or what savage
bird will attack my flesh? You who encompass crimes, accursed Cithaeron, send beasts against me from your forests, send ravening hounds—now send back Agave.[47] My
spirit, why fear death? Death alone can rescue the innocent from Fortune."

[47] The last two phrases allude to the deaths of Actaeon and
Pentheus respectively.

935   Haec fatus aptat impiam capulo manum
ensemque ducit. "Itane? tam magnis breves
poenas sceleribus solvis atque uno omnia
pensabis ictu? moreris: hoc patri sat est;
quid deinde matri, quid male in lucem editis
940 natis, quid ipsi, quae tuum magna luit
scelus ruina, flebili patriae dabis?
solvendo non es! illa quae leges ratas
Natura in uno vertit Oedipoda, novos
commenta partus, supplicîs eadem meis
945 novetur. iterum vivere atque iterum mori
liceat, renasci semper ut totiens nova
supplicia pendas.—utere ingenio, miser!
quod saepe fieri non potest fiat diu;
mors eligatur longa. quaeratur via
950 qua nec sepultis mixtus et vivis tamen
exemptus erres: morere, sed citra patrem.
cunctaris, anime? subitus en vultus gravat
profusus imber ac rigat fletu genas—
et flere satis est? hactenus fundent levem
955 oculi liquorem: sedibus pulsi suis
lacrimas sequantur. hi maritales statim
fodiantur oculi!"

        Dixit atque ira furit:
ardent minaces igne truculento genae
oculique vix se sedibus retinent suis;
960 violentus audax vultus, iratus ferox
iamiam eruentis. gemuit et dirum fremens

---

942 solvendo non es *Grotius*: solvenda non est *EA*
961 iamiam *Sluiter*: tantum *EA*

With these words he fitted his impious hand round the hilt of his sword and drew it. "Is this the way? You pay for such great crimes with so brief a penalty, compensate for them all with a single blow? You die: this is enough for your father. What then will you offer your mother, or your children, so wrongly brought into the light? What will you offer her who pays for your crimes with utter ruin—your pitiful fatherland? You are bankrupt! Nature, who alters her fixed laws in regard to Oedipus alone, by inventing unheard-of procreation, must change yet again to provide my punishment. You must be allowed to live once more and die once more, to be reborn repeatedly so you can pay a new penalty each time. Wretched man, use your cleverness! What cannot happen often must happen slowly; pick out a lingering death. Search for a way to wander without mixing with the dead, and yet removed from the living. Die, but stop short of your father. Do you hesitate, my spirit? See, a sudden flurry of tears burdens my face and wets my cheeks with weeping. And is it enough to weep? No longer shall my eyes pour out this paltry moisture: they must be driven from their seats and follow their tears.[48] Let them be dug out straightway, these eyes of a married man!"

So he spoke, raging with anger. His eyes blazed threateningly with a ravening fire, and their orbs scarcely held fast in their seats. Full of audacious violence was his gaze, of ferocious anger, as he prepared to root it out. He

---

[48] Dryden and Lee (n. above on 558) elaborate: "Yet these [viz. tears] thou think'st are ample satisfaction / For bloodiest Murder, and for burning Lust: / No, Parricide; if thou must weep, weep blood; / Weep Eyes, instead of Tears."

manus in ora torsit; at contra truces
oculi steterunt et suam intenti manum
ultro insequuntur, vulneri occurrunt suo.
965 scrutatur avidus manibus uncis lumina,
radice ab ima funditus vulsos simul
evolvit orbes; haeret in vacuo manus
et fixa penitus unguibus lacerat cavos
alte recessus luminum et inanes sinus,
970 saevitque frustra plusque quam satis est furit:
tantum est periclum lucis. attollit caput
cavisque lustrans orbibus caeli plagas
noctem experitur. quidquid effossis male
dependet oculis rumpit, et victor deos
975 conclamat omnes: "Parcite en patriae, precor:
iam iusta feci, debitas poenas tuli;
inventa thalamis digna nox tandem meis."
rigat ora foedus imber, et lacerum caput
largum revulsis sanguinem venis vomit.

CHORUS

980 Fatis agimur: cedite fatis.
non sollicitae possunt curae
mutare rati stamina fusi.
quidquid patimur mortale genus,
quidquid facimus venit ex alto,
985 servatque suae decreta colus
Lachesis dura revoluta manu.
omnia secto tramite vadunt,
primusque dies dedit extremum.
non illa deo vertisse licet,
990 quae nexa suis currunt causis.
it cuique ratus

groaned, and with a terrible cry he bent his hands towards his face. For their part his eyes stood out wildly, and intently tracked the hands they knew, meeting their wounds halfway. With hooked hands he greedily probed his eyes, and from their base, from their very roots he wrenched the eyeballs and let them roll out together. His hands stayed embedded in the cavities, their nails tearing deeply into the hollow recesses of his eyes, those empty sockets, with fruitless aggression and excessive rage: so great was the threat of the light. He raised his head, and scanning the sky's expanse with hollow orbs he tested the darkness. He broke off the shreds hanging down where the eyes had been incompletely dug out, and in triumph called on all the gods: "Look, spare my fatherland, I pray you: I have done justice, have taken the penalty owed. At last I have found a night suited to my marriage chamber." A hideous flurry of drops wetted his face, and his mutilated head spewed copious blood from the torn veins.

CHORUS

We are driven by fate, and must yield to fate.
No anxious fretting can alter
the threads from that commanding spindle.
All that we mortal beings endure,
all that we do, comes from on high;
Lachesis secures the decrees of her distaff,
things that are spun by her harsh hands.
Everything travels on a path cut for it,
and the first day decides the last.
Not even a god can change events
which run in a woven series of causes.
Each person's commanding thread of life

prece non ulla mobilis ordo.
multis ipsum metuisse nocet,
multi ad fatum venere suum
dum fata timent.
    Sonuere fores,
995   atque ipse suum duce non ullo
molitur iter luminis orbus.

OEDIPUS

Bene habet, peractum est: iusta persolvi patri.
iuvant tenebrae. quis deus tandem mihi
1000   placatus atra nube perfundit caput?
quis scelera donat? conscium evasi diem.
nil, parricida, dexterae debes tuae:
lux te refugit. vultus Oedipodam hic decet.

CHORUS

En ecce, rapido saeva prosiluit gradu
1005   Iocasta vecors, qualis attonita et furens
Cadmea mater abstulit nato caput
sensitve raptum. dubitat afflictum alloqui,
cupit pavetque. iam malis cessit pudor,
sed haeret ore prima vox.

IOCASTA

        Quid te vocem?
1010   natumne? dubitas? natus es: natum pudet.
invite loquere nate. quo avertis caput
vacuosque vultus?

---

[49] *Iusta* also connotes "just dues," viz. for Oedipus' offences against him.

continues unchanged by any prayer.
Many are hurt by fear itself,
many have come upon their fate
through fear of fate.
    A sound from the doors:
he makes his own way with none to guide him,
laboriously, bereft of the light.

OEDIPUS

Good, the task is done: I have paid my father his last rites.[49]
I cherish my darkness. What god, kindly disposed to me at
last, has poured a cloud of blackness over my head? Who
pardons my crimes? I have escaped the witness of the daylight. Parricide, you owe nothing to your right hand: the
light itself fled from you. Such vision as this is right for
Oedipus.

CHORUS LEADER

Look, Jocasta rushes out with urgent steps in violent turmoil, like the frenzied Cadmean mother when she tore
away her son's head, or when she recognised her theft.[50]
She hesitates to speak to the ruined man, desires yet fears
to do so. Now her distress overcomes her shame, but still
the first words stick in her mouth.

JOCASTA

What shall I call you? Son? You object? You *are* my son: it is
my son that feels shame.[51] Speak, my reluctant son! Why
turn away your head and empty eyes?

[50] Again a reference to Agave, who recognised her son's head
when she emerged from her delirium.
[51] I.e. you would not feel shame if you were not my son; your
shame proves the relationship (so Gronovius).

OEDIPUS

    Quis frui et tenebris vetat?
quis reddit oculos? matris, en matris sonus!
perdidimus operam. congredi fas amplius
1015 haud est nefandos. dividat vastum mare
dirimatque tellus abdita, et quisquis sub hoc
in alia versus sidera ac solem avium
dependet orbis alterum ex nobis ferat.

IOCASTA

Fati ista culpa est: nemo fit fato nocens.

OEDIPUS

1020 Iam parce verbis, mater, et parce auribus:
per has reliquias corporis trunci precor,
per inauspicatum sanguinis pignus mei,
per omne nostri nominis fas ac nefas.

IOCASTA

Quid, anime, torpes? socia cur scelerum dare
1025 poenas recusas? omne confusum perît,
incesta, per te iuris humani decus:
morere et nefastum spiritum ferro exige.
non si ipse mundum concitans divum sator
corusca saeva tela iaculetur manu,
1030 umquam rependam sceleribus poenas pares
mater nefanda. mors placet: mortis via
quaeratur.
    Agedum, commoda matri manum,
si parricida es: restat hoc operi ultimum.
—rapiatur ensis. hoc iacet ferro meus

1012 et *CSP*: *omitted by ET*

108

OEDIPUS

Who prevents me from enjoying even the darkness? Who
gives me eyes again? It is my mother's voice, my mother's. I
have wasted my efforts. It is not right for us to come together any more in such corruption. The vast sea should
separate us, a remote land sunder us, and that strange
world that lies opposite this one, facing other stars and a
distant sun, should bear one of us two.

JOCASTA

This fault is fate's; no one becomes guilty by fate.

OEDIPUS

Spare your words now, mother, spare my ears: I beg you by
what remains of my mutilated body, by the inauspicious
bond of my blood,[52] by all that is holy and unholy in our
names.

JOCASTA

Why so sluggish, my spirit? Why refuse to pay the penalty
as accomplice of his crimes? Every decency of human law
has been confounded and destroyed by your incest. Die,
drive out your accursed life with the sword. Even if he who
spurs the heavens, the sire of the gods, should hurl his glittering bolts without mercy, I could never pay a penalty to
match my crimes as an unspeakable mother. Death is my
resolve: the way of death must be found.

[*To Oedipus*] Come now, lend your hand's service to
your mother, if you are a parricide: this task remains to
complete your work. [*To herself*] Let me seize his sword. It

---

[52] This phrase could refer to his blood ties with his mother
and/or to their children; the ambivalence matches the confound-
ing of relationships in this family. The "names" of the next line are
those of mother and son, wife and husband.

1035   coniunx—quid illum nomine haud vero vocas?
         socer est. utrumne pectori infigam meo
         telum an patenti conditum iugulo imprimam?
         eligere nescis vulnus: hunc, dextra, hunc pete
         uterum capacem, qui virum et natos tulit.

CHORUS

1040   Iacet perempta. vulneri immoritur manus
         ferrumque secum nimius eiecit cruor.

OEDIPUS

         Fatidice te, te praesidem veri deum
         compello: solum debui fatis patrem;
         bis parricida plusque quam timui nocens
1045   matrem peremi: scelere confecta est meo.
         o Phoebe mendax, fata superavi impia.
             Pavitante gressu sequere fallentes vias;
         suspensa plantis efferens vestigia
         caecam tremente dextera noctem rege.
1050   —ingredere praeceps, lubricos ponens gradus,
         i profuge vade—siste, ne in matrem incidas.
             Quicumque fessi pectore et morbo graves
         semianima trahitis corpora, en fugio, exeo:
         relevate colla, mitior caeli status
1055   post terga sequitur. quisquis exilem iacens
         animam retentat, vividos haustus levis
         concipiat. ite, ferte depositis opem:
         mortifera mecum vitia terrarum extraho.
         Violenta Fata et horridus Morbi tremor,
1060   Maciesque et atra Pestis et rabidus Dolor,
         mecum ite, mecum. ducibus his uti libet.

1052 pectore *Fitch*: corpore *EA*   1053 corpora *A*: pectora *E*

was this blade that killed my husband. Why call him by an untruthful name? He was my father-in-law. Shall I fasten the weapon in my breast, or drive it deep into my bare throat? You have no skill in choosing a wound! Strike this, my hand, this capacious womb, which bore husband and children.

CHORUS LEADER

She lies slain. Her hand dies as it wounds, and the gushing blood forces the sword out with it.

OEDIPUS

Fate-speaking god, guardian of truth, I reproach you. The only life I owed fate was my father's. I am twice a parricide, more guilty than I feared, in having killed my mother: she was destroyed by my crime. Phoebus, you lied! I have surpassed my sacrilegious fate.

[*To himself*] With shaking steps follow deceptive paths. As you drag yourself away with each hesitant footfall, guide your blind night with trembling hands. No, advance headlong, your steps slipping, go, flee into exile—but stop, lest you fall upon your mother.

All you who are weak at heart and heavy with sickness, dragging frames only half alive, see, I am leaving for exile: lift up your heads, a kindlier condition of the skies will come in behind me. You who feebly retain the breath of life on your sickbeds may freely take in life-giving draughts of air. Go, bring help to those abandoned to die: I am drawing with me the deadly maladies of the land. Savage Fates, the shuddering tremor of Disease, Wasting and black Plague and ravening Pain, come with me, come with me: I rejoice to have such guides as these.

111

AGAMEMNON

INTRODUCTION

Background

In the terrible vendetta between the brothers Atreus and Thyestes over the throne of Argos, Atreus had murdered Thyestes' sons and feasted their unwitting father on their flesh. Thereafter Thyestes was directed by Phoebus to lie with his own daughter Pelopia; the child of this incestuous union, Aegisthus, was fated to take revenge on Atreus' son Agamemnon. During Agamemnon's absence as leader of the Greek expedition to Troy, Aegisthus has become the lover of Agamemnon's wife, Clytemnestra, who has her own reasons for desiring the death of her husband. The Trojan war is now ended, and Agamemnon's arrival home is imminent.

Summary

Act 1
The ghost of Thyestes appears in Argos and foresees the death of Agamemnon.

Ode 1. Royal power is vulnerable to Fortune, whether through the moral corruption fomented by power, or through the inherent instability of all great things.

Act 2
Clytemnestra steels herself for action by dwelling on her

grievances against Agamemnon—his sacrifice of their daughter Iphigenia, his infidelities, and the danger represented by his Trojan mistress Cassandra. When Aegisthus appears, Clytemnestra feels revulsion for her guilty path and longs to recover innocence; finally, however, she resigns herself to colluding with Aegisthus.

Ode 2. The women of Argos sing a thanksgiving ode to Phoebus, Juno, Pallas, Phoebe, and Jupiter for Agamemnon's victory.

Act 3
The herald Eurybates reports Agamemnon's imminent arrival, but also the destruction of much of the Greek fleet by a sea storm during the voyage home from Troy.

Ode 3. A secondary chorus of Trojan women reflects on the human instinct to cling to life even amidst disaster. The women recollect the episode of the Wooden Horse which led to Troy's fall.

Act 4
The Trojan seer Cassandra also mourns for Troy, but then has a vision of coming events as retribution. Agamemnon arrives, and cannot understand Cassandra's comparison of Argos to Troy.

Ode 4. The triumphs of another son of Argos, Hercules.

Act 5
By clairvoyance Cassandra watches the murder of Agamemnon happening in the palace. His children, Electra and Orestes, leave the palace, and Electra entrusts her brother to a faithful friend, Strophius. Defying Clytemnestra and Aegisthus, Electra is led away to prison, while

Cassandra is taken to execution, rejoicing that Troy's fall has been recompensed.

Comment

Like a series of waves breaking on shore, a sequence of falls from success to disaster moves through this play. First we hear from the herald how the Greek fleet, sailing triumphantly from Troy, was devastated by a sea storm at night. The fact that the Argive chorus has just confidently invoked the gods' favour (Ode 2) heightens the contrast between joy and sorrow. The second instance comes in the Trojan chorus' recollection of the thanksgiving in Troy over the apparent departure of the Greeks, followed that very night by the sack of the city. The third instance follows Agamemnon's triumphal arrival home and the celebratory fourth ode, when the banquet in the king's honour turns into a bloodbath.

The play's tragic pattern, then, is multiple: it involves not only Agamemnon but many people, and not only Greeks but also Trojans. And perspectives on it are multiple: the first tragedy is seen though the memories of a Greek participant, the second through the memories of Trojan participants,[1] the third through the vision of an outsider, Cassandra.

---

[1] The secondary chorus of Trojan women arrives together with Cassandra (586–588). Secondary choruses are not uncommon in ancient tragedy; the technique of using such a chorus in association with a single character (often a young woman) is found in Euripides. Seneca's use of that technique here to develop a viewpoint quite different from that of the main chorus is taken up by the authors of both *HO* and *Oct*.

The play is characterised, in fact, by multiple vision. So we view the palace of Argos first through the dark and alien vision of a figure from the underworld, who can see both the guilty feasts of the past (11) and the future feast that will end in death (44–47).[2] And later we look at events through the clairvoyant vision of Cassandra, who can see into the underworld and invite the Trojan dead to watch (758), so that the killing of Agamemnon becomes a spectacle (875) akin to a gladiatorial fight (901). She sees a double image of Argos, as itself but also as Troy (728–729), just as Agamemnon is also Priam (794, cf. 879–880)—images that convey both a similarity in the fall of greatness, and a sense of recompense as the vanquishers are vanquished in turn.

The play's multiple viewpoints offer multiple ways of understanding events. For Thyestes, the coming murder represents revenge on Atreus' descendant; for Clytemnestra, revenge on Agamemnon himself; for Aegisthus, the crisis of his life, a desperate throw of the dice; for Cassandra, a recompense for Troy's doom, which at the same time seals her own fate. None of these ways of understanding appears authoritative, in the sense of excluding others. This situation corresponds to the fact that none of the dramatis personae is central or dominant in the play—least of all Agamemnon himself, who is onstage for only 26 lines.

---

[2] Ghosts are by no means uncommon in ancient tragedy. However, "dramatists of the Renaissance generally knew the ghost-prologue only in Senecan form, and so took the prologues of *Agamemnon* and *Thyestes* as models for scores of later plays" (Tarrant's edition p. 158).

AGAMEMNON

Authority is decentered both in the events of the play and in ways of understanding them.

The first choral ode offers a more general way of understanding the fall of greatness—or rather, characteristically, two ways: Fortune's destructive blows may be due to moral causes or to natural causes (viz. the fact that everything great offers a target to destructive natural forces). This analysis gives the play special cogency for a Roman audience, since each of these two causes of decay—moral degeneration or the vulnerability of greatness—was frequently applied to Rome herself by historians and other writers. The second explanation, especially since it mentions winds as instances of destructive forces (90–93), seems borne out in Act 3 by the devastation of the thousand-strong armada, a devastation attributed here not to divine anger (with the exception of Ajax), but to the power of wind and wave. The first cause, particularly as specified in 79–81 ("Right and shame / and the hallowed loyalties of marriage / abandon palaces") is exemplified in Act 2. Here we find Seneca's characteristic subtlety in depiction of moral and psychological factors, which is worth close examination.

Initially Clytemnestra describes herself as torn between a hopeless desire to revert to the role of chaste wife, and a wish to commit herself fully to the path of violence (108–124). She lists the emotional forces impelling her on the latter path: angry resentment (*dolor*), fear (of retribution), jealousy (of the mistresses), and sexual passion (for Aegisthus); again *pudor* or the impulse to chastity is fighting hopelessly on the other side (133–138). Next the queen tries to justify her murderous plans by listing her grievances against Agamemnon, including his sacrifice of their

119

daughter Iphigenia and his subsequent infidelities up to the present.[3] In this account it would be a distortion to identify any one event, or any one emotion, as primary.

When Aegisthus enters and urges Clytemnestra to remain true to their conspiracy, the queen suddenly reverts to the first impulse she mentioned earlier: desire for a chaste marital relationship with Agamemnon (239–243). The abruptness of this change of heart allows for various readings, but comparison with Seneca's character portrayal in other plays suggests lines of interpretation. As Phaedra, after a debate on similar issues (*pudor* vs guilt), yields to her Nurse's opposition (*Pha* 250–254), so Clytemnestra has been swayed by her Nurse and especially by her most recent and forceful speech (203–225). Why, then, does Seneca set the change *after* Aegisthus' arrival? Here the instances of Megara and Andromache are instructive: the behaviour of each changes drastically in reaction to the arrival of a new figure (respectively Lycus at *Herc* 332 and Ulysses at *Tro* 524). So Clytemnestra's doubts about her guilty path, strengthened by the Nurse, have burgeoned in reaction to the arrival of her lover, whose presence rekindles the guilt of her infidelity (266) and her shame over his unworthiness (291–301).

This portrait of Clytemnestra is much more complex than any other portrait of her known to us from antiquity,

---

[3] During this speech it becomes increasingly clear that Clytemnestra's view is distorted by prejudice. The idea that Cassandra will become the children's stepmother—or indeed that the queen's concern is for her children rather than herself (195–199) —is as unreal as her notion of killing Agamemnon and herself with one blow in a murder-suicide (199–202).

and characteristic of Seneca's interest in the working of the passions. It is indicative of the decentered nature of this play that the moral-psychological viewpoint is not developed further (except arguably in the final scene), as other perspectives supervene.   Even in Act 2 the moral viewpoint is not absolute: Aegisthus provides a different perspective on Clytemnestra's moral calculus by contending that it is irrelevant to the realities of power. He insists that she cannot hope for a reconciliation with her husband based on mutual forgiveness, nor for fair treatment from him, nor for loyalty from her servants, because such things do not exist in palaces; for Aegisthus power engenders other rules, another way of understanding.

The issue of Aegisthus' birth offers yet another perspective, an historical one. He was conceived (as the ghost of his father recalls in Act 1, and Aegisthus himself in Act 2) specifically in order to take revenge on Atreus' descendant: this is the meaning of his life. Events are understood, then, not only through moral issues and issues of power, but also in the light of historical issues that were not resolved in the past and now return to shape the present.

From the moment of the Trojan womens' arrival, the return of history is seen in a different and increasingly strong perspective. Troy's fall returns vividly in their memory in Ode 3, and in turn is seen in the light of more ancient sorrows (670–690). Thereafter Troy's history returns in something more than memory, as Cassandra finds herself cast once again as prophet, seeing Argos as a second Troy and the coming death as both repetition of and recompense for Troy's sufferings. Agamemnon, who in *Trojan Women* sees clearly that the fall of greatness could affect Greeks as much as Trojans, is here blind to Cassandra's parallels with Troy (791–795)—so blind that he dresses for a feast in Priam's gorgeous robes.

Does past move into future in the play's penultimate scene, in which Electra entrusts Orestes for safekeeping to the faithful Strophius? This scene has long been a puzzle, exacerbated by Seneca's tendency to extreme abbreviation of plot action. The scene points forward to Orestes' eventual return, presaged by the emblems of victory in which Strophius dresses him. But nothing in the play suggests a moral or social order, or a divine plan, such as would give grounds for understanding Orestes' return as a new beginning.[4] All that can be said with confidence is that Strophius' *fides* or loyalty contrasts with the lack of *fides* endemic in the palace at Argos.

We are on surer ground in the play's final scene, which features the "defiance of tyrants" (here the new tyrants, Clytemnestra and Aegisthus) so familiar in ancient tragedy. The defiant young women, Electra and Cassandra, both rely on an understanding that under some circumstances death is preferable to life. That perception has occurred in various forms throughout the play. At the very beginning Thyestes, who knows both worlds, prefers that of the dead to that of the living. Even Aegisthus understands death's attraction (233, 996). For the chorus of Trojan women, death represents freedom: potential freedom from their own servitude, perhaps, but more generally

---

[4] The difficulty of judging the scene is illustrated by Shelton's remark (1983, p. 183 n. 61): "Electra may be seen as an exemplum of sisterly love, or as a daughter burning to avenge her father." The last line of the play associates the punishment of the murderers with madness (*furor*) not justice.

freedom from the storms of life, both literal and metaphorical (589–603). Cassandra too sees death as freedom
and safety (796–797). It is the one understanding widely
shared in the play. Indeed it is shared in other plays also,
notably in *Trojan Women* (see vol. 1 pages 23 and 167–
168). From one viewpoint it seems a tragic understanding,
perhaps the darkest of all *Agamemnon's* dark visions. Yet
Seneca as philosopher held and taught it as a source of
strength, in an era when death could come at any time to
slave or senator.

Sources[5]

Aeschylus' celebrated *Agamemnon* is no more than a
distant ancestor of the Senecan play. Seneca's Acts 1 and 2,
and scenes 2 and 3 of Act 5, have no precedent in Aeschylus' drama, and the same is true of the content of Seneca's
choral odes (with the partial exception of Ode 2). Only the
use of Cassandra to describe Agamemnon's murder in the
palace by second sight is reminiscent of Aeschylus, and
even here the similarity is general rather than specific.

Seneca's narration of the Greek fleet's destruction, unlike Aeschylus', contains three distinct episodes: (1) an intense storm, (2) the death of Ajax, (3) Nauplius' treachery.
The first known accounts to contain all three episodes
come from the Hellenistic period. It is noteworthy that
Seneca keeps (1) and (2) separate, whereas some accounts
conflate them into a single event (e.g. Verg. *Aen*. 1.39–45).
Several details found in (1), such as the dolphins' appear-

---

[5] A detailed analysis is given in Tarrant's edition of the play,
pp. 8–23.

ance and the conflict of opposing winds, existed before
Seneca, since they appear in Pacuvius' *Teucer*, a popular
Roman play of the second century B.C.

A confrontation between Electra and her mother after
the murder, not in Aeschylus, is attested for two republican Roman plays, Livius Andronicus' *Aegisthus* and
Accius' *Clytemestra*; in Livius Electra also took sanctuary,
as she does in Seneca. We need not assume, however, that
Seneca drew his scene solely or chiefly from these plays.
As elsewhere we should picture him drawing freely and
eclectically on a rich literary tradition, dramatic and nondramatic.

BIBLIOGRAPHY

Commentary

R. J. Tarrant, *Seneca: Agamemnon, Edited with a Commentary* (Cambridge, 1976).

Criticism

W. M. Calder III, "Seneca's *Agamemnon*," *C Phil*. 71
(1976), 27–36.

D. Henry, B. Walker, "Seneca and the *Agamemnon*. Some
Thoughts on Tragic Doom," *C Phil*. 58 (1963), 1–10.

G. Mader, "*Fluctibus Variis Agor*: an Aspect of Seneca's
Clytemestra Portrait," *Acta Classica* 31 (1988), 51–70.

J.-A. Shelton, "Revenge or Resignation: Seneca's *Agamemnon*," in A. J. Boyle (ed.) *Seneca Tragicus: Ramus Essays
on Senecan Drama* (Victoria, Australia, 1983), 159–183.

DRAMATIS PERSONAE

Ghost of THYESTES, *brother of Atreus and uncle of Agamemnon*
CLYTEMNESTRA, *queen of Argos, wife of Agamemnon*
NURSE *of Clytemnestra*
AEGISTHUS, *son of Thyestes, lover of Clytemnestra*
EURYBATES, *herald of Agamemnon*
CASSANDRA, *daughter of Priam and Hecuba, prophet, slave-mistress of Agamemnon*
AGAMEMNON, *son of Atreus, king of Argos, leader of the Greek expedition against Troy*
ELECTRA, *daughter of Agamemnon and Clytemnestra*
ORESTES (*persona muta*), *brother of Electra*
STROPHIUS *of Phocis, friend of Agamemnon*
PYLADES (*persona muta*), *son of Strophius*
CHORUS *of Argive women*
Secondary CHORUS *of captive Trojan women, accompanying Cassandra*

Scene

The play takes place at the royal palace in the city of Argos (which is also called Mycenae). The action begins shortly before dawn.

125

AGAMEMNON

THYESTIS UMBRA

Opaca linquens Ditis inferni loca
adsum profundo Tartari emissus specu,
incertus utras oderim sedes magis:
fugio Thyestes inferos, superos fugo.
5 en horret animus et pavor membra excutit:
video paternos, immo fraternos lares.
hoc est vetustum Pelopiae limen domus;
hinc auspicari regium capiti decus
mos est Pelasgis, hoc sedent alti toro
10 quibus superba sceptra gestantur manu,
locus hic habendae curiae—hic epulis locus.
    Libet reverti. nonne vel tristes lacus
accolere satius, nonne custodem Stygis
trigemina nigris colla iactantem iubis,
15 ubi ille celeri corpus evinctus rotae
in se refertur, ubi per adversum irritus
redeunte totiens luditur saxo labor,
ubi tondet ales avida fecundum iecur,
et inter undas fervida exustus siti

13 accolere *Bothe*: incolere *EA*

AGAMEMNON

ACT 1

GHOST OF THYESTES

I leave the dark world of infernal Dis and come released from Tartarus' deep cavern, uncertain which abode I hate more: I Thyestes shun those below, and am shunned by those above. Ah, my spirit shudders, my limbs tremble: I see my father's—no, my *brother's* dwelling. This is the ancient threshold of the House of Pelops; here it is the custom for Pelasgians to inaugurate the glory of a royal crown; high on this throne sit those whose proud hand wields the sceptre; this is the place for Senate meetings—this is the place for feasts.[1]

I want to go back. Is it not better to dwell even near those dismal lakes, near the guardian of Styx[2] tossing his triple necks with their black manes? Where the one whose body is bound to a swift wheel circles back on himself;[3] where uphill toil is vain and mocked as the stone repeatedly descends; where the greedy bird crops the ever growing liver; and one parched mid-river with burning

---

[1] The sight of the dining hall recalls that Thyestes was feasted there on the flesh of his own sons by his brother Atreus.

[2] Cerberus.   [3] Ixion; the following references are to Sisyphus, Tityos, and Tantalus respectively.

20   aquas fugaces ore decepto appetit
       poenas daturus caelitum dapibus graves?
           Sed ille nostrae pars quota est culpae senex!
       reputemus omnes quos ob infandas manus
       quaesitor urna Cnosius versat reos:
25   vincam Thyestes sceleribus cunctos meis.
       a fratre vincar, liberis plenus tribus
       in me sepultis? viscera exedi mea.
         Nec hactenus Fortuna maculavit patrem,
       sed maius aliud ausa commisso scelus
30   natae nefandos petere concubitus iubet.
       non pavidus hausi dicta, sed cepi nefas.
       ergo ut per omnes liberos irem parens,
       coacta fatis nata fert uterum gravem
       me patre dignum. versa natura est retro:
35   avo parentem (pro nefas!), patri virum,
       natis nepotes miscui—nocti diem.
           Sed sera tandem respicit fessos malis
       post fata demum sortis incertae fides.
       rex ille regum, ductor Agamemnon ducum,
40   cuius secutae mille vexillum rates
       Iliaca velis maria texerunt suis,
       post decima Phoebi lustra devicto Ilio
       adest—daturus coniugi iugulum suae.
       iam iam natabit sanguine alterno domus.
45   enses secures tela, divisum gravi
       ictu bipennis regium video caput;
       iam scelera prope sunt, iam dolus caedes cruor:
       parantur epulae! causa natalis tui,

---

    [4] Minos, judge of the dead.   [5] The Delphic Oracle directed him to father an avenger (Aegisthus) on his own daughter

thirst seeks the fleeting water with his often cheated lips, doomed to pay dearly for his feast with the gods.

But that old man is as nothing to my guilt! Let us reckon up all those felons sentenced by the Cnossian judge[4] for unspeakable deeds: I Thyestes shall outdo them all by my crimes. Could I be outdone by my brother, when filled with three children buried within me? I have devoured my own flesh and blood!

But Fortune did not stop there in defiling the father: she ventured on another crime greater than that already committed, and bade me seek wicked intercourse with my daughter.[5] I did not take fright at marking her words, but undertook the outrage. And so, in order that I should go as parent through all my children, my daughter bore under fate's duress a heavy womb worthy of me as father. Nature has been inverted: I have confused parent with grandparent (oh outrage!), husband with father, grandchildren with children—day with night.

But at last, though late and after my death, the oracle's uncertain promise is finally paying heed to those wearied by disasters. That famous king of kings, leader of leaders, Agamemnon, behind whose banner a thousand ships hid the seas of Ilium with their sails, has conquered Ilium after ten cycles of Phoebus, and is here—doomed to offer his throat to his own wife. Soon now the house will swim in blood answering blood. I see swords, axes, spears, I see a king's head split by the heavy blow of a double-bladed axe. Now crimes are near, now treachery, slaughter, gore: a feast is being prepared! The reason for your birth has

Pelopia. The promise of revenge is uncertain (38) because unfulfilled, and because oracles equivocate.

Aegisthe, venit. quid pudor vultus gravat?
50 quid dextra dubio trepida consilio labat?
quid ipse temet consulis torques rogas,
an deceat hoc te? respice ad matrem: decet.
    Sed cur repente noctis aestivae vices
hiberna longa spatia producunt mora,
55 aut quid cadentes detinet stellas polo?
Phoebum moramur. redde iam mundo diem.

CHORUS

     O regnorum
     magnis fallax Fortuna bonis,
     in praecipiti dubioque locas
     excelsa nimis.
60   numquam placidam sceptra quietem
     certumve sui tenuere diem;
     alia ex aliis cura fatigat
     vexatque animos nova tempestas.
     non sic Libycis Syrtibus aequor
65   furit alternos volvere fluctus,
     non Euxini
     turget ab imis commota vadis
     unda nivali vicina polo,
     ubi caeruleis immunis aquis
70   lucida versat plaustra Bootes,
     ut praecipites regum casus
     Fortuna rotat.

---

6 These images are paradoxically applied to virtue's vicissitudes in Chapman's *Bussy D'Ambois*: "Not so the Sea raves on the Libyan sands, / Tumbling her billows in each other's neck; / Not so the surges of the euxine Sea / (Near to the frosty Pole, where free

come, Aegisthus. Why is your face heavy with shame? Why does your hand tremble and falter, unsure of its purpose? Why do you consult yourself, torment yourself, ask yourself whether this befits you? Look to your mother: it befits you.

But why is the course of a summer's night suddenly prolonged to the lengthy span of winter? What detains the setting stars in the heavens? I am delaying Phoebus. Now restore daylight to the world.

CHORUS

O Fortune, beguiler
by means of the great blessings of thrones,
you set the exalted
in a sheer, unstable place.
Never do sceptres attain calm peace
or a day that is certain of itself.
They are wearied by care upon care,
their spirits tossed by some new storm.
Not so does the sea in the Libyan Syrtes
roll in rage wave upon wave;
not so in the Euxine
do the waters swell from the lowest depths
—those waters close to the snowy pole
where Bootes turns his shining Wain,
never touching the azure waves—
as Fortune whirls
the fates of kings in headlong movement.[6]

Bootes / From those dark-deep waves turns his radiant Team) / Swell being enrag'd, even from their inmost drop, / As Fortune swings about the restless state / Of virtue, now thrown into all men's hate."

metui cupiunt metuique timent;
non nox illis alma recessus
praebet tutos,
75   non curarum somnus domitor
pectora solvit.
    Quas non arces scelus alternum
dedit in praeceps?
impia quas non arma fatigant?
iura pudorque
80   et coniugii sacrata fides
fugiunt aulas;
sequitur tristis
sanguinolenta Bellona manu
quaeque superbos urit Erinys,
nimias semper comitata domos,
85   quas in planum quaelibet hora
tulit ex alto.
    Licet arma vacent cessentque doli,
sidunt ipso pondere magna
ceditque oneri fortuna suo.
90   vela secundis inflata Notis
ventos nimium timuere suos;
nubibus ipsis inserta caput
turris pluvio vapulat Austro,
densasque nemus spargens umbras
95   annosa videt robora frangi;
feriunt celsos fulmina colles,
corpora morbis maiora patent,
et cum in pastus
armenta vagos vilia currant,
100   placet in vulnus maxima cervix.
quidquid in altum Fortuna tulit,

They desire to be feared and dread to be feared;
no safe respite is afforded them
by gracious night,
no ease comes to their hearts from sleep,
tamer of cares.
   What citadels have answering crimes
not plunged in ruin,
or kindred wars not weakened?
Right and shame
and the hallowed loyalties of marriage
abandon palaces;
in place of these
comes grim Bellona with bloodstained hand
and the Erinys that dogs the proud,
always attending immoderate homes—
homes that any hour can bring
from on high to the ground.
   Though weapons sleep and treacheries cease,
greatness sinks by its very weight,
good fortune is a burden that crushes itself.
Sails that are filled with favouring southerlies
fear the winds that are all too helpful;
with its head thrust up to the very clouds
a tower is thrashed by rainy Auster,
and a grove that casts a heavy shade
sees its ancient tree trunks shattered;
the lofty hills are struck by lightning,
larger physiques are prone to disease,
and while the common
cattle run out to roam and graze,
the loftiest neck is chosen for the axe.
Whatever Fortune raises on high,

ruitura levat.
    Modicis rebus longius aevum est.
felix mediae quisquis turbae
sorte quietus
105   aura stringit litora tuta
timidusque mari credere cumbam
remo terras propiore legit.

CLYTEMESTRA

Quid, segnis anime, tuta consilia expetis?
quid fluctuaris? clausa iam melior via est.
110   licuit pudicos coniugis quondam toros
et sceptra casta vidua tutari fide;
periere mores ius decus pietas fides
et qui redire cum perît nescit pudor.
da frena et omnem prona nequitiam incita:
115   per scelera semper sceleribus tutum est iter.
tecum ipsa nunc evolve femineos dolos,
quod ulla coniunx perfida atque impos sui
amore caeco, quod novercales manus
ausae, quod ardens impia virgo face
120   Phasiaca fugiens regna Thessalica trabe:
ferrum, venena . . . vel Mycenaeas domos
coniuncta socio profuge furtiva rate.
    —quid timida loqueris furta et exilium et fugas?
soror ista fecit; te decet maius nefas.

NUTRIX

125   Regina Danaum et inclitum Ledae genus,
quid tacita versas quidve consilii impotens

---

[7] Cf. "Black deed only through black deed safely flies"
(Marston, *The Malcontent* 5.2).   [8] Medea.   [9] Helen.

she lifts to cast down.
    Modest estate is longer-lived.
Lucky the man content with the lot
of average folk,
who hugs the shore where the breeze is safe,
fears to trust his boat to the sea,
and rows a course close in to land.

ACT 2

CLYTEMNESTRA

Oh sluggish spirit! Why look for safe strategies? Why vacil-
late? The better path is already closed. Once you had the
option of safeguarding your husband's bed and his empty
throne through chastity and loyalty. But integrity, right,
honour, loyalty, faith are lost, and shame, which once lost
cannot return. So loosen the reins, crouch forward, spur on
each form of wickedness. For crimes the safest path is always through crimes.[7] Unfurl now in your mind the tricks
of womankind, all that any faithless wife, crazed with blind
passion, all that stepmothers' hands have dared commit, or
the girl blazing with disloyal lust[8] as she fled her Phasian
kingdom on a Thessalian ship: the steel, poison . . . Or else
take stealthy flight from Mycenae by boat with your partner. But why talk nervously of stealth and exile and escape?
Your sister[9] did such things; you are suited to some greater
outrage.

NURSE

Queen of the Danaans, glorious child of Leda: why ponder
in silence, and keep fierce impulses unchecked in your

tumido feroces impetus animo geris?
licet ipsa sileas, totus in vultu est dolor.
proin quidquid est, da tempus ac spatium tibi:
130   quod ratio non quit, saepe sanavit mora.

CLYTEMESTRA

Maiora cruciant quam ut moras possim pati.
flammae medullas et cor exurunt meum;
mixtus dolori subdidit stimulos timor;
invidia pulsat pectus, hinc animum iugo
135   premit cupido turpis et vinci vetat;
et inter istas mentis obsessae faces
fessus quidem et devictus et pessumdatus
pudor rebellat. fluctibus variis agor,
ut, cum hinc profundum ventus, hinc aestus rapit,
140   incerta dubitat unda cui cedat malo.
proinde omisi regimen e manibus meis:
quocumque me ira, quo dolor, quo spes feret,
hoc ire pergam; fluctibus dedimus ratem.
ubi animus errat, optimum est casum sequi.

NUTRIX

145   Caeca est temeritas quae petit casum ducem.

CLYTEMESTRA

Cui ultima est fortuna, quid dubiam timet?

NUTRIX

Tuta est latetque culpa, si pateris, tua.

CLYTEMESTRA

Perlucet omne regiae vitium domus.

NUTRIX

Piget prioris et novum crimen struis?

fevered mind? Despite your silence, all your pain is in your
face. So whatever it is, give yourself time and space: delay
often cures what reason cannot.

CLYTEMNESTRA

My torments are too great for me to endure delays. Flames
burn my heart and bones; mixed with my pain, fear goads
me on; jealousy pounds in my breast, and again rank lust
oppresses my spirit and will not be controlled. And amid
these fires besetting my mind, though weary and defeated
and ruined, shame fights back. I am driven by conflicting
waves, as when wind and tide pull the sea each way, and the
waters hesitate, uncertain which scourge to yield to. So I
have dropped the rudder from my hands. Wherever anger,
pain, hope carry me, there I shall proceed; I have given up
the boat to the waves. When one's spirit is astray, it is best
to follow chance.

NURSE

It is blind recklessness to look to chance as leader.

CLYTEMNESTRA

If one's fortune is desperate, why fear fortune's uncertain-
ties?

NURSE

Your fault is safe and well hidden, if you let it be so.

CLYTEMNESTRA

Every defect of a royal house is on full view.

NURSE

You detest your former crime *and* plan a new one?

137 devictus *PT*: devinctus *ECS*

CLYTEMESTRA

150   Res est profecto stulta nequitiae modus.

NUTRIX

Quod metuit auget qui scelus scelere obruit.

CLYTEMESTRA

Et ferrum et ignis saepe medicinae loco est.

NUTRIX

Extrema primo nemo temptavit loco.

CLYTEMESTRA

Rapienda rebus in malis praeceps via est.

NUTRIX

155   At te reflectat coniugî nomen sacrum.

CLYTEMESTRA

Decem per annos vidua respiciam virum?

NUTRIX

Meminisse debes subolis ex illo tuae.

CLYTEMESTRA

Equidem et iugales filiae memini faces
et generum Achillem: praestitit matri fidem!

NUTRIX

160   Redemit illa classis immotae moras
et maria pigro fixa languore impulit.

---

10 These *sententiae* are echoed in Hughes, *Misfortunes of Arthur*, "In desperate times the headlong way is best," and in Shakespeare, *Hamlet* 4.3.9–11, "Diseases desperate grown / By desperate appliances are relieved, / Or not at all."

CLYTEMNESTRA

A foolish thing indeed is moderation in crime.

NURSE

To cover up crime with crime is to add to what one fears.

CLYTEMNESTRA

Both fire and steel often serve in place of a cure.

NURSE

No one tries extreme measures at the outset.

CLYTEMNESTRA

In troubles one must seize the head-on path.[10]

NURSE

But you should be turned back by the holy name of marriage.

CLYTEMNESTRA

Single for ten years, shall I give thought to my husband?

NURSE

You should remember your offspring by him.

CLYTEMNESTRA

My memory is also of my daughter's marriage torches and my son-in-law Achilles: he kept true faith with the mother![11]

NURSE

She remedied the delays of the becalmed fleet, and mobilised seas fixed in sluggish idleness.

---

[11] "He" is Agamemnon, and "kept true faith" is said sarcastically. The daughter in question is Iphigenia.

CLYTEMESTRA

Pudet doletque: Tyndaris, caeli genus,
lustrale classi Doricae peperi caput!
revolvit animus virginis thalamos meae
165 quos ille dignos Pelopia fecit domo,
cum stetit ad aras ore sacrifico pater
quam nuptiales! horruit Calchas suae
responsa vocis et recedentes focos.
o scelera semper sceleribus vincens domus!
170 cruore ventos emimus, bellum nece!
sed vela pariter mille fecerunt rates?
non est soluta prospero classis deo:
eiecit Aulis impias portu rates.
     Sic auspicatus bella non melius gerit.
175 amore captae captus, immotus prece,
Sminthea tenuit spolia Phoebei senis,
ardore sacrae virginis iam tum furens.
non illum Achilles flexit indomitus minis,
non ille solus fata qui mundi videt
180 (in nos fidelis augur, in captas levis),
non populus aeger et relucentes rogi.
inter ruentis Graeciae stragem ultimam
sine hoste victus marcet ac veneri vacat
reparatque amores; neve desertus foret
185 a paelice umquam barbara caelebs torus,
ablatam Achilli diligit Lyrnesida,

---

162 doletque *E*: pigetque *A*   163 peperi *E*: peperit *A*

---

[12] The "Sminthean spoil" was Chryseis, Agamemnon's war
prize, daughter of Chryses the priest of Apollo Smintheus. The
more recent "holy virgin" is Cassandra.

CLYTEMNESTRA

Oh shame, oh anguish! I, a Tyndarid, child of heaven, bore a lustral sacrifice for the Dorian fleet! My mind relives my daughter's wedding, celebrated by that man in a manner worthy of the House of Pelops, when he stood as father making sacrificial prayers at the altar—such a bridal altar! Calchas shuddered at his own oracular response, at the cowering altar fires. O house that always outdoes crimes with crimes! We bought the winds with blood, the war with murder! But at least a thousand ships set sail together? No, the fleet was not released with divine favour: Aulis cast the unnatural ships out of its harbour.

He started the war with these auspices, and conducted it no better. Captured by love for a captive, and unmoved by prayer, he kept the Sminthean spoil of Phoebus' old priest, mad even then with passion for a holy virgin.[12] Achilles, though undaunted by threats, could not change his mind, nor could the one who alone sees divine destiny (a trustworthy augur in regard to us, inconsequential in regard to captives!),[13] nor the people's sickness and their blazing pyres. Amidst the final devastation of falling Greece he was conquered, though not by an enemy, enfeebled, with leisure for love, and replaced one mistress with another: lest his bachelor bed should ever be empty of a barbarian mistress, he stole the Lyrnesian from Achilles

---

[13] I.e. Agamemnon believed Calchas' soothsaying concerning the need to sacrifice Iphigenia, but not concerning the need to return Chryseis to her father, Apollo's priest. The sickness mentioned next was visited on the Greek army by Apollo, angered by Agamemnon's flouting of him.

nec rapere puduit e sinu avulsam viri—
en Paridis hostem! nunc novum vulnus gerens
amore Phrygiae vatis incensus furit,
190   et post tropaea Troica ac versum Ilium
captae maritus remeat et Priami gener.
      Accingere, anime: bella non levia apparas.
scelus occupandum est. pigra quem expectas diem?
Pelopia Phrygiae sceptra dum teneant nurus?
195   an te morantur virgines viduae domi
patrique Orestes similis? horum te mala
ventura moveant, turbo quîs rerum imminet!
quid, misera, cessas? en adest natis tuis
furens noverca! per tuum, si aliter nequit,
200   latus exigatur ensis et perimat duos;
misce cruorem, perde pereundo virum:
mors misera non est commori cum quo velis.

NUTRIX

Regina, frena temet et siste impetus
et quanta temptes cogita. victor venit
205   Asiae ferocis, ultor Europae; trahit
captiva Pergama et diu victos Phrygas.
hunc fraude nunc conaris et furto aggredi,
quem non Achilles ense violavit fero,
quamvis procacem torvus armasset manum,
210   non melior Aiax morte decreta furens,
non sola Danais Hector et bello mora,
non tela Paridis certa, non Memnon niger,
non Xanthus armis corpora immixta aggerens

---

[213] immixta aggerens *Gronovius*: immixta gerens *E*: immixte gerens *A*

and loved her, with no shame about tearing her from her man's embrace—look at this enemy of Paris! Now, wounded afresh, he is on fire with mad love for the Phrygian prophet.[14] After routing the Trojans and overthrowing Ilium, he returns as a captive's husband and Priam's son-in-law!

Arm yourself, my spirit: this is no light war you are planning. In crime, one must strike first. What day are you idly waiting for? One when young Phrygian wives hold the sceptre of Pelops? Or are you held back by the thought of unmarried girls at home and Orestes' likeness to his father? The thought of their future troubles should spur you on: a whirlwind is threatening them! Why hesitate, poor woman? See, a mad stepmother is at hand for your children! The sword must be driven through your own side, if it cannot be otherwise, and slaughter two; mingle your blood, destroy your man by self-destruction: to die with someone you want to die with is no wretched death.

NURSE

O queen, rein yourself in, control your impulses, think what you are attempting. He comes as victor over fierce Asia, avenger of Europe; he drags Pergamum prisoner, and the Phrygians whose conquest took so long: and now you attempt to attack him by treachery and stealth? Achilles did not wound him with his savage sword, though the surly fellow armed his presumptuous hand; nor did the better Ajax,[15] raging in his determination to die; not Hector, who alone held up the Danaans and the war, not Paris' unerring arrows, not black Memnon, not Xanthus piling up

---

[14] Cassandra.   [15] I.e. Ajax son of Telamon.

fluctusque Simois caede purpureos agens,
215 non nivea proles Cycnus aequorei dei,
non bellicoso Thressa cum Rheso phalanx,
non picta pharetras et securigera manu
peltata Amazon? hunc domi reducem paras
mactare et aras caede maculare impia?
220 ultrix inultum Graecia hoc facinus feret?
equos et arma classibusque horrens fretum
propone et alto sanguine exundans solum,
et tota captae fata Dardaniae domus
regesta Danais! comprime adfectus truces
225 mentemque tibimet ipsa pacifica tuam.

AEGISTHUS

Quod tempus animo semper ac mente horrui
adest profecto, rebus extremum meis.
quid terga vertis, anime? quid primo impetu
deponis arma? crede perniciem tibi
230 et dira saevos fata moliri deos:
oppone cunctis vile suppliciis caput,
ferrumque et ignes pectore adverso excipe,
Aegisthe: non est poena sic nato mori.
   Tu nos pericli socia, tu, Leda sata,
235 comitare tantum: sanguinem reddet tibi
ignavus iste ductor ac fortis pater.
sed quid trementes circuit pallor genas
iacensque vultu languido obtutus stupet?

CLYTEMESTRA

Amor iugalis vincit ac flectit retro;
240 referimur illuc, unde non decuit prius

240 referimur *M. Müller*: referemus *E*: remeemus *A*

144

bodies jumbled with weapons and Simois running red with blood,[16] not Cycnus the snow-white child of the sea god, not the Thracian squadron with warlike Rhesus, not the Amazon with painted quiver, crescent shield, and axe in hand. Is this the man you plan to sacrifice on his return home, staining the altar with unhallowed blood? Will Greece the avenger leave this deed unavenged? Picture horses, weapons, the sea bristling with warships, the soil flooded deep with blood, and the whole fate of Dardanus' captive house recoiling on the Danaans! Then check your fierce passions, and reconcile your mind to yourself.

AEGISTHUS

[*To himself as he enters*] The time I have always feared in mind and spirit is plainly upon me—the crisis in my affairs. Why turn aside, my spirit? Why lay down arms at the first onslaught? Be sure the cruel gods are engineering destruction and a dire fate for you. So set your worthless life to confront all sufferings, breast fire and steel without flinching, Aegisthus: for one of such birth, death is no hardship.

[*To Clytemnestra*] Partner of my danger, seed of Leda: if *you* will only keep me company, then that cowardly leader and brave father will pay you in blood. But why are your cheeks pale and trembling, your eyes downcast and listless and dazed-looking?

CLYTEMNESTRA

Married love overcomes me and turns me back. I am reverting to the place I should never have left. At least *now* I

---

[16] *Iliad* book 21 portrays these rivers as dangerous in flood, especially when choked with bodies.

abire. sed nunc casta repetatur fides,
nam sera numquam est ad bonos mores via:
quem paenitet peccasse paene est innocens.

AEGISTHUS

Quo raperis amens? credis aut speras tibi
245 Agamemnonis fidele coniugium? ut nihil
subesset animo quod graves faceret metus,
tamen superba et impotens flatu nimis
fortuna magno spiritus tumidos daret.
gravis ille sociis stante adhuc Troia fuit:
250 quid rere ad animum suapte natura trucem
Troiam addidisse? rex Mycenarum fuit,
veniet tyrannus; prospera animos efferunt.
effusa circa paelicum quanto venit
turba apparatu! sola sed turba eminet
255 tenetque regem famula veridici dei.
feresne thalami victa consortem tui?
at illa nolet. ultimum est nuptae malum
palam maritam possidens paelex domum.
nec regna socium ferre nec taedae sciunt.

CLYTEMESTRA

260 Aegisthe, quid me rursus in praeceps agis
iramque flammis iam residentem incitas?
permisit aliquid victor in captam sibi:
nec coniugem hoc respicere nec dominam decet.
lex alia solio est, alia privato in toro.
265 quid, quod severas ferre me leges viro
non patitur animus turpis admissi memor?
det ille veniam facile cui venia est opus.

AEGISTHUS

Ita est? pacisci mutuam veniam licet?

should recover loyalty and chastity, for the path to goodness is never too late. One who repents of wrongdoing is
virtually innocent.

AEGISTHUS

What crazy impulse is this? Do you believe or hope you can
have a faithful marriage with Agamemnon? Even if there
were no secrets in your mind to cause grave fears, yet his
good fortune, haughty and overblown, would give rise to
swollen arrogance. He was overbearing to associates while
Troy still stood: what do you think Troy's fall has added to a
spirit that is naturally harsh? He was king of Mycenae, he
will return as tyrant; success swells men's minds. Around
him spreads a crowd of mistresses, approaching with such
pomp! But one stands out from the crowd and clasps the
king—the handmaid of the prophetic god. Will you endure
being bested and sharing your marriage bed? *She* will not!
The worst disaster for a wife is to have a mistress openly
in control of the marital household. Neither thrones nor
marriages can endure a partner.

CLYTEMNESTRA

Aegisthus, why drive me towards the abyss once more, and
inflame my anger as it dies down? The conqueror has allowed himself some freedom with a captive: one should
not take notice of this either as wife or lady of the house.
There is one law for a throne, another with regard to a private man's bed. Then too my spirit does not allow me to
judge my husband severely, through awareness of my own
dishonour. Forgiveness should be granted readily by one
who needs forgiveness.

AEGISTHUS

Really? Is there a chance of negotiating mutual forgive-

ignota tibi sunt iura regnorum aut nova?
270 nobis maligni iudices, aequi sibi,
id esse regni maximum pignus putant,
si quidquid aliis non licet solis licet.

CLYTEMESTRA
Ignovit Helenae: iuncta Menelao redit
quae Europam et Asiam paribus afflixit malis.

AEGISTHUS
275 Hunc nulla Atriden venere furtiva abstulit
nec cepit animum coniugi obstrictum suae.
iam crimen ille quaerit et causas parat.
nil esse crede turpe commissum tibi:
quid honesta prodest vita, flagitio vacans?
280 ubi dominus odit, fit nocens, non quaeritur.
Spartenne repetes spreta et Eurotan tuum
patriasque sedes profuga? non dant exitum
repudia regum; spe metus falsa levas.

CLYTEMESTRA
Delicta novit nemo nisi fidus mea.

AEGISTHUS
285 Non intrat umquam regium limen fides.

CLYTEMESTRA
Opibus merebor, ut fidem pretio obligem.

AEGISTHUS
Pretio parata vincitur pretio fides.

CLYTEMESTRA
Surgit residuus pristinae mentis pudor;

275 hunc *Damsté*: sed *EA*

148

ness? Are the rules of kingship unknown or strange to you? They are biased judges to us, but fair to themselves; they think it the greatest assurance of their kingship, that they alone are permitted what others are not permitted.

CLYTEMNESTRA

He forgave Helen: she returns alongside Menelaus, though she inflicted equal damage on Europe and on Asia.

AEGISTHUS

But no mistress stole *that* Atreid with clandestine love or captured his heart, which was devoted to his wife. This one is already searching for an accusation and collecting pretexts. Suppose you had committed no dishonour: what use would it be to have lived honorably, free of scandal? A person hated by a master is guilty by fiat, not by trial. Once set aside, will you return to your Sparta and Eurotas and the refuge of your father's house? Divorce from a king allows no escape; you are allaying your fears with false hopes.

CLYTEMNESTRA

Only those loyal to me know of my misconduct.

AEGISTHUS

Loyalty never crosses a king's threshold.

CLYTEMNESTRA

I shall use my wealth to secure loyalty with money.

AEGISTHUS

Loyalty obtained with money is subverted with money.

CLYTEMNESTRA

There is a vestige of my former sense of shame springing

quid obstrepis? quid voce blandiloqua mala
290 consilia dictas? scilicet nubam tibi,
regum relicto rege, generosa exuli?

AEGISTHUS

Et cur Atrida videor inferior tibi,
natus Thyestae?

CLYTEMESTRA

Si parum est, adde et nepos.

AEGISTHUS

Auctore Phoebo gignor: haud generis pudet.

CLYTEMESTRA

295 Phoebum nefandae stirpis auctorem vocas,
quem nocte subita frena revocantem sua
caelo expulistis? quid deos probro addimus?
subripere doctus fraude geniales toros,
quem venere tantum scimus illicita virum,
300 facesse propere ac dedecus nostrae domus
asporta ab oculis; haec vacat regi ac viro.

AEGISTHUS

Exilia mihi sunt haud nova; assuevi malis.
si tu imperas, regina, non tantum domo
Argisve cedo: nil moror iussu tuo
305 aperire ferro pectus aerumnis grave.

---

³⁰⁰ nostrae *E*: clarae* *A*

up again; why do you cry out against it? Why do you keep repeating evil plans in this alluring voice? I suppose I am to be married to you, a noblewoman to an exile, in place of the king of kings?

AEGISTHUS
And why do you think me inferior to Atreus' son, as son of Thyestes?

CLYTEMNESTRA
If that is not enough, add "grandson" too!

AEGISTHUS
I was born at Phoebus' instigation, and am not ashamed of my birth.

CLYTEMNESTRA
You call Phoebus instigator of your evil begetting, though you people drove him from the heavens when he withdrew his chariot in sudden night?[17] Why do we involve the gods in ignominy? You are skilled at stealing married women's love by treachery; it is only by illicit sex that we know you are a man! Begone at once, remove from my sight this disgrace to our house; it is open without hindrance to my king and husband.

AEGISTHUS
Exile is nothing new to me; I am used to suffering. If you command it, my queen, I shall not just leave this house and Argos: I am ready at your bidding to use the sword to open this breast, so heavy with troubles.

[17] "You people" refers to Aegisthus' family: as his father Thyestes unwittingly devoured his sons' flesh, the sun turned back in horror.

CLYTEMESTRA

Siquidem hoc cruenta Tyndaris fieri sinam!
quae iuncta peccat debet et culpae fidem.
secede mecum potius, ut rerum statum
dubium ac minacem iuncta consilia explicent.

CHORUS

310   Canite, o pubes inclita, Phoebum!
         tibi festa caput turba coronat,
         tibi virgineas
         laurum quatiens de more comas
         innuba fudit stirps Inachia.
315   Tu quoque nostros, Parrhasis hospes,
         comitare choros,
         quaeque Erasini gelidos fontes,
         quaeque Eurotan,
         quaeque virenti tacitum ripa
         bibis Ismenon,
         quam fatorum praescia Manto,
320   sata Tiresia,
         Latonigenas monuit sacris
         celebrare deos.

         Arcus, victor, pace relata,
         Phoebe, relaxa,
         umeroque graves levibus telis
325   pone pharetras,
         resonetque manu pulsa citata

---

[315] Parrhasis hospes *Fitch*: thebais hospes *E*: thebana manus *A*

CLYTEMNESTRA

If indeed I could let this happen as a bloodstained Tyndarid! But she who sins with another owes loyalty even to
her offence. Rather withdraw with me, so that our joint
counsels can resolve this critical and threatening situation.

CHORUS

Sing, illustrious folk, of Phoebus!
[*To Phoebus*] For you the festive crowd wears wreaths,
for you unmarried Inachian girls
let down their maiden hair in ritual,
waving the laurel.
You too, Parrhasian guests, must join
our dances,[18] and you
who drink Erasinus' chilly waters,
or the Eurotas
or the Ismenos that flows in silence
between green banks:
for Manto, who has foreknowledge of fate,
Tiresias' seed,
advised you to honour and worship the gods
born of Latona.

With peace restored, unstring your bow,
victorious Phoebus;
take off your shoulder
the quiver burdened with its light arrows,
and let your deft hand play the lyre

18 In this invitation to women visitors, "Parrhasian" designates
those from Arcadia; the river Erasinus, those from the southern
Argolid; the Eurotas, those from Sparta; the Ismenos, those from
Thebes.

vocale chelys.
nil acre velim
magnumque modis intonet altis,
sed quale soles
330 leviore lyra flectere carmen
simplex, lusus
cum docta tuos Musa recenset.
licet et chorda graviore sones,
quale canebas
cum Titanas fulmine victos
videre dei,
335 vel cum montes montibus altis
super impositi
struxere gradus trucibus monstris,
stetit imposita Pelion Ossa,
pinifer ambos pressit Olympus.

340 Ades, o magni, soror et coniunx,
consors sceptri, regia Iuno:
tua te colimus turba Mycenae.
tu sollicitum
supplexque tui numinis Argos
sola tueris,
345 tu bella manu pacemque regis;
tu nunc laurus Agamemnonias
accipe victrix.
tibi multifora tibia buxo
sollemne canit,
tibi fila movent docta puellae
350 carmine molli,
tibi votivam
matres Graiae lampada iactant.

154

with melodious sounds.
I would have no harsh
heroic thundering in lofty measures,
but the kind of song
you modulate to a quieter lyre,
unadorned, when the cultured
Muse runs through your playful verses.
You could sound out too with deeper chords,
as once you sang
when the gods saw Titans overpowered
by the lightning bolt,
or when mountains, piled on top
of lofty mountains,
built a stairway for brutal monsters,
when Pelion stood with Ossa piled on it,
and pine-clad Olympus burdened them both.

Be with us, consort of the mighty sceptre
as wife and sister, royal Juno:
Mycenae, your nation, worships you.
When Argos is troubled
and prays to your godhead in supplication
you alone protect her.
You rule in might over war and peace.
Now receive Agamemnon's laurel
wreaths as victor.
For you the pipe of much-pierced boxwood
plays the anthem;
for you girls pluck the intricate strings
in gentle melody;
for you the votive
torch is tossed by matrons of Greece.

ad tua coniunx candida tauri
delubra cadet,
nescia aratri,
355 nullo collum signata iugo.

Tuque, o magni nata Tonantis,
inclita Pallas,
quae Dardanias cuspide turres
saepe petisti:
te permixto matrona minor
360 maiorque choro
colit et reserat
veniente dea templa sacerdos;
tibi nexilibus turba coronis
redimita venit,
tibi grandaevi lassique senes
365 compote voto
reddunt grates
libantque manu vina trementi.

Et te Triviam
nota memores voce precamur.
tu maternam sistere Delon,
Lucina, iubes,
370 huc atque illuc prius errantem
Cyclada ventis;
nunc iam stabilis
fixa terras radice tenet,
respuit auras religatque rates
assueta sequi.
375 tu Tantalidos funera matris
victrix numeras:

AGAMEMNON

In your temple will fall the white
wife of the bull,
who knows nothing of the plough,
whose neck was never scarred by the yoke.

And you, daughter of the mighty Thunderer,
glorious Pallas,
who often attacked the Dardan towers
with your sharp spear:
you are worshipped by married women, young
and old in a mingled
chorus, and the priestess
opens the temple at your approach.
To you there comes a throng enwreathed
in woven garlands;
to you men weary with length of years,
their prayers now granted,
give thanks, and pour
libations of wine with trembling hands.

You too, Trivia,
we remember in the well-known voice of prayer.
You bade your mother's isle of Delos
stand firm, Lucina,
though once it drifted as a Circling Isle
to and fro in the winds.
Stationary now
it grips the earth with fastened roots,
rebuffs the breezes and anchors ships
that it used to follow.
You numbered the dead of the Tantalid mother
victoriously:

157

stat nunc Sipyli vertice summo
flebile saxum,
et adhuc lacrimas
marmora fundunt antiqua novas.
380   colit impense femina virque
numen geminum.

Tuque ante omnes,
pater ac rector fulmine pollens,
cuius nutu
simul extremi tremuere poli,
385   generis nostri, Iuppiter, auctor,
cape dona libens
abavusque tuam non degenerem
respice prolem.

Sed ecce, vasto concitus miles gradu
manifesta properat signa laetitiae ferens
390   (namque hasta summo lauream ferro gerit),
fidusque regi semper Eurybates adest.

EURYBATES

Delubra et aras caelitum et patrios lares
post longa fessus spatia, vix credens mihi,
supplex adoro. vota superis solvite:
395   telluris altum remeat Argolicae decus
tandem ad penates victor Agamemnon suos.

now she stands on Sipylus' highest peak
a weeping rock,
and still there are tears
poured forth anew from the ancient marble.
Both men and women lavish worship
on your twin godhead.

And you above all,
father and ruler with the lightning's power,
at whose nod the poles
at the ends of the earth tremble together,
Jupiter, source of our nation: graciously
receive our gifts
and give heed to the fourth generation
descended from you[19] and not unworthy.

ACT 3

But see, in tremendous haste a soldier is hurrying this way,
with evident signs of joy (for his spear bears the laurel on
its iron point): it is Eurybates, ever faithful to our king.

EURYBATES

To the shrines and altars of the heavenly ones, and to our
fathers' housegods—though weary after this long span,
and scarcely believing the truth—I give thanks and homage. [*To citizens*] Fulfil your vows to the gods above: the
towering glory of the Argive land, Agamemnon, is returning at last victoriously to his hearth and home.

---

[19] Agamemnon is fourth in descent from Jupiter, after Tantalus, Pelops, and Atreus.

CLYTEMESTRA

Felix ad aures nuntius venit meas.
ubinam petitus per decem coniunx mihi
annos moratur? pelagus an terras premit?

EURYBATES

400   Incolumis, auctus gloria, laude inclitus
reducem expetito litori impressit pedem.

CLYTEMESTRA

Sacris colamus prosperum tandem diem
et si propitios attamen lentos deos.
Tu pande vivat coniugis frater mei,
405   et pande teneat quas soror sedes mea.

EURYBATES

Meliora votis posco et obtestor deos:
nam certa fari sors maris dubii vetat.
ut sparsa tumidum classis excepit mare,
ratis videre socia non potuit ratem.
410   quin ipse Atrides aequore immenso vagus
graviora pelago damna quam bello tulit,
remeatque victo similis, exiguas trahens
lacerasque victor classe de tanta rates.

CLYTEMESTRA

Effare casus quis rates hausit meas,
415   aut quae maris fortuna dispulerit duces.

EURYBATES

Acerba fatu poscis, infaustum iubes
miscere laeto nuntium. refugit loqui

---

414 effare casus quis rates hausit meas *E*: quis fare nostras
hauserit casus rates *A*

CLYTEMNESTRA

Happy the news that has reached my ears. Where then is he delaying, this husband I have sought for ten years? Is his presence felt on sea or on land?

EURYBATES

Unharmed, enhanced in glory, filled with renown, he has set his returning feet on the long-desired shore.

CLYTEMNESTRA

We must honour with sacrifices this day of success at last, and the gods' favour, however tardy. Tell me, does my husband's brother live? And tell me, where is my sister dwelling?

EURYBATES

In my prayers I beg and beseech the gods for better things, for the sea's hazards preclude my speaking with certainty. Once the scattered fleet endured swollen seas, one ship of the group could not see another ship. Even Atreus' son himself, while wandering on the vast expanse, took heavier losses from the sea than from war; he returns, though a conqueror, like one conquered, with a few battered ships in his wake out of that great fleet.

CLYTEMNESTRA

Tell us what chance engulfed my ships, what misfortune at sea scattered the leaders.

EURYBATES

You request what is bitter in the telling; you bid me mix ill-omened news with joyful. My mind balks at speech, sick-

mens aegra tantis atque inhorrescit malis.

CLYTEMESTRA

Exprome: clades scire qui refugit suas
420 gravat timorem; dubia plus torquent mala.

EURYBATES

Ut Pergamum omne Dorica cecidit face,
divisa praeda est, maria properantes petunt.
iamque ense fessum miles exonerat latus,
neglecta summas scuta per puppes iacent;
425 ad militares remus aptatur manus
omnisque nimium longa properanti mora est.
signum recursus regia ut fulsit rate
et clara laetum remigem monuit tuba,
aurata primas prora designat vias
430 aperitque cursus, mille quos puppes secent.
      Hinc aura primo lenis impellit rates
allapsa velis; unda vix actu levi
tranquilla Zephyri mollis afflatu tremit,
splendetque classe pelagus et pariter latet.
435 iuvat videre nuda Troiae litora,
iuvat relicti sola Sigei loca.
properat iuventus omnis adductos simul
lentare remos, adiuvat ventos manu
et valida nisu bracchia alterno movet.
440 sulcata vibrant aequora et latera increpant
dirimuntque canae caerulum spumae mare.
      Ut aura plenos fortior tendit sinus,
posuere tonsas, credita est vento ratis,
fususque transtris miles aut terras procul,
445 quantum recedunt vela, fugientes notat,
aut bella narrat: Hectoris fortis minas

ened and shuddering at such disasters.

Speak out: anyone who shrinks from learning about his calamities increases his fear; disasters torment us more when unconfirmed.

Once all of Pergamum fell to Dorian fire, they shared out the spoils and made in haste for the sea. Now warriors unbuckled swords from their weary sides, and their shields lay disregarded across the ships' decks. Oars were fitted to the soldiers' hands; in their haste any delay seemed too long. When the signal for return shone forth from the king's ship, and the trumpet's clear notes alerted the joyful rowers, the gilded prow marked out the start of the voyage and opened the pathway to be cut by a thousand vessels.

Then a breeze, gentle at first, slipped into the sails and pushed the ships on; the calm waters, with scarcely any current, were ruffled by the soft Zephyr's breath, and the sea was both emblazoned and concealed by the fleet. What a pleasure to see the empty shores of Troy, to see the lonely terrain of deserted Sigeum! The whole army was eager to flex the oars as they pulled together, assisting the winds and moving their stalwart arms with rhythmical power. The furrowed waters glistened, the ships' sides hissed, and white foam sundered the dark blue sea.

Once a stronger breeze filled the bellying sails, they downed their oars and trusted the ships to the wind. Stretched out on the thwarts, the soldiers either pointed out the lands receding in the distance, insofar as gaps opened between the sails, or told stories of the war—the

currusque et empto redditum corpus rogo,
sparsum cruore regis Herceum Iovem.
tum qui iacente reciprocus ludit salo

450 tumidumque pando transilit dorso mare
Tyrrhenus omni piscis exultat freto
agitatque gyros et comes lateri adnatat,
anteire naves laetus et rursus sequi;
nunc prima tangens rostra lascivit chorus,

455 millesimam nunc ambit et lustrat ratem.
        Iam litus omne tegitur et campi latent
et dubia parent montis Idaei iuga;
et iam, quod unum pervicax acies videt,
Iliacus atra fumus apparet nota.

460 iam lassa Titan colla relevabat iugo,
in alta iam lux prona, iam praeceps dies.
exigua nubes sordido crescens globo
nitidum cadentis inquinat Phoebi iubar;
suspecta varius occidens fecit freta.

465 nox prima caelum sparserat stellis, iacent
deserta vento vela. tum murmur grave,
maiora minitans, collibus summis cadit
tractuque longo litus ac petrae gemunt;
agitata ventis unda venturis tumet:

470 cum subito luna conditur, stellae latent.

472 nec una nox est: densa tenebras obruit
caligo et omni luce subducta fretum
caelumque miscet. undique incumbunt simul

475 rapiuntque pelagus infimo eversum solo
adversus Euro Zephyrus et Boreae Notus.

457 parent *EA*: pereunt *Poggio*
461 alta *Damsté*: astra *EA*

threat posed by brave Hector, the chariot, the return of his
body for cremation at a price, the bespattering of Hercean
Jove with the king's blood.[20] Then came the Tyrrhene fish,
that weave playfully in and out of the saltwater when it is
calm, or jump across swells with arching backs: they leapt
out all across the sea, chased in circles, swam up alongside
us, gaily preceded the ships or again followed behind. Now
they tagged the first ship's beak in a frolicking troupe, now
they circled round and round the thousandth ship.

Now all the shoreline was obscured, the lowlands
shrouded, and the peaks of Mt Ida only dimly seen; and
now the one thing visible even to a steadfast gaze was the
smoke from Ilium, showing as a black trace. Now the Titan
was freeing his steeds' weary necks from the yoke, now the
sunlight was sinking towards the deep, now the day was
hastening downward. A small cloud, swelling up into a
dark mass, sullied Phoebus' bright rays as he set; this mix-
ture of colours in the sunset raised misgivings about the
sea. Early night had scattered stars over the sky, the sails
lay forsaken by the wind. Then a deep murmur, carrying
threats of worse, fell from the high hills, and a long-drawn-
out moan came from the shore and cliffs. Waves swelled,
roused by approaching winds. Suddenly the moon was
hidden, the stars invisible. Night was redoubled: a dense
gloom smothered the darkness, stole every trace of light
and confounded sea and sky. Winds fell upon the sea from
all quarters at once, and churned it up violently from its
very bed, Zephyrus against Eurus and Notus against

---

[20] The chariot was that of Achilles, which dragged Hector's
body around Troy; the blood was that of Priam, butchered at Jove's
altar.

sua quisque mittunt tela et infesti fretum
emoliuntur, turbo convolvit mare:
Strymonius altas Aquilo contorquet nives
480 Libycusque harenas Auster ac Syrtes agit,
[nec manet in Austro; fit gravis nimbis Notus]
imbre auget undas; Eurus orientem movet
Nabataea quatiens regna et Eoos sinus;
quid rabidus ora Corus Oceano exerens?
485 mundum revelli sedibus totum suis
ipsosque rupto crederes caelo deos
decidere et atrum rebus induci chaos.
vento resistit aestus, et ventus retro
aestum revolvit. non capit sese mare:
471 in astra pontus tollitur, caelum ferit,
490 undasque miscent imber et fluctus suas.
　　　Nec hoc levamen denique aerumnis datur,
videre saltem et nosse quo pereant malo:
premunt tenebrae lumina et dirae Stygis
inferna nox est. excidunt ignes tamen
495 et nube dirum fulmen elisa micat;
miserisque lucis tanta dulcedo, ut male
hoc lumen optent. ipsa se classis premit
et prora prorae nocuit et lateri latus.
illam dehiscens pontus in praeceps rapit
500 hauritque et alto redditam revomit mari;
haec onere sidit, illa convulsum latus
summittit undis, fluctus hanc decimus tegit;

---

481 *deleted by Richter*　　　　　471 *transposed after* 489 *by*
Tarrant　　　ferit *Zwierlein*: perit *EA*
495f. dulcedo, ut male . . . optent *Fitch*: dulcedo est, male . . .
optant *Bothe*: dulcedo est malae . . . optant *EA*

Boreas. At war, each hurling his own weapons, they heaved up the waters in a whirling tornado. Strymonian Aquilo swirled deep snows; Libyan Auster buffeted the sandy Syrtes,[21] with rain swelling the waves; Eurus struck the East, shaking Nabatean kingdoms and the gulfs of the Dawn—not to mention frenzied Corus, raising his head from Ocean. You would have thought the entire earth was being torn from its place, the very gods falling from the shattered heavens, and black chaos intruding into the world. The wind was resisted by the tide, and again the wind rolled the tide back. The sea overflowed, rose towards the stars, dashed against the heavens; rain and waves combined their billowing waters.

The sufferers were not even granted the relief of at least seeing and knowing the disaster that destroyed them. Darkness weighed on their eyes, the infernal night of terrible Styx. Yet fires did fall, as terrible lightning flashed from shattered clouds; light had such sweetness for those wretches that perversely they longed for this kind of brightness. The fleet did damage to itself, prow crashing on prow and side on side. One ship was pulled down headlong by the yawning sea, swallowed and then spewed up again from the depths; this one foundered under its burden, that one dipped its shattered side under the flood, this one was smothered by a tenth wave.[22] Another, battered

---

21 Line 481 (deleted): "and it did not stay in the south [i.e. as Auster stirring up sand]: it became Notus heavy with rainclouds."

22 A reference to the notion that every tenth wave is exceptionally large.

haec lacera et omni decore populato levis
fluitat, nec illi vela nec tonsae manent
505   nec rectus altas malus antemnas ferens,
sed trunca toto puppis Ionio natat.
      Nil ratio et usus audet; ars cessit malis.
tenet horror artus, omnis officio stupet
navita relicto, remus effugit manus.
510   in vota miseros ultimus cogit timor,
eademque superos Troes et Danai rogant.
quid fata possunt! invidet Pyrrhus patri,
Aiaci Ulixes, Hectori Atrides minor,
Agamemno Priamo: quisquis ad Troiam iacet
515   felix vocatur, cadere qui meruit gradu,
quem fama servat, victa quem tellus tegit.
"Nil nobile ausos pontus atque undae ferent?
ignava fortes fata consument viros?
perdenda mors est? quisquis es, nondum malis
520   satiate tantis, caelitum, tandem tuum
numen serena: cladibus nostris daret
vel Troia lacrimas. odia si durant tua
placetque mitti Doricum exitio genus,
quid hos simul perire nobiscum iuvat,
525   quibus perimus? sistite infestum mare:
vehit ista Danaos classis, et Troas vehit!"
nec plura possunt: occupat vocem mare.
      Ecce alia clades! fulmine irati Iovis
armata Pallas quidquid haud hasta minax,
530   haud aegide et furore Gorgoneo potest,
hoc igne patrio temptat, et caelo novae
spirant procellae. solus invictus malis

529f. haut . . . haut *M. Müller*: aut . . . aut *EA*

and despoiled of all its finery, drifts lightly to and fro; with neither sails nor oars remaining, nor the upright mast with its lofty sailyards, it floats as a mutilated hulk all over the Ionian Sea.

Neither reason nor experience gave courage; skill surrendered to the disaster. Gripped and stupefied by terror, the sailors all abandoned their duties, and let the oars slip from their hands. Extreme fear drove the wretches to prayer, with Trojans and Danaans making the same request of the gods. The strange outcomes of fate! Pyrrhus envies his father, Ulysses Ajax; Atreus' younger son envies Hector, Agamemnon Priam. All who lie at Troy are called fortunate, those who fell worthily at their post and are safeguarded by fame, sheltered by the conquered land. "Have we dared no noble deeds, that the sea waves are to carry us off? Shall an ignoble fate destroy brave men? Must our deaths be wasted? Whichever god you may be that are still unsated by our great sufferings, at last let your godhead be unclouded: even Troy would shed tears for our disasters! But if your hatred endures, and you want the Dorian race destroyed, why do you desire these people, on whose account we are dying, to die with us? Calm the hostile seas: this fleet carries Danaans, but it carries Trojans too!" They could speak no more: the sea cut off their words.

See, another disaster! Pallas arms herself with the thunderbolt of angry Jove. What her enmity cannot achieve with spear or aegis and Gorgon's rage, she attempts with her father's fire. New storms gust across the sky. Ajax alone was still struggling, unconquered by

---

530 et *Gronovius*: aut *EA*   531 hoc *Tarrant*: aut *EA*

luctatur Aiax. vela cogentem hunc sua
tento rudente flamma perstrinxit cadens.
535 libratur aliud fulmen: hoc toto impetu
certum reducta Pallas excussit manu,
imitata patrem. transit Aiacem et ratem
ratisque partem secum et Aiacem tulit.
nil ille motus, ardua ut cautes, salo
540 ambustus exstat, dirimit insanum mare
fluctusque rumpit pectore, et navem manu
complexus ignes traxit et caeco mari
conlucet Aiax; omne resplendet fretum.
tandem occupata rupe furibundum intonat:
545 "Superasse me nunc pelagus atque ignes iuvat,
vicisse caelum Palladem fulmen mare.
non me fugavit bellici terror dei,
[et Hectorem una solus et Martem tuli]
Phoebea nec me tela pepulerunt gradu;
550 cum Phrygibus istos vicimus: tene horream
aliena inerti tela iaculantem manu?
quid si ipse mittat?" plura cum auderet furens,
tridente rupem subruit pulsam pater
Neptunus imis exerens undis caput
555 solvitque montem; quem cadens secum tulit,
terraque et igne victus et pelago iacet.
      Nos alia maior naufragos pestis vocat.
est humilis unda, scrupeis mendax vadis,
ubi saxa rapidis clausa verticibus tegit
560 fallax Caphereus; aestuat scopulis fretum
fervetque semper fluctus alterna vice.

545 me nunc *Düring*: nunc se *A*: nunc *E*: saevum *Delz, Hud-
son-Williams*   548 *deleted by Leo*

170

disaster.[23] As he strained on the ropes to shorten sail, he was grazed by the falling fire. Another bolt was aimed: drawing back her hand, Pallas launched it on target with all her might, imitating her father. It passed through Ajax and his ship, and carried away part of the ship and Ajax himself. Unshaken, though scorched, like a lofty crag he stood out from the saltwater, sundered the maddened sea, broke the waves with his chest. As he grasped his ship tightly he caught fire from it, and in that blind sea Ajax was a source of light; the whole strait was illuminated. Finally, taking his stand on a rock, he thundered in fury: "I glory in having overcome flood and fire, in having conquered heaven, Pallas, lightning, sea. I was not driven off by fear of the war god,[24] nor forced to retreat by Phoebus' arrows; I defeated those foes along with the Phrygians. Should I quail before your feeble-handed hurling of another's weapons? Why not let him fire them himself?" As he dared say more in rage, father Neptune raised his head from the depths of the waves, struck and dislodged the rock with his trident, and toppled the crag. He carried it with him in his fall, and lies conquered by earth and fire and sea.

Already wrecked, we were drawn by another, worse scourge. There are shallows made treacherous by sharp underwater crags, where deceitful Caphereus conceals his rocky base beneath swirling eddies; water boils over the reefs, the waves always seethe in ebb or flow. Above towers

[23] This is Ajax "the Less," son of Oileus.
[24] 548 (deleted): "I alone withstood both Hector and Mars together."

arx imminet praerupta quae spectat mare
utrimque geminum: Pelopis hinc oras tui
et Isthmon, arto qui recurvatus solo
565   Ionia iungi maria Phrixeis vetat;
hinc scelere Lemnon nobilem, hinc et Chalcida
tardamque ratibus Aulida. hanc arcem occupat
Palamedis ille genitor, et clarum manu
lumen nefanda vertice e summo efferens
570   in saxa ducit perfida classem face.
haerent acutis rupibus fixae rates.
has inopis undae brevia comminuunt vada,
pars vehitur huius prima, pars scopulo sedet;
hanc alia retro spatia relegentem ferit
575   et fracta frangit. iam timent terram rates
et maria malunt. cecidit in lucem furor;
postquam litatum est Ilio, Phoebus redit
et damna noctis tristis ostendit dies.

CLYTEMESTRA

Utrumne doleam laeter an reducem virum?
580   remeasse laetor, vulnus et regni grave
lugere cogor. redde iam Graiis, pater
altisona quatiens regna, placatos deos!
nunc omne laeta fronde veletur caput,
sacrifica dulces tibia effundat modos
585   et nivea magnas victima ante aras cadat.
      Sed ecce, turba tristis incomptae comas
Iliades adsunt, quas super celso gradu
effrena Phoebas entheas laurus quatit.

---

566 hinc et Chalcida *recc*.: hinc calchedona *A*: et calchedona *E*

a sheer headland that looks out on two seas, right and left:
on one side to your Pelops' shores and the Isthmus, whose
narrow, recurving ground keeps the Ionian sea apart from
Phrixus'; on the other side to Lemnos, famous for crime,
Chalcis, and Aulis delayer of ships. On this headland
Palamedes' father, that criminal, took up position. Shining
a bright light from the summit, he led the fleet onto the
crags with that treacherous beacon. Ships stuck fast on
the jagged rocks. Some, with insufficient draft, broke up in
the shallows; the front half of one carried away, with the
other half sitting on the reef; one ship, trying to back away,
was struck by another, both wrecked and wrecking. Now
the ships feared the land, and preferred the sea. Towards
dawn the madness subsided. Now that atonement had
been made for Ilium, Phoebus returned, and the gloomy
day revealed the havoc of the night.

CLYTEMNESTRA

Should I grieve or rejoice at my husband's return? I rejoice
at his homecoming, and yet I must mourn the deep wound
to our kingdom. O father who shake the high-resounding
kingdom, at long last restore the gods' favour to the
Greeks! Now every head must be crowned with a joyful
wreath; the flute of sacrifice must pour out its sweet notes,
and a snow-white victim fall before the high altar.

But see, the women of Ilium are here, a sad group,
their hair dishevelled, and pacing tall among them the unbridled priestess of Phoebus[25] shakes the god-filled laurel.

[25] Cassandra; the laurel is associated with prophetic trance.

CHORUS

Heu quam dulce malum mortalibus additum
590   vitae dirus amor, cum pateat malis
effugium et miseros libera mors vocet,
    portus aeterna placidus quiete.
    nullus hunc terror nec impotentis
    procella Fortunae movet aut iniqui
595   flamma Tonantis.
      pax alta nullos civium coetus
    timet aut minaces victoris iras,
    non maria asperis insana Coris,
non acies feras pulvereamve nubem
600   motam barbaricis equitum catervis,
non urbe cum tota populos cadentes
    hostica muros populante flamma
       indomitumve bellum.
    solus servitium perrumpet omne
605   contemptor levium deorum,
     qui vultus Acherontis atri,
     qui Styga tristem non tristis videt
     audetque vitae ponere finem:
    par ille regi, par superis erit.
610   o quam miserum est nescire mori!

    Vidimus patriam ruentem
    nocte funesta, cum Dardana tecta

---

[26] This ode down to line 636, and the whole of the ode at 808–866, is polymetric: see footnote at *Oed* 405.

[27] These lines are elaborated by Mary Sidney in a choral ode of *The Tragedy of Antony*: "Who fearless and with courage bold / Can *Acheron's* black face behold / Which muddy water beareth, /

CHORUS OF TROJAN WOMEN[26]

Oh, the sweet evil implanted in mortals,
this desperate love for life, though escape from troubles
lies open, and death's freedom beckons the wretched—
    a tranquil harbour of eternal calm,
    untouched by any terror, by any storm
    of raging Fortune, by any fire
            from the hostile Thunderer.
      That deep peace fears no throngs
    of citizens, no conqueror's angry menace,
    no seas maddened by wild norwesters,
no ferocious battle lines or clouds of dust
raised by barbarians in horseback squadrons,
no downfall of peoples and whole cities
    as enemy fires ravage the walls,
        no untameable war.
Who can fully break out of bondage?
    Only one who scorns the fickle gods,
    who looks without gloom at gloomy Styx,
    looks upon dark Acheron's face,
    and has courage to set an end to life:
such a one is a match for kings, for gods.[27]
    How wretched to be unschooled in dying!

    We saw our country's downfall
on the fatal night when you Dorian fires

And crossing over in the way / Is not amaz'd at Perruque gray / Old rusty *Charon* weareth . . . / Who freely can himself dispose / Of that last hour which all must close, / And leave this life at pleasure: / This noble freedom more esteems, / And in his heart more precious deems, / Than crown and kingly treasure."

175

Dorici raperetis ignes.
non illa bello victa, non armis,
ut quondam Herculea cecidit pharetra;
615   quam non Pelei Thetidisque natus
carusque Pelidae nimium feroci
vicit, acceptis cum fulsit armis
    fuditque Troas falsus Achilles,
aut cum ipse Pelides animos feroces
620   sustulit luctu celeremque saltu
Troades summis timuere muris,
perdidit in malis extremum decus,
    fortiter vinci:
restitit annis Troia bis quinis
unius noctis peritura furto.

625   Vidimus simulata dona
    molis immensae, Danaumque
fatale munus duximus nostra
creduli dextra; tremuitque saepe
limine in primo sonipes, cavernis
630   conditos reges bellumque gestans.
et licuit dolos versare ut ipsi
    fraude sua caderent Pelasgi:
saepe commotae sonuere parmae,
tacitumque murmur percussit aures
635   ut fremuit male subdolo
    parens Pyrrhus Ulixi.

---

[28] Patroclus, who borrowed Achilles' armour but was killed in battle (hence Achilles' grief, line 620).

plundered our Dardan homes.
    She was not conquered by weapons of war,
as formerly she fell to Hercules' arrows.
The son of Peleus and Thetis could not defeat her,
nor the man beloved by Peleus' ferocious son[28]
    when he gleamed in borrowed armour
       and routed Trojans as a fake Achilles—
nor Achilles himself, when he roused his ferocious spirit
    through grief, and the Trojan women on the high
       walls
shuddered at his swift and springing approach.
Yet amidst her troubles she lost the final glory
       of a valorous defeat;
    Troy resisted for twice five years,
to perish by the subterfuge of a single night.

    We saw the feigned offering
    of that huge body,[29] and trustingly
    we pulled the Danaans' fateful gift
with our own hands; many times the steed
stumbled on the outer gateway, bearing
kings and war hidden in its hollow womb.
And we could have reversed the trick, and made
    the Pelasgians fall in their own trap:
many times there were sounds from moving shields,
and a quiet murmur struck our ears,
    as Pyrrhus grumbled and chafed
       at obeying deceitful Ulysses.

[29] The Wooden Horse: these lines allude to Vergil's famous
account in *Aeneid* book 2.

177

Secura metus Troica pubes
sacros gaudet tangere funes.
hinc aequaevi gregis Astyanax,
640   hinc Haemonio desponsa rogo
ducunt turmas,
haec femineas, ille viriles.
festae matres
votiva ferunt munera divis,
645   festi patres adeunt aras;
unus tota est vultus in urbe;
et, quod numquam
post Hectoreos vidimus ignes,
laeta est Hecabe.

Quid nunc primum, dolor infelix,
650   quidve extremum deflere paras?
moenia divum fabricata manu,
diruta nostra?
an templa deos super usta suos?
non vacat istis lacrimare malis:
655   te, magne parens, flent Iliades.
vidi, vidi senis in iugulo
telum Pyrrhi
vix exiguo sanguine tingui.

CASSANDRA
Cohibete lacrimas omne quas tempus petet,
660   Troades, et ipsae vestra lamentabili

---

[30] With which the Horse was dragged into Troy. *Sacer* can also mean "accursed."   [31] Lit. to the Haemonian, i.e. Thessalian, pyre; she is Polyxena.

178

With no thought of fear, the Trojan youth
delight to touch the sacred ropes.[30]
Here Astyanax,
there the girl betrothed to Achilles' pyre[31]
lead companies of their peers in age,
she of young women, he of young men.
Festive mothers
bear their votive gifts to the gods;
festive fathers approach the altars;
one look is on faces throughout the city;
and—something we never
saw since the burning of Hector's body—
Hecuba is joyful.

Ill-starred grief, what sorrow first,
what last are you now preparing to mourn?
Walls constructed by divine hands,
demolished by ours?
Or temples burnt on top of their gods?
We are not free to lament these troubles:
Ilium's women mourn *you*, great father.
I saw, I saw in the old man's throat
the sword of Pyrrhus
scarcely tinged with his scanty blood.

ACT 4

CASSANDRA

Hold back the tears that will be called for throughout
time,[32] women of Troy, and mourn your own dead with

---

[32] I.e. tears for those subjects (Troy and Priam) that will be
mourned in every age (as the actor in *Hamlet* weeps for Hecuba).

lugete gemitu funera: aerumnae meae
socium recusant. cladibus questus meis
removete: nostris ipsa sufficiam malis.

CHORUS

Lacrimas lacrimis miscere iuvat.
665   magis exurunt
quos secretae lacerant curae;
iuvat in medium deflere suos.
Nec tu, quamvis dura virago
patiensque mali,
poteris tantas flere ruinas.
670   non quae verno mobile carmen
ramo cantat tristis aedon
Ityn in varios modulata sonos,
non quae tectis Bistonis ales
residens summis
impia diri furta mariti
675   garrula narrat,
lugere tuam poterit digne
conquesta domum;
licet ipse velit
clarus niveos inter olores
Histrum cycnus Tanainque colens
680   extrema loqui,
licet alcyones Ceyca suum
fluctu leviter plangente sonent,
cum tranquillo male confisae

[33] The swallow is the metamorphosed form of Procne, wife of
the Thracian Tereus (hence "Bistonian," i.e. Thracian). Tereus re-

180

groans and laments: my sorrows brook no companion.
Keep your keening apart from my tragedies: I shall be adequate to my own troubles.

CHORUS OF TROJAN WOMEN

It helps to mingle tears with tears.
Cares wound more deeply
the people they afflict in private;
it helps to mourn one's losses in common.
Not even you, though heroic and hard
in enduring troubles,
can suffice to mourn such devastation.
Not the sad nightingale that sings
her changeful song from a springtime branch,
inflecting "Itys" in varied notes,
not the Bistonian bird that perches on rooftops
and babbles the story of her monstrous husband's
unnatural secret lust[33]
could suffice to mourn your family
with a fitting lament;
even though Cycnus,
bright amidst the snow-white swans
at home on Hister or Tanais, should choose
to sing his last song;
or though halcyons, to the gentle sorrowful beat
of waves, should sound their Ceyx' name,
when they count unwisely on calm weather,
rashly trusting the sea yet again,

peatedly raped Procne's sister Philomela. Philomela, transformed
into the nightingale, here mourns for Procne's son Itys, killed by
Procne to punish her husband.

credunt iterum pelago audaces
685 fetusque suos
nido pavidae titubante fovent;
non si molles imitata viros
tristis laceret bracchia tecum
quae turritae turba parenti
pectora rauco concita buxo
690 ferit ut Phrygium lugeat Attin.
non est lacrimis, Cassandra, modus,
quia quae patimur vicere modum.

Sed cur sacratas deripis capiti infulas?
miseris colendos maxime superos putem.

CASSANDRA

695 Vicere nostra iam metus omnes mala.
equidem nec ulla caelites placo prece,
nec, si velint saevire, quo noceant habent;
Fortuna vires ipsa consumpsit suas.
quae patria restat, quis pater, quae iam soror?
700 bibere tumuli sanguinem atque arae meum.
quid illa felix turba fraterni gregis?
exhausta nempe. regia miseri senes
vacua relicti, totque per thalamos vident
praeter Lacaenam ceteras viduas nurus.
705 tot illa regum mater et regimen Phrygum
fecunda in ignes Hecuba fatorum novas

---

34 Viz. the Galli, self-castrated devotees of Cybele, who sometimes cut their arms in religious ecstacy. The "crowd" consists of
Cybele's other worshippers; the "mother" is Cybele.

35 Again elaborated by Mary Sidney in an ode of *Antony* (cf.
fn. above on 609): "Our plaints no limits stay, / No more than do

and nestle their young
anxiously in a rocking nest;
not if the crowd should slash their arms
like the unmanned men[34] in sorrow with you—
the crowd that are stirred by the strident flute
and beat their breasts in honour of the tower-
    crowned
mother, to mourn for Phrygian Attis.
There is no limit, Cassandra, to tears,
since what we suffer has surpassed limit.[35]

But why are you ripping the consecrated bands from your
head? I would think the wretched most of all need to re-
vere the gods.

CASSANDRA

My troubles now have surpassed all fears. For my part I
do not try to placate the gods with any prayer: even if
they should want to be brutal, they have no means of
doing harm. Fortune has used up all her resources! Does
any fatherland remain now, any father, any sister? Burial
mounds and altars have drunk my blood. What of that
thriving, thronging group of brothers? All spent, of course.
In the empty palace only sad old men are left, and throughout so many marriage chambers they see all other young
wives widowed except the Spartan.[36] That famous mother
of many princes and guidance for Phrygians, Hecuba, prolific for fires,[37] found fate to have new laws, and put on

our woes; / Both infinitely stray, / And neither measure knows. / In
measure let them plain / Who measured griefs sustain."

[36] Helen.   [37] I.e. prolific of sons who would be cre-
mated. There is also an allusion to the fires of Troy, portended by
her dream of giving birth to a firebrand (*Tro* 36–40).

experta leges induit vultus feros:
circa ruinas rabida latravit suas,
Troiae superstes, Hectori, Priamo, sibi.

CHORUS

710 Silet repente Phoebas et pallor genas
creberque totum possidet corpus tremor;
stetere vittae, mollis horrescit coma,
anhela corda murmure incluso fremunt,
incerta nutant lumina et versi retro
715 torquentur oculi, rursus immoti rigent.
nunc levat in auras altior solito caput
graditurque celsa, nunc reluctantes parat
reserare fauces, verba nunc clauso male
custodit ore, maenas impatiens dei.

CASSANDRA

720 Quid me furoris incitam stimulis novi,
quid mentis inopem, sacra Parnasi iuga,
rapitis? recede, Phoebe, iam non sum tua;
extingue flammas pectori infixas meo.
cui nunc vagor vesana? cui bacchor furens?
725 iam Troia cecidit: falsa quid vates ago?
     Ubi sum? fugit lux alma et obscurat genas
nox alta et aether abditus tenebris latet.
sed ecce gemino sole praefulget dies
geminumque duplices Argos attollit domos.
730 Idaea cerno nemora? fatalis sedet
inter potentes arbiter pastor deas?
timete, reges, moneo, furtivum genus:

bestial form: she barked rabidly around her own ruins, a survivor of Troy, of Hector, of Priam, of herself.

CHORUS LEADER

Suddenly Phoebus' priestess is silent; pallor spreads over her cheeks, continual trembling over her whole body. The holy ribbons stand out, her soft hair bristles. Her panting breast is loud with pent-up utterance; her gaze is unsteady and drooping; her eyes roll backwards, then again are fixed and rigid. Now she raises her head aloft, higher than usual, and walks tall; now she makes ready to unseal her reluctant mouth, now she tries in vain to hold in the words behind closed lips—a maenad unwilling to endure the god.

CASSANDRA

Sacred peaks of Parnassus, why do you goad me with spurs of fresh madness, why sweep me out of control of my mind? Leave me, Phoebus: I am not yours any longer. Smother the flames you have planted in my breast. For whom do I drift in frenzy *now*? For whom do I play the crazed maenad? Now Troy has fallen, what business have I as a failed prophet?

Where am I? The kindly light has vanished, deep night blinds my eyes, heaven is obscured and hidden by darkness. But see now, daylight shines from twofold suns, Argos is twofold and raises up double homes. Do I see the groves of Ida? Is the fatal herdsman sitting as judge between powerful goddesses? You kings, I warn you, fear the clandestine breed: though raised in the backcountry,[38]

[38] These phrases equate Paris (the judge of goddesses) with Aegisthus, each raised in obscurity among herdsmen; "clandestine breed" alludes to the adultery of each, and (since *genus* can also mean "offspring") to Aegisthus' illicit conception.

agrestis iste alumnus evertet domum.
quid ista vecors tela feminea manu
735   districta praefert? quem petit dextra virum
Lacaena cultu, ferrum Amazonium gerens?
quae versat oculos alia nunc facies meos?
victor ferarum colla summissus iacet
ignobili sub dente Marmarici lupi,
740   morsus cruentos passus audacis leae.

      Quid me vocatis sospitem solam e meis,
umbrae meorum? te sequor, tota pater
Troia sepulte. frater, auxilium Phrygum
terrorque Danaum, non ego antiquum decus
745   video aut calentes ratibus ambustis manus,
sed lacera membra et saucios vinclo gravi
illos lacertos. te sequor, nimium cito
congresse Achilli Troile; incertos geris,
Deiphobe, vultus, coniugis munus novae.
750   iuvat per ipsos ingredi Stygios lacus,
iuvat videre Tartari saevum canem
avidique regna Ditis! haec hodie ratis
Phlegethontis atri regias animas vehet,
victamque victricemque. vos, umbrae, precor,
755   iurata superis unda, te pariter precor:
reserate paulum terga nigrantis poli,

738 summissus *Fitch*: sublimis *E*: vexatus *A*

739 Marmarici lupi *or* Marmarici canis *Hendry*: marmaricus
leo *EA*

745 ratibus ambustis *M. Müller*: ruptas bustis *E*: ratibus ex-
ustis *A*

he will overthrow your house! Why is that madwoman's
hand holding an unsheathed weapon? Spartan by dress,[39]
carrying an Amazon's steel, what man does she aim to attack? What different vision is attracting my eyes now? The
conqueror of wild beasts lies with neck bowed beneath the
ignoble jaws of the Marmaric wolf,[40] after suffering the
bloody bites of the daring lioness.

[*Seeing into the underworld*] Spirits of my loved ones,
why do you summon me, the only survivor of my family?
I follow you, father, whose tomb is the whole of Troy.
Brother, support of the Phrygians and terror of the
Danaans, I do not see your splendour of old nor the hands
hot from the firing of the ships, but torn limbs, and those
famous arms wounded by heavy chains. I follow you,
Troilus, who encountered Achilles too soon.[41] Your face
is unrecognisable, Deiphobus, thanks to your new wife.
What joy to embark on the very pools of Styx, what joy to
see the savage hound of Tartarus and the realms of greedy
Dis! Today this boat in black Phlegethon will carry royal
souls, conquered and conqueror. You spirits, I pray you;
you waters that the gods swear by, I pray you as well: draw
back a little the covering of the dark world, so the in-

[39] Clytemnestra is Spartan by birth; perhaps also an allusion to
Spartan women's manlike strength (*Med* 78).

[40] Viz. the hyena (here symbolizing Aegisthus), thought to be
bisexual (cf. 890) and to mate with the lioness (which here sym-
bolizes Clytemnestra).

[41] I.e. as a youth: Troy was destined not to fall if Troilus
reached the age of 20. The previous brother seen by Cassandra is
Hector, his body wounded by being dragged in chains behind
Achilles' chariot.

levis ut Mycenas turba prospiciat Phrygum.
spectate, miseri: fata se vertunt retro!
      Instant sorores squalidae,
760   anguinea iactant verbera,
      fert laeva semustas faces
      turgentque pallentes genae
      et vestis atri funeris
      exesa cingit ilia;
765   strepuntque nocturni metus,
      et ossa vasti corporis
      corrupta longinquo situ
      palude limosa iacent.
        Et ecce, defessus senex
770   ad ora ludentes aquas
      non captat oblitus sitim,
      maestus futuro funere.
      exultat et ponit gradus
      pater decoros Dardanus.

CHORUS

775 Iam pervagatus ipse se fregit furor,
caditque flexo qualis ante aras genu
cervice taurus vulnus incertum gerens.
relevemus artus.
        En deos tandem suos
victrice lauru cinctus Agamemnon adit,
780 et festa coniunx obvios illi tulit
gressus, reditque iuncta concordi gradu.

substantial throng of Phrygians can look out at Mycenae.
Watch, you poor folk: fate is reversing itself!

> The scabrous sisters[42] advance,
> they brandish snaky whips,
> their left hands bear charred torches,
> their cheeks are pale and bloated,
> and black funereal garments
> girdle their wasted flanks.
> The terrors of darkness howl,
> and the bones of a giant body
> rotted by long decay
> lie in the slimy marsh.
>   And see, the tired old man
> does not snatch at the fooling waters
> near his lips, forgets his thirst,
> grieving at death to come.[43]
> But Father Dardanus exults
> and treads a stately dance.

CHORUS LEADER

Now her madness has spent itself with its ramblings, and
she sinks down, as a bull sinks on bent knees before the
altar, bearing an ill-aimed wound in its neck. Let us lift her
body.

See, at last Agamemnon comes before his own gods,
crowned with the victor's laurel; his wife went out to meet
him in festive mood, and returns walking in concord at his
side.

42 The Furies.
43 Tantalus mourns the imminent death of his great-grandson
Agamemnon.

189

AGAMEMNON

Tandem revertor sospes ad patrios lares.
o cara salve terra! tibi tot barbarae
dedere gentes spolia, tibi felix diu
785 potentis Asiae domina summisit manus.
    Quid ista vates corpus effusa ac tremens
dubia labat cervice? famuli, attollite,
refovete gelido latice. iam recipit diem
marcente visu. Suscita sensus tuos:
790 optatus ille portus aerumnis adest.
festus dies est.

CASSANDRA

Festus et Troiae fuit.

AGAMEMNON

Veneremur aras.

CASSANDRA

Cecidit ante aras pater.

AGAMEMNON

Iovem precemur pariter.

CASSANDRA

Herceum Iovem?

AGAMEMNON

Credis videre te Ilium?

CASSANDRA

Et Priamum simul.

AGAMEMNON

795 Hic Troia non est.

AGAMEMNON

AGAMEMNON

At long last I return in safety to my father's housegods.
Greetings, my dear land! To you so many barbarian peoples have yielded spoils, to you the long-thriving mistress of powerful Asia has surrendered.

Why is the priestess lying there trembling and fainting, her neck drooping? Servants, raise her, revive her with cold water. Now she sees the light again, but with dull eyes. [*To Cassandra*] Gather your senses: the longed-for haven from sufferings is here at hand. This is a festive day!

CASSANDRA
It was festive too at Troy.

AGAMEMNON
Let us do reverence at the altar.

CASSANDRA
Father fell before an altar.

AGAMEMNON
Let us pray to Jove together.

CASSANDRA
Hercean Jove?

AGAMEMNON
You think you see Ilium?

CASSANDRA
Yes, and Priam as well.[44]

AGAMEMNON
Here is not Troy.

44 I.e. a king fated to be murdered in his own palace, viz. Agamemnon.

SENECA

CASSANDRA
Helena ubi est, Troiam puto.

AGAMEMNON
Ne metue dominam famula.

CASSANDRA
Libertas adest.

AGAMEMNON
Secura vive!

CASSANDRA
Mihi mori est securitas.

AGAMEMNON
Nullum est periclum tibimet.

CASSANDRA
At magnum tibi.

AGAMEMNON
Victor timere quid potest?

CASSANDRA
Quod non timet.

AGAMEMNON
800   Hanc, fida famuli turba, dum excutiat deum,
retinete, ne quid impotens peccet furor.
    At te, pater, qui saeva torques fulmina
pellisque nubes, sidera et terras regis,
ad quem triumphi spolia victores ferunt,
805   et te sororem cuncta pollentis viri,

---

45 I.e. Clytemnestra, as Helen's sister and an adulteress and
bringer of death like her. (Helen herself is not present.) That

AGAMEMNON

CASSANDRA

Where Helen is,[45] I think it Troy.

AGAMEMNON

Do not fear your mistress, though a slave.

CASSANDRA

Freedom is close.

AGAMEMNON

Live in security!

CASSANDRA

For me death is security.

AGAMEMNON

There is no danger for you.

CASSANDRA

But great danger for you.

AGAMEMNON

What can a conqueror fear?

CASSANDRA

What he does not fear.

AGAMEMNON

My loyal band of servants, restrain her until she throws off the god's influence, lest her wayward madness should commit some offence.

But you, father, who hurl fierce thunderbolts, who drive the clouds and rule the stars and earth, to whom conquerors bring triumphal spoils, and you, sister of your

Cassandra glances at Clytemnestra is suggested by Agamemnon's reply.

Argolica Iuno, pecore votivo libens
Arabumque donis supplice et fibra colam.

CHORUS

Argos nobilibus nobile civibus,
    Argos iratae carum novercae,
810   semper ingentes educans alumnos,
    imparem aequasti numerum deorum.
tuus ille bis seno meruit labore
      allegi caelo magnus Alcides,
      cui lege mundi Iuppiter rupta
815   roscidae noctis geminavit horas
         iussitque Phoebum
    tardius celeres agitare currus
    et tuas lente remeare bigas,
        candida Phoebe.
    * * * rettulitque pedem
820   nomen alternis stella quae mutat
      seque mirata est Hesperum dici.
      Aurora movit
ad solitas vices caput, et relabens
    imposuit seni collum marito.
      sensit ortus, sensit occasus
825   Herculem nasci: violentus ille
    nocte non una poterat creari.
    tibi concitatus substitit mundus,
      o puer subiture caelum.

810 educans *Fitch*: educas *EA*
819 *lacuna recognised by Zwierlein*

---

[46] Juno, angry at the number of Jove's bastard children, her "stepchildren."

all-powerful husband, Argive Juno: I shall gladly worship you with votive animals, with offerings from Arabia, and with entrails burnt in thanksgiving.

CHORUS

Argos famed for famous citizens,
  Argos dear to the angry stepmother,[46]
  always nurturing mighty sons:
  you rounded the uneven number of the gods.
That hero of yours earned admission to heaven
      by his twice six labours—great Alcides,
      for whom Jove broke the laws of the cosmos,
  doubled the hours of dewy night,
          and ordered Phoebus
  to drive his speeding chariot more slowly
  and your two horses to return at a walk,
          radiant Phoebe.
    The star that alternates its name[47]
        . . . and then stepped back,
      amazed to find itself called Hesper.
          Aurora raised
her head in time for the usual shift, then sinking back
  pillowed her neck on her ancient husband.
      The lands of sunrise and sunset were aware
  of Hercules' genesis; that aggressive hero
  could not have been sired in a single night.
For you the hastening skies stood still,
  child with the destiny of entering heaven.

[47] The dawn star, Lucifer, was sometimes regarded as identical with the evening star, Hesperus. The gist of the missing words must be that the star prepared to shine as Lucifer.

Te sensit Nemeaeus arto
830   pressus lacerto fulmineus leo
       cervaque Parrhasis,
   sensit Arcadii populator agri,
       gemuitque taurus
   Dictaea linquens horridus arva.
835   morte fecundum domuit draconem
   vetuitque collo pereunte nasci,
       geminosque fratres
   pectore ex uno tria monstra natos
   stipite incusso fregit insultans
840   duxitque ad ortus Hesperium pecus,
       Geryonae spolium triformis.
       egit Threicium gregem,
quem non Strymonii gramine fluminis
       Hebrive ripis pavit tyrannus:
845   hospitum dirus stabulis cruorem
   praebuit saevis, tinxitque crudos
   ultimus rictus sanguis aurigae.
       vidit Hippolyte ferox
       pectore e medio rapi
850   spolium, et sagittis nube percussa
       Stymphalis alto decidit caelo;
   arborque pomis fertilis aureis
   extimuit manus insueta carpi
   fugitque in auras leviore ramo.
855 audivit sonitum crepitante lamna

---

[48] The chorus list Hercules' labours in the following order: Nemean lion, Arcadian hind, Erymanthian boar, Cretan bull, Lernaean hydra, cattle of Geryon, horses of Diomedes, baldric of

Your power was felt by the lightning-like
Nemean lion, crushed in your tightened arms,[48]
     and the Parrhasian hind,
and felt by the plunderer of Arcadian fields;
     and the fearsome bull
  bellowed at leaving Dictaean lands.
He subdued the snaky creature, fertile in death,
and stopped it arising from dying necks;
     the twinned brothers
that rose as three monsters from a single breast
  he crushed as he leapt with blows from his club,
and he brought east the Hesperian cattle,
    spoil from three-formed Geryon.
  He drove the Thracian herd
that the tyrant had fed not on the grassy banks
    of the Strymon River or Hebrus:
the fiend purveyed the gore of strangers
to his savage beasts, but the last blood to redden
those brutish jaws was their charioteer's.
     From her very breast the fierce
     Hippolyte watched him wrench
the spoil; when the clouds were struck by arrows
    the Stymphalids fell from the high heavens.
The tree prolific of golden apples
  shrank from his hands, unused to being plucked,
  and recoiled upwards with lightened branches.
The clink of metallic leaves was heard

Hippolyte, Stymphalian birds, apples of Hesperides, Cerberus.
(Details are given in the Index.) To these eleven they add the expedition against Troy and omit the Augean stables, maintaining
the canonical number of twelve.

197

       frigidus custos nescius somni,
      linqueret cum iam nemus omne fulvo
      plenus Alcides vacuum metallo.
      tractus ad caelum canis inferorum
860   triplici catena
      tacuit nec ullo latravit ore,
      lucis ignotae metuens colorem.
           te duce succidit
        mendax Dardanidae domus
      et sensit arcus iterum timendos;
865   te duce concidit totidem diebus
          Troia quot annis.

CASSANDRA

  Res agitur intus magna, par annis decem.
  eheu quid hoc est? anime, consurge et cape
  pretium furoris: vicimus victi Phryges.
870 bene est, resurgis, Troia; traxisti iacens
  pares Mycenas, terga dat victor tuus!
  tam clara numquam providae mentis furor
  ostendit oculis: video et intersum et fruor;
  imago visus dubia non fallit meos.
875 spectemus! epulae regia instructae domo,
  quales fuerunt ultimae Phrygibus dapes,
  celebrantur; ostro lectus Iliaco nitet
  merumque in auro veteris Assaraci trahunt.
  et ipse picta veste sublimis iacet,
880 Priami superbas corpore exuvias gerens.

---

[49] The Dardanid was Laomedon, who cheated Hercules of a promised reward. Hercules' arrows would threaten Troy again in the hands of Philoctetes.

by the chill guard that knew no sleep,
as Alcides was leaving the grove entirely empty
of the tawny metal that filled his arms.
The hound of the underworld, dragged aloft
         with triple chains,
fell silent, barked with none of his mouths,
fearing the colour of the unknown light.
      When you led the attack,
   the Dardanid's perjured house collapsed,
and felt the arrows that would threaten again;[49]
when you led the attack, it fell in as many days
        as Troy took years to fall.

ACT 5

CASSANDRA

A great deed is being done inside, a match for those ten years. Oh no, what is this? Rise up, my spirit, and enjoy the rewards of your madness! We have conquered, we conquered Phrygians! Good, you are rising again, Troy. While fallen you have dragged down your adversary, Mycenae; your conqueror turns and runs! My prophetic madness has never shown things to my eyes so clearly. I see the scene, I am there, I relish it; this is no hazy picture deceiving my sight. Let us watch! A feast is being held, laid out in the royal house—like that last banquet for the Phrygians. The couch is replendent with purple cloths from Ilium, and they quaff their wine from the gold of old Assaracus. He himself lies in state in an embroidered robe, his body clothed in proud spoils from Priam.

Detrahere cultus uxor hostiles iubet,
induere potius coniugis fidae manu
textos amictus. horreo atque animo tremo!
regemne perimet exul et adulter virum?
885 venere fata. sanguinem extremae dapes
domini videbunt, et cruor Baccho incidet.
mortifera vinctum perfidae tradit neci
induta vestis: exitum manibus negant
caputque laxi et invii claudunt sinus.
890 haurit trementi semivir dextra latus,
nec penitus egit: vulnere in medio stupet.
at ille, ut altis hispidus silvis aper
cum casse vinctus temptat egressus tamen
artatque motu vincla et in cassum furit,
895 cupit fluentes undique et caecos sinus
dissicere et hostem quaerit implicitus suum.
armat bipenni Tyndaris dextram furens,
qualisque ad aras colla taurorum popa
designat oculis antequam ferro petat,
900 sic huc et illuc impiam librat manum.
habet, peractum est! pendet exigua male
caput amputatum parte, et hinc trunco cruor
exundat, illinc ora cum fremitu iacent.
nondum recedunt: ille iam exanimem petit
905 laceratque corpus, illa fodientem adiuvat.
uterque tanto scelere respondet suis:
est hic Thyestae natus, haec Helenae soror.
stat ecce Titan dubius emerito die,
suane currat an Thyestea via.

898 popa *Bentley*: prius *EA*

His wife bids him take off this enemy attire, and put on instead a mantle woven by her hand, his faithful spouse. I shudder and tremble in spirit! Shall the king be murdered by an exile, the husband by an adulterer? The hour of fate has come. The feast's last course will see the master's blood—yes, blood will drop into the wine. The deadly garment he has put on binds him and delivers him to death by treachery. Its loose, impenetrable folds imprison his head and give his hands no way out. The half-man gouges his side with a trembling hand—but he has not thrust deep, he freezes in the very act of wounding! As in deep woods a bristling boar caught fast in a net still attempts to escape, tightening his bonds by his movements and raging in vain, so the king tries to part the blinding folds that pour around him, and searches for his enemy while ensnared. The Tyndarid madly arms herself with a double-bladed axe, and tries aiming at various points with those wicked hands, just as an attendant at the altar marks out the bulls' necks by eye before striking with the steel. He's hit,[50] it's all over! The head hangs by a small segment, not cleanly cut off. Here blood pours from the torso, there lies the face with its mouth still shouting. They are not yet stepping away: *he* attacks Agamemnon now he is dead and mutilates his body, *she* assists in the stabbing. Both show themselves true to family by such a crime: he is Thyestes' son, she is Helen's sister. But see, with his day's work ended the Titan halts in confusion: should he run his own course, or a Thyestean course?[51]

[50] Literally "he has it" (the wound), a phrase taken from gladiatorial fights.   [51] After Thyestes' gruesome feast the sun turned and ran counter to its normal direction.

ELECTRA

910 Fuge, o paternae mortis auxilium unicum,
fuge et scelestas hostium evita manus.
eversa domus est funditus, regna occidunt.
     Quis iste celeres concitus currus agit?
germane, vultus veste furabor tuos.
915 —quid, anime demens, refugis? externos times?
domus timenda est! pone iam trepidos metus,
Oresta: amici fida praesidia intuor.

STROPHIUS

Phocida relictam Strophius Elea inclitus
palma revertor. causa veniendi fuit
920 gratari amico, cuius impulsum manu
cecidit decenni marte concussum Ilium.
     Quaenam ista lacrimis lugubrem vultum rigat
pavetque maesta? regium agnosco genus.
Electra, fletus causa quae laeta in domo est?

ELECTRA

925 Pater peremptus scelere materno iacet,
comes paternae quaeritur natus neci,
Aegisthus arces venere quaesitas tenet.

STROPHIUS

O nulla longi temporis felicitas!

ELECTRA

Per te parentis memoriam obtestor mei,
930 per sceptra terris nota, per dubios deos:
recipe hunc Oresten ac pium furtum occule.

ELECTRA

[*Entering with Orestes and speaking to him*] Escape! You are the only hope of redress for our father's death—escape and elude our enemies' wicked hands. Our house is utterly overthrown, our royal power brought low.

Who is this, driving a chariot here in such haste? Brother, I shall conceal your face behind my cloak. [*To herself*] What craziness, to shrink back and fear outsiders! Our home is what we must fear! No more panic now, Orestes: I see a loyal friend and protector.

STROPHIUS

[*Entering in a chariot with his son Pylades*] I am returning home to Phocis, my name Strophius made famous through winning the palm at Elis. My purpose in coming was to congratulate my friend, whose hand has toppled Ilium after ten years of warfare had shaken her.

Who is this with tears of sorrow on her face, fearful and sad? I recognise her royal lineage. Electra, what cause is there for tears in your joyful house?

ELECTRA

Our father lies murdered by our mother's criminal act; they are searching for the son to join his father in death; and Aegisthus holds sway over the city, gained by adultery.

STROPHIUS

Oh, the transience of all happiness!

ELECTRA

By my father's memory I implore you, by his world-renowned sceptre, and by the fickle gods: take Orestes here, and conceal the righteous theft.

STROPHIUS

Etsi timendum caesus Agamemnon docet,
aggrediar et te, Oresta, furabor libens.
[fidem secunda poscunt, adversa exigunt]
935 cape hoc decorum ludicri certaminis,
insigne frontis; laeva victricem tenens
frondem virenti protegat ramo caput,
et ista donum palma Pisaei Iovis
velamen eadem praestet atque omen tibi.
940 Tuque, o paternis assidens frenis comes,
condisce, Pylade, patris exemplo fidem.
Vos Graecia nunc teste veloces equi
infida cursu fugite praecipiti loca.

ELECTRA

Excessit, abiit, currus effreno impetu
945 effugit aciem. tuta iam opperiar meos
hostes et ultro vulneri opponam caput.
    Adest cruenta coniugis victrix sui,
et signa caedis veste maculata gerit.
manus recenti sanguine etiamnunc madent
950 vultusque prae se scelera truculenti ferunt.
concedam ad aras.—Patere me vittis tuis,
Cassandra, iungi paria metuentem tibi.

CLYTEMESTRA

Hostis parentis, impium atque audax caput,
quo more coetus publicos virgo petis?

934 *deleted by Peiper*

AGAMEMNON

STROPHIUS

Even though Agamemnon's murder teaches the need for fear, I shall gladly brave the task and steal you away, Orestes.[52] Take this prize from the athletic games to adorn your brow. Your left hand must hold the branch of victory and screen your head with its green foliage: so the palm bestowed by Pisaean Jove shall offer you both concealment and a good omen. And Pylades, sitting close by your father as he drives: learn loyalty from your father's example. Now, you horses, whose speed all Greece has witnessed, gallop away from this place where loyalty is lost.

ELECTRA

He is off, he has gone, the chariot sped headlong, already out of sight! Now I am safe,[53] I shall await my enemies and willingly offer my neck to the death blow.

Here she is, the bloodthirsty conqueror of her own husband, with the signs of murder on her stained clothes. Her hands are still wet with fresh blood, and her truculent expression reveals her criminality. I shall withdraw to the altar. Let me share your protecting chaplets,[54] Cassandra, since my danger is equal to yours.

CLYTEMNESTRA

Enemy of your mother, unnatural, brazen creature: what behaviour is this, to seek public converse as a virgin girl?

---

[52] 934 (deleted): "Good fortune calls for loyalty, but adversity demands it."

[53] Because Orestes is out of danger, and she is unafraid to face death herself (cf. e.g. *Tro* 574).

[54] The reference is to the woollen bands identifying those under the aegis of the gods, such as priests and suppliants.

ELECTRA

955 Adulterorum virgo deserui domum.

CLYTEMESTRA

Quis esse credat virginem—

ELECTRA

Natam tuam?

CLYTEMESTRA

Modestius cum matre.

ELECTRA

Pietatem doces?

CLYTEMESTRA

Animos viriles corde tumefacto geris;
sed agere domita feminam disces malo.

ELECTRA

960 Nisi forte fallor, feminas ferrum decet.

CLYTEMESTRA

Et esse demens te parem nobis putas?

ELECTRA

Vobis? quis iste est alter Agamemnon tuus?
ut vidua loquere: vir caret vita tuus.

CLYTEMESTRA

Indomita posthac virginis verba impiae
965 regina frangam; citius interea mihi
edissere ubi sit natus, ubi frater tuus.

ELECTRA

Extra Mycenas.

ELECTRA

As a virgin girl I have quit the home of adulterers.

CLYTEMNESTRA

Who would believe you a virgin?

ELECTRA

Your daughter?

CLYTEMNESTRA

More modestly with your mother!

ELECTRA

Are you teaching right relationships?

CLYTEMNESTRA

You carry a man's spirit in your puffed-up heart, but when tamed by suffering you will learn to play the woman.

ELECTRA

If I am not mistaken, women have an aptitude for steel.

CLYTEMNESTRA

And do you have the crazy notion that you are a match for us?

ELECTRA

For you two? Who is that other Agamemnon of yours? Speak as a widow: your husband has lost his life.

CLYTEMNESTRA

These unbridled words from an undutiful virgin—I shall break them later as queen. Meanwhile tell me quickly where is my son, your brother.

ELECTRA

Outside Mycenae.

CLYTEMESTRA
Redde nunc natum mihi.

ELECTRA
Et tu parentem redde.

CLYTEMESTRA
Quo latitat loco?

ELECTRA
Tuto quietus, regna non metuens nova:
970   dixi parenti satis.

CLYTEMESTRA
At iratae parum.
morieris hodie.

ELECTRA
Dummodo hac moriar manu.
recedo ab aris. sive te iugulo iuvat
mersisse ferrum, praebeo iugulum tibi;
seu more pecudum colla resecari placet,
975   intenta cervix vulnus expectat tuum.
scelus paratum est: caede respersam viri
atque obsoletam sanguine hoc dextram ablue.

CLYTEMESTRA
Consors pericli pariter ac regni mei,
Aegisthe, gradere. nata genetricem impie
980   probris lacessit, occulit fratrem abditum.

AEGISTHUS
Furibunda virgo, vocis infandae sonum
et aure verba indigna materna opprime.

---

[970] dixi *E*: iustae* *A*   [973] tibi *E*: volens *A*

CLYTEMNESTRA

Restore my son to me now.

ELECTRA

And you restore my father.

CLYTEMNESTRA

Where is he hiding?

ELECTRA

In peace and safety, with no fear of the new regime. I have said enough for a mother.

CLYTEMNESTRA

But not enough for an angry one. You shall die this day.

ELECTRA

So long as I die by this hand of yours! I am moving away from the altar. If you please to sink the steel in my throat, I offer you my throat; or if you want my neck to be severed like cattle, my neck is stretched out to await your death-blow. The crime is ready-made. Since your hand is spattered and tarnished with your husband's gore, cleanse it with this blood!

CLYTEMNESTRA

You who share my danger as well as my throne, Aegisthus, come! My daughter is insulting her mother outrageously, and keeping her brother hidden away.

AEGISTHUS

Demented girl, hush this infamous talk, these words unfit for a mother's ears.

ELECTRA

Etiam monebit sceleris infandi artifex,
per scelera natus, nomen ambiguum suis,
985   idem sororis natus et patris nepos?

CLYTEMESTRA

Aegisthe, cessas impium ferro caput
demetere? fratrem reddat aut animam statim.

AEGISTHUS

Abstrusa caeco carcere et saxo exigat
aevum; per omnes torta poenarum modos
990   referre quem nunc occulit forsan volet.
inops egens inclusa, paedore obruta,
vidua ante thalamos, exul, invisa omnibus
aethere negato sero succumbet malis.

ELECTRA

Concede mortem.

AEGISTHUS

                    Si recusares, darem:
995   rudis est tyrannus morte qui poenam exigit.

ELECTRA

Mortem aliquid ultra est?

AEGISTHUS

                          Vita, si cupias mori.
Abripite, famuli, monstrum, et avectam procul
ultra Mycenas ultimo in regni angulo
vincite saeptam nocte tenebrosi specus,
1000   ut inquietam virginem carcer domet.

210

ELECTRA

Is he really going to give reprimands, this architect of
infamous crime, a man born through crime, ambiguously
related to his own family—both son of his sister and grandchild of his father?

CLYTEMNESTRA

Aegisthus, why hesitate to strike off the undutiful creature's head with your sword? She must give up her brother
or her life immediately.

AEGISTHUS

She shall live out her life buried in an unlit, rocky dungeon.
Tormented by all manner of punishments, she will perhaps
agree to return the one she is now hiding. Helpless, starv-
ing, imprisoned, overwhelmed with filth, bereft before
being married, exiled, hated by all, denied the daylight,
she will succumb at long last to her sufferings.

ELECTRA

Grant me death!

AEGISTHUS

If you said no to it, I would confer it. One who punishes by
death is an inept tyrant.

ELECTRA

Is anything worse than death?

AEGISTHUS

Life, if you long to die. Slaves, hurry this monster away,
carry her far outside Mycenae, and in the kingdom's remotest corner chain and confine her in the darkness of an
unlit cave, so that prison may tame this turbulent virgin.

211

SENECA

CLYTEMESTRA

At ista poenas capite persolvet suo
captiva coniunx, regii paelex tori.
Trahite, ut sequatur coniugem ereptum mihi.

CASSANDRA

Ne trahite, vestros ipsa praecedam gradus.
1005 perferre prima nuntium Phrygibus meis
propero: repletum ratibus eversis mare,
captas Mycenas, mille ductorem ducum,
ut paria fata Troicis lueret malis,
perisse dono, feminae stupro, dolo.
1010 nihil moramur, rapite, quin grates ago:
iam, iam iuvat vixisse post Troiam, iuvat.

CLYTEMESTRA

Furiosa, morere!

CASSANDRA
Veniet et vobis furor.

212

CLYTEMNESTRA

But this one shall pay the death penalty—this prisoner-wife, mistress of the royal bed. Drag her away to follow the husband she stole from me.

CASSANDRA

Do not drag me, I shall walk before you. I am eager to reach my Phrygians first with the news: how the sea was filled with capsized ships, how Mycenae was taken, how the leader of a thousand leaders—to meet a fate commensurate with Troy's sufferings—perished by a gift, by a woman's lust, by a trick. I make no delay, hurry me away, indeed I thank you. *Now* I am happy to have outlived Troy—yes, happy!

CLYTEMNESTRA

Die in your madness!

CASSANDRA

Madness will come upon you too.[55]

---

[55] I.e. vengeance will come upon both of you (*vobis* plural) at Orestes' hands: madness (furor) and revenge are closely connected through the Furies.

THYESTES

INTRODUCTION

Background

Tantalus, a human son of Jupiter, served the flesh of his son Pelops to the gods to test them. They perceived the trick, restored Pelops to life, and sentenced Tantalus to eternal torment by hunger and thirst in the underworld. Later Pelops came to Greece, and was challenged by Oenomaus to a mortal chariot race. Pelops bribed his opponent's charioteer Myrtilus to sabotage his master's chariot; when Myrtilus claimed his reward, Pelops drowned him. Afterwards Pelops established a kingdom in Greece south of the Isthmus, which became known as the Peloponnese or "island of Pelops."

The family's history of wrongdoing continues in Pelops' sons Atreus and Thyestes. Thyestes seduced Atreus' wife Aerope; consequently Atreus is uncertain of the paternity of his sons Agamemnon and Menelaus. With Aerope's help, Thyestes obtained the golden-fleeced ram which was the talisman of the Argive throne; so he became king, and drove Atreus into exile. Now Atreus has gained the throne, and is preparing to take revenge on his banished brother.

Summary

Act 1
The ghost of Tantalus is brought from the underworld, and forced by a Fury to infect the royal house of Argos with his evil influence.

Ode 1. The chorus prays that the gods will end the sequence of evildoing among Tantalus' descendants. Description of Tantalus' punishment in the underworld.

Act 2
Atreus goads himself to take revenge on his brother, and settles on the scheme of the feast. First he will invite Thyestes and his sons back from exile in a pretence of reconciliation.

Ode 2. True kingship consists not of temporal power but governance of the self. The chorus expresses its ideal of a simple life in seclusion.

Act 3
Thyestes thinks better of returning to Argos, but is persuaded by his son to continue. Atreus welcomes him effusively and dresses him in royal robes.

Ode 3. The chorus comments on the drastic change from war preparations to peace. No situation or good fortune is enduring.

Act 4
A messenger describes Atreus' sacrifice of Thyestes' sons, his cooking of their flesh, and its consumption by Thyestes.

218

Ode 4. The chorus reacts to the turning back of the sun. Does it signal the imminent fall of the constellations and destruction of the cosmos?

Act 5

The still ignorant Thyestes attempts to enjoy the feast, but cannot dispel misgivings. After mocking him, Atreus reveals what he has done. Thyestes' prayers to the gods for retribution meet with no response.

Comment

The play's central theme is tantalising, insatiable desire. The eponymous embodiment of such desire is Tantalus, ancestor of the royal house of Argos, whose punishment in the underworld is appropriately to "catch at vanishing food with his avid mouth" (line 2). When the Fury bids him "fill the whole house with Tantalus," she means "fill it with insatiable desire" (53). Hunger and thirst, emptiness and fulness are constant motifs of the play, sometimes literal and physical as in Tantalus, sometimes metaphors for other desires and attempts to satisfy them. Supreme power above all tantalises those who desire it: "Let kingship slip from the brothers when in their pride, and pull them back when in exile" (32–33).

In keeping with the insatiable nature of desire, Atreus does not enjoy the supreme power he holds, but wants more. Specifically he wants revenge, which he regards as the right and almost the duty of a despot. But how to encompass a revenge that will be adequate, in the sense of outdoing all previous achievements? Here as in *Medea* and elsewhere we find the old heroic drive for competitive accomplishment, "to be best and to be outstanding among others"; but that drive has now become an obsessive desire, and one devoid of any moral content. The longing to "fill" the self with transcendent passion (253) suggests hollowness, not heroism. And the wish "to be outstanding among others" has been transformed into (or revealed as) a desire to vindicate one's selfhood by domination of others. Hence the connection in Atreus' mind between supreme power and revenge. As his subjects must be forced not just to tolerate but to praise his acts (206–07), so the threat posed (allegedly) by Thyestes' existence must be brought under control. The issue of mastery is clear in Atreus' image of Thyestes as a beast caught in a net, and of the crown placed on Thyestes' head as a bond (491, 544). Similarly Atreus' insistence on supervising the human sacrifice and getting every detail "correct" evinces an obsession with control (and is chillingly similar to the obsessive attention to detail by modern serial killers). The sacrifice demonstrates Atreus' control in other ways too: as a sacrifice *to himself* (713) it places him in the position of a god, and simultaneously proves that the gods cannot prevent his usurpation of their rights.

Ode 2, with its calm teaching that self-governance is the only true kingship, presents so attractive a contrast to Atreus' understanding of kingship that it has been taken as an authorial statement controlling interpretation of the play. Seneca as a philosopher was, after all, aligned with Stoicism, and the best known of the Stoic paradoxes held that "the wise man alone is king." But there were differences of emphasis and doctrine within Stoicism, as within

Christianity. Seneca as philosopher nowhere endorses the paradox of the wise man as king.[1] His ideal of kingship is rather that of the *rex iustus*, i.e. of one who holds temporal power but exercises it with justice and clemency (see his essay *On Clemency*). The doctrine that "the wise man alone is king" has the potential to lead to a radical and non-Stoic repudiation of temporal power and of involvement in affairs of state: it is significant that this very ode shifts into a desire for retirement and enjoyment of the passing day (391–403) that is certifiably Epicurean, not Stoic. As elsewhere, the chorus' moral pronouncements shed light on the drama, but should not be read as authorial.

In contrast to the single-minded Atreus, Thyestes is torn between desire on the one hand and knowledge on the other hand. In this he recalls Ovid's Medea: "Desire urges one course, knowledge another; I see the better path and endorse it, but I follow the worse" (*Metamorphoses* 7.19–21). References in Thyestes' opening speech to wealth, acclaim, and the throne reveal that he has not lost his hunger for those things. On the other hand he knows how delusive and dangerous they are, and how much peace lies in the simple life—a life lived according to nature, a life "among the beasts and comparable to theirs" (413–414). In some ways his understanding echoes the philosophical ideas of Ode 2, though his knowledge is based on personal experience not philosophy, and his behaviour shows that he has not in fact "put aside" ambition and other desires. Consequently he follows his sons, trusts

[1] He does however recount—with evident irony—that his Stoic teacher Attalus claimed such philosophical kingship (*Letter* 108.13).

his brother, and accepts a crown, knowing full well that he should do none of these things, and wallows in food and drink exactly where he knows danger lurks.

Both brothers, then, are in the grip of tantalising desire. In what sense is it inspired by their grandfather Tantalus, as Act 1 suggests? His role can be understood symbolically: as he rises from the depths of the underworld, so desire rises from the irrational depths of the mind. Correspondingly the dark, sinister valley in the palace grounds is like a black hole of irrational drives within the psyche. But Act 1 also symbolises a causal relationship between Tantalus' desire and his grandsons', since the family's history has shaped the present generation, including its insatiable desires. By both nature and nurture this generation is driven to desire, imitating and emulating the examples of its forebears.

Desire is so boundless that it perverts not only human relationships but also the natural world and the order of the cosmos. The turning back of the sun in horror, traditional to the myth, brings darkness at noon, and raises fears of a universal cataclysm (such as was predicted by the physical science of Seneca's day, both Stoic and Epicurean). Already in the prologue the earth's moisture is parched, its greenery withered, by the presence of Tantalus/desire (106–121); consequently the chorus' hope in Ode 1, that nature's beauty will inspire divine protection, is already undermined for the audience. Similarly fire recoils from involvement in Atreus' evil (768–772).[2] Such

---

[2] In ancient myth and religion, nature is seen as reacting to evil in the human world by omens and portents; in Seneca that traditional picture may take on some philosophical colouring through

unintended consequences of human desire are matched by its intended results. Atreus wants the whole world to be convulsed by his revenge, with fields and cities blazing everywhere (180–183)—and he has the power, like his Roman counterparts, to put at least some of that into effect. The high and mighty of Argos/Rome contravene nature systematically, building out into the sea, planting forests on rooftops, turning day into night—and making themselves gods in place of Jove, to show that they recognise no limit to their power (455–467). There is no missing the relevance of these themes to our own situation two millennia later, in which a mania for consumption threatens every natural system on earth, and the desire for political dominion has led to development of weapons that could devastate the world.

Allusions and references to the world of Rome are prominent in the middle stretch of this play (from Ode 2 on), almost all having to do with power and dominion. The examples of ostentatious greed cited by Thyestes—the building of villas out into the sea, and so on—are familiar in Roman satire and moralising, while the reference to supplanting Jove's worship cannot fail to suggest the worship of Roman emperors (see e.g. Suetonius' *Life of Caligula* 22). The Messenger's description of the Tantalid palace in Act 4 strongly evokes Vergil's depiction of a hilltop palace-temple in early Rome (*Aeneid* 7.170–186), a prototype of the actual imperial palace of Vergil's and Seneca's day atop the Palatine Hill; what is a place of benign power in Vergil has become a place of tyranny in Seneca.

the Stoic doctrine of *sympatheia*, i.e. the interconnection and interaction of all parts of the cosmos.

And particularly in Odes 2 and 3 there are references to foreign peoples at or beyond the borders of Rome's empire, peoples of importance in the geopolitical struggles of the first century A.D. This plethora of references leaves no doubt that the play's themes of megalomania, lust for power, violation of family relationships, and oppression of citizens have a direct relevance to the experience of imperial Rome.

The story of Atreus and Thyestes had, in fact, long been found particularly relevant to Roman potentates and their boundless hunger for power. The notorious tag *oderint dum metuant*, "let them hate as long as they fear me," comes from Accius' *Atreus* (perhaps 140 B.C.); it was quoted by Cicero to suggest Antony's tyrannical ambition, and by Seneca in reference to the age of Sulla and Marius; Caligula allegedly liked to utter it with perverse approval. The *Atreus* of Aemilius Scaurus so offended Tiberius that it cost the author his life. Later in the century, Curiatius Maternus planned a *Thyestes* specifically as a vehicle for dissident comment under the autocratic Domitian. If Seneca did indeed write *Thyestes* in the later years of Nero's reign, he can have had little doubt about the dangerous relevance of its subject. *Fortem facit vicina libertas senem*: "The closeness of freedom makes the aged brave" (*Pha* 139).

Thyestes is remarkable for its integration of many facets into a unified whole: dramaturgy, rhetoric, themes, imagery, moral and political issues. Because of this integration it is often and rightly regarded as Seneca's masterpiece (though one should add that Seneca did not necessarily seek unity of this kind in the other plays). *Thyestes* also has other characteristics of greatness: an ability to resonate with meaning at many levels, and an ability to speak directly to ages other than its own.

But though unmistakably a masterpiece, is its effect that of tragedy? It does not evoke that sympathy for the victims of disaster on which many Greek tragedies base their emotional effect; for Thyestes is too weak-willed, too gross in his feasting, too dim-witted in comparison with his brother, to command much sympathy. Atreus himself is paradoxically far more attractive, at least initially: in his exuberant ruthlessness, in his frank devotion to power as the only good, in his macabre wit, in his command of words and rhetoric, he has an appeal like that of Shakespeare's Richard III. But he becomes repellent in his demented sacrificing of the youngsters, and in his sadistic toying with Thyestes. The play's effect is likely to be horror and shock—shock in particular that the play ends in Atreus' triumph, with no prospect of his punishment in sight. Admittedly his insatiable desire is unlikely to remain satisfied for long, indeed is already dissatisfied (1053–1068). And admittedly we know, unlike the chorus, that the cosmos will survive. But that knowledge is hardly reassuring, since the pathological desire for domination will also survive, in the Tantalid family and in Atreus' metaphorical descendants, a Caligula or a Nero, a Hitler or a Hussein. Perhaps part of tragedy's role is to confront us with the darkest elements in our experience of the world and of ourselves. The experience may not be comfortable or therapeutic. But in a tough-minded age largely unaccustomed to religious comfort, it may not seem as intolerable as it did to some earlier ages.

The greatest horror, the killing and eating of the children, was part of the myth long before Seneca, and is parallelled in other Greek myths such as those of Saturn, Procne, and Tantalus himself. The killing of children or young people by the older generation, often their parents, is a prominent motif of ancient tragedy, present in most of the Senecan dramas. A structural contrast may be made with comedy: in a familiar comic pattern, young people escape the control of their elders and establish themselves as adults, potential parents in turn. In tragedy that natural succession is often denied.[3] The inversion of natural processes is particularly clear when children are thrust back into the body of the parent in a travesty of birth and pregnancy (see 999–1000, 1041–1044), unable to achieve separation (978–979, 998). However extreme this element in *Thyestes* may appear from a moral viewpoint, it has a structural centrality to the tragic genre.

Sources

The widespread view of *Thyestes* as the most Senecan of the Senecan plays is largely attributable to the loss of so many dramas from antiquity. The strife between Thyestes and Atreus was one of the most popular themes of ancient tragedy. We know of eight Greek dramatists who wrote on it, including Sophocles and Euripides, and six Roman dramatists other than Seneca himself (see Tarrant [1985] 40–

[3] The triumphant success of the leading character at the end of *Thyestes* is structurally comparable with the pattern of comedy—as is the use of wit, cunning, and humour in the process of achieving it—but inverts the implications and values of comedy. Similarly the feast, in comedy a celebration of community, here becomes inversely a feast for one man.

43). Most of these plays are lost beyond recall. The only
one that can be reconstructed with any confidence is the
Atreus of Accius (probably performed 140 B.C.). It appears
to have been similar in outline to Seneca's play, and even to
have shared the theme of tyranny, to judge by its best
known surviving words, quoted above. The probable explanation of the similarities is not that Seneca followed
Accius in particular, but that the main elements of plot and
character had become thoroughly traditional—with each
dramatist free, of course, to adjust them according to his
own emphases.

Seneca also draws on a wealth of nondramatic poetry,
particularly Augustan. There are several resonances with
scenes of Vergil's *Aeneid* that have underworld connotations: Aeneas' descent to the underworld (Book 6),
Faunus' oracular grove (7.81–91), and the Fury Allecto's
ascent to earth (7.323–571). And there are echoes
throughout of Seneca's master Ovid, especially his re-
counting of the myth of Procne (*Metamorphoses* 6, chiefly
609–666), with its relevance to the subject of the play. "In
his overt awareness of the Procne-Tereus story, and particularly in his desire to surpass it, [Atreus] resembles Seneca
himself in his relationship to Ovid. The challenge and anxiety of *imitatio* are shared by author and character"
(Tarrant [1985] 130).

BIBLIOGRAPHY

Commentary

R. J. Tarrant, *Seneca's Thyestes, Edited with Introduction
and Commentary* (Atlanta, 1985).

Criticism

A. J. Boyle, "*Hic Epulis Locus*: The Tragic Worlds of Seneca's *Agamemnon* and *Thyestes*," in A. J. Boyle (ed.) *Seneca Tragicus: Ramus Essays on Senecan Drama* (Victoria, Australia, 1983), 199–228.

H. Hine, "The Structure of Seneca's *Thyestes*," *Papers of the Liverpool International Latin Seminar 3* (1981), 259–275.

C. J. Littlewood, "Seneca's *Thyestes*: the Tragedy with No Women," *MD* 38 (1997), 57–86.

G. Meltzer, "Dark Wit and Black Humor in Seneca's *Thyestes*," *TAPA* 118 (1988) 309–330.

R. G. M. Nisbet, "The Dating of Seneca's Tragedies, with Special Reference to *Thyestes*," *Papers of the Leeds International Latin Seminar 6* (1990), 95–114.

J. P. Poe, "An Analysis of Seneca's *Thyestes*," *TAPA* 100 (1969), 355–376.

DRAMATIS PERSONAE

Ghost of TANTALUS, *grandfather of Atreus and Thyestes*
FURY *from the underworld*
ATREUS, *king of Argos, grandson of Tantalus and son of Pelops*
ASSISTANT *to Atreus*
THYESTES, *banished brother of Atreus*
SONS *of Thyestes*: TANTALUS, PLISTHENES, and a third (*the last two personae mutae*)
MESSENGER
CHORUS

Scene

The action takes place outside and (in Act 5) inside the royal palace in the city of Argos (which is also called Mycenae). The action begins shortly before dawn.

THYESTES

TANTALI UMBRA

Quis inferorum sede ab infausta extrahit
avido fugaces ore captantem cibos?
quis male deorum Tantalo invisas domos
ostendit iterum? peius inventum est siti
5 arente in undis aliquid et peius fame
hiante semper? Sisyphi numquid lapis
gestandus umeris lubricus nostris venit,
aut membra celeri differens cursu rota,
aut poena Tityi, qui specu vasto patens
10 vulneribus atras pascit effossis aves
et nocte reparans quidquid amisit die
plenum recenti pabulum monstro iacet?
in quod malum transcribor? o quisquis nova
supplicia functis durus umbrarum arbiter
15 disponis, addi si quid ad poenas potest
quod ipse custos carceris diri horreat,
quod maestus Acheron paveat, ad cuius metum
nos quoque tremamus, quaere! iam nostra subit
e stirpe turba quae suum vincat genus
20 ac me innocentem faciat et inausa audeat.

3 invisas *Heinsius*: visas *E*: vivas *A*

230

THYESTES

ACT 1

GHOST OF TANTALUS

From the accursed abode of the underworld, who drags forth the one that catches at vanishing food with his avid mouth? Who perversely lets Tantalus see once more the hated homes of the gods? Has something worse been devised than thirst parched amidst water, worse than hunger that gapes forever? Can it be that Sisyphus' stone comes to be carried—so slippery—on my shoulders, or the wheel that racks limbs in its swift rotation?[1] Or the punishment of Tityos, who with his cavernous vast opening feeds dark birds from his quarried wounds—who regrows by night what he lost by day, and lies as a full meal for the fresh monster? What evil am I being reassigned to? Whoever you are that allot new penalties to the dead, harsh judge of the shades: if anything can be added to my punishment that would make the very guardian of that dire prison[2] shudder, make gloomy Acheron afraid, make even *me* tremble in fear of it, seek it out! Now from my stock there is rising a crew that will outdo its own family, make me innocent and dare the undared. Any space unused in the

---

[1] The wheel is usually Ixion's punishment.
[2] Cerberus.

regione quidquid impia cessat loci
complebo; numquam stante Pelopea domo
Minos vacabit.

FURIA
Perge, detestabilis
umbra, et penates impios furiis age.
25   certetur omni scelere et alterna vice
stringatur ensis. nec sit irarum modus
pudorve; mentes caecus instiget furor,
rabies parentum duret et longum nefas
eat in nepotes. nec vacet cuiquam vetus
30   odisse crimen: semper oriatur novum,
nec unum in uno, dumque punitur scelus,
crescat. superbis fratribus regna excidant
repetantque profugos; dubia violentae domus
fortuna reges inter incertos labet;
35   miser ex potente fiat, ex misero potens,
fluctuque regnum casus assiduo ferat.
ob scelera pulsi, cum dabit patriam deus
in scelera redeant, sintque tam invisi omnibus
quam sibi. nihil sit ira quod vetitum putet:
40   fratrem expavescat frater et natum parens
natusque patrem; liberi pereant male,
peius tamen nascantur; immineat viro
43a,46b infesta coniunx: impia stuprum in domo
47   levissimum sit facinus. et fas et fides
48a,43b iusque omne pereat. bella trans pontum vehant,
effusus omnes irriget terras cruor,
45   supraque magnos gentium exultet duces

46b-48a *transposed after* 43a *by Fitch*

quarter of unnatural crimes I shall fill up; while the House of Pelops stands, Minos will never be empty-handed.

FURY

Proceed, loathsome shade: goad this unnatural house into vengeful rage. Let them compete in crime of every kind, and take turns to unsheathe the sword. Let there be no limit to their anger, no shame in it; let blind rage incite their minds, let the parents' frenzy last and the long-lived evil pass into the grandchildren. Let there be no space for anyone to loathe an old offence: let new ones always arise, and many within each one, and while crime is being punished, let it grow. Let kingship slip from the brothers when in their pride, and pull them back when in exile. Let the shaky fortunes of this violent house crumble between the insecure brothers. Let the ruler be ruined and the ruined turn ruler; let chance toss the throne on incessant waves. Exiled for crimes, when god restores their homeland let them return to crimes, and let them be as hateful to themselves as they are to all. Let there be nothing that anger regards as forbidden. Let brother be afraid of brother, parent of son, son of father; let death come to children vilely, but birth more vilely; let husband be menaced by wife's enmity; in this unnatural home let adultery be the lightest of misdeeds.[3] Let right, faithfulness and law perish utterly. Let them carry war overseas, let spilt blood drench all lands, and over the mighty leaders of nations let Lust exult

---

[3] Some of the Fury's words allude clearly to future events. The vile deaths are those of Thyestes' sons; the vile birth is that of Aegisthus, conceived in incest; the rancorous wife is Clytemnestra, and her deed worse than adultery is murder of her husband. The overseas war of the following lines is the Trojan War.

Libido victrix. non sit a vestris malis
immune caelum—cur micant stellae polo
50 flammaeque servant debitum mundo decus?
nox alia fiat, excidat caelo dies.

Misce penates, odia caedes funera
accerse et imple Tantalo totam domum.
ornetur altum columen et lauro fores
55 laetae virescant, dignus adventu tuo
splendescat ignis—Thracium fiat nefas
maiore numero. dextra cur patrui vacat?
nondum stuprator liberos deflet suos?
et quando tollet? ignibus iam subditis
60 spument aëna, membra per partes eant
discerpta, patrios polluat sanguis focos,
epulae instruantur. non novi sceleris tibi
conviva venies. liberum dedimus diem
tuamque ad istas solvimus mensas famem:
65 ieiunia exple! mixtus in Bacchum cruor
spectante te potetur. inveni dapes
quas ipse fugeres. siste, quo praeceps ruis?

TANTALI UMBRA

Ad stagna et amnes et recedentes aquas
labrisque ab ipsis arboris plenae fugas.
70 abire in atrum carceris liceat mei
cubile; liceat, si parum videor miser,
mutare ripas: alveo medius tuo,

51 alia *E*: alta *PT*: atra *CS*
58 stuprator *suggested as a possibility by Fitch*: Thyestes *EA*

---

4 The Thracian outrage involved the feeding of Itys' flesh to

victorious. And let heaven not be immune to your evil. Why are the stars glittering in the sky, their fires maintaining their due of glory in the firmament? Let there be another night, let daylight be lost from the heavens.

Bring havoc on the housegods, summon hatred, slaughter, death, fill the whole house with Tantalus. Let the high roofbeams be festooned, the doors verdant and cheerful with laurel; let the fire blaze up brightly in keeping with your arrival—and let the Thracian outrage be performed with larger numbers![4] Why is the uncle's hand empty? Does the adulterer not yet weep for his own children? And when will he lift them up?[5] Now let cauldrons foam with fires lit beneath them, let rent limbs go piece by piece, let blood pollute the ancestral hearth, let a banquet be furnished. You will join the diners at a crime that is not new to you. We have given you a day of freedom, and released your hunger for this meal: fill up your fasting! Let blood mingled with wine be drunk while you watch. I have found a dinner that even you would run from. Stop, where are you rushing wildly?

GHOST OF TANTALUS

To the pools and rivers and retreating waters, and the full tree's recoil from my very lips. Give me leave to return to my prison's black lair; give me leave, if I seem not wretched enough, to change rivers: let me be left amidst your chan-

his unwitting father Tereus in revenge for the latter's infidelity. So it closely matches Atreus' coming revenge on Thyestes—but Thyestes has more sons.   [5] To lift up a child (*tollere*) was a gesture recognising it as one's own—as Thyestes will recognise his children (line 1005) after "lifting" them to his mouth. The verb can also mean "do away with."

Phlegethon, relinquar igneo cinctus freto.
Quicumque poenas lege fatorum datas
75   pati iuberis, quisquis exeso iaces
pavidus sub antro iamque venturi times
montis ruinam, quisquis avidorum feros
rictus leonum et dira Furiarum agmina
implicitus horres, quisquis immissas faces
80   semustus abigis, Tantali vocem excipe
properantis ad vos: credite experto mihi,
amate poenas! quando continget mihi
effugere superos?

FURIA

                Ante perturba domum,
inferque tecum proelia et ferri malum
85   regibus amorem; concute insano ferum
pectus tumultu.

TANTALI UMBRA

            Me pati poenas decet,
non esse poenam! mittor ut dirus vapor
tellure rupta vel gravem populis luem
sparsura pestis? ducam in horrendum nefas
90   avus nepotes? magne divorum parens
nosterque (quamvis pudeat), ingenti licet
taxata poena lingua crucietur loquax,
nec hoc tacebo. Moneo, ne sacra manus
violate caede neve furiali malo
95   aspergite aras. stabo et arcebo scelus.

---

6 The Ghost of Sylla in Ben Jonson's *Catiline* echoes Tantalus'
ghost: "Behold, I come, sent from the Stygian sound, / As a dire

nel, Phlegethon, surrounded by your fiery stream. All you who are forced to endure punishments assigned by fate's law, all who lie in terror in hollowed caves, fearing the mountain's imminent collapse, all who tremble in bonds at the fierce jaws of avid lions and the dread troops of Furies, all who half-burnt try to fend off torches thrust at you: take in Tantalus' words as he hurries to you: trust my experience, love your punishments! When shall I have the chance to escape the upper world?

FURY

First, disorder this house; along with yourself instil battles and the evil love of the sword in its kings; rouse their fierce hearts to mad turmoil.

GHOST OF TANTALUS

My proper role is to suffer punishments, not to *be* a punishment! Am I sent forth like some dread exhalation from a fissure in the earth, or as a plague to scatter foul contagion among the nations?[6] As grandfather am I to lead my grandchildren into terrible evil? Great father of the gods—my father too, even if ashamed of it: though my tongue is assessed a huge penalty and tortured for being talkative, I shall not keep quiet about *this* either.[7] [*As if to his descendants*] I warn you, do not defile your hands with accursed bloodshed, and do not sprinkle the altars with the evil of avenging fury. I shall stand and block the crime. [*To Fury*]

vapour that had cleft the ground, / To ingender with the night and blast the day; / Or like a pestilence that should display / Infection through the world."

[7] As earlier he had blabbed secrets of the gods to humans—one reason for his punishment in the underworld.

Quid ora terres verbere et tortos ferox
minaris angues? quid famem infixam intimis
agitas medullis? flagrat incensum siti
cor et perustis flamma visceribus micat.
100   sequor.

FURIA

Hunc, hunc furorem divide in totam domum.
sic, sic ferantur et suum infensi invicem
sitiant cruorem. sentit introitus tuos
domus et nefando tota contactu horruit.
105   actum est abunde. gradere ad infernos specus
amnemque notum. iam tuum maestae pedem
terrae gravantur: cernis ut fontes liquor
introrsus actus linquat, ut ripae vacent
ventusque raras igneus nubes ferat?
110   pallescit omnis arbor, ac nudus stetit
fugiente pomo ramus; et qui fluctibus
illinc propinquis Isthmos atque illinc fremit,
vicina gracili dividens terra vada,
longe remotos latus exaudit sonos.
115   iam Lerna retro cessit et Phoronides
latuere venae, nec suas profert sacer
Alpheos undas; et Cithaeronis iuga
stant parte nulla cana deposita nive,
timentque veterem nobiles Argi sitim.
120   en ipse Titan dubitat an iubeat sequi
cogatque habenis ire periturum diem.

CHORUS
Argos de superis si quis Achaicum

Why do you menace my face with your whip and threaten me fiercely with entwined snakes? Why do you rouse the hunger set in my bones' marrow? My heart is fired and ablaze with thirst, and flames dart through my burnt flesh. I follow!

FURY

Distribute *this* very frenzy throughout the house! They must be driven just like *this*, and in enmity thirst for blood of their blood by turns. The house feels you entering, and shudders throughout at this accursed contact. It is done, and amply! Go to the infernal caverns and the river you know. Already the sad earth is oppressed by your step: do you see how water deserts the springs, forced back within? How rivers are empty, and a fiery wind carries off the sparse clouds? Every tree fades, the branches stand bare as the fruit vanishes, and the Isthmus, which booms to waves close by on each side, as it divides neighbouring gulfs with its strip of land, grows wide and catches their sounds far off. Now Lerna has shrunk back, the Phoronean streams have disappeared, holy Alpheus does not bring forth its waters; Cithaeron's ridges stand nowhere white, their snow sloughed off; and renowned Argos fears its ancient thirst.[8] See, even the Titan hesitates whether to bid the daylight follow him, and to force it with the reins to come forth to its ruin.

CHORUS

If any god loves Achaean Argos,

[8] Argos was said to have suffered drought early in its history. In this context literal thirst can hardly be distinguished from the thirst for power of the Tantalids.

Pisaeasque domos curribus inclitas,
Isthmi si quis amat regna Corinthii,
125 et portus geminos et mare dissidens;
si quis Taygeti conspicuas nives,
quas cum Sarmaticus tempore frigido
in summis Boreas composuit iugis,
aestas veliferis solvit Etesiis;
130 quem tangit gelido flumine lucidus
Alpheos, stadio notus Olympico:
advertat placidum numen et arceat,
alternae scelerum ne redeant vices
nec succedat avo deterior nepos
135 et maior placeat culpa minoribus.

Tandem lassa feros exuat impetus
sicci progenies impia Tantali.
peccatum satis est! fas valuit nihil
aut commune nefas. proditus occidit
140 deceptor domini Myrtilus, et fide
vectus qua tulerat nobile reddidit
mutato pelagus nomine: notior
nulla est Ioniis fabula navibus.
exceptus gladio parvulus impio
145 dum currit patrium natus ad osculum,
immatura focis victima concidit
divisusque tua est, Tantale, dextera,
mensas ut strueres hospitibus deis.
hos aeterna fames persequitur cibos,
150 hos aeterna sitis; nec dapibus feris

---

9 The line uses two senses of *maior* and *minor*: more literally,
"and greater/older wrong attract those who are younger/lesser."

or the Pisan district famed for chariots;
or loves the realm of Corinth's Isthmus,
its twofold harbours and divided sea;
if any loves the far-seen snows
piled on Taygetus' lofty ridges
by Sarmatian Boreas in the chill season,
then melted by summer's sail-filling Etesians;
any touched by the ice-cold current of bright
Alpheus, famed for Olympic races:
let his kindly power be with us, and forbid
that a cycle of answering crimes return,
that grandsire be followed by worse grandchild
and the young strive to be elders in evil.[9]

   Spent at last, parched Tantalus' unnatural
issue must drop its savage aggression.
Enough of iniquity! Right achieved nothing—
nor collective wrong. Myrtilus, his master's
betrayer, fell betrayed; conveyed as disloyally
as he conveyed others, he made the sea
renowned through its changed name; no tale
is better known on Ionian ships.[10]
The little son running for his father's kiss
was received with a cold-blooded sword
and fell at the hearth, an unripe victim;
your hand, Tantalus, sectioned him
to furnish the table for your guests the gods.
Such food is avenged by eternal hunger,
eternal thirst; for that savage feast

[10] The Myrtoan Sea, east of Argos, was sometimes said to
be named for Myrtilus, who was thrown into it by Pelops and
drowned. "Ionian" here = Aegean (see Index).

decerni potuit poena decentior.
    Stat lassus vacuo gutture Tantalus.
impendet capiti plurima noxio
Phineis avibus praeda fugacior.
155   hinc illinc gravidis frondibus incubat
et curvata suis fetibus ac tremens
alludit patulis arbor hiatibus.
haec, quamvis avidus nec patiens morae,
deceptus totiens tangere neglegit
160   obliquatque oculos oraque comprimit
inclusisque famem dentibus alligat.
sed tunc divitias omne nemus suas
demittit propius, pomaque desuper
insultant foliis mitia languidis
165   accenduntque famem, quae iubet irritas
exercere manus. has ubi protulit
et falli libuit, totus in arduum
autumnus rapitur silvaque mobilis.
instat deinde sitis non levior fame;
170   qua cum percaluit sanguis et igneis
exarsit facibus, stat miser obvios
fluctus ore petens; quos profugus latex
avertit sterili deficiens vado
conantemque sequi deserit. hic bibit
175   altum de rapido gurgite pulverem.

ATREUS

Ignave, iners, enervis et (quod maximum
probrum tyranno rebus in summis reor)
inulte, post tot scelera, post fratris dolos

no apter penalty could have been appointed.
    Tantalus stands spent and empty-throated.
Over his guilty head in abundance
hangs prey more fleeting than Phineus' birds.
Leaning around him with gravid branches,
curved and trembling with what it bears,
the tree mocks at his gaping jaws.
Though impatient and avid, he makes no effort
(deceived so often) to touch the fruit,
but averts his eyes and seals his lips
and fetters his hunger behind clenched teeth.
But then the whole orchard lowers its riches
closer still, and the fruits from above
taunt him, so mellow, with drooping leaves,
and inflame his hunger, which bids him busy
his hands in vain. As he stretches them out,
consents to be cheated, the entire harvest
is whisked on high with the nimble trees.
Next thirst attacks, no weaker than hunger.
Once it heats his blood and fires it with torches
of flame, the wretch stands chasing the offered
waters with his mouth; but the fleeing stream
turns away, and dwindles to a barren channel
and leaves him trying to follow. He drinks
the deeps left from the whirling flood: deep dust.

ACT 2

ATREUS

Idle, inert, impotent, and (what I count the greatest reproach for a tyrant in high matters) unavenged: after so
many crimes, after your brother's treachery and the break-

243

fasque omne ruptum questibus vanis agis
180　iratus Atreus? fremere iam totus tuis
debebat armis orbis, et geminum mare
utrimque classes agere; iam flammis agros
lucere et urbes decuit, ac strictum undique
micare ferrum. tota sub nostro sonet
185　Argolica tellus equite; non silvae tegant
hostem nec altis montium structae iugis
arces. relictis bellicum totus canat
populus Mycenis. quisquis invisum caput
tegit ac tuetur, clade funesta occidat.
190　haec ipsa pollens incliti Pelopis domus
ruat vel in me, dummodo in fratrem ruat.

　　　Age, anime, fac quod nulla posteritas probet,
sed nulla taceat. aliquod audendum est nefas
atrox, cruentum, tale quod frater meus
195　suum esse mallet. scelera non ulcisceris,
nisi vincis.—et quid esse tam saevum potest
quod superet illum? numquid abiectus iacet?
numquid secundis patitur in rebus modum,
fessis quietem? novi ego ingenium viri
200　indocile: flecti non potest—frangi potest.
proinde antequam se firmat aut vires parat,
petatur ultro, ne quiescentem petat.
aut perdet aut peribit: in medio est scelus
positum occupanti.

SATELLES
Fama te populi nihil
205　adversa terret?

ing of every principle, do you act with futile complaints—
you, Atreus in anger? By now the whole world should be
resounding to your weapons, fleets on each coast should
be stirring up the twin seas; by now fields and cities should
be alight with flames, and the drawn sword glinting everywhere. Let the whole Argive land ring beneath my cavalry;
let forests not hide the enemy, nor strongholds built on
high hilltops. Let the whole populace leave Mycenae and
sound the trumpets for war. Let all who hide and protect
that hated creature perish in a blood bath. This mighty
house of famous Pelops itself—let it fall even on me, so
long as it falls on my brother.

Come, my spirit, do what no future age will endorse,
but none fail to talk about. I must dare some fierce, bloody
outrage, such as my brother would have wished his own.[11]
You do not avenge crimes unless you surpass them. And
what could be cruel enough to vanquish him? Does he lie
downcast? Can he abide moderation in success, or inaction
in failure? I know the man's intractable nature: he cannot
be bent, but he can be broken. So, before he strengthens
himself or marshalls his powers, he must be attacked first,
lest he attack me at rest. He will either destroy or be destroyed. Crime is set between us, for the one who seizes it
first.

ASSISTANT

You have no fear of hostile talk among the people?

---

[11] Cf. Ben Jonson, *Sejanus* II.2: "A race of wicked acts / Shall
flow out of my anger, and o'erspread / The world's wide face,
which no posterity / Shall e'er approve, nor yet keep silent: things /
That for their cunning, close and cruel mark, / Thy father would
wish his."

ATREUS

Maximum hoc regni bonum est,
quod facta domini cogitur populus sui
tam ferre quam laudare.

SATELLES

Quos cogit metus
laudare, eosdem reddit inimicos metus.
at qui favoris gloriam veri petit
210   animo magis quam voce laudari volet.

ATREUS

Laus vera et humili saepe contingit viro,
non nisi potenti falsa. quod nolunt velint.

SATELLES

Rex velit honesta: nemo non eadem volet.

ATREUS

Ubicumque tantum honesta dominanti licent,
215   precario regnatur.

SATELLES

Ubi non est pudor
nec cura iuris sanctitas pietas fides,
instabile regnum est.

ATREUS

Sanctitas pietas fides
privata bona sunt: qua iuvat reges eant.

246

ATREUS

This is the greatest value of kingship: that the people are compelled to praise as well as endure their master's actions.[12]

ASSISTANT

When fear compels them to praise, fear also turns them into enemies. But one who seeks the tribute of sincere support will want praise from the heart rather than the tongue.

ATREUS

Sincere praise often comes even to a lowly man; false praise comes only to the mighty. They must want what they do not want!

ASSISTANT

Let a king want what is honorable: everyone will want the same.

ATREUS

Where a sovereign is permitted only what is honorable, he rules on sufferance.[13]

ASSISTANT

Where there is no shame, no concern for the law, no righteousness, goodness, loyalty, rule is unstable.

ATREUS

Righteousness, goodness, loyalty are private values: kings should go where they please.

---

[12] Cf. "It is the greatest glory of a king / When, though his subjects hate his wicked deeds, / Yet they are forced to bear them all with praise" (Anon., *The Tragical Reign of Selimus* [1594]).

[13] Cf. "Where only honest deeds to kings are free, / It is no empire, but a beggary" (Marston, *Antonio & Mellida Part I* IV.1).

SATELLES

Nefas nocere vel malo fratri puta.

ATREUS

220 Fas est in illo quidquid in fratre est nefas.
     quid enim reliquit crimine intactum aut ubi
     sceleri pepercit? coniugem stupro abstulit
     regnumque furto; specimen antiquum imperi
     fraude est adeptus, fraude turbavit domum.
225 Est Pelopis altis nobile in stabulis pecus,
     arcanus aries, ductor opulenti gregis,
     cuius per omne corpus effuso coma
     dependet auro, cuius e tergo novi
     aurata reges sceptra Tantalici gerunt;
230 possessor huius regnat, hunc tantae domus
     fortuna sequitur. tuta seposita sacer
     in parte carpit prata, quae claudit lapis
     fatale saxeo pascuum muro tegens.
     hunc facinus ingens ausus assumpta in scelus
235 consorte nostri perfidus thalami avehit.
     Hinc omne cladis mutuae fluxit malum:
     per regna trepidus exul erravi mea,
     pars nulla nostri tuta ab insidiis vacat,
     corrupta coniunx, imperi quassa est fides,
240 domus aegra, dubius sanguis; est certi nihil
     nisi frater hostis. quid stupes? tandem incipe
     animosque sume. Tantalum et Pelopem aspice;
     ad haec manus exempla poscuntur meae.
     Profare, dirum qua caput mactem via.

     238 nostri *A*: generis *E*

ASSISTANT

Consider it wrong to harm even a wicked brother.

ATREUS

All that is wrong in dealing with a brother is right in dealing with him. What has he left untouched by guilt, when has he refrained from crime? He stole my wife by adultery and my kingdom by theft; by deceit he obtained our ancient symbol of power, by deceit he brought turmoil on the house. In Pelops' high stalls there is a purebred beast, a mysterious ram, leader of a prosperous flock. All over his body there hangs down a luxuriant fleece of gold, and from this coat new Tantalid kings have their sceptres gilded. The one who possesses him reigns, the fortune of this great house follows him. Hallowed, he grazes on safe meadows in a secluded area, enclosed by a rocky stone wall that conceals the fateful pasture. Risking a flagrant crime, and taking the partner of my bed as accomplice, that betrayer carried him off. From this act flowed all the evil of our mutual destruction. Throughout my own realm I have wandered fearfully in exile; no part of what is mine is safe from treachery; my wife is defiled, my confidence in power shaken, my house tainted, its blood uncertain;[14] nothing is sure—except my brother's enmity. Why paralysed? At long last rouse your heart and begin. Look to Tantalus and Pelops: my hands are called to follow their examples. [*To assistant*] Tell me how to slay that fearsome creature.

14 Because of Thyestes' seduction of Aerope, Atreus is uncertain of his sons' paternity (which he characteristically refers to as "blood").

SATELLES

245   Ferro peremptus spiritum inimicum expuat.

ATREUS

De fine poenae loqueris; ego poenam volo.
perimat tyrannus lenis; in regno meo
mors impetratur.

SATELLES

Nulla te pietas movet?

ATREUS

Excede, Pietas, si modo in nostra domo
250   umquam fuisti. dira Furiarum cohors
discorsque Erinys veniat et geminas faces
Megaera quatiens: non satis magno meum
ardet furore pectus, impleri iuvat
maiore monstro.

SATELLES

Quid novi rabidus struis?

ATREUS

255   Nil quod doloris capiat assueti modum;
nullum relinquam facinus et nullum est satis.

SATELLES

Ferrum?

ATREUS

Parum est.

SATELLES

Quid ignis?

ATREUS

Etiamnunc parum est.

ASSISTANT

Let him die by the sword and spew out his hateful life.

ATREUS

You talk about punishment's conclusion: I want the punishment! Slaying is for a lenient tyrant; in my kingdom death is something people beg for.

ASSISTANT

Does no affection move you?

ATREUS

Begone, Affection, if ever you existed at all in our house! Let the dread band of Furies come, and the Erinys of strife and Megaera brandishing her twin torches. The madness firing my heart is not big enough, I want to be filled with some greater monstrosity.

ASSISTANT

What new scheme is your rage devising?

ATREUS

Nothing conforming to the limits of ordinary bitterness. I shall leave no deed undone—and none is enough.

ASSISTANT

The sword?

ATREUS

Insufficient.

ASSISTANT

What about fire?

ATREUS

Still insufficient.

SATELLES

Quonam ergo telo tantus utetur dolor?

ATREUS

Ipso Thyeste.

SATELLES

Maius hoc ira est malum.

ATREUS

260 Fateor. tumultus pectora attonitus quatit
penitusque volvit; rapior et quo nescio,
sed rapior.—imo mugit e fundo solum,
tonat dies serenus ac totis domus
ut fracta tectis crepuit et moti Lares
265 vertere vultum. fiat hoc, fiat nefas
quod, di, timetis!

SATELLES

Facere quid tandem paras?

ATREUS

Nescioquid animo maius et solito amplius
supraque fines moris humani tumet
instatque pigris manibus. haud quid sit scio,
270 sed grande quiddam est! ita sit. hoc, anime, occupa.
dignum est Thyeste facinus et dignum Atreo:
uterque faciat! vidit infandas domus
Odrysia mensas—fateor, immane est scelus,
sed occupatum: maius hoc aliquid dolor

267 animo *Leo*: animus *EA*
272 uterque *A*: quod uterque *E*

ASSISTANT

Then what *will* such bitterness use as its weapon?

ATREUS

Thyestes himself.

ASSISTANT

This evil goes beyond anger.

ATREUS

I admit it. A tumult of frenzy is shaking my breast, and churning it deep within. I am swept along, and know not where, but I am swept along. —The ground moans from its lowest depths, the sky thunders though cloudless, the house cracks throughout its structure as if shattered, and the housegods shake and avert their faces. Let it be done, let it be done, this outrage that makes you gods afraid!

ASSISTANT

What *are* you planning to do?

ATREUS

Something greater, larger than usual, beyond normal human limits, is swelling in my spirit and jolting my sluggish hands. What it is I do not know, but it is something mighty![15] So be it. Seize on it, my spirit! The deed is worthy of Thyestes and worthy of Atreus: let each perform it. The Odrysian house saw an unspeakable feast[16]—that crime is monstrous, admittedly, but already taken. My bitterness

---

[15] Cf. Shakespeare, *King Lear* II.4.280–282: "I will do such things—/What they are yet I know not, but they shall be/The terrors of the earth."   [16] See fn. 4: "Odrysian" is a synonym for "Thracian." The "Daulian mother and sister" (275) is Procne, who served her son Itys' flesh to his father Tereus, to avenge Tereus' rape of her sister Philomela.

275 inveniat. animum Daulis inspira parens
sororque; causa est similis: assiste et manum
impelle nostram. liberos avidus pater
gaudensque laceret et suos artus edat.
bene est, abunde est: hic placet poenae modus
280 tantisper.
           Ubinam est? tam diu cur innocens
versatur Atreus? tota iam ante oculos meos
imago caedis errat, ingesta orbitas
in ora patris—anime, quid rursus times
et ante rem subsidis? audendum est, age:
285 quod est in isto scelere praecipuum nefas,
hoc ipse faciet.

SATELLES

           Sed quibus captus dolis
nostros dabit perductus in laqueos pedem?
inimica credit cuncta.

ATREUS

           Non poterat capi,
nisi capere vellet. regna nunc sperat mea:
290 hac spe minanti fulmen occurret Iovi,
hac spe subibit gurgitis tumidi minas
dubiumque Libycae Syrtis intrabit fretum,
hac spe, quod esse maximum retur malum,
fratrem videbit.

SATELLES

           Quis fidem pacis dabit?
295 cui tanta credet?

---

[290] *in this position A: after* 292 *MF: after* 293 *E*

must find something greater than this. Breathe your spirit into me, you Daulian mother and sister: our cause is comparable. Stand by me, drive my hand. Let the father rend his children avidly, gleefully, and eat his own flesh. This is good, this is ample. This measure of revenge pleases me—for the present.

Where in the world is he? Why has Atreus remained innocent so long? Now the whole picture of the carnage hovers before my eyes—childlessness stuffed down the father's throat![17] Why take fright again, my spirit, and slacken before the event? Come, you must be bold. *He* will be the one that commits the principal outrage in this crime.

ASSISTANT

But what ruse will catch him and induce him to walk into our snare? He sees enemies everywhere.

ATREUS

He could not be caught, unless he wanted to catch others. But as it is, he desires my kingdom. In this desire he will confront Jove's threat of the thunderbolt; in this desire he will face the threats of the swelling flood, or enter the treacherous straits of the Libyan Syrtes; in this desire he will do what he thinks the greatest evil: see his brother.

ASSISTANT

Who will give him assurance of peace? Whom will he trust so greatly?

---

[17] The Latin can mean also "thrust in the father's face" (as happens at 1005).

ATREUS

Credula est spes improba.
natis tamen mandata quae patruo ferant
dabimus, relictis exul hospitiis vagus
regno ut miserias mutet atque Argos regat
ex parte dominus. [si nimis durus preces
300 spernet Thyestes, liberos eius rudes
malisque fessos gravibus et faciles capi
prece commovebo.] hinc vetus regni furor,
illinc egestas tristis ac durus labor
quamvis rigentem tot malis subigent virum.

SATELLES

305 Iam tempus illi fecit aerumnas leves.

ATREUS

Erras: malorum sensus accrescit die.
leve est miserias ferre, perferre est grave.

SATELLES

Alios ministros consili tristis lege.
peiora iuvenes facile praecepta audiunt;
310 in patre facient quidquid in patruo doces.
saepe in magistrum scelera redierunt sua.

ATREUS

Ut nemo doceat fraudis et sceleris vias,
regnum docebit. ne mali fiant times?
nascuntur. istud quod vocas saevum asperum,
315 agique dure credis et nimium impie,
fortasse et illic agitur.

299b-302a *deleted by Courtney*
309 *part of Assistant's speech in A: spoken by Atreus in E*

ATREUS

Greedy desire trusts readily. However, I shall give my sons a mandate to take to their uncle: that he should leave a wandering exile's lodgings, trade his wretchedness for a throne, and reign in Argos as co-ruler.[18] On the one side his old passion for power, on the other grim poverty and hard toils, will subdue the fellow, however toughened by so many troubles.

ASSISTANT

By now time has made affliction light to him.

ATREUS

You are wrong. The sense of hardship accumulates day by day. To bear wretchedness is a light thing; to keep bearing it is heavy.

ASSISTANT

Select other agents for your grim plan. Young men readily listen to worse precepts. All that you teach them in dealings with their uncle, they will do in dealings with their father. Crimes often return upon the teacher.[19]

ATREUS

Though no one teaches them the ways of deceit and crime, kingship will teach it. You fear their becoming evil? They are born so. What you call cruel and savage, and consider too harsh and unnatural a step, is perhaps being taken on that side too.

[18] Lines 299b–302a (deleted): "If Thyestes is too hard and scorns my appeal, my appeal will move his children, inexperienced and weary of hardship and easily deceived."

[19] Cf. Shakespeare, *Macbeth* I.7.7–10: "But in these cases / We still have judgment here, that we but teach / Bloody instructions, which, being taught, return / To plague th'inventor."

SATELLES

                  Hanc fraudem scient

nati parari?

ATREUS

           Tacita tam rudibus fides

non est in annis; detegent forsan dolos.

tacere multis discitur vitae malis.

SATELLES

320   Ipsosque per quos fallere alium cogitas

falles?

ATREUS

           Ut ipsi crimine et culpa vacent.

quid enim necesse est liberos sceleri meo

inserere? per nos odia se nostra explicent.

—male agis, recedis, anime: si parcis tuis,

325   parces et illis. consili Agamemnon mei

sciens minister fiat, et fratri sciens

Menelaus adsit. prolis incertae fides

ex hoc petatur scelere: si bella abnuunt

et gerere nolunt odia, si patruum vocant,

330   pater est. eatur.—multa sed trepidus solet

detegere vultus, magna nolentem quoque

consilia produnt: nesciant quantae rei

fiant ministri. Nostra tu coepta occule.

SATELLES

Haud sum monendus: ista nostro in pectore

335   fides timorque, sed magis claudet fides.

317b-319 *spoken by Atreus in E: by Assistant in A*

ASSISTANT

Are your sons to know this deception is planned?

ATREUS

Reliable discretion is not found in such tender years; perhaps they will reveal the plot; silence is a lesson learned through life's many sufferings.

ASSISTANT

So you will deceive the very people by whom you plan to deceive others?

ATREUS

Yes, so they themselves may be free of guilt. What need is there to involve my children in my crime? Let my hatred unfold through me. —You are going wrong, you are retreating, my spirit! If you spare your own, you will spare those too. Agamemnon must serve my scheme knowingly, and Menelaus assist his brother knowingly. Let me gain assurance about my questionable issue from this crime: if they refuse to engage in this war of hatred, if they call him uncle, he is their father. They must go. —But a nervous expression often reveals much; great schemes betray a person even against his will. They must not know how great a business they are agents in. And you, keep my venture secret.

ASSISTANT

I need no warning. Loyalty and fear will hide it in my heart—but chiefly loyalty.

CHORUS

Tandem regia nobilis,
antiqui genus Inachi,
fratrum composuit minas.
   Quis vos exagitat furor,
340   alternis dare sanguinem
et sceptrum scelere aggredi?
nescitis, cupidi arcium,
regnum quo iaceat loco.
   Regem non faciunt opes,
345   non vestis Tyriae color,
non frontis nota regia,
non auro nitidae trabes.
rex est qui posuit metus
et diri mala pectoris;
350   quem non ambitio impotens
et numquam stabilis favor
vulgi praecipitis movet,
non quidquid fodit Occidens
aut unda Tagus aurea
355   claro devehit alveo,
non quidquid Libycis terit
fervens area messibus;
quem non concutiet cadens
obliqui via fulminis,
360   non Eurus rapiens mare
aut saevo rabidus freto
ventosi tumor Hadriae,
quem non lancea militis,

---

[20] The Chorus presumably means "settled," i.e. they are igno-

CHORUS

At last this famed royal house,
issue of ancient Inachus,
has arranged[20] the brothers' threats.
    What is this frenzy that drives you
to spill your blood by turns
and beset the sceptre with crime?
In your greed for strongholds, you mistake
the place where kingship lies.
    A king is not made by wealth
nor the colour of Tyrian robes
nor the sign of royalty on his brow
nor roofbeams gleaming with gold.
A king is one rid of fear
and the evil of an ugly heart;
one that no wilful ambition
or the ever shifting favour
of the hasty mob can affect,
nor all that is mined in the West
or that golden-flowing Tagus
carries down in its bright bed,
nor all that is threshed from Libyan
harvests on scorching floors;
one that the zigzag lightning
cannot shake in its falling track,
nor Eurus whirling the sea,
nor the violent raging swell
of the windswept Adriatic;
one that no soldier's lance,

rant of Atreus' real intention in recalling Thyestes. But for the
audience *composuit* holds another meaning, "set face to face."

261

non strictus domuit chalybs;
365   qui tuto positus loco
infra se videt omnia
occurritque suo libens
fato nec queritur mori.
      Reges conveniant licet
370   qui sparsos agitant Dahas,
qui rubri vada litoris
et gemmis mare lucidis
late sanguineum tenent,
aut qui Caspia fortibus
375   recludunt iuga Sarmatis;
certet Danuvii vadum
audet qui pedes ingredi
et (quocumque loco iacent)
Seres vellere nobiles:
380   mens regnum bona possidet.
nil ullis opus est equis,
nil armis et inertibus
telis, quae procul ingerit
Parthus, cum simulat fugas;
385   admotis nihil est opus
urbes sternere machinis
longe saxa rotantibus:
[rex est qui metuit nihil,
rex est qui cupiet nihil]

388–389 *deleted by Leo*

---

21 *Ruber* ("Red") is a general term for the seas around the
Arabian peninsula, including the modern Red Sea. Seneca here
relates it to the colour of the gems.

no naked steel has subdued;
one set in a place of safety
who sees all things beneath him
and willingly goes to meet
his fate, with no protest at death.

 Let kings forgather—those
who rouse the scattered Dahae,
who control the waters of the ruby
coast,[21] the sea blood-reddened
far and wide by gleaming gems,
or those who open the Caspian
heights to the bold Sarmatians;[22]
let him compete, who dares
to walk on the Danube River,[23]
and the Seres famed for silk
(in whatever place they lie):
wisdom secures the kingship.
There is no need of cavalry,
no need of weapons, the craven
arrows poured from a distance
by the Parthian in feigned flight,
no need to flatten cities
by moving up siege engines
that whirl rocks from afar:[24]

[22] I.e. the kings of Iberia (modern Georgia), who let the Sarmatians enter from the north through a pass in the Caucasus to attack their enemies.

[23] I.e. its frozen surface (cf. *Pha* 59).

[24] Lines 388–389 (deleted); "A king is one who fears nothing, / a king is one who will want nothing."

263

390   hoc regnum sibi quisque dat.
              Stet quicumque volet potens
          aulae culmine lubrico:
          me dulcis saturet quies.
          obscuro positus loco
395   leni perfruar otio,
          nullis nota Quiritibus
          aetas per tacitum fluat.
          sic cum transierint mei
          nullo cum strepitu dies,
400   plebeius moriar senex.
          illi mors gravis incubat
          qui, notus nimis omnibus,
          ignotus moritur sibi.

THYESTES

      Optata patriae tecta et Argolicas opes
405   miserisque summum ac maximum exulibus bonum,
      tractum soli natalis et patrios deos
      (si sunt tamen di) cerno, Cyclopum sacras
      turres, labore maius humano decus,
      celebrata iuveni stadia, per quae nobilis
410   palmam paterno non semel curru tuli.
      occurret Argos, populus occurret frequens—
      sed nempe et Atreus. repete silvestres fugas
      saltusque densos potius et mixtam feris

---

²⁵ A passage naturalized in English poetry. The best known
rendering is Andrew Marvell's. "Climb at court for me that will /
Giddy favour's slippery hill; / All I seek is to lie still. / Settled in
some secret nest, / In calm leisure let me rest, / And far off from
public stage / Pass away my silent age. / Thus when without noise,
unknown, / I have lived out all my span, / I shall die, without a

each grants himself this kingship.
　Who wishes may stand in power
on a palace's slippery peak:
let sweet repose sate me.
Set in an obscure place
let me bask in gentle leisure;
unknown to any Quirites
let my life flow on through peace.
So, when my days have passed
without turmoil, let me die
an old plebeian man.
Death weighs heavy on one
who, too well known to all,
dies unknown to himself.[25]

ACT 3

THYESTES

At last I see the long-desired housetops of my homeland, the wealth of Argos, and what seems to miserable exiles the greatest and highest good—the reaches of my native soil and the gods of my fathers (if there really *are* gods); the Cyclopes' sacred towers, a glory too great for human labour, and the racetrack I frequented in youth, through which I carried the palm in glory more than once on my father's chariot. Argos will come to meet me, the people will come in crowds—but so will Atreus, of course. Better hurry back to your forest refuges, to those dense woods

groan, / An old honest countryman. / Who exposed to others' eyes, / Into his own heart ne'er pries, / Death's to him a strange surprise."

similemque vitam. clarus hic regni nitor
415 fulgore non est quod oculos falso auferat.
cum quod datur spectabis, et dantem aspice.
modo inter illa, quae putant cuncti aspera,
fortis fui laetusque. nunc contra in metus
revolvor: animus haeret ac retro cupit
420 corpus referre, moveo nolentem gradum.

TANTALUS

Pigro (quid hoc est?) genitor incessu stupet
vultumque versat seque in incerto tenet.

THYESTES

Quid, anime, pendes, quidve consilium diu
tam facile torques? rebus incertissimis,
425 fratri atque regno, credis ac metuis mala
iam victa, iam mansueta, et aerumnas fugis
bene collocatas? esse iam miserum iuvat.
reflecte gressum, dum licet, teque eripe.

TANTALUS

Quae causa cogit, genitor, a patria gradum
430 referre visa? cur bonis tantis sinum
subducis? ira frater abiecta redit
partemque regni reddit et lacerae domus
componit artus teque restituit tibi.

THYESTES

Causam timoris ipse quam ignoro exigis.
435 nihil timendum video, sed timeo tamen.
placet ire, pigris membra sed genibus labant,
alioque quam quo nitor abductus feror.
sic concitatam remige et velo ratem
aestus resistens remigi et velo refert.

THYESTES

and your life among the beasts and comparable to theirs.
There is no reason for this bright lustre of kingship to blind
your eyes with its false glitter. When you examine a gift,
look at the giver too. Just now, amid what everyone consid-
ers hardships, I was courageous and happy. But now I am
relapsing into fears; my spirit falters and wants to turn my
body back, my steps are forced and reluctant.

TANTALUS

What is it? Father walks listlessly, in a daze; he keeps looking round and hesitating.

THYESTES

Why the impasse, my spirit? Why wrestle so long with such
an easy decision? Can you trust the most unreliable of
things, a brother and a throne? Are you afraid of evils you
have already conquered and tamed? Running from hardships you have turned to advantage? By now it is pleasant
to be "wretched"! Turn back while you may, and rescue
yourself.

TANTALUS

What is forcing you, father, to walk away from sight of your
fatherland? Why fold your arms against such blessings?
Your brother returns to you with his anger cast aside, gives
you back a share in the throne, joins together the limbs of
this dismembered family, and restores you to yourself.

THYESTES

You ask the reason for my fear: I do not know it myself. I
see nothing fearful, but I fear nonetheless. My intention is
to proceed, but my body is weak-kneed and faltering, and I
am pulled away from the goal I struggle towards. Just so a
ship, urged on by oar and sail, is carried back by the tide
resisting oar and sail.

TANTALUS

440 Evince quidquid obstat et mentem impedit
reducemque quanta praemia expectent vide.
pater, potes regnare.

THYESTES

Cum possim mori.

TANTALUS

Summa est potestas—

THYESTES

Nulla, si cupias nihil.

TANTALUS

Natis relinques.

THYESTES

Non capit regnum duos.

TANTALUS

445 Miser esse mavult esse qui felix potest?

THYESTES

Mihi crede, falsis magna nominibus placent,
frustra timentur dura. dum excelsus steti,
numquam pavere destiti atque ipsum mei
ferrum timere lateris. o quantum bonum est
450 obstare nulli, capere securas dapes
humi iacentem! scelera non intrant casas,
tutusque mensa capitur angusta scyphus;
venenum in auro bibitur. expertus loquor:

452 scyphus *Axelson*: cibus *EA*

---

26 The option of death guarantees self-determination, i.e.
kingship over oneself (cf. *Phoen* 105).

TANTALUS

Whatever this check and hindrance is in your mind, overcome it. Think what rewards await your return. Father, you
can be king!

THYESTES

Yes, since I can die.[26]

TANTALUS

The highest power is—

THYESTES

No power, if you want nothing.

TANTALUS

You will leave it to your sons.

THYESTES

A throne has no room for two.

TANTALUS

A person who can be happy prefers to be wretched?

THYESTES

Believe me, they are false names that make "greatness" attractive; the fear of "hardship" is groundless. While I stood
on high, I never ceased to feel terror, or to fear the very
sword at my side. Oh, what a blessing it is to stand in no
one's way, to take carefree meals lying on the ground!
Crimes do not enter huts, and one takes a cup safely at a
humble table; poison is drunk in gold.[27] I speak from ex-

---

[27] John Crowne rings variations on these themes in his version
of *Thyestes* (1681): "Things are miscall'd, I ne're was blest till
now— / When I was great, I had not one delight: / Who needs a
Taster has small joy in taste: / Who needs a guard for safety, ne're
are safe: / And who needs watching, has but little rest."

malam bonae praeferre fortunam licet.
455   Non vertice alti montis impositam domum
et imminentem civitas humilis tremit,
nec fulget altis splendidum tectis ebur,
somnosque non defendit excubitor meos.
non classibus piscamur et retro mare
460   iacta fugamus mole, nec ventrem improbum
alimus tributo gentium; nullus mihi
ultra Getas metatur et Parthos ager.
non ture colimur nec meae excluso Iove
ornantur arae. nulla culminibus meis
465   imposita nutat silva, nec fumant manu
succensa multa stagna, nec somno dies
Bacchoque nox iungenda pervigili datur.
sed non timemur, tuta sine telo est domus
rebusque parvis magna praestatur quies.
470   immane regnum est posse sine regno pati.

TANTALUS

Nec abnuendum est, si dat imperium deus,
nec appetendum est. frater ut regnes rogat.

THYESTES

Rogat? timendum est. errat hic aliquis dolus.

TANTALUS

Redire pietas unde summota est solet,
475   reparatque vires iustus amissas amor.

THYESTES

Amat Thyesten frater? aetherias prius
perfundet Arctos pontus et Siculi rapax

perience: one may legitimately prefer "bad" fortune to "good."

No house of mine is set lowering on a high hilltop, making the lowly citizenry tremble; there is no bright ivory gleaming on high ceilings of mine, no bodyguard protecting my sleep. I do not take whole fleets fishing, or drive back the sea by dumping rock,[28] or feed a gluttonous belly with the tribute of nations; no fields are harvested for me beyond the Getae or Parthians. I am not worshipped with incense, no altars of mine are adorned to the exclusion of Jove. I have no woodland planted on my rooftop and swaying in the breeze, no steaming pools heated by many hands; my day is not given over to sleep, nor my night forthwith to sleepless drinking. But I am not feared, my house is safe without weapons, and my small domain is supplied with great peace. It is a vast kingdom, to be able to cope without a kingdom.

TANTALUS

Power is not to be refused, if god offers it, nor to be sought. Your brother is *asking* you to rule.

THYESTES

Asking? Fearful! Some trickery is skulking here.

TANTALUS

Family feeling often returns where it has been banished, and rightful love regains its lost strength.

THYESTES

Thyestes loved by his brother? Sooner the ocean will soak the Bears of heaven, and the whirling waves of Sicily's tides

---

[28] I.e. as a foundation for a luxurious villa built out into the sea. This and other details of Thyestes' satire are overtly Roman.

consistet aestus unda et Ionio seges
matura pelago surget et lucem dabit
480 nox atra terris; ante cum flammis aquae,
cum morte vita, cum mari ventus fidem
foedusque iungent.

TANTALUS

Quam tamen fraudem times?

THYESTES

Omnem: timori quem meo statuam modum?
tantum potest quantum odit.

TANTALUS

In te quid potest?

THYESTES

485 Pro me nihil iam metuo: vos facitis mihi
Atrea timendum.

TANTALUS

Decipi cautus times?

THYESTES

Serum est cavendi tempus in mediis malis.
eatur. unum genitor hoc testor tamen:
ego vos sequor, non duco.

TANTALUS

Respiciet deus
490 bene cogitata. perge non dubio gradu.

ATREUS

Plagis tenetur clausa dispositis fera:
et ipsum et una generis invisi indolem
iunctam parenti cerno. iam tuto in loco
versantur odia. venit in nostras manus

will halt; ripe grain will grow on the Ionian Sea, and black night give light to the earth; sooner will water join flame, life join death, wind join sea in a bond of allegiance.

TANTALUS

But what kind of deceit do you fear?

THYESTES

Every kind! What limit can I set on my fear? His capacity is as great as his hatred.

TANTALUS

What can he do to you?

THYESTES

For myself I fear nothing now: you are the ones that make Atreus fearful to me.

TANTALUS

Despite caution, you fear being deceived?

THYESTES

The time for caution is past in the midst of evil. Onward! But this one thing I affirm as your father: I am following you, not leading.

TANTALUS

God will look kindly on our well-considered plans. Step forward without hesitation.

ATREUS

[*Aside*] The beast is held fast in the nets I set out. I see both the man and, along with him, the hopes of that detested line, joined with their father. Now my hatred is on a firm

495 tandem Thyestes, venit, et totus quidem.
vix tempero animo, vix dolor frenos capit.
sic, cum feras vestigat et longo sagax
loro tenetur Umber ac presso vias
scrutatur ore, dum procul lento suem
500 odore sentit, paret et tacito locum
rostro pererrat; praeda cum propior fuit,
cervice tota pugnat et gemitu vocat
dominum morantem seque retinenti eripit.
cum sperat ira sanguinem, nescit tegi—
505 tamen tegatur. aspice, ut multo gravis
squalore vultus obruat maestos coma,
quam foeda iaceat barba.—praestetur fides.
    Fratrem iuvat videre. complexus mihi
redde expetitos. quidquid irarum fuit
510 transierit; ex hoc sanguis ac pietas die
colantur, animis odia damnata excidant.

THYESTES

Diluere possem cuncta, nisi talis fores.
sed fateor, Atreu, fateor, admisi omnia
quae credidisti. pessimam causam meam
515 hodierna pietas fecit. est prorsus nocens
quicumque visus tam bono fratri est nocens.
lacrimis agendum est: supplicem primus vides;
hae te precantur pedibus intactae manus:
ponatur omnis ira et ex animo tumor
520 erasus abeat. obsides fidei accipe
hos innocentes, frater.

ATREUS

                    A genibus manum
aufer meosque potius amplexus pete.

footing. At last Thyestes has come into my hands, he has come—yes, in his entirety. I can scarcely restrain my spirit, my rancour can scarcely be reined in. So with a keen-nosed Umbrian hound tracking beasts, held on a long leash, his snout bent down to probe the trails: while he scents the boar far off and faintly, he is obedient and silent in scouring the place; but when the prey is closer, he struggles with all the force of his neck and bays to hurry his slow master and fights free of restraint. When anger senses blood, it knows no concealment. But concealed it must be. See how his hair is heavy with grime and shrouds his dismal face, how foul and limp his beard. —But good faith must be demonstrated.

I am delighted to see my brother. Let me feel once more the embrace I have longed for! Any anger that existed must be in the past. From this day ties of blood and family must be cherished, and hatred be condemned and expelled from our hearts.

I could explain everything away, if you were not like this. But I confess, Atreus, I confess, I committed all that you thought I had. The fraternal affection you show today has made my case indefensible. A man is obviously guilty if he seems guilty to such a good brother. I must plead with tears. You are the first to see me supplicate. These hands, that have touched no one's feet before, implore you; let all anger be set aside, let passion be erased and gone. As hostages of my good faith take these innocents, brother.

Take your hand from my knees, and come to my embrace

Vos quoque, senum praesidia, tot iuvenes, meo
pendete collo. Squalidam vestem exue,
525   oculisque nostris parce, et ornatus cape
pares meis, laetusque fraterni imperi
capesse partem. maior haec laus est mea,
fratri paternum reddere incolumi decus;
habere regnum casus est, virtus dare.

THYESTES

530   Di paria, frater, pretia pro tantis tibi
meritis rependant. regiam capitis notam
squalor recusat noster et sceptrum manus
infausta refugit. liceat in media mihi
latere turba.

ATREUS

Recipit hoc regnum duos.

THYESTES

535   Meum esse credo quidquid est, frater, tuum.

ATREUS

Quis influentis dona Fortunae abnuit?

THYESTES

Expertus est quicumque quam facile effluant.

ATREUS

Fratrem potiri gloria ingenti vetas?

THYESTES

Tua iam peracta gloria est, restat mea.
540   respuere certum est regna consilium mihi.

instead. You too, protectors of old men—so *many* youngsters!—come cling about my neck. [*To Thyestes*] Off with
these filthy clothes—have pity on our eyes—and accept
finery equal to mine; prosper and take on a share of your
brother's power. Mine is the greater glory in restoring our
father's grandeur to my safely returned brother. To hold a
throne is luck; to bestow it, virtue.

THYESTES
The gods grant you, brother, the rewards you deserve so
richly. But my foul state unfits my head for the royal emblem, and my luckless hand shrinks from the sceptre. Let
me just blend in with the common people.

ATREUS
This throne has room for two.

THYESTES
All that is yours, brother, I regard as mine.[29]

ATREUS
Who would refuse the inflow of Fortune's gifts?

THYESTES
Anyone who has experienced how easily they flow away.

ATREUS
You forbid your brother to win great glory?

THYESTES
Your glory is already complete, mine still to be won. It is
my fixed purpose to reject the throne.

[29] Thyestes implies diplomatically "I do not need to share
power formally, since I enjoy it through you." But the words could
have another meaning, of which Thyestes is presumably unaware.

ATREUS

Meam relinquam, nisi tuam partem accipis.

THYESTES

Accipio. regni nomen impositi feram,
sed iura et arma servient mecum tibi.

ATREUS

Imposita capiti vincla venerando gere;
545   ego destinatas victimas superis dabo.

CHORUS

Credat hoc quisquam? ferus ille et acer
nec potens mentis truculentus Atreus
fratris aspectu stupefactus haesit.
nulla vis maior pietate vera est;
550   iurgia externis inimica durant,
quos amor verus tenuit, tenebit.
ira cum magnis agitata causis
gratiam rupit cecinitque bellum,
cum leves frenis sonuere turmae,
555   fulsit hinc illinc agitatus ensis,
quem movet crebro furibundus ictu
sanguinem Mavors cupiens recentem,
opprimit ferrum manibusque iunctis
ducit ad pacem Pietas negantes.
560   Otium tanto subitum e tumultu
quis deus fecit? modo per Mycenas
arma civilis crepuere belli.
pallidae natos tenuere matres;

THYESTES

ATREUS

I shall abandon my share, unless you accept yours.

THYESTES

Then I accept. I shall bear the title of king imposed on me,
but the laws and army will be subject to you, along with
myself.[30]

ATREUS

Wear this bond set on your venerable head. For my part, I
shall offer the designated victims to the gods above.

CHORUS

Who could believe it? That savage man,
the wild, irrational, truculent Atreus,
was awed and arrested by sight of his brother.
No force is greater than true love of family.
Disputes among strangers persist in rancour,
but those it has held, true love will hold.
When anger, roused by mighty causes,
breaks off friendship and trumpets war,
when harnesses jangle on wheeling squadrons
and the roused sword gleams in opposing ranks,
stirred to repeated blows by furious
Mars in his longing for fresh blood,
then family love overwhelms the steel,
joins hands, and leads the reluctant to peace.

What god has created sudden calm
out of such uproar? Just now the weapons
of civil war clattered throughout Mycenae;
ashen-faced mothers clasped their children;

---

[30] Another unintended and unfortunate ambiguity from Thyestes (cf. note on 534).

uxor armato timuit marito,
565 cum manum invitus sequeretur ensis,
sordidus pacis vitio quietae.
ille labentes renovare muros,
hic situ quassas stabilire turres,
ferreis portas cohibere claustris
570 ille certabat, pavidusque pinnis
anxiae noctis vigil incubabat:
peior est bello timor ipse belli.

    Iam minae saevi cecidere ferri,
iam silet murmur grave classicorum,
575 iam tacet stridor litui strepentis:
alta pax urbi revocata laetae est.
sic, ubi ex alto tumuere fluctus
Bruttium Coro feriente pontum,
Scylla pulsatis resonat cavernis
580 ac mare in portu timuere nautae
quod rapax haustum revomit Charybdis;
et ferus Cyclops metuit parentem
rupe ferventis residens in Aetnae,
ne superfusis violetur undis
585 ignis aeternis resonans caminis;
et putat mergi sua posse pauper
regna Laertes Ithaca tremente.
si suae ventis cecidere vires,
mitius stagno pelagus recumbit;
590 alta, quae navis timuit secare,
592 strata ludenti patuere cumbae,
591 hinc et hinc fusis speciosa velis;

592 *transposed before* 591 *by Fitch*

wives feared for their husbands in arms,
as the sword reluctantly came to hand
dulled with the rust of tranquil peace.
Some men struggled to repair the sagging
walls, others to strengthen derelict
towers, others to lock the gates
with iron bars; guards crouched in dread
on the battlements to watch the anxious night.
Worse than war is the fear of war.

　　Now the menace of savage steel is fallen,
now hushed the trumpets' blaring din,
now quiet the strident clarion's scream;
deep peace is restored to the joyful city.
So, when waves swell out of the deep
as Corus buffets the Bruttian Sea,
Scylla roars at the pounding of her caves,
and sailors in harbour dread the seas
swallowed, then spewed by whirling Charybdis;
and a bestial Cyclops, perched on a crag
of seething Etna, fears his parent[31]
may violate with his flooding waves
the fire that roars in undying forges;
and as Ithaca trembles, Laertes thinks
his meagre kingdom could be submerged.
But if their force has failed the winds,
the sea sinks down calmer than a pond;
the deeps that ships were afraid to cleave
are smooth and open to pleasure craft,
arrayed with sails spread far and wide;

---

[31] Neptune; the Cyclopes tend Vulcan's forges within Mt Etna.

et vacat mersos numerare pisces
hic ubi ingenti modo sub procella
595   Cyclades pontum timuere motae.
      Nulla sors longa est: dolor ac voluptas
invicem cedunt; brevior voluptas.
ima permutat levis hora summis.
Ille qui donat diadema fronti,
600   quem genu nixae tremuere gentes,
cuius ad nutum posuere bella
Medus et Phoebi propioris Indus
et Dahae Parthis equitem minati,
anxius sceptrum tenet et moventes
605   cuncta divinat metuitque casus
mobiles rerum dubiumque tempus.
Vos quibus rector maris atque terrae
ius dedit magnum necis atque vitae,
ponite inflatos tumidosque vultus.
610   quidquid a vobis minor expavescit,
maior hoc vobis dominus minatur;
omne sub regno graviore regnum est.
quem dies vidit veniens superbum,
hunc dies vidit fugiens iacentem.
615   Nemo confidat nimium secundis,
nemo desperet meliora lassis:
miscet haec illis prohibetque Clotho
stare Fortunam, rotat omne fatum.
nemo tam divos habuit faventes,
620   crastinum ut posset sibi polliceri.
res deus nostras celeri citatas
      turbine versat.

there is freedom to count the fish below water
where just now, under the mighty storm,
the shaken Cyclades feared the sea.
    No state is lasting; pain and pleasure
give way in turn: pleasure is briefer.
A short hour switches high and low.
Even he who crowns the heads of princes,
before whom nations kneel and tremble,
at whose nod wars are set aside
by Medes and Indians close to Phoebus
and Dahae whose horsemen threaten the Parthians—
he grips the sceptre tensely, and tries
in his fear to divine the changes of chance
that changes all, and the hazards of time.
You, whom the ruler of earth and sea
has granted dread power over life and death:
drop your puffed-up, arrogant airs.
Whatever a lesser man fears from you
threatens you from a greater master;
all power is under a weightier power.
Rising day sees a man in pride:
retreating day sees him brought low.
    No one should trust too much in success,
no one despair of misfortune improving.
Clotho mixes the two, forbidding Fortune
to rest, and spins each destiny around.
No one has enjoyed such favouring gods
that he could promise himself the morrow.
God keeps our lives hastening, turning
      in a speeding whirlwind.

NUNTIUS

Quis me per auras turbo praecipitem vehet
atraque nube involvet, ut tantum nefas
625   eripiat oculis? o domus Pelopi quoque
et Tantalo pudenda!

CHORUS
Quid portas novi?

NUNTIUS

Quaenam ista regio est? Argos et Sparte, pios
sortita fratres, et maris gemini premens
fauces Corinthos, an feris Hister fugam
630   praebens Alanis, an sub aeterna nive
Hyrcana tellus, an vagi passim Scythae?
quis hic nefandi est conscius monstri locus?

CHORUS
Effare, et istud pande, quodcumque est, malum.

NUNTIUS

Si steterit animus, si metu corpus rigens
635   remittet artus. haeret in vultu trucis
imago facti. Ferte me insanae procul,
illo, procellae, ferte quo fertur dies
hinc raptus.

CHORUS
Animos gravius incertos tenes.
quid sit quod horres ede et auctorem indica.
640   non quaero quis sit, sed uter. effare ocius.

THYESTES

ACT 4

MESSENGER

Will some whirlwind carry me headlong through the air and wrap me in black cloud, to wrest such an outrage from my sight? This house would shame even Pelops and Tantalus!

CHORUS LEADER

What news do you bring?

MESSENGER

What country is this? Argos, and Sparta blessed with devoted brothers,[32] and Corinth that closes the throats of two seas? Or the Danube that offers escape to barbarous Alani, or the Hyrcanian land under its eternal snow, or the far-wandering Scythians? What is this place that knows such a terrible enormity?

CHORUS LEADER

Speak out and reveal this evil, whatever it is.

MESSENGER

Once my mind slows down, once my fear-frozen body loosens its limbs. The picture of that savage deed sticks in my eyes. Bear me far away, you mad cyclones, bear me where the daylight is borne, now stolen from here.[33]

CHORUS LEADER

You hold our minds in deeper uncertainty. Tell us the source of your horror and name the culprit. I do not ask who it might be, but which of the two. Speak out quickly.

---

[32] Castor and Pollux, exemplars of brotherly devotion.
[33] By the Sun's turning back in horror (cf. 776ff.).

NUNTIUS

In arce summa Pelopiae pars est domus
conversa ad austros, cuius extremum latus
aequale monti crescit atque urbem premit
et contumacem regibus populum suis
645   habet sub ictu. fulget hic turbae capax
immane tectum, cuius auratas trabes
variis columnae nobiles maculis ferunt.
post ista vulgo nota, quae populi colunt,
in multa dives spatia discedit domus.
650   arcana in imo regio secessu iacet,
alta vetustum valle compescens nemus,
penetrale regni, nulla qua laetos solet
praebere ramos arbor aut ferro coli,
sed taxus et cupressus et nigra ilice
655   obscura nutat silva, quam supra eminens
despectat alte quercus et vincit nemus.
hinc auspicari regna Tantalidae solent,
hinc petere lassis rebus ac dubiis opem.
affixa inhaerent dona: vocales tubae
660   fractique currus, spolia Myrtoi maris,
victaeque falsis axibus pendent rotae
et omne gentis facinus; hoc Phrygius loco
fixus tiaras Pelopis, hic praeda hostium
et de triumpho picta barbarico chlamys.
665   fons stat sub umbra tristis et nigra piger
haeret palude: talis est dirae Stygis
deformis unda quae facit caelo fidem.
hinc nocte caeca gemere ferales deos
fama est, catenis lucus excussis sonat
670   ululantque manes. quidquid audire est metus

MESSENGER

On the summit of the citadel is a section of the House of
Pelops that faces south. Its outer flank rises up like a
mountain, hemming in the city and holding in its range
a populace defiant to its kings. Here is a vast gleaming
hall, room enough for a multitude, its gilded roofbeams
supported by columns with conspicuous varied markings.
Behind these public rooms, where whole peoples pay
court, the wealthy house goes back a great distance. At the
farthest and lowest remove there lies a secret area that
confines an age-old woodland in a deep vale—the inner
sanctum of the realm. There are no trees here such as
stretch out healthy branches and are tended with the
knife, but yews and cypresses and a darkly stirring thicket
of black ilex, above which a towering oak looks down from
its height and masters the grove. Tantalid kings regularly
inaugurate their reigns here, and seek help here in disasters and dilemmas. Here votive gifts are fastened: hanging
up are bruiting trumpets and wrecked chariots, spoils
from the Myrtoan Sea, wheels defeated because of rigged
axles,[34] and all the exploits of the clan. In this place is
pinned the Phrygian cap of Pelops, here are spoils from
his enemies and an embroidered cape from his triumph
over barbarians. In the gloom is a dismal stagnant spring,
oozing slowly in the black swamp. Such is the unsightly
stream of dread Styx, which generates trust in heaven.
Here in the blind darkness rumour has it that death gods
groan; the grove resounds to the rattling of chains, and
ghosts howl. Anything fearful to *hear* can be *seen* there. A

[34] The reference is to Oenomaus' chariot, wrecked and defeated in the race with Pelops.

illic videtur. errat antiquis vetus
emissa bustis turba et insultant loco
maiora notis monstra. quin tota solet
micare silva flamma, et excelsae trabes
675 ardent sine igne. saepe latratu nemus
trino remugit, saepe simulacris domus
attonita magnis. nec dies sedat metum:
nox propria luco est, et superstitio inferum
in luce media regnat. hinc orantibus
680 responsa dantur certa, cum ingenti sono
laxantur adyto fata et immugit specus
vocem deo solvente.
              Quo postquam furens
intravit Atreus liberos fratris trahens,
ornantur arae. quis queat digne eloqui?
685 post terga iuvenum nobiles revocat manus
et maesta vitta capita purpurea ligat.
non tura desunt, non sacer Bacchi liquor
tangensve salsa victimam culter mola.
servatur omnis ordo, ne tantum nefas
690 non rite fiat.

CHORUS
Quis manum ferro admovet?

NUNTIUS
Ipse est sacerdos, ipse funesta prece
letale carmen ore violento canit.
stat ipse ad aras, ipse devotos neci
contrectat et componit et ferro apparat;
695 attendit ipse: nulla pars sacri perit.
Lucus tremescit, tota succusso solo

hoary crowd walks abroad, released from their ancient tombs, and things more monstrous than any known caper about the place. In addition, flames repeatedly flicker throughout the wood, and the lofty treetrunks burn without fire. Often the grove booms with threefold barking, often the house is awed by huge apparitions. Daytime does not allay the fear: the grove has a night all its own, and an eerie sense of the underworld reigns in broad daylight. Here those seeking oracles are granted infallible answers; words of destiny are loosed from the sanctuary amidst thunderous noise, and the hollow space booms as a god unleashes his voice.

Once Atreus enters the place in frenzy, dragging his brother's children, the altar is fitted out. Who could express it properly? He pulls the youths' princely hands behind their backs, and binds their sorrowful heads with a purple band of wool. The incense is not missing, nor Bacchus' holy liquid nor the knife that touches the victims with salted meal. Every part of the ritual is kept, to ensure that such an outrage is performed by the rules.

CHORUS LEADER

Who sets his hand to the knife?

MESSENGER

He himself is priest, he himself makes sinister prayers and sings the death chant in a bloodthirsty voice. He stands by the altar himself, himself handles and arranges those doomed to slaughter and readies them for the knife; he himself checks details—no part of the ritual is forgotten. The grove begins to tremble; as the earth shakes the whole

---

694 apparat *Axelson*: admovet *EA*

nutavit aula, dubia quo pondus daret
ac fluctuanti similis; e laevo aethere
atrum cucurrit limitem sidus trahens.
700 libata in ignes vina mutato fluunt
cruenta Baccho; regium capiti decus
bis terque lapsum est; flevit in templis ebur.
movere cunctos monstra, sed solus sibi
immotus Atreus constat, atque ultro deos
705 terret minantes.
                    Iamque dimissa mora
adsistit aris, torvum et obliquum intuens.
ieiuna silvis qualis in Gangeticis
inter iuvencos tigris erravit duos,
utriusque praedae cupida, quo primum ferat
710 incerta morsus; flectit hoc rictus suos,
illo reflectit et famem dubiam tenet:
sic dirus Atreus capita devota impiae
speculatur irae. quem prius mactet sibi
dubitat, secunda deinde quem caede immolet.
715 nec interest, sed dubitat et saevum scelus
iuvat ordinare.

CHORUS
Quem tamen ferro occupat?

NUNTIUS
Primus locus (ne desse pietatem putes)
avo dicatur: Tantalus prima hostia est.

CHORUS
Quo iuvenis animo, quo tulit vultu necem?

NUNTIUS
720 Stetit sui securus et non est preces

palace sways, uncertain which way to topple and seeming to waver. From the sky's left quarter races a comet, leaving a black trail. Wine poured in libation on the fires changes as it flows to blood; the royal emblem slips repeatedly from his head; ivory statues weep in the temples. All are affected by these prodigies, but Atreus alone remains unaffected and constant; he counter-threatens the menacing gods.

And now he dismisses delays and takes his stand at the altar, with a forbidding sidelong glare. As in the woods by the Ganges a hungry tigress wavers between two young bulls, craving each prey and uncertain where to sink her teeth first; she turns her gaping jaws here, turns them back there and keeps her hunger in suspense: so dread Atreus surveys the victims consecrated to his godless anger. He hesitates: which shall he sacrifice first to himself, then which shall he offer up as the second killing? It makes no difference, yet he hesitates and takes pleasure in ordering the savage crime.

CHORUS LEADER

Which one *does* he catch first with the sword?

MESSENGER

First place (lest you think him lacking in family feeling) is dedicated to his grandfather: Tantalus is the first victim.

CHORUS LEADER

What was the young man's attitude and expression in facing murder?

MESSENGER

He stood firm without concern for himself, and refused to

perire frustra passus; ast illi ferus
in vulnere ensem abscondit, et penitus premens
iugulo manum commisit: educto stetit
ferro cadaver, cumque dubitasset diu
725   hac parte an illa caderet, in patruum cadit.
     Tunc ille ad aras Plisthenem saevus trahit
adicitque fratri. colla percussa amputat;
cervice caesa truncus in pronum ruit,
querulum cucurrit murmure incerto caput.

CHORUS

730   Quid deinde gemina caede perfunctus facit?
  puerone parcit, an scelus sceleri ingerit?

NUNTIUS

Silva iubatus qualis Armenia leo
in caede multa victor armento incubat;
cruore rictus madidus et pulsa fame
735   non ponit iras: hinc et hinc tauros premens
vitulis minatur, dente iam lasso piger:
non aliter Atreus saevit atque ira tumet.
ferrumque gemina caede perfusum tenens,
oblitus in quem fureret, infesta manu
740   exegit ultra corpus; ac pueri statim
pectore receptus ensis e tergo exstitit.
cadit ille et aras sanguine extinguens suo
per utrumque vulnus moritur.

CHORUS

O saevum scelus!

---

741 e *Tarrant*: in *EA*

waste breath on futile prayers. The brute buried his sword in the wound he made, the hand meeting the throat as it thrust deep. When the steel was pulled out the corpse stayed upright; after long hesitation whether to fall this way or that, it fell on its uncle.

Then that savage drags Plisthenes to the altar, and adds him to his brother. With a mortal stroke he chops off the head; with the neck severed the trunk falls forward, while the head rolls away, mumbling some unintelligible protest.

CHORUS LEADER

Then what does he do after accomplishing two murders? Spare the boy, or pile crime on crime?

MESSENGER

As in the forests of Armenia a maned lion falls victoriously on a herd amidst much slaughter; though his jaws are bloodsoaked and his hunger checked he does not abandon his anger, but attacks the bulls in one direction and another and threatens the calves, though sluggishly and with weary jaws: just so Atreus rages, swollen with anger. Holding a blade soaked in two killings, and regardless of the target of his rage, he drives it violently out beyond the body: taken on the chest, the sword projects at once from the boy's back. He falls, and dies from both wounds as his blood douses the altar fire.

CHORUS LEADER

What a savage crime!

SENECA

NUNTIUS

Exhorruistis? hactenus si stat nefas,
745   pius est.

CHORUS

An ultra maius aut atrocius
natura recipit?

NUNTIUS

Sceleris hunc finem putas?
gradus est.

CHORUS

Quid ultra potuit? obiecit feris
lanianda forsan corpora atque igne arcuit?

NUNTIUS

Utinam arcuisset! ne tegat functos humus
750   nec solvat ignis! avibus epulandos licet
ferisque triste pabulum saevis trahat—
votum est sub hoc quod esse supplicium solet:
pater insepultos spectet! o nullo scelus
credibile in aevo quodque posteritas neget!
755   erepta vivis exta pectoribus tremunt
spirantque venae corque adhuc pavidum salit;
at ille fibras tractat ac fata inspicit
et adhuc calentes viscerum venas notat.
Postquam hostiae placuere, securus vacat
760   iam fratris epulis. ipse divisum secat
in membra corpus, amputat trunco tenus
umeros patentes et lacertorum moras,
denudat artus durus atque ossa amputat;
tantum ora servat et datas fidei manus.
765   haec veribus haerent viscera et lentis data

294

MESSENGER

You shudder? If this is where the outrage stops, he is a righteous man.

CHORUS LEADER

Does nature have room for anything still greater or more atrocious?

MESSENGER

You think this is the endpoint of crime? It is just a step!

CHORUS LEADER

What could he do beyond this? Perhaps toss the bodies to wild beasts to tear, and deny them fire?

MESSENGER

I wish he *had* denied them! Let earth not hide the dead, nor fire consume them! Let him drag them out for birds to feast on, as ghastly feed for savage animals! Under him what is normally a punishment becomes a prayer. May their father look upon them unburied! No age could believe such a crime: the future will deny it. Torn from the living chests the organs are still trembling, the veins pulsing and the hearts throbbing in terror. But he handles the entrails and looks into destiny and takes note of the still-hot veins on the viscera. Once the victims prove satisfactory, he relaxes and takes time for his brother's feast. With his own hands he cuts and separates the bodies limb by limb: working back to the trunk he chops away the resisting arms and broad shoulders; heartlessly he lays bare the joints and bones and chops them away; just the faces he keeps, and the hands given in trust. Some of the flesh is stuck on spits, and sits dripping over slow burners; other

stillant caminis, illa flammatus latex
candente aëno iactat.

                   Impositas dapes
transiluit ignis, inque trepidantes focos
bis ter regestus et pati iussus moram

770   invitus ardet. stridet in veribus iecur;
nec facile dicam corpora an flammae magis
gemuere. piceos ignis in fumos abit;
et ipse fumus, tristis ac nebula gravis,
non rectus exit seque in excelsum levat:

775   ipsos penates nube deformi obsidet.

    O Phoebe patiens, fugeris retro licet
medioque raptum merseris caelo diem,
sero occidisti! lancinat natos pater
artusque mandit ore funesto suos.

780   nitet fluente madidus unguento comam
gravisque vino est; saepe praeclusae cibum
tenuere fauces. in malis unum hoc tuis
bonum est, Thyesta, quod mala ignoras tua.
sed et hoc peribit. verterit currus licet

785   sibi ipse Titan obvium ducens iter,
tenebrisque facinus obruat taetrum novis
nox missa ab ortu tempore alieno gravis,
tamen videndum est. tota patefient mala.

CHORUS

    Quo, terrarum superumque potens,

790   cuius ad ortus
    noctis opacae decus omne fugit,
    quo vertis iter

---

771 magis *E*: gemant *A*   777 raptum *recc*.: ruptum *EA*

parts are tossed about by kindled water in a boiling cauldron.

The fire leaps past the food placed on it; though forced back again and again onto the trembling hearth and commanded to stay in place, it burns grudgingly. The liver hisses on the spit; I could not easily say whether the bodies or flames groan more loudly. The fire turns into pitchy smoke, and the smoke itself, in a heavy, gloomy fog, will not go straight up or rise into the air: it smothers the very house gods in an unsightly cloud.

O long-suffering Phoebus! Though you have fled backward, snatched the day from mid-heaven and drowned it, you set too late! The father is mangling his sons, gnawing his own limbs with entombing teeth. He is glistening, with hair soaked in flowing unguent, and he is heavy with wine. Often his blocked throat holds the food. In your troubles there is this one boon, Thyestes, that you are ignorant of your troubles! But this too will perish. Though the Titan has turned his chariot, tracing a path counter to himself, and though the foul deed is smothered in strange darkness by this oppressive night, released from the East and at an alien time, yet see you must. All your troubles will be revealed.

CHORUS

Where, you master of earth and heaven
—at whose rising all
the glory retreats of shadowed night—
where do you turn,

---

781 est *inserted by Tränkle*
789 potens *Heinsius*: parens *EA*

medioque diem perdis Olympo?
cur, Phoebe, tuos rapis aspectus?
nondum serae nuntius horae
795   nocturna vocat lumina Vesper;
nondum Hesperiae flexura rotae
iubet emeritos solvere currus;
nondum in noctem vergente die
tertia misit bucina signum;
800   stupet ad subitae tempora cenae
nondum fessis bubus arator.
    Quid te aetherio pepulit cursu?
quae causa tuos limite certo
deiecit equos?
805   numquid aperto carcere Ditis
victi temptant bella Gigantes?
numquid Tityos pectore fesso
renovat veteres saucius iras?
num reiecto
latus explicuit monte Typhoeus?
810   numquid struitur
via Phlegraeos alta per hostes
et Thessalicum
Thressa premitur Pelion Ossa?
    Solitae mundi periere vices;
nihil occasus, nihil ortus erit.
815   stupet Eoos
assueta deo tradere frenos
genetrix primae roscida lucis
perversa sui limina regni;

---

[35] This implies a regular signal marking the last portion of the day, but the details are uncertain.

annulling the day while still in mid-sky?
Why do you snatch your face from us, Phoebus?
Not yet is the sign of eventide,
Vesper, summoning the lights of night;
not yet does the turning of the western wheel
bid you loose your steeds, their task completed;
not yet, at the sinking of day towards night,
has the third trumpet voiced its signal;[35]
the ploughman, his oxen not yet weary,
stands in amazement: suddenly suppertime!
    What has driven you out of your heavenly course?
What cause has forced your horses down
from their fixed path?
Can it be that the prison of Dis is open
and the conquered Giants are venturing war?
Can it be that wounded Tityos renews
his ancient rage in his weary breast?
Can Typhon have thrown
the mountain off and stretched his limbs?
Can it be that a soaring
path is built by Phlegraean foes,[36]
and that Pelion in Thessaly
is burdened with the weight of Thracian Ossa?
    The regular cycles of heaven are lost;
sunset and sunrise will not exist.
The dewy mother of dawning light,
accustomed to hand the eastern reins
to the god, is stunned
by such disorder on her kingdom's threshold;

[36] The Giants, who fought the Olympian gods at Phlegra, and
tried to storm heaven by piling up mountains.

nescit fessos tinguere currus
820 nec fumantes sudore iubas
mergere ponto.
ipse insueto novus hospitio
Sol Auroram videt occiduus,
tenebrasque iubet
surgere nondum nocte parata:
825 non succedunt astra nec ullo
micat igne polus,
non Luna graves digerit umbras.
        Sed quidquid id est, utinam nox sit!
trepidant, trepidant
pectora magno percussa metu,
830 ne fatali cuncta ruina
quassata labent
iterumque deos hominesque premat
deforme chaos,
iterum terras et mare cingens
et vaga picti sidera mundi
Natura tegat.
835   Non alternae facis exortu
dux astrorum saecula ducens
dabit aestatis brumaeque notas,
non Phoebeis obvia flammis
demet nocti Luna timores
840 vincetque sui fratris habenas
curvo brevius limite currens.
ibit in unum congesta sinum
turba deorum.
hic qui sacris pervius astris

835 alternae *Heinsius*: aeternae* *EA*

she does not know how to bathe tired steeds
or plunge their smoking, sweaty manes
into the sea.
Startled himself by such strange welcome
the Sun beholds Aurora as he sets;
he bids the darkness rise, yet night
is not yet ready:
no stars appear in their turn, no fires
gleam in the ether,
no moon disperses the heavy shadows.
    But whatever the cause, may this be night only!
Our hearts are shaken and trembling, trembling
with enormous fear
lest the shattered cosmos fall in the ruin
ordained by fate,
lest gods and humans be engulfed once more
in formless chaos,
and once more earth and girdling sea
and the wandering stars of the jewelled sky
be hidden by Nature.
    No longer in successive fiery dawns
will the leader of stars,[37] who leads the ages,
give indications of summer and winter;
no longer, facing Phoebus' flames,
will the Moon relieve the night of terrors,
as she outstrips her brother's chariot,
riding more shortly on her curving path.
Into one gulf will fall in a heap
the throng of gods.
This highway of the holy planets,

[37] The Sun.

301

845   secat obliquo tramite zonas,
                flectens longos signifer annos,
                lapsa videbit sidera labens.
                hic qui nondum vere benigno
                reddit Zephyro vela tepenti
850   Aries praeceps ibit in undas,
                per quas pavidam vexerat Hellen.
                hic qui nitido Taurus cornu
                praefert Hyadas,
                secum Geminos
                trahet et curvi bracchia Cancri.
855   Leo flammiferis aestibus ardens
                iterum e caelo cadet Herculeus;
                cadet in terras Virgo relictas,
                iustaeque cadent pondera Librae
                secumque trahent Scorpion acrem.
860   et qui nervo tenet Haemonio
                pinnata senex spicula Chiron,
                rupto perdet spicula nervo.
                pigram referens hiemem gelidus
                cadet Aegoceros,
865   frangetque tuam, quisquis es, urnam;
                tecum excedent
                ultima caeli sidera Pisces.
                    Monstraque numquam perfusa mari
                merget condens omnia gurges.
                et qui medias dividit Ursas,
870   fluminis instar lubricus Anguis

---

[38] In Latin the zodiac is called *signifer*, "bearer of the signs" (constellations). Seneca here plays on the military sense of *signifer*, as if the zodiac were "standard-bearer" to the years.

that crosses the zones with its slanting track,
Sign-Bearer, guide of the lengthy years,[38]
will see the fallen stars as it falls.
This *Ram*, that before spring weather is kind
restores sails to the balmy Zephyr,
will fall headlong into the waves
over which it carried the frightened Helle.
This *Bull*, that displays the *Hyades*
on his gleaming horn, will drag down with him
the *Twins*, and the claws of the curving *Crab*.
Hercules' *Lion*, blazing with fiery
heat, will fall once more from heaven;
the *Virgin* will fall to the earth she left,
the weights of the even-handed *Scales* will fall
and drag sharp *Scorpion* down with them.
The one who holds feathered darts against
his bowstring, old Haemonian *Chiron*,[39]
will lose his darts, the bowstring broken.
The chill restorer of sluggish winter,
Goat's horn, will fall,
and smash *your* urn, whoever you are;[40]
with you will depart
the last of heaven's stars, the *Fish*.

     And the monsters that never bathe in the sea
will be drowned by the all-engulfing flood.
Both the one that glides like a river between
the *Bears* and keeps them apart, the *Snake*,

---

[39] Here the Archer (Sagittarius) is identified as the centaur
Chiron.
[40] The Water Carrier (Aquarius) was variously identified.

magnoque minor iuncta Draconi
frigida duro Cynosura gelu,
custosque sui tardus plaustri
iam non stabilis ruet Arctophylax.
875   Nos e tanto visi populo
digni, premeret
quos everso cardine mundus?
in nos aetas ultima venit?
o nos dura sorte creatos,
880   seu perdidimus solem miseri,
sive expulimus!
Abeant questus, discede timor:
vitae est avidus quisquis non vult
mundo secum pereunte mori.

ATREUS

885 Aequalis astris gradior et cunctos super
altum superbo vertice attingens polum.
nunc decora regni teneo, nunc solium patris.
dimitto superos: summa votorum attigi.
bene est, abunde est, iam sat est etiam mihi.
890 sed cur satis sit? pergam et implebo patrem
funere suorum. ne quid obstaret pudor,
dies recessit: perge dum caelum vacat.
utinam quidem tenere fugientes deos
possem et coactos trahere, ut ultricem dapem
895 omnes viderent. quod sat est, videat pater.
etiam die nolente discutiam tibi

---

41 Snake and Serpent are one and the same. Cynosura is a
name for the Lesser Bear.

and the great *Serpent's* lesser neighbour,
Cynosura,[41] chilled by icy frost,
and the slow guard of the *Wain*, no longer
standing firm, will fall—the *Bear-Ward*.

    Out of so many people, is it judged that *we*
deserve to be crushed
by the overthrow of the axis of heaven?
Has the final age come upon *us*?
O, we were born with a heavy fate,
whether we lost the sun through misfortune
or drove him away!
But let laments go, let fear depart:
a glutton for life is one that is loath
to die when the whole world perishes with him.[42]

ACT 5

ATREUS

Peer of the stars I stride, out-topping all, my proud head
reaching to the lofty sky. *Now* I hold the kingdom's glories,
now my father's throne. I discharge the gods: I have
reached the pinnacle of my prayers. This is good, this is
ample, this is enough now, even for me. But why should it
be enough? I shall go on, and fill the father with the death
of his sons. Lest shame should present any obstacle, daylight has withdrawn: go on while heaven is empty! Indeed I
wish I could stop the gods fleeing, round them up and drag
them all to see this feast of vengeance. But it is enough that
the father see it. Even though the daylight is unwilling, I

---

[42] "Who would not fall with all the world about him?" (Ben
Jonson, *Catiline* III.1).

tenebras, miseriae sub quibus latitant tuae.
nimis diu conviva securo iaces
hilarique vultu; iam satis mensis datum est
900 satisque Baccho: sobrio tanta ad mala
opus est Thyeste.
                         Turba famularis, fores
templi relaxa, festa patefiat domus.
libet videre, capita natorum intuens
quos det colores, verba quae primus dolor
905 effundat aut ut spiritu expulso stupens
corpus rigescat. fructus hic operis mei est.
miserum videre nolo, sed dum fit miser.
      Aperta multa tecta conlucent face.
resupinus ipse purpurae atque auro incubat,
910 vino gravatum fulciens laeva caput.
eructat. o me caelitum excelsissimum,
regumque regem! vota transcendi mea.
satur est; capaci ducit argento merum—
ne parce potu: restat etiamnunc cruor
915 tot hostiarum; veteris hunc Bacchi color
abscondet. hoc, hoc mensa claudatur scypho.
mixtum suorum sanguinem genitor bibat:
meum bibisset. ecce, iam cantus ciet
festasque voces, nec satis menti imperat.

THYESTES

920   Pectora longis hebetata malis,
      iam sollicitas ponite curas.
      fugiat maeror fugiatque pavor,
      fugiat trepidi comes exilii
      tristis egestas

shall dispel for you the darkness that conceals your sorrows. Too long you have lain there feasting with a carefree, cheerful expression. Enough devotion now to the board, enough to wine: for suffering so great, we need Thyestes sober.

You throng of slaves, unbar the temple doors, let the revels of the house be revealed.[43] [*Aside*] I long to see what colour he turns as he looks on his sons' heads, what words his first torment pours forth, how his body stiffens, breathless with shock. This is the fruit of my work: I do not want to see him broken, but to see him *being* broken.

Opened up, the house is bright with myriad torches. *He* is lying on purple and gold, sprawled backwards, propping his wine-heavy head on his left hand. He belches! Oh, I am highest of heavenly gods, and king of kings! I have surpassed my own prayers. He is stuffed, he imbibes pure wine from a great silver cup. Do not stint your drinking! There still remains the blood of so many victims; the colour of vintage wine will disguise it. Yes, let this be the cup to close the feast! Let the father drink the blended blood of his sons: he would have drunk mine. See, now he is raising his voice in festive songs, with little control over his wits.

THYESTES

Heart made dreary by long troubles,
now set aside your fretful cares.
Away with grief, away with fear,
away with the comrade of anxious exile,
gloomy poverty,

---

[43] As the doors open, the indoor scene is wheeled out onstage. Similar dramaturgy at *Herc* 1123 (see note), *Pha* 384, 863.

925   rebusque gravis pudor afflictis.
    magis unde cadas quam quo refert.
    magnum, ex alto culmine lapsum
    stabilem in plano figere gressum;
    magnum, ingenti strage malorum
930   pressum fracti pondera regni
    non inflexa cervice pati,
    nec degenerem victumque malis
    rectum impositas ferre ruinas.
    sed iam saevi nubila fati
935   pelle ac miseri temporis omnes
    dimitte notas;
    redeant vultus ad laeta boni,
    veterem ex animo mitte Thyesten.
       Proprium hoc miseros sequitur vitium,
    numquam rebus credere laetis;
940   redeat felix fortuna licet,
    tamen afflictos gaudere piget.
    quid me revocas
    festumque vetas celebrare diem,
    quid flere iubes,
    nulla surgens dolor ex causa?
    quis me prohibet
945   flore decenti vincire comam,
    prohibet, prohibet?
    vernae capiti fluxere rosae,
    pingui madidus crinis amomo
    inter subitos stetit horrores,
950   imber vultu nolente cadit,
    venit in medias voces gemitus.
    maeror lacrimas amat assuetas,

and shame that weighs upon misfortune.
Where you fall *from* matters more than where you
    fall *to*.
It's great, when you slip from a lofty peak,
to plant your feet firmly on the ground;
great, when a huge havoc of troubles
engulfs you, to keep your neck unbowed
while enduring the burden of broken kingship
—not to be conquered ignobly by troubles
but to stand and bear the infliction of ruin.
But now dispel the clouds of cruel
destiny, and put aside every token
of unhappy days;
smile once more at happiness,
cast from your heart the old Thyestes.
    Yet the wretched are dogged by this special fault
of never trusting in happy times.
Although good fortune comes round again,
yet rejoicing grates on those who have suffered.
Why hold me back
and forbid my celebrating this festive day,
why bid me weep,
pain arising without a cause?
Who prevents me
from binding my hair properly with flowers,
prevents me, prevents me?
The roses of spring slide from my head,
my hair, though soaked in heavy myrrh,
bristles in sudden shivering fits,
teardrops fall from my eyes unbidden,
amidst my words there comes a groan.
Sorrow loves its familiar tears,

flendi miseris dira cupido est.
libet infaustos mittere questus,
955 libet et Tyrio
saturas ostro rumpere vestes,
ululare libet.
　　Mittit luctus signa futuri
mens ante sui praesaga mali:
instat nautis fera tempestas,
960 cum sine vento tranquilla tument.
　　—Quos tibi luctus quosve tumultus
fingis, demens?
credula praesta pectora fratri:
iam, quidquid id est,
vel sine causa vel sero times.
965 　　—Nolo infelix,
sed vagus intra terror oberrat,
subitos fundunt oculi fletus,
nec causa subest.
dolor an metus est?
an habet lacrimas magna voluptas?

ATREUS

970 Festum diem, germane, consensu pari
celebremus. hic est sceptra qui firmet mea
solidamque pacis alliget certae fidem.

THYESTES

Satias dapis me nec minus Bacchi tenet.
augere cumulus hic voluptatem potest,
975 si cum meis gaudere felici datur.

---

44 Cf. Shakespeare, *Richard III* II.3.42–44: "By a divine in-

the unhappy have a fearful craving to weep.
I long to utter ill-omened laments,
I long to rend these garments steeped
in Tyrian purple,
I long to howl.
    Signs of grief to come are sent
by the mind, foreboding its own misfortune:
sailors are threatened by a savage storm
when a calm sea heaves without any wind.[44]
—What griefs, what upheavals are you conjuring
for yourself, you madman?
Show your brother a trustful heart!
Your fear of *whatever* is either groundless
or too late now.
—Poor me, I resist,
but terror roves and prowls inside me,
my eyes pour forth these sudden tears,
based on no cause.
Is it grief or fear?
Or does great pleasure make for weeping?

ATREUS

My own brother, we must celebrate this festive day in mutual harmony. This is the day that will strengthen my sceptre, and lock up solid confidence in reliable peace.

THYESTES

I am stayed by a surfeit of fine fare, and equally of wine. The final addition that could increase my pleasure would be the chance to enjoy my happiness with my boys.

stinct men's minds mistrust / Ensuing danger; as by proof we see / The water swell before a boist'rous storm."

ATREUS

Hic esse natos crede in amplexu patris.
hic sunt eruntque; nulla pars prolis tuae
tibi subtrahetur. ora quae exoptas dabo
totumque turba iam sua implebo patrem.
980   satiaberis, ne metue! nunc mixti meis
iucunda mensae sacra iuvenilis colunt;
sed accientur. poculum infuso cape
gentile Baccho.

THYESTES

           Capio fraternae dapis
donum. paternis vina libentur deis,
985   tunc hauriantur. —sed quid hoc? nolunt manus
parere, crescit pondus et dextram gravat.
admotus ipsis Bacchus a labris fugit
circaque rictus ore decepto fluit,
et ipsa trepido mensa subsiluit solo.
990   vix lucet ignis; ipse quin aether gravis
inter diem noctemque desertus stupet.
quid hoc? magis magisque concussi labant
convexa caeli. spissior densis coit
caligo tenebris noxque se in noctem abdidit;
995   fugit omne sidus. quidquid est, fratri precor
natisque parcat, omnis in vile hoc caput
abeat procella. Redde iam natos mihi!

ATREUS

Reddam, et tibi illos nullus eripiet dies.

THYESTES

Quis hic tumultus viscera exagitat mea?
1000   quid tremuit intus? sentio impatiens onus
meumque gemitu non meo pectus gemit.

ATREUS

Consider your sons as here in their father's embrace. Here
they are, and will stay. No portion of your offspring will be
taken from you. I shall show you shortly the faces you long
for, and give the father his fill of his own dear throng. You
will be surfeited, never fear! At the moment, in company
with mine, they are observing the sweet communion of the
young men's table. But they will be summoned. Take this
cup of our bloodline, with an infusion of wine.

THYESTES

I take the gift, as part of my brother's feast. The wine shall
be poured to our fathers' gods, then drained. —But what is
this? My hands will not obey, the weight increases and burdens my hand. When raised, the wine flees from my very
lips, cheats my mouth and swirls around my open jaws. The
table itself jumps with the ground's trembling. The fire
scarcely gives light. Even the skies are sluggish and dazed,
left abandoned between day and night. What is this? More
and more heaven's vault is shaking and lurching. Darkness
gathers more thickly amidst dense shadows, and night bur-
ies itself in night; every star is in flight. Whatever it is, I
pray it may spare my brother and sons, and the whole
storm spend itself on this worthless head of mine. Now
return my sons to me!

ATREUS

I shall return them, and no day will steal them from you.

THYESTES

What is this turmoil that shakes my guts? What trembles
inside me? I feel a restless burden, and my breast groans
with groaning not my own. Come, sons, your unhappy

Adeste, nati, genitor infelix vocat,
adeste. visis fugiet hic vobis dolor—
unde obloquuntur?

ATREUS

                Expedi amplexus, pater:

1005   venere. natos ecquid agnoscis tuos?

THYESTES

Agnosco fratrem. Sustines tantum nefas
gestare, Tellus? non ad infernam Styga
te nosque mergis, rupta et ingenti via
ad chaos inane regna cum rege abripis?

1010   non tota ab imo tecta convellens solo
vertis Mycenas? stare circa Tantalum
uterque iam debuimus. hinc compagibus
et hinc revulsis, si quid infra Tartara est
avosque nostros, hoc tuam immani sinu

1015   demitte vallem, nosque defossos tege
Acheronte toto. noxiae supra caput
animae vagentur nostrum, et ardenti freto
Phlegethon harenas igneus tostas agens
exilia supra nostra violentus fluat.

1020   immota, Tellus, pondus ignavum iaces?
fugere superi.

ATREUS

               Iam accipe hos potius libens
diu expetitos: nulla per fratrem est mora.
fruere, osculare, divide amplexus tribus.

1018 tostas *Raphelengius*: totas *EA*

314

THYESTES

father calls you, come! Once I see you this pain will vanish. They interrupt—but from where?

ATREUS

Unfold your welcoming arms, father. They have come. [The severed heads are revealed]⁴⁵ I suppose you recognise your sons?

THYESTES

I recognise my brother. Earth, can you bear to support such a weight of outrage? Do you not plunge us down with you into infernal Styx—break open a huge passageway and drag this kingdom with its king into the empty void? Not uproot every building from its base and overturn Mycenae? We two should have been set long ago on each side of Tantalus. Wrench your frame apart here and here; if there is anything below Tartarus and our ancestors, hollow out an immense ravine within yourself to plummet down that far: bury us and hide us beneath the whole of Acheron. Over our heads let guilty souls roam, and let fiery Phlegethon, that carries charred sands in its burning stream, flow violently over our place of exile. Do you lie motionless, Earth, just a stolid mass? The gods above have fled.

ATREUS

Come now, rather than this, receive with joy the boys you missed so long. Your brother is not stopping you. Enjoy them, kiss them, split your embraces among the three of them.

^{45} There are various staging possibilities. A vessel containing the heads could be opened (as in the story of Harpagus in Herodotus 1.119) at this moment by Atreus or attendants or Thyestes. Or the heads could be carried onstage at this point.

THYESTES

Hoc foedus? haec est gratia, haec fratris fides?
1025 sic odia ponis? non peto, incolumes pater
natos ut habeam; scelere quod salvo dari
odioque possit, frater hoc fratrem rogo:
sepelire liceat. redde quod cernas statim
uri; nihil te genitor habiturus rogo,
1030 sed perditurus.

ATREUS

Quidquid e natis tuis
superest habes, quodcumque non superest habes.

THYESTES

Utrumne saevis pabulum alitibus iacent,
an beluis vorantur, an pascunt feras?

ATREUS

Epulatus ipse es impia natos dape.

THYESTES

1035 Hoc est deos quod puduit, hoc egit diem
aversum in ortus. quas miser voces dabo
questusque quos? quae verba sufficient mihi?
abscisa cerno capita et avulsas manus
et rupta fractis cruribus vestigia:
1040 hoc est quod avidus capere non potuit pater.
Volvuntur intus viscera, et clausum nefas
sine exitu luctatur et quaerit fugam:
da, frater, ensem (sanguinis multum mei
habet ille): ferro liberis detur via.
1045 negatur ensis? pectora inliso sonent

1033 vorantur *Axelson*: servantur *EA*

316

THYESTES

Is this our agreement? Is this your goodwill, your brotherly promise? Is this how you set aside hatred? I do not ask as a father to have my sons safe. What can be granted with no damage to your crime and hatred, I ask you brother to brother: let me bury them. Return what you can watch being burnt at once. I ask you for nothing to keep as a father, only something to lose.

ATREUS

All that remains of your children you have, all that does not remain you have.

THYESTES

Are they lying as fodder for cruel birds, or being devoured by monsters, or feeding beasts of the field?

ATREUS

You yourself banqueted on your sons—a sacrilegious meal.

THYESTES

This was what shamed the gods, *this* drove the day back to where it rises. What words shall I utter in such wretchedness, what laments? What speech will suffice me? I see the lopped-off heads, the wrenched-off hands, the feet torn from broken legs. This is what the greedy father could not take in![46] The flesh churns within me, the imprisoned horror struggles with no way out, seeking to escape. Give me your sword, brother—it already has much of my blood: the blade must give my children a path. You refuse the sword? Let me batter my breast, smash resounding blows against

---

[46] Either physically (since he was full) or mentally (by understanding Atreus' riddles).

contusa planctu—sustine, infelix, manum,
parcamus umbris. Tale quis vidit nefas?
quis inhospitalis Caucasi rupem asperam
Heniochus habitans, quisve Cecropiis metus
1050   terris Procrustes? genitor en natos premo
premorque natis! sceleris est aliquis modus!

ATREUS
Sceleri modus debetur ubi facias scelus,
non ubi reponas. hoc quoque exiguum est mihi:
ex vulnere ipso sanguinem calidum in tua
1055   defundere ora debui, ut viventium
biberes cruorem. verba sunt irae data
dum propero. ferro vulnera impresso dedi,
cecidi ad aras, caede votiva focos
placavi, et artus, corpora exanima amputans,
1060   in parva carpsi frusta, et haec ferventibus
demersi aënis, illa lentis ignibus
stillare iussi; membra nervosque abscidi
viventibus, gracilique traiectas veru
mugire fibras vidi et aggessi manu
1065   mea ipse flammas: omnia haec melius pater
fecisse potuit. cecidit in cassum dolor:
scidit ore natos impio, sed nesciens,
sed nescientes.

THYESTES
Clausa litoribus vagis
audite maria; vos quoque audite hoc scelus,
1070   quocumque, di, fugistis; audite inferi,
audite terrae. Noxque Tartarea gravis
et atra nube, vocibus nostris vaca:
tibi sum relictus, sola tu miserum vides,

it—no, hold your hand, poor wretch, we must spare the dead. Who has ever seen such horror? What Henioch, dwelling on the rough crags of inhospitable Caucasus, or what Procrustes, terror of Cecropian lands? See, a father burdening his sons, and burdened by his sons. There is *some* limit to crime!

ATREUS

Crime is owed some limit when you commit crime, not when you repay it. Even this is too little for me. Straight from the wound I should have poured the hot blood into your mouth, so you could drink their lifeblood while they lived. I have cheated my anger in my haste. I dealt wounds, pressing the blade home, I slaughtered at the altar, I propitiated the hearth with votive killing, I chopped up the lifeless bodies, pulled the flesh into small pieces and plunged some into boiling cauldrons, bade others drip over slow fires; I cut away limbs and sinews from the living bodies, pierced the organs with thin spits and watched them moan, piled up fires with my own hands: all this the father could have done better. My anger was to no avail. He tore his sons in his sacrilegious mouth, but he did not know it, they did not know it.

THYESTES

Seas enclosed by winding shores, listen; listen to this crime too, you gods, wherever you have fled; listen, hell; listen, earth. Night, black and heavy with Tartarean fogs, be open to my words: I am abandoned to you, you alone see my

319

etiam sine astris. vota non faciam improba,
1075 pro me nihil precabor—et quid iam potest
pro me esse? vobis vota prospicient mea.

    Tu, summe caeli rector, aetheriae potens
dominator aulae, nubibus totum horridis
convolve mundum, bella ventorum undique
1080 committe et omni parte violentum intona,
manuque non qua tecta et immeritas domos
telo petis minore, sed qua montium
tergemina moles cecidit et qui montibus
stabant pares Gigantes, hac arma expedi
1085 ignesque torque. vindica amissum diem,
iaculare flammas, lumen ereptum polo
fulminibus exple. causa, ne dubites diu,
utriusque mala sit; si minus, mala sit mea:
me pete, trisulco flammeam telo facem
1090 per pectus hoc transmitte. si natos pater
humare et igni tradere extremo volo
ego sum cremandus. si nihil superos movet
nullumque telis impios numen petit,
aeterna nox permaneat et tenebris tegat
1095 immensa longis scelera. nil, Titan, queror,
si perseveras.

ATREUS

    Nunc meas laudo manus,
nunc parta vera est palma. perdideram scelus,
nisi sic doleres. liberos nasci mihi
nunc credo, castis nunc fidem reddi toris.

1074 etiam *Fitch*: tu quoque *EA*

misery—even with no starlight. I shall make no wicked prayers, no prayers to my own benefit—and what can be to my benefit now? My prayers will be in all *your* interests.

You exalted ruler of the skies, mighty master of heaven's court: enfold all the world in fearsome clouds, bring winds from every direction together in warfare, thunder ferociously in every quarter. Not as you strike at innocent homes and buildings with lighter weapons, but as you made the triple mass of mountains[47] fall, along with the Giants who stood tall as mountains: with such force deploy your weapons and launch your fires. Avenge the lost daylight, hurl flames, restore the light stolen from heaven with your bolts of lightning! To save you lengthy deliberation, let each of us be judged guilty. If not, let *me* be judged guilty. Strike at me, hurl the fiery brand of your three-forked weapon through this chest! If I would bury my sons as father and commit them to the final fire, I must be burnt up myself. But if nothing moves the gods, if no divinity strikes with his weapons at the wicked, let night remain forever, and hide these immeasurable crimes in lasting darkness. I make no protest, Titan, if you continue as you are.

ATREUS

Now I commend my hands, now the true palm is won. My crime would have been wasted if you did not feel pain like this. Now I believe that the children are mine, and that my bed is faithful and chaste once more!

[47] Pelion, Ossa, and Olympus, piled up by the Giants (cf. lines 811–812).

THYESTES

1100 Quid liberi meruere?

ATREUS
Quod fuerant tui.

THYESTES

Natos parenti—

ATREUS
Fateor, et, quod me iuvat,
certos.

THYESTES
Piorum praesides testor deos.

ATREUS

Quid coniugales?

THYESTES
Scelere quis pensat scelus?

ATREUS
Scio quid queraris: scelere praerepto doles;
1105 nec quod nefandas hauseris angit dapes:
quod non pararis! fuerat hic animus tibi
instruere similes inscio fratri cibos
et adiuvante liberos matre aggredi
similique leto sternere. hoc unum obstitit:
1110 tuos putasti.

THYESTES
Vindices aderunt dei:
his puniendum vota te tradunt mea.

ATREUS
Te puniendum liberis trado tuis.

THYESTES

What was my children's guilt?

ATREUS

That they were yours.

THYESTES

You gave sons to their father . . .

ATREUS

I admit it—and definitely your own sons, I am delighted to say.

THYESTES

I call to witness the gods that protect the righteous.

ATREUS

What about the marriage gods?

THYESTES

Who repays crime with crime?

ATREUS

I know why you complain: you are hurt at being forestalled in crime. What irks you? Not that you swallowed an unspeakable feast: that you did not arrange one! This had been your purpose, to provide similar food for your unwitting brother, to attack my children with their mother's help and put them to a similar death. The one obstacle was this: you thought them yours!

THYESTES

The gods of vengeance will come: my prayers consign you to them for punishment.

ATREUS

I consign you to your children for punishment.

HERCULES ON OETA

INTRODUCTION

Background

Hercules was once travelling through Greece with his newly won bride Deianira, when he found the river Evenus in flood. He entrusted her to the centaur Nessus, who knew the river, to carry her across. But Nessus attempted to abduct her, whereupon Hercules shot him with his poison-tipped arrows. The dying Nessus told the young bride to save some of his poisoned blood, for use as a love philtre if Hercules' affections should ever wander.

Many years later, after completion of his labours, Hercules conceived a desire for the young Iole, princess of the town of Oechalia. When her father Eurytus denied her to him, Hercules sacked her town, killed her father and brother, and sent Iole to his home in Trachis, where Deianira was waiting.[1]

Summary

Act 1

Hercules impatiently states his readiness and his qualifications for deification.

[1] This myth is not compatible with that which makes Megara the wife of Hercules at the completion of the labours, as in Seneca's *Hercules* and its antecedents. The adaptability of the myths,

Ode 1. The women of Oechalia lament the destruction of their town, and Hercules' hardness of heart and body. Iole mourns her murdered family.

Act 2

Deianira expresses her rage and anguish over Hercules' infidelities, most recently Iole. She impregnates a robe with the supposed love philtre from Nessus, and sends it to Hercules via the messenger Lichas.

Ode 2. Deianira's attendants express loyalty to her in this crisis, and see her danger as an inevitable concomitant of high status.

Act 3

Deianira realises belatedly that the philtre was probably deadly. Hyllus arrives and describes how the robe began to consume the body of Hercules, who killed Lichas in rage. Near death, Hercules is being transported home. Deianira prepares to commit suicide out of guilt and grief.

Ode 3. Orpheus' teaching that everything perishes is confirmed for the chorus by Hercules' downfall; they envisage the collapse of the cosmos as imminent.

Act 4

Hercules, brought in by bearers, is distraught over so inglorious a downfall, and rages against Deianira even after hearing of her suicide. Only when he learns that his death is in accordance with prophecy does he regain self-control and order a pyre to be built on Mt Oeta.

i.e. the absence of canonical versions, makes for such inconsistencies.

[SENECA]

Ode 4. The chorus envisages two possibilities, that Hercules' spirit has descended to the underworld or ascended to heaven.

Act 5
Philoctetes, who has inherited Hercules' bow and arrows, returns from Oeta and describes the hero's triumphant endurance of the final fire. Hercules' mother, Alcmene, mourns his death, but he appears from above to assure her that he has joined the gods in heaven.

Comment

This is the longest tragedy surviving from antiquity. It is composed on a monumental scale, which matches the hero's colossal physique and endurance and achievements. A drama about a superman, particularly a drama which ends by affirming his greatness, is appropriately a super-drama.

The more Hercules' greatness is emphasised, the more titanic he seems, and the more dangerous to ordinary humans around him. There was ambivalence in antiquity both about the nature of Hercules' heroism and about the nature of his afterlife. The earliest Greek accounts spoke of him as descending after death to the house of Hades, like an ordinary mortal. By the mid-fifth century B.C., on the other hand, it was generally believed that he had joined the gods on Olympus. But Sophocles' *Women of Trachis*, which portrays him as callous and self-centered, ends with preparations for his death on Mt Oeta, and so leaves us uncertain what fate awaits him beyond death, and whether such a hero deserves deification. Seneca's *Hercules* shows a hero who expects deification as the promised reward for the just-completed labours, but who is so full of violent aggression and megalomania that he falls into a bout of madness in which he kills his family.

Hercules on Oeta (= *HO*) dramatises the end of Hercules' life, and makes clear allusions to the two plays just mentioned. Inevitably, then, our attention is focussed on the question of deification and whether it is deserved. What answers does the play suggest? Some critics see Hercules as portrayed in an essentially favourable light, from his claim in the opening lines to have pacified the world, to his elevation to heaven at the end. They tend, therefore, to palliate or ignore elements of the play that reveal less admirable aspects of his heroism. Such a reading takes its orientation from a passing reference in Seneca's *On Steadfastness* (*De Constantia* 2.1) to Hercules as a Stoic exemplar. That reference, however, is brief and general, and qualified by the statement that Cato the Younger is a more reliable exemplar than Hercules; indeed, it can hardly be reconciled, except by drastic allegorization, with the details of the Hercules myth.

Other readers acknowledge negative elements in the portrayal of Hercules: ominous reminiscences in Act 1 of his madness in *Hercules*; monstrous cruelty and lust, as seen through the eyes of the Oechalian women and Deianira; anger and lack of endurance (by Herculean standards) in suffering the torment of the poisoned robe. There is a causal nexus inherent in the myth, with which this reading accords. Hercules' bestial lust goads Deianira into using the supposed love philtre, while his use of the hydra's poison on his arrows, which aligns him thematically with the beast, contributes to the philtre's toxic effect on him. In both respects his monstrousness contributes to his death.

One benefit of the latter reading is to yield a strong onward impetus in the play, as our views of Hercules change in accordance with his behaviour and the reactions of other characters. The play takes on a dramatic movement from high to low to high: internally, from vainglorious heroics through weakness to steadfast heroism; externally, from apparent success to disaster to supreme good fortune. That the play aims at such a *gradual* unfolding is confirmed by the fact that Hercules' deification is confirmed only at the very end, after considerable doubt (as in ode 4) about whether he has descended to the underworld or ascended to heaven. A difficulty of such a reading—which perhaps constitutes a criticism of the play itself—is that Hercules' failings are revealed to the audience, but not to himself: he barely acknowledges the damaging impact of his actions on others, nor at the end does he define the mortal part of himself, consumed in the flames, as the part that engendered his failings and passions.

However we read the earlier scenes, the steadfast heroism which Hercules displays from line 1472 can be securely understood in the light of popular Stoicism, such as runs through Seneca's prose works. There, examples of endurance of physical torment are held up as praiseworthy in themselves and as analogues for endurance of spiritual trials. In fact Hercules' self-immolation as a conscious *exhibition* of courage (in his case, to a double audience, divine and human) resembles Seneca's own enforced suicide as described by the historian Tacitus in his *Annals* (15.62–64), with its display of calmness, absence of haste, concern for friends rather than self. Stoicism sheds light also on Hercules' sudden access of endurance at the end of Act 4.

A prime Stoic duty is willing acceptance of fate: "to obey the gods, not to flare up at sudden misfortunes or deplore one's lot, but to accept fate patiently and do its commands" (Seneca, *Epistle* 76.23). Correspondingly Hercules finds courage to accept death without complaint, even with joy, at exactly the moment when he realises that it is fated (lines 1471–1480). It is worth adding that the philosophical and didactic colouring of these elements would not *per se* mark them as alien from the context of imaginative literature for a Roman audience, as they might for a modern audience. In Vergil's *Aeneid*, for example, endurance is embodied in the image of Aeneas as an oak tree, buffeted but unshakeable; acceptance of fate, in the image of Aeneas hoisting on his shoulder the shield that depicts "the fame and fate of his descendants" (respectively 4.441–449 and 8.731). The Vergilian image of the oak lies behind the description in *HO* of a mighty oak on Oeta, which resists robustly but finally falls (1623–1630), just as Hercules' great physique is destroyed. Complexity is increased by the fact that the oak, together with other sacred trees, indeed a whole forest, is felled at Hercules' own command (1483–1484, 1618–1641): the titanic aspect of the hero's greatness is kept before our eyes even at his death.

What of the doctrine enunciated at the end of *HO*, that Hercules' mortal part has been consumed by the fire, while his divine part has risen to heaven? Though Hercules' case was special because of his mortal-divine parentage, it could be seen in antiquity as suggesting the possibility that ordinary mortals' souls might similarly rejoin their proper element, the divine heavens, after release from the body. Such body-soul dualism is not in itself Stoic: it belongs to a much broader current of belief going back to Plato and beyond. But it often appears in Seneca's popular philosophy as an inducement to fighting the good fight on earth. Similarly in *HO* deification rewards Hercules' Stoic endurance on the pyre and, by extension, in the labours.

It would be a mistake, however, to see the play's ending in doctrinaire terms. The idea in *HO* (1565, 1942, 1971) that the soul's ascent is earned by the display of *virtus*/valour in great deeds is also seen, for example, in Cicero's *Dream of Scipio*, in Horace's *Odes* 3.2, and in the famous *sic itur ad astra* of *Aeneid* 9.641. Some such belief is implicit in the Roman practice of deifying emperors after death. Indeed the role of Jupiter's representative on earth, claimed by Hercules in *HO* (3, 1143), was often associated with the position of the emperor. The nexus of ideas bound up with Hercules' deification, then, is part of mainstream Roman cultural thinking under the empire.

The choral odes of this play are attractive, their contemplative lyric tenor contrasting with the *Sturm und Drang* of the Acts. By expressing the viewpoint of ordinary humans rather than *Übermenschen* (note the evocation of childhood in 583–599) and by generalising the tragedy into themes of mutability, mortality, and the fragility of power, the odes enable the audience to see the applicability of the tragedy to their own situation. Ode 3 gains great power by placing the theme of mortality in the mouth of Orpheus, thus evoking while changing such passages as Ode 2 of *Hercules* and the end of Vergil's *Georgics*.

Authorship

Hercules on Oeta differs in many respects from the other plays of the corpus. It repeatedly borrows phrases and echoes passages from the other plays, particularly from *Hercules*. These echoes can enrich the meaning of the drama; often, however, the effect is cento-like, making one wonder whether the author is in command of the material or vice versa. Phrasing is sometimes remarkably awkward; was Latin not the author's first language? The play's scale is unique in the corpus. There is no sense of a "Cloud of Evil" such as hangs over the other plays; on the contrary, the happy ending with its positive Stoic overtones, and the benign light it sheds on what preceded it, is quite foreign to the rest of the corpus. Consequently many authorities believe that *HO* was not written by Seneca. Certain close similarities of phrasing to the poetry of Statius and Silius Italicus may indicate that *HO* was composed in the last decade of the first century A.D. or early in the second century, but this dating is far from certain. On the relationship of *HO* to Seneca's tragedies, see below under "Sources."

Sources

The development of Acts 1–4 runs parallel to that of Sophocles' *Women of Trachis*, but with significant differences. The opening speech is now by Hercules, not Deianira, and raises immediately the issue of deification. Iole and her companions speak of their sufferings at Hercules' hands, whereas in Sophocles they are silent. The Deianira of *HO* is very different from the gentle, wistful woman of Sophocles: modelled on the great passion figures of Seneca's plays such as Medea, she becomes a person at Hercules' own level, at least in the scope of her thinking if not in her strength, as willing to take on Juno's role as he is to take on Jupiter's.

Like Seneca, the *HO* author took full advantage of Ovid's treatments of the myth in question: they included Deianira's letter to Hercules (*Heroides* 9), and the narration of the story, from Hercules' winning of Deianira to his death and apotheosis, in Book 9 of the *Metamorphoses*.

In the composition of Roman poetry the twin imperatives of imitation and emulation often involved borrowing the work of predecessors and incorporating it into a new whole. The relationship of *HO* to Seneca's dramas can be seen as a particular manifestation of this practice. The *HO* author constantly borrows phrases, and remodels passages and scenes, from Seneca's work, but he also goes beyond his model, in the scale of his work and in its positive Stoic message. Similarly he goes beyond Sophocles by including Hercules' death on the pyre and his apotheosis, material which Sophocles had notably avoided. Whether the process of going beyond produces a real advance in this case is a matter of opinion, but certainly it generates a drastically new and intriguing development in the history of ancient drama. It is the last substantial new development in tragedy known to us until Albertino Mussato composed his *Ecerinis* in 1315—likewise in imitation of Seneca.

BIBLIOGRAPHY

J. G. Fitch, "Textual Notes on *Hercules Oetaeus* and on Seneca's *Agamemnon* and *Thyestes*," *CQ* 54 (2004), 240–254.

G. K. Galinsky, *The Herakles Theme* (Oxford, 1972).

R. Nisbet, "The Oak and the Axe: Symbolism in Seneca, *Hercules Oetaeus* 1618ff.," in *Homo Viator: Classical Essays for John Bramble* (Bristol 1987), 243–251.

C. Walde, *Herculeus labor: Studien zum pseudosenecanischen Hercules Oetaeus* (Studien zur klassischen Philologie, 64; Frankfurt am Main 1992).

DRAMATIS PERSONAE

HERCULES, *son of Jupiter and a mortal mother,*
  Alcmene; mightiest hero of Greece
IOLE, *princess of Oechalia, taken captive by Hercules*
NURSE *of Deianira*
DEIANIRA, *wife of Hercules*
HYLLUS, *son of Hercules and Deianira*
ALCMENE, *mother of Hercules*
PHILOCTETES, *one of Hercules' companions*
LICHAS *(persona muta), messenger serving Hercules*
CHORUS *of captive women from Oechalia, accompany-*
  ing Iole
CHORUS *of Aetolian women, attendants of Deianira*

Scene

*Ode 1 is probably set near Iole's sacked city of Oechalia in
Thessaly; the same may be true of Act 1, though its setting
is indeterminate (and immaterial). The rest of the play is
set before Hercules' palace in Trachis, near Mt Oeta.*

HERCULES OETAEUS

Sator deorum, cuius excussum manu
utraeque Phoebi sentiunt fulmen domus,
secure regna: protuli pacem tibi,
quacumque Nereus porrigi terras vetat.
5   non est tonandum: perfidi reges iacent,
saevi tyranni. fregimus quidquid fuit
tibi fulminandum. sed mihi caelum, parens,
adhuc negatur? parui certe Iove
ubique dignus, teque testata est meum
10 patrem noverca. quid tamen nectis moras?
numquid timemur? numquid impositum sibi
non poterit Atlas ferre cum caelo Herculem?
quid astra, genitor, quid negas? mors me tibi
certe remisit, omne concessit malum
15 quod terra genuit, pontus aer inferi.
nullus per urbes errat Argolicas leo,
Stymphalis icta est, Maenali nulla est fera;

16 Argolicas *Jac. Gronovius*: arcadias *EA*

---

1 I.e. in the far east and west, implying "and everywhere in between." Similarly line 4, connoting "on every shore," implies "in every land."

HERCULES ON OETA

ACT 1

HERCULES

Sire of the gods, whose hand launches the thunderbolts
felt by both homes of Phoebus:[1] rule with ease of mind.
I have brought forth peace for you, wherever Nereus
forbids the land to spread further. No need to thunder:
treacherous kings are laid low, and cruel tyrants. I have
crushed all that required your lightning bolt. But father, is
heaven denied me even now? Surely I have proved myself
worthy of Jove the world over; and your fatherhood of me
is attested by my stepmother![2] Why do you nonetheless
weave delays? Can it be that I am feared? Or that Atlas will
be unable to bear the burden of Hercules along with that
of heaven? Why, father, why deny me the stars? Certainly
Death restored me to you;[3] and every evil produced by
earth, sea, air, underworld has surrendered. No lion prowls
through Argive cities, the Stymphalian birds are struck
down, the beast of Maenalus is no more; the serpent spat-

[2] I.e. attested by Juno's persecution of her husband's bastard
son (cf. *Herc* 36).

[3] I.e. Hercules returned from the underworld to the earth and
the sight of heaven.

337

sparsit peremptus aureum serpens nemus,
et hydra vires posuit, et notos Hebro
20 cruore pingues hospitum fregi greges,
hostique traxi spolia Thermodontiae.
vidi silentum fata, nec tantum redî,
sed trepidus atrum Cerberum vidit dies
et ille solem. nullus Antaeus Libys
25 animam resumit, cecidit ante aras suas
Busiris, una Geryon sparsus manu
taurusque populis horridus centum pavor.
quodcumque tellus genuit infesta occidit
meaque fusum est dextera; iratis deis
30 non licuit esse. si negat mundus feras,
animum noverca, redde nunc nato patrem
vel astra forti. nec peto ut monstres iter;
permitte tantum, genitor: inveniam viam.
vel si times ne terra concipiat feras,
35 properet malum quodcumque, dum terra Herculem
habet videtque: nam quis invadet mala
aut quis per urbes rursus Argolicas erit
Iunonis odio dignus?
                              In tutum meas
laudes redegi, nulla me tellus silet:
40 me sensit Ursae frigidum Scythicae genus
Indusque Phoebo subditus, Cancro Libys.
te, clare Titan, testor: occurri tibi

22 silentum *E*: regentem *A*

---

4 The serpent guarded the golden apples of the Hesperides.

tered the golden grove in death,[4] the hydra lost its might. I crushed the herds famed on Hebrus that fattened on the blood of strangers, and I wrested spoils from Thermodon's warlike queen.[5] I saw the fate of the silent dead, and not only did I return, but the daylight quailed at seeing black Cerberus, and he at seeing the Sun. No longer does Libyan Antaeus draw new life; Busiris fell before his own altar; Geryon was spattered by me single-handedly, and the bristling bull, terror of a hundred communities.[6] All that earth engendered in hostility has been felled and mown down by my right hand; the gods were not permitted to be angry![7] If the world denies me wild beasts, and my stepmother her anger, now vouchsafe the father to the son, or heaven to the hero. I do not ask you to show the path; just give permission, father, I shall find the way. Or, if you fear that earth may conceive beasts, let the evil come quickly, whatever it may be, while the earth holds Hercules and sees him: for who will attack evils, or who will ever again be worthy of Juno's hatred throughout Argive cities?

I have made my glory impregnable. Every land speaks of me: the chill tribes of the Scythian Bear have met me, and Indians lying beneath Phoebus, and Libyans beneath the Crab. You shall be my witness, bright Titan: I have en-

[5] The herds were Diomedes' horses; the queen was Hippolyte the Amazon.

[6] Antaeus gained strength by contact with his mother Earth, so Hercules killed him while holding him aloft. "Single-handedly" implies a contrast with the triple-bodied Geryon. The bull was that of Crete, island of a hundred cities.

[7] I.e. they had no occasion to take arms against these monsters, as they did against the Giants.

quacumque fulges, nec meos lux prosequi
potuit triumphos; solis excessi vices
45 intraque nostras substitit metas dies.
natura cessit, terra defecit gradum,
lassata prior est. nox et extremum chaos
in me incucurrit; inde ad hunc orbem redî,
nemo unde retro est. tulimus Oceani minas,
50 nec ulla valuit quatere tempestas ratem
quamcumque pressi. pars quota est Perseus mei!
    Iam vacuus aether non potest odio tuae
sufficere nuptae, quasque devincam feras
tellus timet concipere, nec monstra invenit.
55 ferae negantur: Hercules monstri loco
iam coepit esse. quanta nunc fregi mala,
quot scelera nudus! quidquid immane obstitit,
solae manus stravere; nec iuvenis feras
timui nec infans. quidquid est iussum leve est,
60 nec ulla nobis segnis illuxit dies.
o quanta fudi monstra quae nullus mihi
rex imperavit! institit virtus mihi
Iunone peior.
           Sed quid impavidum genus
fecisse prodest? non habent pacem dei.
65 purgata tellus omnis in caelo videt
quodcumque timuit; transtulit Iuno feras.
ambit peremptus cancer ardentem plagam
Libyaeque sidus fertur et messes alit;
annum fugacem tradit Astraeae leo,
70 at ille, iactans fervidam collo iubam,

---

[8] Perseus was proverbial for travelling far and fast with his

340

countered you wherever you shine—but the light could not keep pace with my triumphs; I outran the sun's orbit, the daylight stopped short of my bounds. Nature gave way, the earth failed my steps and grew tired first. Night and deepest Chaos beset me; yet I returned to this world from the place whence no one returns. I endured the menace of Ocean, and no storm could shake any ship I freighted. How small Perseus looks against me![8]

The emptied sky cannot now meet the needs of your wife's hatred,[9] the earth dare not conceive beasts for me to conquer, and cannot find monsters. Now beasts are denied, Hercules begins to take the place of a monster. What evils, how many crimes, have I now crushed unarmed! These hands unaided have demolished every monstrous opponent; I feared no beasts as man or child.[10] All commands were easy for me, no idle day ever dawned for me. How many monsters I slew without orders from any king![11] My heroism drove me on more relentlessly than Juno.

But what use is it to have made people unafraid? The gods have no peace. The earth, though completely cleansed, sees all that it feared in the heavens; Juno has transferred the beasts! The slain Crab, known as Libya's constellation, goes round the torrid zone and nurtures harvests; the Lion passes the fleeting year on to Astraea[12]— the Lion, who, tossing the blazing mane on his neck, dries

winged sandals. The implication is, "though less of a world-ranger than I, he has entered heaven." [9] The Nemean lion and other beasts were sometimes said to have fallen to earth from the moon. [10] In infancy he crushed the snakes sent against him by Juno. [11] I.e. Eurystheus, the taskmaster of the Labours themselves. [12] I.e. the sun passes from Leo into Virgo.

austrum madentem siccat et nimbos rapit.
invasit omnis ecce iam caelum fera
meque antecessit; victor e terris meos
specto labores! astra portentis prius
75 ferisque Iuno tribuit, ut caelum mihi
faceret timendum. sparserit mundum licet
caelumque terris peius ac peius Styge
irata faciat, dabitur Alcidae locus.
87 Da, da tuendos, Iuppiter, saltem deos.
88 illa licebit fulmen a parte auferas,
89 ego quam tuebor. sive glacialem polum
90 seu me tueri fervidam partem iubes,
91 hac esse superos parte securos puta.
79 Si post feras, post bella, post Stygium canem
80 hauddum astra merui, Siculus Hesperium latus
tangat Pelorus: una iam tellus erit,
illinc fugabo maria. si iungi iubes,
committat undas Isthmos, et iuncto salo
nova ferantur Atticae puppes via.
85 mutetur orbis, vallibus currat novis
86 Hister novasque Tanais accipiat vias.
92   Cirrhaea Paean templa et aetheriam domum
serpente caeso meruit; o quotiens iacet
Python in hydra! Bacchus et Perseus deis
95 iam se intulere; sed quota est mundi plaga
oriens subactus aut quota est Gorgon fera!
quis astra natus laudibus meruit suis
ex te et noverca? quem tuli mundum peto.
    Sed tu, comes laboris Herculei, Licha,

87–91 *placed after* 78 *by Fitch*

342

the damp south wind and carries off the clouds. See, each and every beast has now invaded heaven and forestalled me. Though victor, I gaze from earth at my own Labours! Juno has granted stars to prodigies and beasts first, to make heaven fearful to me. But though she has strewn the sky, and makes heaven worse than earth and worse than Styx in her anger, yet Alcides[13] shall be granted a place. At least grant me, Jove, to *protect* the gods. You may remove your lightning bolt from whatever region I shall protect. Whether you bid me protect the icy pole or the torrid region, consider the gods secure in that region.

Yet if after facing beasts, battles, the hound of Styx, I have not yet earned a place in the stars, let Sicilian Pelorus touch the Hesperian coast: it will be all one land, I shall drive the seas thence. If you bid them be united, let the Isthmus connect up the straits, and let Attic ships travel a new path on the united waters. Let the world be changed, let the Hister run in new valleys and the Tanais accept new channels.

Paean earned a temple at Cirrha and a home in the heavens by slaying the serpent; oh, how many times over was Python slain in the hydra! Bacchus and Perseus have already arrived among the gods; but how small a tract of the earth is the conquered East,[14] how small a fraction of wild beasts is the Gorgon! What son of you and my stepmother has earned a place in the heavens by his worthy deeds? I bore the heavens:[15] now I claim them!

But you, Lichas, companion of Hercules' toils, take

13 Alcides = Hercules.
14 Scene of Bacchus' triumphs.
15 When he relieved Atlas of his burden.

100   perfer triumphos, Euryti victos lares
      stratumque regnum. Vos pecus rapite ocius
      qua templa tollens ora Cenaei Iovis
      aestu timendum spectat Euboicum mare.

CHORUS

      Par ille est superis cui pariter dies
105   et fortuna fuit; mortis habet vices
      lente cum trahitur vita gementibus.
      quisquis sub pedibus fata rapacia
      et puppem posuit fluminis ultimi,
      non captiva dabit bracchia vinculis
110   nec pompae veniet nobile ferculum:
      numquam est ille miser cui facile est mori.
      illum si medio decipiat ratis
      ponto, cum Borean expulit Africus
      aut Eurus Zephyrum, cum mare dividunt,
115   non puppis lacerae fragmina colligit,
      ut litus medio speret in aequore:
      vitam qui poterit reddere protinus,
      solus non poterit naufragium pati.
          Nos turpis macies et lacrimae tenent
120   et crinis patrio pulvere sordidus.
      nos non flamma rapax, non fragor obruit:
      felices sequeris, mors, miseros fugis.
      stamus, sed patriae messibus heu locus
      et silvis dabitur, lapsaque sordidae

      102 ora *Bothe*: ara *EA*
      103 aestu *Axelson*: austro *E*: astro *A*
      123 sed *Gronovius*: nec *EA*   patriae* *A*: patriis *E*   messibus *E*: moenibus* *A*

news of my triumphs, the defeat of Eurytus' house and conquest of his kingdom. [*To other attendants*] You, quickly drive the cattle to where the shore of Cenaean Jove raises his temple, and looks out on the Euboean sea with its fearsome tides.

CHORUS OF OECHALIAN WOMEN

Equal of the gods is one whose days and fortunes
end equally; but a life dragged slowly on,
amidst laments, becomes a kind of death.
Once a person has set beneath his feet the rapacious
fates, and the boat that sails the final river,[16]
he will not yield his wrists to chains as a prisoner,
nor walk in a victor's parade as a signal trophy:
one for whom dying is easy need never suffer.
If his ship betrays him in the midst of the deep,
when the southern wind has driven off the northern,
or the eastern wind the western, as they rend the sea,
he does not gather fragments of his wrecked vessel,
to cling to hope of shore in the midst of ocean.
One who can yield his life without delay
is the only person immune from suffering shipwreck.

But we linger on amid dismal wasting and weeping,
our hair begrimed with the dust of our fatherland.
We were not buried in that greedy, crashing inferno:
death follows the fortunate, but shuns the wretched.
We stand, but the place where our city stood will be
    given
to crops and trees, and its fallen temples will turn

---

[16] I.e. once he has overcome fear of death.

125 fient templa casae; iam gelidus Dolops
hac ducet pecudes qua tepet obrutus
stratae qui superest Oechaliae cinis.
illo Thessalicus pastor in oppido
indocta referens carmina fistula
130 cantu nostra canet tempora flebili;
et dum pauca deus saecula contrahet,
quaeretur patriae quis fuerit locus.
felix incolui non steriles focos
nec ieiuna soli iugera Thessali;
135 ad Trachina vocor, saxa rigentia
et dumeta iugis horrida torridis,
vix gratum pecori montivago nemus.
at si quas melior sors famulas vocat,
illas aut volucer transferet Inachus
140 aut Dircaea colent moenia, qua fluit
Ismenos tenui flumine languidus—
142 hic mater tumidi nupserat Herculis!
147   Falsa est de geminis fabula noctibus,
aether cum tenuit sidera longius
commisitque vices Lucifer Hespero
150 et Solem vetuit Delia tardior.
143 quae cautes Scythiae, quis genuit lapis?
num Titana ferum te Rhodope tulit,
145 te praeruptus Athos, te fera Caspia,
146 quae virgata tibi praebuit ubera?
151 nullis vulneribus pervia membra sunt:

---

17 "Chill" as living by cold Mt Pindus (493)—and in contrast to the warm ash.

18 I.e. they will be sent to Argos or Thebes, two other cities associated with Hercules.

into grubby shacks; the chill Dolopian[17] soon
will drive his livestock here where the buried ash
lies warm, last remnant of Oechalia's fall.
At this famed city's site a Thessalian herdsman,
playing over songs on his untutored pipe,
will sing an elegy for these our times;
and before the gods have sped a few generations,
folk will be asking where our country lay.
I thrived as I dwelt in a far from barren home,
on fruitful acres of Thessalian soil;
but now I am called to Trachis—rugged rocks
and baking hillsides covered in rough bush,
scrubland unfit for mountain-roaming goats.
But those slavewomen called to a better lot
will either cross swift-running Inachus
or dwell within Dircean walls, where flows
sluggish Ismenos with its meagre stream[18]—
where the mother of arrogant Hercules once wed.

  False is the story of the double night[19]
when the heavens kept the stars beyond their time,
when Lucifer's shift ran into that of Hesper
and Delia's tardiness detained the Sun!
What boulder gave you birth, what Scythian crag?
Did Rhodope bring you forth like a wild Titan,
or cliffbound Athos, or some brindled beast[20]
that offered you her teats by the Caspian Sea?
Impervious his limbs to any wound.

[19] After mention of Hercules' mother Alcmene, the chorus rejects the story that Jove fathered Hercules on her during a double night.

[20] A tigress.

ferrum sentit hebes, lentior est chalybs;
in nudo gladius corpore frangitur
et saxum resilit, fataque neglegit
155 et mortem indomito pectore provocat.
non illum poterant figere cuspides,
non arcus Scythica tensus harundine,
non quae tela gerit Sarmata frigidus
aut qui soliferae suppositus plagae
160 vicino Nabatae vulnera derigit
Parthus Cnosiacis certior ictibus.

    Muros Oechaliae corpore propulit;
nil obstare valet. vincere quod parat
iam victum est—quota pars vulnere concidit!
165 pro fato potuit vultus iniquior,
et vidisse sat est Herculeas minas.
quis vastus Briareus, quis tumidus Gyges,
supra Thessalicum cum stetit aggerem
caeloque insereret vipereas manus,
170 hoc vultu riguit? commoda cladibus
magnis magna patent: nil superest mali,
iratum miserae vidimus Herculem.

IOLE

At ego infelix
non templa suis collapsa deis
sparsosve focos,
175 natis mixtos arsisse patres
hominique deos, templa sepulcris—
nullum querimur commune malum.

---

155 pectore *L. Müller*: corpore *EA*
167 Gyges *Ascensius*: gigas* *EA* (*cf.* 1139)

He senses iron as dull, steel is too soft;
a sword is shattered on his unarmed body,
a rock rebounds. He scorns the power of fate
and challenges death with his unconquered breast.
He never could be pierced by sharpened spears
nor Scythian shafts discharged from tautened bows
nor arrows that the chill Sarmatian bears
or Parthians, set beneath the zone of dawn,
who train wounds on their Nabataean neighbours
and strike more surely than any Cretan archer.
    His body's thrust pushed down Oechalia's walls;
nothing could stand in his way. What he planned to
    conquer
was as good as conquered—How few fell to his wounds!
His angry visage carried a power like death;
to have seen the threatening Hercules was enough.
What giant Briareus or swollen Gyges,
standing on mountains piled in Thessaly
and reaching snaky hands towards the sky,
glared so ferociously? Yet from great disasters
great gains emerge: no further evil remains,
we have seen the anger of Hercules to our sorrow.

IOLE

But my sad theme
is not temples fallen on their gods
or hearths demolished,
the burning of fathers together with sons,
gods with men, temples with tombs:
no shared disaster is my lament.

alio nostras fortuna vocat
lacrimas, alias flere ruinas
180   mea fata iubent.
quae prima querar? quae summa gemam?
pariter cunctos deflere iuvat,
nec plura dedit pectora sexus,
ut digna sonent verbera fatis.
185   Me vel Sipyli flebile saxum
fingite, superi,
vel in Eridani ponite ripis,
ubi maesta sonat
Phaethontiadum silva sororum;
me vel Siculis addite saxis,
190   ubi fata gemam Thessala Siren,
vel in Edonas tollite silvas,
qualis natum Daulias ales
solet Ismaria flere sub umbra.
formam lacrimis aptate meis
195   resonetque malis aspera Trachin.
Cypria lacrimas Myrrha tuetur,
raptum coniunx Ceyca gemit,
sibi Tantalis est facta superstes;
fugit vultus Philomela suos
200   natumque sonat flebilis Atthis:
cur mea nondum

182 cunctos *Peiper*: cuncta *A*: *omitted by E*
183 sexus *Fitch*: tellus *EA*
185 siphili *PT*: sisiphi *CS*: si syphum *E*

21 Like Niobe.

Fortune directs my tears elsewhere,
my destiny bids me weep for ruin
of a different kind.
What first shall I mourn? What grieve for last?
I want to weep for all together,
but my sex did not grant me breasts enough
to resound with blows worthy of my fate.
    Into a weeping rock on Sipylus[21]
transform me, gods;
or set me on Eridanus' banks
where sadly sigh
the woodland trees, Phaethon's sisters;[22]
or add me to those on Sicily's rocks
to keen my fate, a Thessalian Siren;
or bear me into Edonian forests
like the Daulian bird[23] that ever weeps
for her son in the shade of Ismarian trees.
Give me a form to match my tears,
and let rough Trachis re-echo my woes.
Cyprian Myrrha keeps her tears,[24]
the wife of Ceyx still mourns his loss,
the Tantalid became her own survivor,
Philomela escaped her rightful form
and the Attic mourner laments her son.
Why do *my* arms

[22] Transformed into poplars while grieving for Phaethon.
[23] Procne, here transformed to a nightingale.
[24] I.e. the drops of gum resin from the myrrh tree into which she was transformed. Alcyone (197) metamorphosed into a halcyon, Niobe (198) into a rock, Philomela and Procne (199–200) into birds.

351

capiunt volucres bracchia plumas?
felix, felix,
cum silva domus nostra feretur
patrioque sedens ales in agro
205 referam querulo murmure casus
volucremque Iolen fama loquetur.
    Vidi, vidi
miseranda mei fata parentis,
cum letifero stipite pulsus
tota iacuit sparsus in aula;
210 pro, si tumulum fata dedissent,
quotiens, genitor, quaerendus eras!
potuine tuam spectare necem,
nondum teneras vestite genas
necdum forti sanguine, Toxeu?
215   Quid vestra queror fata, parentes,
quos in tutum mors aequa tulit?
mea me lacrimas fortuna rogat:
iam iam dominae captiva colos
fusosque legam.
pro saeve decor
220 formaque mortem paritura mihi,
tibi cuncta domus concidit uni,
dum me genitor negat Alcidae
atque Herculeus socer esse timet.
Sed iam dominae tecta petantur.

CHORUS

225 Quid regna tui clara parentis
proavosque tuos respicis amens?

226 proavosque *A*: casusque *E*

not yet transform to feathered wings?
Happy, happy
shall I be when the woodland is called my home,
and alighting as a bird in my native fields
I recount my ruin in plaintive tones,
and fame shall speak of winged Iole.
    I saw, I saw
the pitiful fate my father met:
struck by that death-bearing club
his body lay spattered throughout the hall.
Ah, if fate had granted you burial
how repeated the search would have been for you,
    father!
Could I bear to watch *your* butchery,
your cheeks still tender, not yet bearded,
and your heartblood not yet valiant, Toxeus?
    But why lament my family's fate,
when kindly death has borne them to safety?
My own fortune calls for tears from me.
Soon as a captive I shall spin the distaff
and spindle for my mistress.
Ah, cruel beauty,
lovely form that will bring forth death for me:
for you alone my whole house fell
as my father refused me to Alcides,
afraid to be Hercules' kin by marriage.
But now I must make for my lady's house.

CHORUS

Why look back on your ancestry
and the glorious throne of your father? Folly!

[SENECA]

fugiat vultus fortuna prior.
felix quisquis novit famulum
regemque pati
230   vultusque suos variare potest.
rapuit vires pondusque mali
casus animo qui tulit aequo.

NUTRIX

O quam cruentus feminas stimulat furor,
cum patuit una paelici et nuptae domus!
235   Scylla et Charybdis Sicula contorquens freta
minus est timenda, nulla non melior fera est.
namque ut reluxit paelicis captae decus
et fulsit Iole qualis innubis dies
purisve clarum noctibus sidus micat,
240   stetit furenti similis ac torvum intuens
Herculea coniunx, feta ut Armenia iacens
sub rupe tigris hoste conspecto exilit,
aut iussa thyrsum quatere conceptum ferens
Maenas Lyaeum dubia quo gressus agat
245   haesit parumper. tum per Herculeos lares
attonita fertur, tota vix satis est domus;
incurrit, errat, sistit, in vultus dolor
processit omnis, pectori paene intimo
nihil est relictum; fletus insequitur minas.
250   nec unus habitus durat aut uno furit
contenta vultu: nunc inardescunt genae,
pallor ruborem pellit et formas dolor
errat per omnes; queritur implorat gemit.

246 attonita fertur *E*: lymphata rapitur *A*

354

Your bearing must renounce your former fortunes.
Happy are those who can endure
to be slave or king
and adjust their bearing accordingly.
To bear misfortunes with a tranquil mind
robs hardship of its strength and weight.

ACT 2

NURSE

What a bloodthirsty rage there is that goads women when a
single house is opened to a mistress as well as a wife! Scylla
and Charybdis, churning the Sicilian strait, are not more
fearsome, no wild beast is worse. When the captive mistress' beauty shone forth—Iole shimmering like the gleam
of unclouded daylight or a bright star in the clear night—
Hercules' wife stood like a madwoman, glaring grimly. She
resembled a whelped tigress, lying beneath a crag in Armenia, that leaps up at sight of the foe; or a Maenad, called
to brandish the thyrsus, quickened and ridden by Lyaeus,
who hesitates briefly, unsure where to direct her steps.
Then she rushed in frenzy through Hercules' house, the
whole building scarcely giving room enough; she charged
forward, swerved, stopped. All her pain came into her face,
almost nothing was left hidden in her breast. Tears followed hard on threats. No single attitude lasted long, no
single expression of rage satisfied her: now her cheeks
flamed, now pallor expelled the colour. Her pain ranged
through every possible form, she lamented, entreated,
groaned.

Sonuere postes; ecce praecipiti gradu
255 secreta mentis ore confuso exerit.

DEIANIRA

Quamcumque partem sedis aetheriae premis,
coniunx Tonantis, mitte in Alciden feram
quae mihi satis sit! si qua fecundum caput
palude tota vastior serpens movet,
260 ignara vinci, si quid excessit feras
immane dirum horribile, quo viso Hercules
avertat oculos, hoc specu immenso exeat.
vel si ferae negantur, hanc animam, precor,
converte in aliquod—quodlibet possum malum
265 hac mente fieri. commoda effigiem mihi
parem dolori: non capit pectus minas.
quid excutis telluris extremae sinus
orbemque versas? quid rogas Ditem mala?
omnes in isto pectore invenies feras
270 quas timeat: odiis accipe hoc telum tuis,
272 perfer manus quocumque. quid cessas, dea?
utere furente! quod iubes fieri nefas?
274 peperi, quid haeres? ipsa iam cesses licet:
271 ego sum noverca perdere Alciden potens;
275 haec ira satis est.

NUTRIX

Pectoris sani parum,
alumna, questus comprime et flammas doma,
frena dolorem. coniugem ostende Herculis.

270 timeat *A*: timuit *E*
271 *placed after* 274 *by Fitch*   potens *Bentley*: potes *EA*
274 peperi *EA*: reperi *recc.*

A sound from the doors! See, she is rushing headlong, flinging out her mind's secrets in confused words.

DEIANIRA

Wife of the Thunderer: wherever you stand in the heavenly abode, send against Alcides a beast that will satisfy *me*! If some snaky creature lifts its prolific heads, invincible and vaster than a whole marsh[25]—or if there is something that surpasses beasts, something monstrous, dreadful, terrible, a sight to make Hercules avert his eyes—let it come from its vast lair! Or if beasts are denied, change this spirit into something, I pray; in this mood I can be made into anything at all. Provide me with a shape to match my pain; this breast cannot contain all its menace. Why search the remotest ends of the earth and ransack the world? Why ask Dis for evils? In this breast you will find every wild thing for him to fear: accept it as the instrument of your hatred. Convey my hands anywhere you wish. Why hold back, goddess? Use my rage! What enormity do you bid occur? I have given birth![26] Why are you at a loss? You yourself may hold back now: I am a stepmother who *can* destroy Hercules;[27] this anger of mine suffices.

NURSE

Your heart is scarcely sane, my child: restrain its outcry, quench its flames, bridle its pain. Show yourself the wife of Hercules.

[25] I.e. a superior form of the hydra.

[26] I.e. I am mature and capable of anything (cf. *Med* 50 "Greater crimes become me now, after giving birth").

[27] I.e. in contrast to Juno herself. Deianira is "stepmother" to Hercules' bastard child Lamus (Ovid, *Heroides* 9.54).

DEIANIRA

Iole meis captiva germanos dabit
natis, Iovisque fiet ex famula nurus?
280 num flamma cursus pariter et torrens feret
et Ursa pontum sicca caeruleum bibet?
non ibo inulta. gesseris caelum licet
totusque pacem debeat mundus tibi,
est aliquid hydra peius: iratae dolor
285 nuptae. quis ignis tantus in caelum furit
ardentis Aetnae? quidquid est victum tibi
hic vincet animus. capta praeripiet toros?
adhuc timebam monstra; iam nullum est malum,
cessere pestes, in locum venit ferae
290 invisa paelex.
            Summe pro rector deum
et clare Titan, Herculis tantum fui
coniunx timentis; vota quae superis tuli
cessere captae, paelici felix fui,
illi meas audistis, o superi, preces,
295 incolumis illi remeat! o nulla dolor
contente poena, quaere supplicia horrida,
incogitata, infanda, Iunonem doce
quid odia valeant: nescit irasci satis.
      Pro me gerebas bella, propter me vagas
300 Achelous undas sanguine infecit suo,
cum lenta serpens fieret, in taurum trucem
nunc flecteret serpente deposita minas,
et mille in hoste vinceres uno feras.
iam displicemus, capta praelata est mihi.
305 —non praeferetur: qui dies thalami ultimus
nostri est futurus, hic erit vitae tuae.
      Quid hoc? recedit animus et ponit minas,

DEIANIRA

Shall Iole the captive produce brothers for my sons? Shall a slave become daughter-in-law to Jove? Can it be that fire and torrent will take the same course, or the dry Bear drink of the deep-blue sea? I shall not go unavenged. Though you have borne the heavens and the whole world owes its peace to you, there is something worse than a hydra: the pain of an angry wife. Does any fire as great as that rage toward heaven from burning Etna? Anything you have conquered, this spirit will conquer. Is a mistress to steal my marriage bed? I was still fearing monsters, but now such evils are no more, scourges have vanished, and in place of a beast has come this hateful mistress.

In the name of the gods' high ruler and the bright Titan! I was Hercules' wife only in his danger, the vows I offered the gods worked for the captive, I was successful for the mistress; for her you gods heard my prayers, for her he returns unscathed. O pain that no vengeance can satisfy, look for horrible, unthought-of, unspeakable punishments! Teach Juno the power of hate: she is incapable of sufficient anger.

You used to wage war for me; it was on my account that Achelous stained his meandering stream with his blood, when he turned into a lithe serpent, then dropped the serpent and changed his menace to that of a grim bull: you conquered a thousand beasts in one enemy! Now I no longer please you; a captive is preferred to me. But she shall not be preferred: the last day of our marriage will be the last of your life.

What is this? My spirit is retreating, dropping its men-

iam cessat ira. quid miser langues dolor?
perdis furorem, coniugis tacitae fidem
310 mihi reddis iterum. quid vetas flammas ali?
quid frangis ignes? hunc mihi serva impetum,
pares eamus. non erit votis opus:
aderit noverca quae manus nostras regat
nec invocata.

NUTRIX

Quod paras demens scelus?
315 perimes maritum, cuius extremus dies
primusque laudes novit et caelo tenus
erecta terras fama suppositas habet?
Argea in istos terra consurget lares,
domusque soceri prima et Aetolum genus
320 sternetur omne, saxa iam dudum ac faces
in te ferentur, vindicem tellus suum
defendet omnis: una quot poenas dabis!
effugere terras crede et humanum genus
te posse: fulmen genitor Alcidae gerit!
325 iam iam minaces ire per caelum faces
specta et tonantem fulmine excusso diem.
mortem quoque ipsam, quam putes tutam, time:
dominatur illic patruus Alcidae tui.
quocumque perges, misera, cognatos deos
330 illi videbis.

DEIANIRA

Maximum fieri scelus
et ipsa fateor, sed dolor fieri iubet.

309 tacitae *E*: sanctae* *A*
318 Argea *Fitch*: angor *E*: rogos *A*

ace, my anger ebbing. My sorry pain, why are you flagging? You are losing rage, and returning me once more to the loyalty of a wife who keeps silent. Why do you stop the flames being fed? Why allay the fire? Maintain this impetus I have now, let us advance side by side. There will be no need of prayers: a stepmother will stand by to guide my hands, without being invoked.

NURSE

What mad crime are you planning? Will you murder this husband, whose renown is known where the day begins and ends, whose glory is raised far above the earth and reaches heaven? The Argive land will quickly rise up against your home: first your father's house[28] and all the folk of Aetolia will be destroyed, and straightway rocks and firebrands will be aimed at you; the whole world will support its champion. One woman suffering so many punishments! But suppose you can evade the earth and the human race: Alcides' father wields the lightning! Watch dangerous bolts immediately crossing the heavens, and the sky thundering as the lightning is launched. Even death itself, which you might think safe, you must fear: your Alcides' uncle[29] is lord there. Wherever you travel, poor woman, you will see gods related to him.

DEIANIRA

I myself admit that it is an enormous crime, but my pain insists on it.

---

[28] Lit. "the house of his father-in-law," i.e. Deianira's father Oeneus.   [29] Dis, brother of Jupiter.

---

[327] putes *Zwierlein*: putas *EA*   [330] illi *Gronovius*: illic *EA*

NUTRIX

Moriere.

DEIANIRA

Moriar Herculis nempe incliti
coniunx, nec ullus nocte discussa dies
viduam notabit, nec meos paelex toros
335   captiva capiet. ante ab occasu dies
nascetur, Indos ante glacialis polus
Scythasve tepida Phoebus inficiet rota,
quam me relictam Thessalae inspiciant nurus.
meo iugales sanguine extinguam faces.
340   aut pereat aut me perimat. elisis feris
et coniugem addat, inter Herculeos licet
me quoque labores numeret: Alcidae toros
moritura certe corpore amplectar meo.
ire, ire ad umbras Herculis nuptam libet,
345   sed non inultam: si quid ex nostro Hercule
concepit Iole, manibus evellam meis
ante et per ipsas paelicem invadam faces.
me nuptiali victimam feriat die
infestus, Iolen dum supra exanimem ruam:
350   felix iacet quicumque quos odit premit.

NUTRIX

Quid ipsa flammas pascis et vastum foves
ultro dolorem? misera, quid cassum times?
dilexit Iolen nempe cum staret parens
regisque natam peteret. in famulae locum
355   regina cecidit; perdidit vires amor

344 herculis nuptam libet *E*: herculi iunctam licet *A*
353 cum staret parens *E*: dum starent lares *A*

NURSE

You will die!

DEIANIRA

I shall die, you see, as wife of the glorious Hercules. No day as it dispels night will see me husbandless, and no captive mistress will capture my marriage rights. Sooner shall daylight be born from the west, sooner shall the icy pole colour Indians' skin, or Phoebus colour Scythians with his chariot's warmth, than young Thessalian brides will behold me abandoned. I shall quench the marriage torches with my own blood. He must either be killed or kill me. Let him add his wife to the beasts he has crushed, let him count me among the Herculean labours: be sure that I shall cling to Alcides' marriage bed with my dying body. I am glad to go to the shades as Hercules' bride—but not without taking revenge! First, if Iole has conceived some by-blow from Hercules, I shall drag it out with my own hands, strike at his mistress amidst her marriage torches. Let him smite me in anger as the sacrifice on his wedding day, so long as I can fall on the lifeless Iole! To crush those one hates is to lie happy in death.

NURSE

Why do you feed the flames and deliberately foster your swelling pain? Poor soul, why endure pointless fear? He loved Iole, you see, when her father prospered and he was wooing a king's daughter. But the princess has fallen to a slave's status; love has lost its power, and her abject posi-

multumque ab illa traxit infelix status.
illicita amantur, excidit quidquid licet.

DEIANIRA

Fortuna amorem peior inflammat magis.
amat vel ipsum quod caret patrio lare,
360   quod nudus auro crinis et gemma iacet—
ipsas misericors forsan aerumnas amat.
hoc usitatum est Herculi: captas amat.

NUTRIX

Dilecta Priami nempe Dardanii soror
concessa famula est; adice quot nuptas prius,
365   quot virgines dilexit: erravit vagus.
Arcadia nempe virgo, Palladios choros
dum nectit, Auge, vim stupri passa excidit,
nullamque amoris retinet Herculei notam.
referam quid alias? nempe Thespiades vacant,
370   brevique in illas arsit Alcides face.
hospes Timoli Lydiam fovit nurum
et amore captus ad leves sedit colos,
tenerum feroci stamen intorquens manu.
nempe illa cervix spolia deposuit ferae
375   crinemque mitra pressit et famulus stetit,
hirtam Sabaea marcidus myrrha comam.
ubique caluit, sed levi caluit face.

DEIANIRA

Haerere amantes post vagos ignes solent.

368 retinet herculei *A*: retinet herculis *E*: Hercules retinet *Leo*
373 tenerum *Birt*: colum *E*: unum *A*

tion has devalued her greatly. The unattainable is loved, the attainable is disregarded.

DEIANIRA

No, a fall from fortune makes love burn hotter. He loves the very fact that she is homeless, that her hair lies stripped of gold and gems. Perhaps he loves her very troubles out of compassion. This is customary with Hercules: he loves captive women.

NURSE

He loved the sister of Dardanian Priam[30]—but gave her up as a slave, you see. Think too of all the brides and maidens he has loved previously. He has been a roving wanderer! The Arcadian girl Auge, you see, weaver of dances in Pallas' honour, was forgotten after suffering his rape; she retains no vestige of Hercules' love. Why mention others? Thespius' daughters are clear, you see, and Alcides' flame of passion for them was short-lived. When a guest on Tmolus he fondled the young Lydian woman,[31] and sat as love's captive at the light distaff, twisting the soft thread with his fierce hand. He took the beast-spoil off that famous neck, you see, bound his hair in a turban and stood as a slave, his shaggy hair limp with Sabaean myrrh. He has burned with love everywhere, but burned with an inconstant flame.

DEIANIRA

But after wandering in their passions, lovers usually cleave to one.

[30] Hesione.
[31] Omphale.

NUTRIX

Famulamne et hostis praeferet natam tibi?

DEIANIRA

380   Ut alta silvas forma vernantes habet,
quas nemore nudo primus investit tepor,
at cum solutos expulit Boreas Notos
et saeva totas bruma discussit comas,
deforme solis aspicis truncis nemus:
385   sic nostra longum forma percurrens iter
deperdit aliquid semper et fulget minus,
nec illa venus est. quidquid in nobis fuit
olim petitum cecidit, et pariter soror
materque multum rapuit ex illo mihi,
390   aetas citato senior eripiet gradu.
vides ut altum famula non perdat decus?
cessere cultus penitus et paedor sedet;
tamen per ipsas fulget aerumnas decor
nihilque ab illa casus et fatum grave
395   nisi regna traxit. hic meum pectus timor,
altrix, lacessit, hic rapit somnos pavor.
praeclara totis gentibus coniunx eram
thalamosque nostros invido voto nurus
optabat omnis, quae nimis quicquam deos
400   orabat ullos: nuribus Argolicis fui
mensura voti. quem Iovi socerum parem,
altrix, habebo? quis sub hoc mundo mihi
dabitur maritus? ipse qui Alcidae imperat
facibus suis me iungat Eurystheus licet,

---

380 alta *EA*: laeta *Bentley*   383 discussit *E*: decussit *A*
388 pariter soror *Fitch*: pariter labat *E*: partu labat *A*

NURSE

Will he prefer a slave, an enemy's daughter, to you?

DEIANIRA

As a high beauty fills the springtime trees, when the first
warm days clothe them in the naked forest; but when the
norther has driven away the languid south winds, and
fierce winter has scattered all the foliage, you see the forest
without beauty, its trunks exposed: so our beauty, as it runs
its long course, always suffers some loss and shines less
brightly, without that attractiveness it used to have. All that
was once desirable in me is diminished; sisterhood[32] and
motherhood both stole much of it from me, and much will
be stolen by quickly advancing age. But you see how this
slave has not lost her high grace. She is completely without
adornment, covered in grime, yet her loveliness shines
through her very troubles; chance and harsh fate have
taken nothing from her except her realm. This is the fear
that besets my heart, nurse, this is the dread that robs me
of sleep. I used to be famed as a wife among all nations;
every young woman that asked intensely for anything from
any gods would long for my marriage with envy in her
prayers; for Argive women's prayers, I was the standard!
What father-in-law shall I have to equal Jove? What such
husband will be given me under this sky? Though Eurystheus himself, who gives Alcides orders, should take me in

---

[32] She and Meleager's other sisters were grief-stricken by his
death (Ovid, *Metamorphoses* 8.533–546).

---

390 eripiet *Grotius*: eripuit *EA*
399 quae* nimis *A*: quaeve mens *E*

405 minus est. toris caruisse regnantis leve est;
alte illa cecidit quae viro caret Hercule.

NUTRIX

Conciliat animos coniugum partus fere.

DEIANIRA

Hic ipse forsan dividet partus toros.

NUTRIX

Famula illa trahitur interim donum tibi.

DEIANIRA

410 Hic quem per urbes ire praeclarum vides
et viva tergo spolia gestantem ferae,
qui regna miseris donat et celsis rapit
vasta gravatus horridam clava manum,
cuius triumphos ultimi Seres canunt
415 et quisquis alius orbe consaepto iacet,
levis est, nec illum gloriae stimulat decor.
errat per orbem, non ut aequetur Iovi
nec ut per urbes magnus Argolicas eat:
quod amet requirit, virginum thalamos petit.
420 si qua est negata, rapitur; in populos furit,
nuptas ruinis quaerit et vitium impotens
virtus vocatur. cecidit Oechalia inclita,
unusque Titan vidit atque unus dies
stantem et cadentem; causa bellandi est amor.
425 totiens timebit Herculi natam parens
quotiens negabit, hostis est quotiens socer
fieri recusat; si gener non est, ferit.

---

415 consepto *recc.*: concepto A *(407–439 omitted by E)*

marriage, it would be a falling-off. Not to have been wife of a ruler is a slight thing; to lose Hercules as one's husband is to fall far.

NURSE

Having children generally secures husbands' affection.

DEIANIRA

Perhaps in this case having children[33] will itself break up the marriage.

NURSE

But for now she is hauled here as a slave, a gift to you.

DEIANIRA

This man you see marching through cities in glory, wearing the living[34] spoil from the beast on his back, who grants thrones to the oppressed and takes them from the mighty, his rugged hand burdened with the massive club, whose triumphs are sung by the remote Seres and whoever else lies at the world's edge—he is a trifler, not spurred by the attraction of renown. He wanders through the world, not in order to match Jove, nor to walk tall through Argive cities: he is searching for love objects, looking for girls to bed. If any is denied him, he takes her by force; he rages against whole peoples, seeks out brides amid destruction. And this uncontrolled vice is called heroism! Famous Oechalia fell, a single day's sun saw it standing and falling: the cause of war was love. Whenever a parent denies Hercules his daughter, he must be afraid; anyone who refuses to be his father-in-law is his foe; if he is not son-in-law, he strikes.

---

[33] I.e. by Iole.   [34] Primarily meaning that, unlike most spoils, this one is "natural, not manmade," but also suggesting that the pelt looks lifelike when worn.

Post haec quid istas innocens servo manus?
donec furentem simulet ac saeva manu
430   intendat arcus meque natumque opprimat?
sic coniuges expellit Alcides suas,
haec sunt repudia. nec potest fieri nocens:
terris videri sceleribus causam suis
fecit novercam. quid stupes segnis, furor?
435   scelus occupandum est: perge, dum fervet manus.

NUTRIX

Perimes maritum?

DEIANIRA
Paelicis certe meae.

NUTRIX

At Iove creatum.

DEIANIRA
Nempe et Alcmena satum.

NUTRIX

Ferrone?

DEIANIRA
Ferro.

NUTRIX
Si nequis?

DEIANIRA
Perimam dolo.

NUTRIX

Quis iste furor est?

After all this, why am I keeping my hands free of guilt? Waiting for the time when he feigns madness, levels his bow with that cruel hand and overwhelms me and my son?[35] This is how Alcides throws out his wives, this is his style of divorce! And nothing can make him guilty: he has made the world believe the cause of his crimes is his stepmother. Why dazed and idle, my rage? In crime one must strike first. Go ahead, while your hand is hot!

NURSE

You will kill this husband?

DEIANIRA

My rival's? Certainly!

NURSE

But one fathered by Jove.

DEIANIRA

Begotten by Alcmene too, you see.

NURSE

With the sword?

DEIANIRA

The sword.

NURSE

If you cannot?

DEIANIRA

I shall kill by guile.

NURSE

What is this rage?

---

[35] As he did with Megara and her sons.

DEIANIRA

Quem meus coniunx docet.

NUTRIX

440 Quem nec noverca potuit, hunc perimes virum?

DEIANIRA

Caelestis ira quos premit, miseros facit:
humana nullos.

NUTRIX

Parce, miseranda, et time.

DEIANIRA

Contempsit omnes ille qui mortem prius;
libet ire in enses.

NUTRIX

Maior admisso tuus,
445 alumna, dolor est; culpa par odium exigat.
cur saeva modicis statuis? ut laesa es, dole.

DEIANIRA

Leve esse credis paelicem nuptae malum?
quidquid dolorem pascit, hoc nimium puta.

NUTRIX

Amorne clari fugit Alcidae tibi?

DEIANIRA

450 Non fugit, altrix, remanet et penitus sedet
fixus medullis, crede; sed magnus dolor
iratus amor est.

DEIANIRA

What my husband teaches.

NURSE

Will you kill a hero not even his stepmother could kill?

DEIANIRA

Heavenly anger plagues its targets, human anger destroys them.

NURSE

Hold back, you pitiable woman, in fear.

DEIANIRA

One who scorns death first, scorns all. I want to charge against swords!

NURSE

Your pain, my child, is too great for the fault. An offence should not arouse more than its share of hate. Why judge something ordinary so fiercely? Let your pain match your injury!

DEIANIRA

You think a mistress is a trivial wrong to a wife? What you should consider excessive is what feeds the pain.[36]

NURSE

Has your love for glorious Alcides vanished?

DEIANIRA

Not vanished, nurse; it remains rooted deep in my bones, believe me. But anger in love is a source of great pain.

---

[36] I.e. its cause, Hercules' infidelity.

[SENECA]

NUTRIX

Artibus magicis fere
coniugia nuptae precibus admixtis ligant.
vernare iussi frigore in medio nemus
455 missumque fulmen stare; concussi fretum
cessante vento, turbidum explicui mare
et sicca tellus fontibus patuit novis.
habuere motum saxa, discussi fores
umbrasque Ditis, et mea iussi prece
460 manes loquuntur, siluit infernus canis;
[mare terra caelum et Tartarus servit mihi]
nox media solem vidit et noctem dies,
nihilque leges ad meos cantus tenet.
flectemus illum, carmina invenient iter.

DEIANIRA

465 Quas Pontus herbas generat aut quas Thessala
sub rupe Pindus, aut ubi inveniam malum
cui cedat ille? carmine in terras mago
descendat astris Luna desertis licet
et bruma messes videat et cantu fugax
470 stet deprehensum fulmen et versa vice
medius coactis ferveat stellis dies,
nil flectet illum.

459 umbrasque Ditis *Richter*: umbrae stetistis *EA*
460 siluit *Axelson*: sonuit *A*: novit *E*
461 *omitted by* E: *placed after* 462 *by Bothe*: *deleted by Fitch*
466 aut ubi *A*: aluit ubi *E*
472 nil *Fitch*: non *EA*

---

37 Line 461 (deleted): "Sea, land, heaven, and Tartarus serve
me."

374

NURSE

Wives often bind their spouses by magic arts combined
with prayers. I have bidden trees to burgeon in midwinter,
and the thunderbolt to halt in flight; I have stirred up the
straits when the wind was still, and levelled a turbulent
sea; in the dry earth new springs have opened; rocks have
started to move; I have shattered the doors and darkness of
Dis; at the bidding of my prayers the shades spoke and the
infernal dog fell silent;[37] midnight has seen the sun, and
the day night, and at my chants nothing keeps its nature.[38]
We shall change his heart, the spells will find a way.

DEIANIRA

What herbs are engendered in Pontus or beneath crags on
Thessalian Pindus, or where could I find a bane to master
him? Though the moon might abandon the stars through
magic and descend to earth, and winter see harvests, and
the winging thunderbolt halt intercepted by a spell, and
the midday sky blaze unnaturally with stars under con-
straint, nothing will change his heart.

---

[38] These claims to supernatural power are echoed in Chapman, *Byron's Conspiracy* II.1.114–127: "And tell him this too: if in
midst of winter / To make black groves grow green, to still the
thunder / And cast out able flashes from mine eyes, / To beat the
lightning back into the skies, / Prove power to do it, I can make it
good. / And tell him this too: if to lift the sea / Up to the stars, when
all the winds are still, / And keep it calm, when they are most enraged, / To make earth's driest plains sweat humorous springs, / To
make fixed rocks walk and loose shadows stand, / To make the
dead speak, midnight see the sun, / Midday turn midnight, to dissolve all laws / Of nature and of order, argue power / Able to work
all, I can make all good."

NUTRIX
Vicit et superos Amor.

DEIANIRA
Vincetur uni forsan et spolium dabit
Amorque summus fiet Alcidae labor.
475   sed te per omne caelitum numen precor,
per hunc timorem: quidquid arcani apparo
penitus recondas et fide tacita premas.

NUTRIX
Quid istud est quod esse secretum petis?

DEIANIRA
Non tela sunt, non arma, non ignis minax.

NUTRIX
480   Praestare fateor posse me tacitam fidem,
si scelere careat: interim scelus est fides.

DEIANIRA
Circumspice agedum, ne quis arcana aucupet,
partemque in omnem vultus inquirens eat.

NUTRIX
En locus ab omni tutus arbitrio vacat.

DEIANIRA
485   Est in remoto regiae sedis loco
arcana tacitus nostra defendens specus.
non ille primos accipit soles locus,
non ille seros, cum premens Titan diem
lassam rubenti mergit Oceano rotam.

482 aucupet *Scaliger*: occupet *EA*
488 premens *Axelson*: ferens *EA*

376

NURSE

Love has conquered even the gods.[39]

DEIANIRA

Perhaps it will be conquered and plundered by this one man, and Love become Alcides' final labour! But I pray you by every single divinity, and by this my fear: any occult preparations I make you must conceal completely and wrap in loyal silence.

NURSE

What is it you want kept secret?

DEIANIRA

Not weapons, not arms, not menacing fire.

NURSE

I agree that I can offer loyal silence, provided no crime is involved; but sometimes loyalty is criminal.

DEIANIRA

Come, look around, lest someone eavesdrop on the secret; cast your gaze attentively in each direction.

NURSE

See, the place is clear and safe from any observation.

DEIANIRA

In a remote corner of the royal demesne there is a hidden cave that guards my secret. That corner does not receive the sun's first rays, nor its last, when the Titan, closing the day, sinks his weary chariot in the crimson Ocean.

---

[39] And equally a love potion will be able to conquer Hercules.

490 illic amoris pignus Herculei latet.
altrix, fatebor: auctor est Nessus mali
quem gravida Nephele Thessalo genuit duci,
qua gelidus astris inserit Pindus caput
ultraque nubes Othrys eductus riget.
495 namque ut subactus Herculis clava horridi
Achelous, omnes facilis in species dari,
tandem peractis omnibus patuit feris
unoque turpe subdidit cornu caput,
me coniugem dum victor Alcides habet,
500 repetebat Argos. forte per campos vagus
Evenos altum gurgitem in pontum ferens
iam paene summis turbidus ripis erat.
transire Nessus verticem solitus vadis
pretium poposcit; meque iam dorso ferens
505 qua iungit hominem spina deficiens equo,
frangebat ipsas fluminis tumidi minas.
    Iam totus undis Nessus exierat ferox
medioque adhuc errabat Alcides vado,
vasto rapacem verticem scindens gradu;
510 ast ille, ut esse vidit Alciden procul,
"Tu praeda nobis" inquit "et coniunx eris;
prohibetur undis," meque complexu ferens
gressum citabat. non tenent undae Herculem:
"Infide vector," inquit "immixti licet
515 Ganges et Hister vallibus iunctis eant,
vincemus ambos, consequar telo fugam."
praecessit arcus verba; tum longum ferens
harundo vulnus tenuit haerentem fugam

493 gelidus *Axelson*: trepidus *E*: celsus *A*
502 ripis *A*: silvis *E*

378

There lies concealed a surety of Hercules' love. I will admit, nurse, the source of the bane was Nessus, born of Nephele's womb to the Thessalian leader,[40] where chill Pindus thrusts its head among the stars and frozen Othrys rises beyond the clouds. For Achelous, deft at changing to any form, was subdued by rugged Hercules' club and finally stood revealed, all his beast forms used up, bowing his head marred by loss of a horn. By this victory Alcides had gained me as his wife, and was heading for Argos. As it happened the Evenus, whose deep swirling waters wander through fields to the sea, was then foaming almost at the top of its banks. Nessus asked a fee for his experience in fording the torrent; and bearing me on his back just where the horse's spine ends and joins the human,[41] he began to break the swollen river's menace.

And now, while Alcides was still straggling in mid-river, parting the whirling torrent with his huge steps, fierce Nessus had completely emerged from the water. When he saw that Alcides was at a distance, he said, "You shall be my prize and my wife: *he* is kept away by the waters." And clasping me he began to hurry away. But water does not stop Hercules. "Treacherous ferryman!" said he. "Though Ganges and Hister should flow combined in a joint river-bed, I would overcome them both—and I shall catch your flight with an arrow!" The bowshot preceded the words; then the shaft, with its far-reaching wound, stopped his

[40] Ixion.
[41] Nessus was a centaur, half human and half horse.

mortemque fixit. ille, iam quaerens diem,
520　tabem fluentis vulneris dextra excipit
traditque nobis ungulae insertam suae,
quam forte saeva sciderat avulsam manu.
tunc verba moriens addit: "Hoc" inquit "magae
dixere amorem posse defigi malo;
525　hoc docta Mycale Thessalas docuit nurus,
unam inter omnes Luna quam sequitur magas
astris relictis. inlitas vestes dabis
hac" inquit "ipsa tabe, si paelex tuos
invisa thalamos tulerit et coniunx levis
530　aliam parenti dederit altisono nurum.
hoc nulla lux conspiciat, hoc tenebrae tegant
tantum remotae: sic potens vires suas
sanguis tenebit." verba deprendit quies,
mortemque lassis intulit membris sopor.
535　　Tu, quam meis admittit arcanis fides,
perge ut nitentem virus in vestem datum
mentem per artus adeat et tacitum intimas
intret medullas.

NUTRIX
Ocius iussa exequar,
alumna; precibus tu deum invictum advoca
540　qui certa tenera tela dimittit manu.

DEIANIRA
Te te precor, quem mundus et superi timent
et aequor et qui fulmen Aetnaeum quatit,
timende Marti teliger saevo puer:

537 tacitum intumas *Gronovius*: tacitus mas *E*: tactus sinus *A*
543 Marti . . . saevo *Axelson*: matri . . . saevae* *EA*

380

stalled flight and implanted death. Already losing the light of day, he caught in his hand the gore from the flowing wound, and passed it to me encased in his own hoof, opportunely wrenched off and split open by his savage hand. Then he added these dying words: "By this bane," he said, "sorceresses say love can be bound fast. This skill was taught to Thessalian wives by skilled Mycale, who alone of all sorceresses makes the moon follow her and abandon the stars. You shall give him garments smeared with this very gore," he said, "if a hateful rival takes your marriage bed, and your husband's straying affections present his high-thundering father with another daughter-in-law. Only let no light see it, let deepest darkness hide it: in this way the potent blood will retain its power." Silence overtook his words, and sleep prefaced death in his languid limbs.

[*To Nurse*] Your loyalty gives you access to my secret. Proceed, so the venom once placed on the shining clothes may make its way to his mind through his body, and stealthily pass into his very marrow.

NURSE

I shall do your bidding speedily, my child. *You* must invoke the invincible god whose tender hands discharge unerring arrows.[42] [*Exit*]

DEIANIRA

To you I pray, whom earth and heaven fear, and sea and the wielder of Etna's bolt,[43] young weapon-bearer whom

[42] Cupid.

[43] Jupiter, whose bolts were forged by the Cyclopes within Mt Etna.

intende certa spiculum velox manu,
545 non ex sagittis levibus: e numero, precor,
graviore prome quod tuae nondum manus
misere in aliquem; non levi telo est opus,
ut amare possit Hercules. rigidas manus
intende et arcum cornibus iunctis para.
550 nunc, nunc sagittam prome qua quondam horridus
Iovem petisti, fulmine abiecto deus
cum fronte subita tumuit et rabidum mare
taurus puellae vector Assyriae scidit.
immitte amorem: vincat exempla omnia,
555 amare discat coniuges! si quas decor
Ioles inussit pectori Herculeo faces,
extingue totas, perbibat formam mei.
tu fulminantem saepe domuisti Iovem,
tu furva nigri sceptra gestantem poli,
560 turbae ducem maioris et dominum Stygis,
tuque, o noverca gravior irata deus,
cape hunc triumphum: solus evince Herculem.

NUTRIX

Prolata vis est quaeque Palladia colu
lassavit omnem texta famularem manum.
565 nunc ingeratur virus et vestis bibat
Herculea pestem; precibus augebo malum.
    In tempore ipso navus occurrit Lichas:
celanda vis est dira, ne pateant doli.

550 horridus *A*: horridum *E*
562 evince *A*: et vince *E*
564 texta *EA*: tela *recc.*
565 ingeratur *Axelson*: congeratur *E*: congregetur *A*

382

savage Mars must fear. Aim a swift dart with unerring hand—not one of your lighter arrows: from the heavier sort I pray you bring out one that your hands have not yet fired at anyone; no light weapon is needed to make Hercules capable of love. Stretch out your hands rock-firm, bend the bow so its tips join. *Now* you must bring out the arrow that once in ferocious mood you shot at Jove, when the god cast aside his thunderbolt, and with suddenly distended brows cut through the raging sea as a bull ferrying the Assyrian girl.[44] Fire love into him, let him surpass all precedents—and let him learn to love his wives![45] If Iole's beauty has burnt firebrands into Hercules' heart, quench them completely; let him drink in the beauty of me. You have often mastered thundering Jove, and the bearer of the black world's dusky sceptre, commander of the greater throng and lord of Styx; o deity harsher than the angry stepmother, win this triumph too: be Hercules' only conqueror.

NURSE

[*Returning*] Your arsenal is brought out, and the woven garment that wearied every servant's hands with Pallas' distaff. Now the venom must be poured onto Hercules' clothing, so it drinks in the poison. I shall strengthen the bane with my prayers. [*They prepare the robe. Lichas approaches*]

At a timely moment here comes the busy Lichas. But our dread arsenal must be hidden, or our ruse is revealed.

44 Europa.
45 The plural suggests habitual failings, i.e. towards both Megara and herself.

DEIANIRA

O quod superbae non habent umquam domus,
570 fidele semper regibus nomen Licha:
cape hos amictus, nostra quos nevit manus
dum vagus in orbe fertur et victus mero
tenet feroci Lydiam gremio nurum,
dum poscit Iolen. sed iecur fors horridum
575 flectam merendo: merita vicerunt malos.
non ante vestes induat coniunx iube
quam ture flammas pascat et placet deos,
cana rigentem populo cinctus comam.
    Ipsa ad penates regios gressus feram
580 precibusque Amoris horridi matrem colam.
Vos, quas paternis extuli comites focis,
Calydoniae, lugete deflendam vicem.

CHORUS

Flemus casus, Oenei, tuos,
comitum primos turba per annos;
585 flemus dubios, miseranda, toros.
nos Acheloi
tecum solitae pulsare vadum,
cum iam tumidas vere peracto
poneret undas
gracilisque gradu serperet aequo,
590 nec praecipitem volveret amnem
flavus rupto fonte Lycormas.
nos Palladias ire per aras
et virgineos celebrare choros,
nos Cadmeis orgia ferre

585 miseranda *A*: venerande (*sic*) *E*

DEIANIRA

Lichas, name of constant loyalty to your rulers—something proud houses never possess: take this garment, spun by my hands while he was wandering the earth, while he clasped the young Lydian woman in his fierce embrace when worse for wine, and while he demanded Iole. But perhaps I can change his violent passion by serving him; service can prevail on the unkind. Before my husband puts the garment on, bid him feed incense into the fire and propitiate the gods, his stiff hair circled with grey poplar leaves.

I myself shall go inside the royal house, and make prayers to the mother of ferocious Love. You Calydonian women, whom I brought as friends from my father's hearth: lament this grievous situation.

CHORUS OF AETOLIAN WOMEN

We grieve for your plight, daughter of Oeneus,
your group of friends through your childhood years;
poor woman, we grieve for your threatened marriage.
With you we used
to splash in the shallows of Achelous,
once he allayed at the end of spring
his swollen waves
and glided calmly in a narrow channel,
and Lycormas no longer poured his tawny
headlong river from bursting springs.
We used to visit Pallas' altars
and perform together the maidens' dances;
with you we carried the mystic symbols

595   tecum solitae condita cistis,
    cum iam pulso sidere brumae
    tertia soles evocat aestas
    et spiciferae concessa deae
    Attica mystas claudit Eleusin.
600   nunc quoque casum quemcumque times,
    fidas comites accipe fatis;
    nam rara fides
    ubi iam melior fortuna ruit.
       Tu quicumque es qui sceptra tenes:
605   licet omne tua vulgus in aula
    centum pariter limina pulset;
    cum tot populis stipatus eas,
    in tot populis vix una fides.
    tenet auratum limen Erinys,
610   et cum magnae patuere fores,
    intrant fraudes cautique doli
    ferrumque latens;
    cumque in populos prodire paras,
    comes Invidia est.
    noctem quotiens summovet Eos,
615   regem totiens credite nasci.
       Pauci reges, non regna colunt;
    plures fulgor concitat aulae.
    cupit hic regi proximus ipsi
    clarus totas ire per urbes
620   (urit miserum gloria pectus);

---

46 The reference is to a Bacchic festival held every three years by inclusive counting (i.e. every two years by modern reckoning). "Cadmean" = of Thebes, Bacchus' birthplace and centre of worship; the "star," i.e. constellation, of winter is Pisces. The "god-

concealed inside Cadmean baskets
when each third summer had driven off
the star of winter and summoned the sun,[46]
and the grain-bearing goddess' own demesne,
Attic Eleusis, enclosed the initiates.
Now too, in any plight you fear,
take us loyal friends to share your fate;
for loyalty is rare
once good fortune begins to fail.

    You that hold a sceptre, whoever you are:
granted, the whole population together
may knock at the hundred doors of your palace;
but though so many people throng around you,
among so many people there is scarcely one loyal.
The Erinys holds the gilded doorway,
and when the great doors open wide,
in come betrayals and cagey tricks
and the hidden sword;
and when you prepare to go out in public,
at your side is Envy.
Each time the dawn supplants the night,
each time consider a king newborn.[47]

    Few cherish kings and not their thrones;
most are drawn by the glitter of court.
One man longs to walk resplendent
through every city at the king's own side;
such glory inflames his pathetic breast.

---

dess" mentioned next is Ceres, worshipped in the Eleusinian
Mysteries.

[47] The danger of assassination is so great that each day represents a new lease on life.

cupit hic gazis implere famem,
nec tamen omnis
plaga gemmiferi sufficit Histri
nec tota sitim Lydia vincit
625 nec quae Zephyro subdita tellus
stupet aurato flumine clarum
radiare Tagum,
nec si totus serviat Hebrus
ruraque dives iungat Hydaspes
intraque suos currere fines
630 spectet toto flumine Gangen:
avidis, avidis natura parum est.
  Colit hic reges regumque lares,
non ut presso vomere semper
numquam cesset curvus arator,
635 vel mille secent arva coloni:
solas optat quas ponat opes.
colit hic reges, calcet ut omnes
perdatque aliquos nullumque levet:
tantum ut noceat cupit esse potens.
640   Quota pars moritur tempore fati!
quos felices Cynthia vidit,
vidit miseros enata dies;
rarum est felix idemque senex.
  Caespes Tyrio mollior ostro
645 solet impavidos ducere somnos;
aurea rumpunt texta quietem

646 texta *Axelson*: tecta *EA*

---

48 The version of this ode attributed to Queen Elizabeth I (and

Another wants treasure to fill his hunger;
but all the tract of jewelled Hister
cannot suffice
not the whole of Lydia slake his thirst,[48]
nor the land facing the western winds
that is dazzled by the radiance from bright Tagus'
golden river—
not even if the whole of Hebrus served him
and rich Hydaspes added its lands,
and he saw the whole of Ganges' river
flowing within his own domains.
The greedy, the greedy find Nature too little.

One man courts kings and kingly abodes,
not so his ploughman shall hunch forever
down on his plough and never rest,
or a thousand tenants till his fields:
he craves wealth only to put it by.
Another courts kings to trample on all,
destroying some and supporting none:
he covets power for harm's sake only.

How few of them die at the fated time!
Those seen in good fortune by the Cynthian
are seen in misery by the budding day.
To be old *and* fortunate is rare.

The greensward, softer than Tyrian sheets,
brings slumbers that are free from fear;
golden fabrics break one's rest,

intriguingly relevant to her court) rises to eloquence here: "Not all
the coast where Istrus' trade doth haunt, / With gems bedecked
through hue of diverse kind, / Nor Lydia fair with sweetest
streams suffice / To quench or answer all such thirst by half."

	vigilesque trahit purpura noctes.
	o si pateant pectora ditum!
	quantos intus
650	sublimis agit fortuna metus!
	Bruttia Coro pulsante fretum
	lenior unda est.
652	pectora pauper secura gerit:
655	carpit faciles vilesque cibos,
656	sed non strictos respicit enses;
653	tenet e patula pocula fago,
654	sed non trepida tenet illa manu:
657	aurea miscet pocula sanguis.
	Coniunx modico nupta marito
	non disposito clara monili
660	gestat pelagi dona rubentis,
	nec gemmiferas detrahit aures
	lapis Eoa lectus in unda,
	nec Sidonio mollis aëno
	repetita bibit lana rubores,
665	nec Maeonia distinguit acu
	quae Phoebeis subditus Euris
	legit Eois Ser arboribus.
	quaelibet herbae tinxere colus
	quas indoctae nevere manus,
670	sed non dubios fovet illa toros.
	sequitur dira lampade Erinys
	quarum populi coluere diem.
	[nec sibi felix pauper habetur
	nisi felices cecidisse videt]

655–656 *placed after* 652 *by Zwierlein*
673–674 *deleted by Schrader*

the purple has a train of sleepless nights.
If only the hearts of the rich were revealed!
How great the fears
that lofty fortune stirs within them!
Less fierce are the Bruttian
waves when a norther pounds the strait.
The poor man's heart is free of care.
He gathers food at hand and cheap,
but keeps no lookout for drawn swords.
His cup is carved from the spreading beech,
but the hand that holds it does not tremble;
golden cups are mixed with blood.

The wife whose spouse has modest means
does not carry about the gifts of the ruby
sea[49] in bright array on her necklace;
her ears are not bejewelled and burdened
with stones collected in eastern waters;
her wool is not softened in Sidonian vats,
drinking twice over the crimson dyes;
she does not embroider Maeonian-style
threads that the Ser collected from eastern
trees in a land of orient winds.
Her yarn is dyed with everyday herbs
and spun by hands that have no training;
but the marriage bed she keeps is stable.
The Erinys pursues with her baleful torch
women whose days are attended by crowds.[50]

[49] See *Thyestes* lines 371–373 with note.
[50] Lines 673–74 (deleted): "And the poor man thinks himself unfortunate / unless he sees the fortunate fallen."

675 Quisquis medium defugit iter
     stabili numquam tramite curret.
     dum petit unum praebere diem
     patrioque puer constitit axe
     nec per solitum decurrit iter,
680 sed Phoebeis
     ignota petit sidera flammis
     errante rota,
     secum pariter perdidit orbem.
     medium caeli dum sulcat iter,
     tenuit placidas Daedalus oras
685 nullique dedit nomina ponto;
     sed dum volucres vincere veras
     Icarus audet
     patriasque puer despicit alas
     Phoeboque volat proximus ipsi,
690 dedit ignoto nomina ponto.
     male pensantur magna ruinis.
     felix alius magnusque sonet;
     me nulla vocet turba potentem.
     stringat tenuis litora puppis,
695 nec magna meas aura phaselos
     iubeat medium scindere pontum:
     transit tutos Fortuna sinus,
     medioque rates quaerit in alto

678 patrioque puer constitit axe *E*: patriosque puer concitat axes *A*
681 petit *Fitch*: petens *E*: secat *A*

Those who avoid the middle path
will never run on a stable course.
A boy bestrode his father's chariot,[51]
seeking to furnish one day's light;
since he would not run on the usual path,
but sought out stars
unknown before to Phoebus' fire
with wayward wheels,
he ruined himself and the world as well.
Since Daedalus cleaved a middle path
through the sky, he reached a tranquil shore
and bestowed his name upon no sea.
But Icarus—
since he dared to rise above real birds,
a boy looking down on his father's wings
and flying right up to Phoebus' side—
bestowed his name on an unknown sea.[52]
Great deeds are harshly repaid with ruin.
Let another resound as great and fortunate,
but let no crowd hail me as powerful.
My modest boat should hug the shore,
and no great breezes urge a yacht
of mine to cleave the midst of the sea.
Misfortune passes by safe coves
and searches in mid-sea for ships

[51] The boy is Phaethon, his father Phoebus.
[52] I.e. unknown to the world until named "Icarian," but also
paradoxically unknown to the source of its name.

quarum feriunt sipara nubes.

700   Sed quid pavido territa vultu,
    qualis Baccho saucia maenas,
    fertur rapido regina gradu?
    Quae te rursus fortuna rotat?
    miseranda, refer:
    licet ipsa neges,
705   vultus loquitur quodcumque tegis.

DEIANIRA

Vagus per artus errat excussos tremor,
erectus horret crinis, impulsis adhuc
stat terror animis et cor attonitum salit
pavidumque trepidis palpitat venis iecur.
710 ut fractus austro pontus etiamnum tumet,
quamvis quiescat languidis ventis dies,
ita mens adhuc vexatur excusso metu.
semel profecto premere felices deus
cum coepit, urget. hos habent magna exitus.

CHORUS

715 Quis tam impotens, miseranda, te casus rotat?

DEIANIRA

Ut missa palla est tabe Nessea inlita

701 maenas *E*: thyas *A*
715 *attributed to Chorus by A, to Nurse (with 713–714) by E*

---

53 The last lines are vigorously rendered by John Studley in his
translation of the play (published 1566): "Let other mount aloft,
let other soar, / As happy man in great estate to sit. / By flattering
name of Lord I set no store; / For under shore my little keel should

whose topsails strike the very clouds.[53]

ACT 3

But why is the queen rushing out in fear,
panic in her face, with hasty steps
like a maenad driven in pain by Bacchus?
What whirlwind of new misfortune drives you?
Poor woman, tell us:
though you say nothing,
your face speaks clearly of what you are hiding.

DEIANIRA

Shudders run here and there through my shaking limbs, my hair bristles up on end, terror still lodges in my stricken spirit, my heart beats hard in shock, and my liver pulses in fear, its veins trembling. As a sea churned up by the south wind continues to heave though the weather grows calm and the winds drop, so my mind is still agitated though the fear is shaken off. Assuredly when god once begins to attack the fortunate, he harries them. This is how greatness ends.

CHORUS LEADER

What is this violent whirlwind of mischance, poor woman?

DEIANIRA

After I had sent off the robe smeared with Nessus' gore, as

flit, / And from rough winds my sails fain would I keep, / Lest I be driven into the dangerous deep. / Proud Fortune's rage doth never stoop so low / As little roads, but them she overflies / And seeks amid main seas her force to show / On argosies, whose tops do reach the skies."

thalamisque maerens intuli gressum meis,
nescioquid animus timuit: ⟨an moriens viro
poenas parat Centaurus⟩ et fraudem struit?
libet experiri. solibus virus ferum
720 flammisque Nessus sanguinem ostendi arcuit:
hic ipse fraudes esse praemonuit dolus.
et forte, nulla nube respersus iubar,
laxabat ardens fervidum Titan diem
—vix ora solvi patitur etiamnunc timor.
725 medios in ignes solis et claram facem,
quo tincta fuerat palla vestisque inlita,
abiectus horret villus et Phoebo comam
tepefactus arsit—vix queo monstrum eloqui.
nives ut Eurus solvit aut tepidus Notus,
730 quas vere primo lucidus perdit Mimas,
utque evolutos frangit Ionio salo
opposita fluctus Leucas et lassus tumor
in litore ipso spumat, aut caelestibus
aspersa tepidis tura laxantur focis,
735 sic languet omne vellus et perdit comas.
dumque ista miror, causa mirandi perit;
quin ipsa tellus spumeos motus agit,
et quidquid illa tabe contactum est labat
tumensque tacita * * *
        ⟨Quis ille maestum lugubris⟩ quassat caput?
740 natum paventem cerno et ardenti pede
gressus ferentem. Prome quid portes novi.

718 *Lacuna recognised and supplement proposed by Leo*
727 villus *Richter*: virus *A*: sanguis *E*   Phoebo *Fitch*:
Phoebi* *EA*

I sadly walked into my bedchamber, my mind felt a vague fear: ‹did the dying centaur plan revenge on my husband› and devise some treachery? I wanted to check. Nessus had forbidden that the dangerous blood and venom should be exposed to sunlight or flames. This very stratagem gave forewarning of treachery. As it happened the fiery Titan was loosing the blazing daylight, his rays unsullied by any cloud—fear scarcely allows me to speak even now. A wool cloth, used to impregnate the robe and smear the clothes, had been thrown aside full in the bright, burning sunlight. It shuddered, and as its pile was heated by Phoebus it burst into flames—I can scarely speak of something so monstrous! As the east wind or warm south wind melts the snows that vanish in early spring on bright Mimas, and as the spent swell foams right on the shore when waves rolling in from the Ionian Sea break against the barrier of Leucas, or as incense strewn to the gods melts in altar fires, so the whole cloth wilted and lost its pile. And while I wondered at it, the cause of my wonder was destroyed. Indeed the very ground heaved and foamed; anything touched by that gore languished, and swelling with the stealthy ‹bane› . . .

‹But who is this,› pounding his head ‹in grief and sorrow?› I see my son in panic, coming hotfoot towards us. Tell me what news you bring.

---

739 *E writes* tumensque tacita *and* quassat caput *on separate lines: A links them by writing* tumensque tacita sequitur et quassat caput. *Supplement by Fitch*

HYLLUS

I, profuge, quaere si quid ulterius patet
terris freto sideribus Oceano inferis;
ultra labores, mater, Alcidae fuge.

DEIANIRA

745 Nescioquod animus grande praesagit malum.

HYLLUS

Spolium triumphi templa Iunonis pete:
haec tibi patent, delubra praeclusa omnia.

DEIANIRA

Effare quis me casus insontem premat.

HYLLUS

Decus illud orbis atque praesidium unicum,
750 quem fata terris in locum dederant Iovis,
o mater, abiit. membra et Herculeos toros
urit lues nescioqua; qui domuit feras,
ille ille victor vincitur maeret dolet.
quid quaeris ultra?

DEIANIRA

            Miserias properant suas
755 audire miseri. fare, quo posita in statu
iam nostra domus est? o lares, miseri lares!
nunc vidua, nunc expulsa, nunc ferar obruta.

HYLLUS

Non sola maeres Herculem, toto iacet
mundo gemendus. fata nec, mater, tua
760 privata credas: iam genus totum obstrepit.

---

[746] spolium *Fitch*: certae *Damsté*: regna *E*: 746–747 *omitted
by A*

HYLLUS

Go, escape, try to find some haven beyond earth, sea, stars, Ocean, underworld: beyond Alcides' labours, mother, is where you must flee.

DEIANIRA

My mind forebodes some great evil.

HYLLUS

As Juno's spoil of triumph, run for her temples! They are open to you, but all other shrines are barred.

DEIANIRA

Tell me what undeserved mischance is falling on me.

HYLLUS

That glory of the world, its sole defence, whom fate gave to the earth in lieu of Jove, is gone, mother! Those muscular limbs of Hercules are being burnt away by some strange blight. He who tamed wild beasts, that famous conqueror is conquered, in grief, in pain. Why ask further?

DEIANIRA

The sorrowful are eager to hear about their sorrows. Tell me, what is the situation now with our house? O my home, my unhappy home! Now I shall go forth widowed, banished, ruined.

HYLLUS

You are not alone in mourning Hercules: his death deserves the whole world's grief. Do not think your fate a private one, mother; the whole race cries out in protest. This

hunc ecce luctum quem gemis cuncti gemunt;
commune terris omnibus pateris malum.
luctum occupasti: prima, non sola, Herculem,
miseranda, maeres.

DEIANIRA

        Quam prope a leto tamen
765 ede, ede quaeso iaceat Alcides meus.

HYLLUS

Mors refugit illum, victa quae in regno suo
semel est, nec audent Fata tam vastum nefas
admittere. ipsa forsitan trepida colos
Clotho manu proiecit et fata Herculis
770 timet peragere. pro diem, infandum diem!
hocne ille summo magnus Alcides erit?

DEIANIRA

Ad fata et umbras atque peiorem polum
praecedere illum dicis? an possum prior
mortem occupare? fare, si nondum occidit.

HYLLUS

775 Euboica tellus vertice immenso tumens
pulsatur omni latere: Phrixeum mare
scindit Caphereus, servit hoc Austro latus;
at qua nivosi patitur Aquilonis minas,
Euripus undas flectit instabilis vagas
780 septemque cursus volvit et totidem refert,
dum lassa Titan mergit Oceano iuga.
hic rupe celsa, nulla quam nubes ferit,
annosa fulgent templa Cenaei Iovis.

761 ecce luctum *Richter*: ecce luctu *E*: eiulatu (-i *PT*) *A*
768 ipsa *A*: ipsas *E*

very grief which you mourn, all mourn; the trouble you suffer is common to every land. You have anticipated their grief—Hercules' first mourner, poor woman, but not his sole mourner.

DEIANIRA

But tell me, tell me, I pray, how close to death my Alcides lies.

HYLLUS

Death, defeated once in its own kingdom,[54] flies from him, and the Fates dare not commit so great an outrage. Clotho herself perhaps let the distaff drop from her trembling hands, afraid to wind up Hercules' fate. Oh this day, this unspeakable day! Will it be the last of mighty Hercules' life?

DEIANIRA

Do you mean he precedes me to doom and the shades and the darker world? Or can I reach death first? Tell me if he has not yet perished.

HYLLUS

The Euboean land, swelling to an immense height, is buffeted on every side. Cape Caphereus juts into the Sea of Phrixus, and this side is open to the southerlies; but where it feels the blustery, snowy norther, the restless Euripus switches its vagrant tides, flowing seven times one way and seven times the other before the Titan plunges his weary team in Ocean. Here, on a high crag unscathed by clouds, gleams an age-old temple to Cenaean Jove.

---

54 When Hercules took Cerberus from the world of the dead.

Ut stetit ad aras omne votivum pecus
785   totumque tauris gemuit auratis nemus,
spolium leonis sordidum tabo exuit
posuitque clavae pondus et pharetra graves
laxavit umeros. veste tunc fulgens tua,
cana revinctus populo horrentem comam,
790   succendit aras. "Accipe has" inquit "focis
non false messes genitor et largo sacer
splendescat ignis ture, quod Phoebum colens
dives Sabaeis colligit truncis Arabs.
pacata tellus" inquit "et caelum et freta,
795   feris subactis omnibus victor redî:
depone fulmen"—gemitus in medias preces
stupente et ipso cecidit; hinc caelum horrido
clamore complet. qualis impressa fugax
taurus bipenni vulnus et telum ferens
800   delubra vasto trepida mugitu replet,
aut quale mundo fulmen emissum tonat,
sic ille gemitu sidera et pontum ferit,
et vasta Chalcis sonuit et voces Cyclas
excepit omnis; hinc petrae Capherides,
805   hinc omne voces reddit Herculeas nemus.
flentem videmus. vulgus antiquam putat
rabiem redisse; tunc fugam famuli petunt.
At ille, vultus ignea torquens face,
unum inter omnes sequitur et quaerit Lichan.
810   complexus aras ille tremebunda manu
mortem metu consumpsit et parvum sui
poenae reliquit. dumque tremebundum manu
tenuit cadaver, "Hac manu, hac" inquit "ferar,

Once all the votive cattle were stationed at the altar, and the grove was filled with the bellows of gilded bulls,[55] he took off the lionskin, soiled with gore, set down the heavy club, and relieved his burdened shoulders of the quiver. Then, resplendent in your robe, and with his rough hair wreathed in grey poplar leaves, he kindled the altar. "Accept these thank offerings," said he, "you who are rightly called my father; let the holy flame blaze up with abundant incense, collected from Sabaean branches by the rich sun-worshipping Arabs. Earth has been pacified," he said, "and sky and sea; after subduing all beasts I have returned victorious. Lay down your thunderbolt!" The prayer was interrupted by a groan that astonished even him; then he filled the sky with fearful shouts. As a runaway bull with the axe embedded, bearing both wound and weapon, fills a startled shrine with tremendous bellows, or as a bolt thunders when launched from heaven, so he smote stars and sea with his groans. Chalcis resounded mightily, and all the Cyclades heard his cries. On one side the crags of Caphereus, on the other the whole grove echoed to Hercules' cries. We beheld him weeping! People thought his old madness had returned; then his servants made their escape.

But with eyes rolling from the fiery heat, he pursued and sought Lichas alone among them all. He, clutching the altar with trembling hands, spent his death through terror and left little of himself for retribution. With the trembling corpse in his grip he said, "Is this the hand, you fates, by

55 Bulls' horns were sometimes gilded before sacrifice.

o fata, victus? Herculem vicit Lichas?
815 ecce alia clades: Hercules perimit Lichan.
facta inquinentur: fiat hic summus labor."
in astra missus fertur et nubes vago
spargit cruore; talis in caelum exilit
harundo Getica iussa dimitti manu
820 aut quam Cydon excussit—inferius tamen
et tela fugient. truncus in pontum cadit,
in saxa cervix: unus ambobus iacet.
     "Resistite" inquit, "non furor mentem abstulit,
furore gravius istud atque ira malum est:
825 in me iuvat saevire." vix pestem indicat
et saevit: artus ipse dilacerat suos
et membra vasta carpit avellens manu.
exuere amictus quaerit: hoc solum Herculem
non posse vidi. trahere conatus tamen
830 et membra traxit: corporis palla horridi
pars est et ipsa, vestis immiscet cutem.
nec causa dirae cladis in medio patet,
sed causa tamen est. vixque sufficiens malo
nunc ore terram languidus prono premit,
835 nunc poscit undas—unda non vincit malum;
fluctisona quaerit litora et pontum occupat:
famularis illum retinet errantem manus—
o sortem acerbam! fuimus Alcidae pares.
     Nunc puppis illum litore Euboico refert
840 Austerque lenis pondus Herculeum rapit.
destituit animus membra, nox oculos premit.

814 vicit *E*: perimit *A*
822 cervix *CSV*: coniunx *PT*: versus *E*: vertex *Gronovius*
unus *Grotius*: funus *EA*

404

which history will say I was conquered? Lichas has conquered Hercules? See, another defeat: Hercules slays Lichas! My deeds must be sullied, and this must be my final labour." Hurled towards the stars, he[56] spattered the clouds with a spray of blood. So a shaft leaps skyward when released on command by a Getic hand, or shot by a Cydonian—yet even arrows would fly lower. His body fell into the sea, his head onto rocks: one death in two elements.

"Wait!" he said to us. "My mind is not seized with madness, this evil is deeper than madness or wrath: *I* am the target of my rage!" Scarcely had he described his affliction when he vented his rage. He rent his own body, plucked and tore at his limbs with his mighty hands. He was trying to take off the garment—the one task in which I have seen Hercules fail. But in trying to tear it off, he tore his limbs too: the robe was part of his rugged body, the garment merged with the skin. The cause of the terrible havoc was not clear to all, yet this was the cause. Scarcely able to endure the pain, now he fell face-down on the ground in weakness, now demanded water—but water did not master the pain. He made for the wave-loud shore and plunged into the sea; the band of servants restrained him as he lurched about. Cruel fate!—we were Alcides' equals.

Now a ship is bringing him back from the shore of Euboea, with a light south wind speeding Hercules' bulky body. His spirit is forsaking his limbs, night pressing on his eyes.

[56] I.e. Lichas' body.

DEIANIRA

Quid, anime, cessas? quid stupes? factum est scelus.
natum reposcit Iuppiter, Iuno aemulum;
⟨ille urbium defensor et victor mali⟩
reddendus orbi est. quod potest reddi, exhibe:
845   eat per artus ensis exactus meos.
sic, sic agendum est—tam levis poenas manus
tantas reposcit? perde fulminibus, socer,
nurum scelestam. nec levi telo manus
armetur: illud fulmen exiliat polo,
850   quo, nisi fuisset genitus Alcides tibi,
hydram cremasses; pestem ut insolitam feri
et ut noverca peius irata malum.
emitte telum quale in errantem prius
Phaethonta missum est: perdidi erepto Hercule
855   et ipsa populos.   Quid rogas telum deos?
iam parce socero! coniugem Alcidae necem
optare pudeat: haec erit voto manus,
a me petatur. occupa ferrum ocius—
cur deinde ferrum? quidquid ad mortem trahit
860   telum est abunde. rupe ab aetheria ferar.
haec, haec renatum prima quae poscit diem
Oeta eligatur; corpus hinc mitti placet.—
866   levis una mors est—levis, at extendi potest:
863   abrupta cautes scindat et partem mei
ferat omne saxum, pendeant lacerae manus
865   totumque rubeat asperi montis latus.

Before 844 *lacuna recognised by Zwierlein; supplement by* Fitch   854 erepto Hercule *A:* sola Herculem *E:* in solo Hercule *Heinsius*   866 *placed after* 862 *by Zwierlein*

DEIANIRA

Why hesitant, why stunned, my spirit? The crime is done! Jove demands back his son, Juno her antagonist; ‹that great defender of cities and conqueror of evil› ought to be given back to the world. But provide what *can* be given back.[57] The sword must be thrust through my body—yes, this is what must be done. But can so slight a hand lay claim to such weighty restitution? Use your thunderbolts, father-in-law, to destroy your criminal daughter-in-law! And do not arm your hand with a light weapon: the bolt leaping from the sky must be the one you would have used—if Alcides had not been born to you—to incinerate the hydra. Strike me like some unexampled scourge, like an evil worse than the angry stepmother.[58] Launch a weapon like that launched once against the straying Phaethon: I too have ruined nations,[59] by robbing them of Hercules.

Why ask the gods for a weapon? Give your father-in-law some respite! Alcides' wife should be ashamed to *pray* for death. My prayer must be to myself, this hand will serve it. Quick, seize a sword. But then, why a sword? Anything that leads to death is ample as a weapon. I shall leap from a soaring crag. My choice shall be this very Oeta, which first claims the reborn daylight: yes, I shall fling my body from here. Yet a single death is light punishment—light, but it can be prolonged: let the steep cliff rend me and every rock take part of me, let my broken hands hang there, and the whole jagged flank of the mountain be encrimsoned.

[57] The recompense of her death.
[58] Juno.
[59] Phaethon ruined nations and cities when he lost control of the sun chariot.

867   Eligere nescis, anime, cui telo incubes!
      utinam esset, utinam fixus in thalamis meis
      Herculeus ensis: huic decet ferro immori.—
870   una perire dextera nobis sat est?
      coite, gentes, saxa et immensas faces
      iaculetur orbis, nulla nunc cesset manus,
      corripite tela: vindicem vestrum abstuli.
      impune saevi sceptra iam reges gerent,
875   impune iam nascetur indomitum malum;
      reddentur arae cernere assuetae hostiam
      similem colenti. sceleribus feci viam;
      ego vos tyrannis regibus monstris feris
      saevisque rapto vindice opposui deis.
880   cessas, Tonantis socia? non spargis facem
      imitata fratrem et mittis ereptam Iovi
      meque ipsa perdis? laus tibi erepta inclita est,
      ingens triumphus: aemuli, Iuno, tui
      mortem occupavi.

NUTRIX

              Quid domum impulsam trahis?
885   erroris est hic omne quodcumque est nefas.
      haud est nocens quicumque non sponte est nocens.

DEIANIRA

Quicumque fato ignoscit et parcit sibi,
errare meruit: morte damnari placet.

NUTRIX

Nocens videri, qui mori quaerit, cupit.

<hr>

885 est hic *E*: istic *A*

408

O my spirit, you are inept in choosing a weapon to fall on! I wish, I wish there was a sword of Hercules' lodged in my bedchamber; that would be a fitting blade for me to die upon. But is it enough for me to be killed by a single hand? Gather, you nations! The whole world must hurl rocks and firebrands without number, no hand must be idle now; seize your weapons! I have stolen your defender. Now cruel kings will wield their sceptres in safety, now some invincible scourge will be born in safety. Altars will be restored that regularly see victims resembling the worshippers.[60] I have made a path for crimes; I have exposed you all to tyrants, kings, monsters, wild animals, and cruel gods by removing your defender. Are you slow to act, partner of the Thunderer? Not showering fire in your brother's style, stealing it from Jove, hurling it and destroying me yourself? Glorious renown, a huge triumph has been stolen from you: I have outstripped you, Juno, in killing your antagonist.

NURSE
Why pull down a house that is already shaken? Such iniquity as exists here is entirely due to error. A person is not guilty unless guilty by intent.

DEIANIRA
A person who condones his fate and pardons himself *deserved* to make the error. My sentence on myself is death.

NURSE
One who seeks to die *wants* to look guilty.

[60] A reference to human sacrifice such as was practiced by Busiris.

DEIANIRA

890   Mors innocentes sola deceptos facit.

NUTRIX

Titana fugies?

DEIANIRA

Ipse me Titan fugit.

NUTRIX

Vitam relinques?

DEIANIRA

Miseram, ut Alciden sequar.

NUTRIX

Superest et auras ille caelestes trahit.

DEIANIRA

Vinci Hercules cum potuit, hinc coepit mori.

NUTRIX

895   Natum relinques fataque abrumpes tua?

DEIANIRA

Quamcumque natus sepelit haec vixit diu.

NUTRIX

Virum sequeris?

DEIANIRA

Praegredi castae solent.

NUTRIX

Si te ipsa damnas, scelere te misera arguis.

DEIANIRA

Only death establishes the innocence of those that were
duped.

NURSE

You will run from the Titan?[61]

DEIANIRA

The Titan himself runs from me.

NURSE

You will leave your life?

DEIANIRA

This wretched life, yes, to follow Alcides.

NURSE

He still survives and breathes the air of heaven.

DEIANIRA

From the moment he became vincible, he began to die.

NURSE

Will you leave your son and break off your own destiny?

DEIANIRA

A woman buried by her son has had a long life.

NURSE

You will follow your husband?

DEIANIRA

Chaste wives go before.

NURSE

If you sentence yourself, you show yourself guilty of crime,
poor woman.

---

[61] I.e. leave the daylight. Deianira's answer suggests that the
Sun avoids the sight of her because of her guilt.

411

DEIANIRA

Nemo nocens sibi ipse poenas irrogat.

NUTRIX

900   Multis remissa est vita quorum error nocens,
non dextra fuerat. fata quis damnat sua?

DEIANIRA

Quicumque fata iniqua sortitus fuit.

NUTRIX

Hic ipse Megaram nempe confixam suis
stravit sagittis atque natorum indolem,
905   Lernaea flectens tela furibunda manu;
ter parricida factus ignovit tamen
sibi, non furori: fonte Cinyphio scelus
sub axe Libyco tersit et dextram abluit.
quo, misera, pergis? cur tuas damnas manus?

DEIANIRA

910   Damnat meas devictus Alcides manus:
placet scelus punire.

NUTRIX

       Si novi Herculem,
aderit cruenti forsitan victor mali,
dolorque fractus cedet Alcidae tuo.

DEIANIRA

Exedit artus virus, ut fama est, hydrae;
915   immensa pestis coniugis membra abstulit.

899 irrogat *A*: abrogat *E*
905 flectens *A*: figens *E*
907 non furori *E*: nam furoris *A*

412

DEIANIRA

No guilty person imposes punishment on himself.

NURSE

Many whose guilt lay in their mistake, not their act, have been allowed to live. Who passes sentence on his own fate?

DEIANIRA

Everyone that has drawn an unjust fate.

NURSE

He himself, you see, shot and killed Megara and their fine children with his arrows, directing his Lernaean shafts with crazed hands. Though a filicide thrice over he never-theless forgave himself—not his madness: he washed away the crime in the Cinyphian spring beneath the Libyan sky, and purified his right hand. What are you trying to do, poor woman? Why condemn *your* hands?

DEIANIRA

It is Alcides' overthrow that condemns my hands. I am resolved to punish the crime.

NURSE

If I know Hercules, he will perhaps arrive victorious over that bloody scourge; pain will be broken and submit to your Alcides.

DEIANIRA

But the hydra's venom has wasted his body, they say; that myriad scourge[62] has destroyed my husband's limbs.

---

[62] An allusion to the hydra's multiple heads.

[SENECA]

NUTRIX

Serpentis illi virus enectae autumas
haud posse vinci, qui malum vivum tulit?
elisit hydram, dente cum fixo stetit
media palude victor effuso obrutus
920   artus veneno. sanguis hunc Nessi opprimet,
qui vicit ipsas horridi Nessi manus?

DEIANIRA

Frustra tenetur ille qui statuit mori:
proinde lucem fugere decretum est mihi.
vixit satis quicumque cum Alcide occidit.

NUTRIX

925   Per has aniles ecce te supplex comas
atque ubera ista paene materna obsecro:
depone tumidas pectoris laesi minas,
mortisque dirae expelle decretum horridum.

DEIANIRA

Quicumque misero forte dissuadet mori,
930   crudelis ille est: interim poena est mori,
sed saepe donum; pluribus veniae fuit.

NUTRIX

Defende saltem dexteram, infelix, tuam,
fraudisque facinus esse, non nuptae, sciat.

DEIANIRA

Defendar illic: inferi absolvent ream.
935   a me ipsa damnor, purget has Pluton manus.
stabo ante ripas, immemor Lethe, tuas
et umbra tristis coniugem excipiam meum.

---

931 veniae* fuit *EA*: venia obfuit *Grotius*

414

NURSE

You reckon the venom of the slaughtered serpent cannot be conquered by one who endured the living scourge? He crushed the hydra, standing victoriously in the midst of the marsh, with its fangs fixed in him and his body smothered with the flowing poison! Shall Nessus' blood overpower one who conquered the savage Nessus' own hands?

DEIANIRA

It is useless to restrain a person committed to dying. Accordingly my decision is to flee the light. One who dies with Alcides has lived long enough.

NURSE

See, by this old woman's hair and these breasts, virtually your mother's, I supplicate and beseech you: renounce these swelling threats coming from your wounded heart, and banish this fearful purpose of dread death.

DEIANIRA

Anyone who chances to dissuade the wretched from dying acts cruelly. Sometimes death is a punishment, but often a gift; for many it means forgiveness.

NURSE

At least vindicate your action, ill-fated woman: let him know the deed arose from treachery, not his wife.

DEIANIRA

I shall be vindicated *there*: those below will absolve me at my trial. I condemn myself; let Pluto absolve these hands. O Lethe of oblivion, I shall stand before your banks and wait as a sad shade to greet my husband.

Sed tu, nigrantis regna qui torques poli,
para laborem. scelera quae quisque ausus est
940 hic vincet error; Iuno non ausa Herculem est
eripere terris: horridam poenam para.
Sisyphia cervix cesset et nostros lapis
impellat umeros; me vagus fugiat latex
meamque fallax unda deludat sitim;
945 merui manus praebere turbinibus tuis,
quaecumque regem Thessalum torques rota;
effodiat avidus hinc et hinc vultur fibras;
vacat una Danais: has ego explebo vices.
laxate, manes! recipe me comitem tibi,
950 Phasiaca coniunx: peior haec, peior tuo
utroque dextra est scelere, seu mater nocens
seu dira soror es; adde me comitem tuis,
Threicia coniunx, sceleribus; natam tuam,
Althaea mater, recipe, nunc veram tui
955 agnosce prolem—quid tamen tantum manus
vestrae abstulerunt?
                    Claudite Elysium mihi,
quaecumque fidae coniuges nemoris sacri
lucos tenetis. si qua respersit manus
viri cruore nec memor castae facis
960 stricto cruenta Belias ferro stetit,
in me suas agnoscat et laudet manus:
in hanc abire coniugum turbam libet—
sed et illa fugiet turba tam diras manus.
Invicte coniunx, innocens animus mihi,
965 scelesta manus est. pro nimis mens credula,
pro Nesse fallax atque semiferi doli!

---

940 vincet *E*: vicit *A*   948 vacat *Raphelengius*: vacet *EA*

But you who rack the realm of the dark world, prepare me some suffering. This mistake will surpass the crimes dared by anyone; even Juno did not dare rob the world of Hercules. So prepare some fearful punishment. Let Sisyphus' neck rest, and his stone push down on my shoulders. Let the inconstant water flee, the fraudulent stream delude my thirst.[63] I deserve to surrender my hands to the spinning of the wheel that racks the Thessalian king. Let a greedy vulture on each side root out my guts. One Danaid is missing: I shall fill her role. Make room, you shades! Take me as your companion, wife from Phasis: this hand is worse than either of your crimes, whether as guilty mother or monstrous sister.[64] Let me accompany your crimes, Thracian wife. Receive your daughter, mother Althaea, and recognise your true child now. Yet did your hands destroy anything as great?

Bar Elysium to me, you loyal wives who dwell in the groves of the sacred wood. But each wife that stained her hands with her husband's blood, dismissed chaste love and stood with drawn sword as a bloodstained Beliad, should recognise and praise her own hands in mine. I want to join this group of wives—but even that group will shun such monstrous hands.

O invincible husband, my spirit is innocent, but my hand bears the crime. Oh for my credulous mind, oh for Nessus' deceit and half-bestial guile! In trying to take you

[63] This is Tantalus' punishment; next mentioned are Ixion's wheel and Tityos' vultures.

[64] The wife from Phasis is Medea, who killed her children and brother; the Thracian wife is Procne, who killed her son; Althaea was responsible for her son Meleager's death.

417

[SENECA]

auferre cupiens paelici eripui mihi.
recede, Titan, tuque quae blanda tenes
in luce miseros vita: cariturae Hercule
970 lux vilis ista est. exigam poenas tibi
reddamque vitam—fata an extendo mea
mortemque, coniunx, ad tuas servo manus?
virtusne superest aliqua et armatae manus
intendere arcum tela missurum valent?
975 an arma cessant teque languenti manu
non audit arcus? si potes letum dare,
animosa coniunx dexteram expecto tuam.
mors differatur: frange ut insontem Lichan,
alias in urbes sparge et ignotum tibi
980 immitte in orbem; perde ut Arcadiae nefas
et quidquid aliud cessit—at ab illis tamen,
coniunx, redisti.

HYLLUS
Parce iam, mater, precor,
ignosce fatis; error a culpa vacat.

DEIANIRA
Si vera pietas, Hylle, quaerenda est tibi,
985 iam perime matrem! pavida quid tremuit manus?
quid ora flectis? haec erit pietas scelus.
ignave dubitas? Herculem eripui tibi.
haec, haec peremit dextra, cui debes patri
avum Tonantem. maius eripui decus,
990 quam luce tribui. si tibi ignotum est nefas,

969 cariturae* *A*: caritura *E*   970 exigam . . . tibi *A*: exigat
. . . sibi *E*   977 animosa *A*: animose *E*   987 eripui *A*:
eripuit *E*   990 quam *Heinsius*: quam in *EA*

418

from my rival, I wrested you from myself! Depart, Titan,
and life that holds the wretched in the beguiling sunlight: for one facing life without Hercules, that light has no
value. I shall exact recompense on your behalf, and pay
with my life. Or should I prolong my lifespan and reserve
my death for your hands, husband? Have you some
strength left, are your hands once armed capable of drawing a bow to fire arrows? Or do weapons fail you, and the
bow not heed your feeble-handed efforts? If you can bestow death, I await your hand as a courageous wife; my
death must be postponed. Crush me like the innocent
Lichas; scatter me abroad into other regions, hurl me into
some world unknown to you; destroy me like the Arcadian
monster[65] and all your other conquests—but from them,
husband, you came back.

HYLLUS

Stop now, mother, I beg you; forgive your fate! A mistake
involves no guilt.

DEIANIRA

If you want to pursue true devotion, Hyllus, you must kill
your mother now! Why does your hand tremble with fear?
Why do you look away? This crime will be an act of devotion. Are you uncertain and fainthearted? I have robbed
you of Hercules! This very hand killed the father through
whom you have the Thunderer as grandfather. I have
robbed you of a greater glory than I gave you by birth. If
villainy is unknown to you, learn it from your mother.

---

[65] The Erymanthian boar.

a matre disce. seu tibi iugulo placet
mersisse ferrum, sive maternum libet
invadere uterum, mater intrepidum tibi
praebebit animum. non erit tantum scelus
995   a te peractum: dextera sternar tua,
sed mente nostra. natus Alcidae times?
ita nulla perages iussa, nec franges mala
referens parentem? dexteram intrepidam para.
1000   patet ecce plenum pectus aerumnis: feri.
      Scelus remitto, dexterae parcent tuae
Eumenides ipsae: verberum crepuit sonus.
quaenam ista torquens angue vibrato comam
temporibus atras squalidis pinnas quatit?
1005   quid me flagranti, dira, persequeris face,
Megaera? poenas poscis Alcidae? dabo.
iamne inferorum, diva, sedere arbitri?
sed ecce apertas carceris video fores.
quis iste saxum immane detritis gerit
1010   iam senior umeris? ecce iam victus lapis
quaerit relabi. membra quis praebet rotae?
hic ecce pallens dira Tisiphone stetit,
causam reposcit. parce verberibus, precor,
Megaera, parce, sustine Stygias faces:
1015   scelus est amoris.
             Sed quid hoc? tellus labat

997–999a *The text printed is that of E, with* referes *corrected to*
referens (*Bentley*). *A's text includes the interpolated line* 998: ita
nulla peragas iussa, nec peragens mala / erres per orbem, si qua
nascetur fera / referas parentem.
1003 vibrato *Peiper*: vipereo *EA*
1007 diva *A*: dira *E*

420

Whether you decide to plunge your sword in my throat, or wish to assault your mother's womb, your mother will offer you unshrinking courage. Such a terrible crime will not be done wholly by you: it will be your hand that strikes me down, but my will. Alcides' son afraid? So will you not carry out orders or crush evils after your father's style? Prepare your hand fearlessly![66] See, my sorrowful breast is open: strike!

I release you from the crime, the Eumenides themselves are going to spare your right hand. There is the sound of their cracking whips! Who is this whose hair writhes with quivering snakes, who flails the black wings at her fetid temples? Why do you pursue me with that blazing torch, dread Megaera? Demanding retribution for Alcides? I shall pay it. Are the underworld's judges already seated, goddess? But look, I see the prison doors open. Who is that man, now old, carrying a huge rock on his grazed shoulders? See, though mastered the boulder is already trying to roll back. Who surrenders his body to the wheel?[67] See here, dread Tisiphone stands white-faced and demands my account of myself. Spare your lashes, I pray, Megaera, spare them, hold off your Stygian torches: my crime is one of love.

But what is this? The ground is trembling, the palace

---

[66] A's text of 997–999, with the interpolated line 998, seems to mean: "May you carry out no orders, nor wander through the world carrying out evils, but may you evoke your father whenever some wild beast arises—with this proviso: that you prepare your hand fearlessly."

[67] She again alludes to the punishments of Sisyphus and Ixion.

et aula tectis crepuit excussis. minax
unde iste coetus? totus in vultus meos
decurrit orbis, hinc et hinc populi fremunt,
totusque poscit vindicem mundus suum.
1020 iam parcite, urbes! quo fugam praeceps agam?
mors sola portus dabitur aerumnis meis.
testor nitentis flammeam Phoebi rotam
superosque testor: Herculem in terris adhuc
moritura linquo.

HYLLUS
Fugit attonita, ei mihi.
1025 peracta iam pars matris est: statuit mori;
nunc nostra superest, mortis auferre impetum.
o misera pietas! si mori matrem vetas,
patri es scelestus; si mori pateris tamen,
in matre peccas: urget hinc illinc scelus.
1030 inhibenda tamen est; pergam et eripiam neci.

CHORUS
Verum est quod cecinit sacer
Thressae sub Rhodopes iugis
aptans Pieriam chelyn
Orpheus, Calliopae genus,
1035 aeternum fieri nihil.
Illius stetit ad modos
torrentis rapidi fragor,
oblitusque sequi fugas
amisit liquor impetum;
1040 et dum fluminibus mora est,
defecisse putant Getae
Hebrum Bistones ultimi.

buildings shaking and rattling. Where has this threatening crowd come from? The whole world is rushing to confront me, peoples are clamouring on every side, the whole earth demands its defender. Stop now, you nations! Where can I flee in haste? The only haven granted my troubles will be death. Witness bright Phoebus' fiery chariot, witness the gods above: in going to my death I leave Hercules still here on earth.

HYLLUS

Alas, she has rushed off in despair. Mother's part is concluded, she has decided to die; now mine remains, to thwart her impulse to die. Unhappy devotion! If you prevent your mother's death, you are culpable towards your father; yet if you allow her death, you offend against your mother. Wrongdoing threatens on each side. Yet she must be stopped; I shall go ahead and save her from suicide.

CHORUS

The holy man sang true
to his Pierian lyre
below Rhodope's heights in Thrace
—Orpheus, Calliope's child—
that nothing is made for ever.
    At the strains of his music the roar
of the whirling torrent stopped;
forgetting to chase in flight
the waters lost their headway;
and as the rivers tarried
the Getae, far into Bistonia,
thought the Hebrus had failed.

1030 pergam *A*: verum *E*   neci *Garrod*: scelus *EA*

advexit volucrem nemus
et silva residens venit;
1045 aut si qua aëra pervolat
auditis vaga cantibus
ales deficiens cadit.
abrumpit scopulos Athos
Centauros obiter ferens,
1050 et iuxta Rhodopen stetit
laxata nive cantibus;
et quercum fugiens suam
ad vatem properat Dryas.
ad cantus veniunt tuos
1055 ipsis cum latebris ferae,
iuxtaque impavidum pecus
sedit Marmaricus leo,
nec dammae trepidant lupos
et serpens latebras fugit
1060   tunc oblita veneni.
   Quin per Taenarias fores
manes cum tacitos adît
maerentem feriens chelyn,
cantu Tartara flebili
1065 et tristes Erebi deos
vicit, nec timuit Stygis
iuratos superis lacus.
haesit non stabilis rota
victo languida turbine;
1070 increvit Tityi iecur,
1071 dum cantus volucres tenet;
1081 et vinci lapis improbus

The woodland brought winged creatures,
perched in the trees they came;
but those flying in the open
veered at the sound of his songs
with faltering wings, and fell.
Athos tore its crags free,
carrying Centaurs along,
and stopped near Rhodope,
its snows melted by song.
Dryads escaped from their oaks
and hurried to hear the bard.
Wild beasts came to your songs
with their very hiding places;
close to unterrified cattle
sat the Marmaric lion;
deer were not panicked by wolves,
and serpents abandoned their lairs,
for once forgetting their venom.

   He even approached the silent
shades through Taenarus' gates,
plucking his mournful lyre.
With his tearful song he vanquished
Tartarus and the sombre gods
of Erebus, and braved the pools
of Styx, the oath of heaven.
The restless wheel stayed put,
inert, its spinning quelled;
Tityos' liver grew
as the vultures were held by song;
and the shameless stone could at last

1082	et vatem potuit sequi.
1075	tunc primum Phrygius senex
	undis stantibus immemor
	excussit rabidam sitim
1078	nec pomis adhibet manus.
1072	audis tu quoque, navita:
	inferni ratis aequoris
1074	nullo remigio venit.
1079	sic cum blanda per inferos
1080	Orpheus carmina funderet,
1083	consumptos iterum deae
	supplent Eurydices colos.
1085	sed dum respicit immemor
	nec credens sibi redditam
	Orpheus Eurydicen sequi,
	cantus praemia perdidit:
	quae nata est iterum perit.
1090	Tunc solamina cantibus
	quaerens flebilibus modis
	haec Orpheus cecinit Getis:
	leges in superos datas
	et qui tempora digerens
1095	quattuor praecipitis deus
	anni disposuit vices;
	nulli non avidi colus
	Parcas stamina nectere:

.

1072–1074 *placed after* 1078 *by Richter*; 1081–1082 *placed after* 1071 *by Peiper*

1079 blanda per *Fitch*: inquirens *E*: linqueret *A*

1095 praecipitis *A*: praecipites *E*

be mastered and follow the bard.[68]
For the first time then the old Phrygian,
heedless of now still waters,
shook off his rabid thirst,
did not stretch his hands to the fruit.
Boatman, you heard too:
the ship of the underworld sea
travelled without being rowed.
When Orpheus poured such enchanting
songs through the underworld,
the goddesses filled again
Eurydice's spent distaff.[69]
But in looking back, unmindful,
not believing Eurydice
restored and behind him, Orpheus
lost the reward for his songs;
reborn, she perished once more.

    Then looking for solace in song
Orpheus in tearful measures
sang these themes to the Getae:
laws are established for heaven,
even for the god who arranges
the seasons, and sets in order
the headlong year's four changes;
the Parcae spin the greedy
distaff's threads for all;

[68] The reference to Sisyphus' "shameless stone" echoes an Homeric phrase. Below, the old Phrygian is Tantalus, and the boatman Charon.
[69] I.e. the Fates (called the Parcae below, 1098) replenished her life thread.

quod natum est iterum mori.
1100 vati credere Thracio
devictus iubet Hercules.

  Iam, iam legibus obrutis
mundo cum veniet dies,
australis polus obruet
1105 quidquid per Libyam iacet
et sparsus Garamas tenet;
arctous polus obruet
quidquid subiacet axibus
et siccus Boreas ferit.
1110 amisso trepidus polo
Titan excutiet diem.
caeli regia concidens
ortus atque obitus trahet,
atque omnes pariter deos
1115 perdet mors aliqua et chaos;
et Mors fata novissima
in se constituet sibi.

  Quis mundum capiet locus?
discedet via Tartari,
1120 fractis ut pateat polis?
an quod dividit aethera
a terris spatium sat est
et mundi nimium malis?
quis tantum capiet nefas
1125 fati, quis superus locus
pontum Tartara sidera
regna unus capiet tria?

1099 iterum *Fitch*: poterit *EA*   1125 fati *recc.*: fatum *A*:
fratrum *E*   superus *Ascensius*: superis *EA*

what is born, dies once more.
Hercules' overthrow bids us
believe the Thracian bard.

Soon, when all laws are buried,
when the day comes for the cosmos,
the southern skies will bury
all that lies in Libya's compass
and is held by the sparse Garamantes;
the northern skies will bury
all that lies beneath the pole
and is flailed by parching Boreas.
In fear, with the firmament lost,
the Titan will jettison daylight.
The foundering palace of heaven
will drag down East and West;
Chaos and death of a kind
will destroy all gods together;
and Death will assign itself
the final fate as its own.

What place will receive the cosmos?
Will the path to Tartarus part
to make room for the fractured skies?
Or is the space that divides
heaven from earth sufficient,
bigger than the ruined cosmos?
What place in heaven will hold
such fate-wrought havoc—what single
place will hold three realms,
Tartarus, sea, and stars?

Sed quis non modicus fragor
aures attonitas movet?
1130   est est Herculeus sonus.

HERCULES

Converte, Titan clare, anhelantes equos,
emitte noctem. pereat hic mundo dies
quo morior, atra nube inhorrescat polus:
obsta novercae! nunc, pater, caecum chaos
1135   reddi decebat, hinc et hinc compagibus
ruptis uterque debuit frangi polus;
quid parcis astris? Herculem amittis, pater.
nunc partem in omnem, Iuppiter, specta poli,
ne quis Gyges Thessalica iaculetur iuga
1140   et fiat Othrys pondus Encelado leve.
laxabit atri carceris iam iam fores
Pluton superbus, vincula excutiet patri
caelumque reddet. ille qui pro fulmine
tuisque facibus natus in terris eram,
1145   ad Styga revertor. surget Enceladus ferox
mittetque quo nunc premitur in superos onus.
regnum omne, genitor, aetheris dubium tibi
mors nostra faciet. antequam spolium tui
caelum omne fiat, conde me tota, pater,
1150   mundi ruina, frange quem perdis polum.

CHORUS

Non vana times, nate Tonantis:
nunc Thessalicam Pelion Ossam
premet, et Pindo congestus Athos

1139 Gyges *West*: gigas *EA* (*cf.* 167)

430

But what intemperate clamour
strikes and astounds our ears?
The sound of Hercules!

[*He is carried in on a litter by servants*]

ACT 4

HERCULES

Bright Titan, turn around your panting horses, release the
night! Let the world lose this day of my death, let heaven
be roiled with black clouds: block my stepmother's view!
Now, father, blind chaos should be restored; both poles
should be smashed, the firmament shattered from end to
end. Why spare the stars? You are losing Hercules, father.
Now, Jupiter, look to every quarter of heaven, lest some
Gyges hurl Thessalian peaks, and Othrys prove a light
weight for Enceladus. Proud Pluto will shortly open the
doors of his black prison, strike off his father's[70] chains and
restore him to heaven. I, the one born on earth in lieu of
your fiery thunderbolt, am returning to the Styx. Fierce
Enceladus will arise and hurl at the gods the burden that
now oppresses him. My death, father, will put the entire
realm of the sky at risk for you. Before you are completely
despoiled of the heavens, hide me, father, in the utter ruin
of the cosmos, smash the sky that you are losing.

CHORUS

Your fears are not empty, son of the Thunderer.
Now Ossa in Thessaly will bear the weight
of Pelion, and Athos piled on Pindus

---

[70] Saturn.

nemus aetheriis inseret astris;
1155 vincet scopulos inde Typhoeus
et Tyrrhenam feret Inarimen;
feret Aetnaeos inde caminos
scindetque latus montis aperti
nondum Enceladus fulmine victus.
1160 iam te caeli regna sequuntur.

HERCULES

Ego qui relicta morte, contempta Styge,
per media Lethes stagna cum spolio redî
quo paene lapsis excidit Titan equis,
ego quem deorum regna senserunt tria,
1165 morior; nec ullus per meum stridet latus
transmissus ensis aut meae telum necis
saxum est nec instar montis abrupti lapis
aut totus Othrys, non truci rictu gigas
Pindo cadaver obruit toto meum:
1170 sine hoste vincor, quodque me torquet magis
(o misera virtus!) summus Alcidae dies
nullum malum prosternit; impendo, ei mihi,
in nulla vitam facta. pro mundi arbiter
superique quondam dexterae testes meae,
1175 pro cuncta tellus, Herculis vestri placet
mortem perire? dirus o nobis pudor,
o turpe fatum: femina Herculeae necis
auctor feretur! morior Alcides quibus!
invicta si me cadere feminea manu
1180 voluere fata perque tam turpes colos
mea mors cucurrit, cadere potuissem (ei mihi!)

1181 potuissem *A*: potuisset *E* ei mihi *Lipsius*: mihi *EA*

will poke its trees among heaven's stars.
Then Typhon will prevail and lift
the crags of Tyrrhene Inarime;[71]
Enceladus, still not quelled by the lightning,
will lift the forges of Etna then
and rend the gaping mountain's flank.
Heaven's realm is following you already.[72]

HERCULES

I who left the world of death, who scorned the Styx and returned straight through Lethe's pools with my spoil, at sight of which the Titan was almost thrown by his stumbling horses—I, whose presence the gods' three realms have felt—am dying. Yet there is no grating sword thrust through my side; the weapon of my death is not a rock, nor a boulder big as a sheer mountain, nor the whole bulk of Othrys; no fiercely grimacing Giant buried my body beneath the whole of Pindus. I am defeated without an enemy, and as a greater torment—such grief to my valour!—Alcides' last day strikes down no evil; I am not expending my life, alas, on any deeds. O ruler of the universe, and gods above who once witnessed my handiwork, o entire earth: are you resolved that your Hercules' death should be wasted? What a dire disgrace for me, what an ignominious fate: a woman will be called the author of Hercules' death! Alcides dies—at whose hands! If the unyielding fates wished me to fall by a woman's hand, if my death ran on such an ignominious thread, I could have fallen (what

71 Beneath which he is pinned, as Enceladus is beneath Mt Etna.
72 I.e. into ruin.

Iunonis odio; feminae caderem minis,
sed caelum habentis. si nimis superis fuit,
Scythico sub axe genita domuisset meas
1185 vires Amazon. feminae cuius manu
Iunonis hostis vincor! hinc gravior tui,
noverca, pudor est. quid diem hunc laetum vocas?
quid tale tellus genuit iratae tibi?
mortalis odia femina excessit tua.
1190 adhuc furebas esse te Alcidae imparem:
victa es duobus. pudeat irarum deos!

    Utinam meo cruore satiasset suos
Nemeaea rictus pestis, aut centum anguibus
vallatus hydram tabe pavissem mea!
1195 utinam fuissem praeda Centauris datus,
aut inter umbras vinctus aeterno miser
saxo sederem! spolia nunc traxi ultima
Fato stupente, nunc ab inferna Styge
lucem recepi, Ditis evici moras,
1200 ubique mors me fugit—ut titulo inclitae
mortis carerem. pro ferae, victae ferae!
non me triformis sole conspecto canis
ad Styga reduxit, non sub Hesperio polo
Hibera vicit turba pastoris feri,
1205 non gemina serpens; perdidi mortem, ei mihi,
totiens honestam: titulus extremus quis est!

1183 superis *A*: superi *E*
1190 furebas *Gruter*: ferebas *EA*
1197 nunc *Leo*: cum *EA*
1200 titulo *Heinsius*: leto *EA*
1201 mortis *E*: fortis *A*: sortis *Leo*

torment!) to Juno's hatred; my fall would have come through the onslaught of a female, but one who holds heaven. If that was too much for the gods, an Amazon born beneath the Scythian sky could have tamed my strength. But what a woman it is whose hand defeats *me*, the opponent of Juno! Yet the shame of this is more grievous for you, stepmother! Why do you call this a happy day? Did earth produce anything comparable to serve your anger? A mortal woman has surpassed your hatred. You were still enraged at being unequal to Alcides: now you are bested by two. The gods should be ashamed of their anger!

If only the Nemean scourge had sated its gaping jaws on my blood, or I had fed the hydra with my gore, walled in by its hundred snakes! If only I had been given to Centaurs as pillage, or were seated among the shades, bound pitifully fast to eternal rock![73] As it is, I dragged forth the remotest spoil (to Fate's amazement), reached the daylight once more from infernal Styx, won past the barriers of Dis, everywhere death has fled from me—so I should lack the distinction of a glorious death. Ah, those wild beasts, the beasts I conquered! The triform hound could not take me back to the Styx when he glimpsed the sun; under western skies the savage herdsman's Spanish throng[74] could not defeat me, nor could the twin serpents. Alas, I have squandered an honourable death so often: and look at my final claim to glory!

[73] An allusion to the duress in the underworld from which he rescued Theseus.

[74] I.e. the cattle of Geryon. The twin serpents were sent by Juno against Hercules in his cradle.

435

[SENECA]

CHORUS

Viden ut laudis conscia virtus
non Lethaeos horreat amnes?
pudet auctoris, non morte dolet;
1210   cupit extremum finire diem
vasta tumidi mole gigantis
et montiferum Titana pati
rabidaeque necem debere ferae.
sed tua causa est, miserande, manus,
1215   quod nulla fera est nullusque gigas.
iam quis dignus necis Herculeae
superest auctor nisi dextra tui?

HERCULES

Eheu quis intus scorpios, quis fervida
plaga revulsus cancer infixus meas
1220 urit medullas? aëris quondam capax
tumidi specus pulmonis arentes fibras
distendit, ardet felle siccato iecur,
totumque lentus sanguinem avexit vapor.
primam cutem consumpsit, hinc aditum nefas
1225 in membra fecit, abstulit pestis latus,
exedit artus penitus et totas malum
hausit medullas; ossibus vacuis sedet.
nec ossa durant ipsa, sed compagibus
discussa ruptis mole collapsa fluunt.
1230 defecit ingens corpus et pesti satis
Herculea non sunt membra. pro, quantum est malum
quod esse vastum fateor, o dirum nefas!

1214 miserande *Bentley*: miseranda *EA*
1216 iam *A*: nam *E*   1220 aëris *Fitch*: sanguinis *EA*
1221 specus *Fitch*: iecur *EA*

436

CHORUS

You see how valour is alert to fame
and has no dread of Lethe River?
Not grieved by death, but shamed by its source,
he longs to end his final day
crushed by a maddened, hulking giant,
to succumb to a mountain-bearing Titan
or owe his demise to a ravening beast.
But your hand is the cause, pitiable man,
of the fact that there is no beast, no giant.
What fitting source of Hercules' death
remains except your own right hand?

HERCULES

Ah, what scorpion inside me, what crab torn from the torrid zone[75] and embedded in me scorches my vitals? Once
capable of taking in air, my hollow lungs as they inhale now
strain the dry tissue; my liver burns, its gall dried up, and
the smouldering heat has driven off all my blood. The
fiendish thing first consumed my skin, and from there
made its way into my body; the scourge wasted my flanks,
the bane completely devoured my limbs; it drained all
the marrow from my bones, and is lodged in their hol-
lows. The bones themselves cannot stay firm, they pull
apart as the joints rupture, lose their mass and dissolve. My
huge body has become insufficient, the Herculean limbs
are not enough for this scourge. Oh how great is the bane
that I acknowledge as vast! Oh terrible fiend!

[75] I.e. the equatorial zone of the heavens, in which the constellation Cancer lies. Scorpio is traditionally described as "blazing."

[SENECA]

En cernite, urbes, cernite ex illo Hercule
quid iam supersit. Herculem agnoscis, pater?
1235 hisne ego lacertis colla Nemeaei mali
elisa pressi? tensus hac arcus manu
astris ab ipsis detulit Stymphalidas?
his ego citatam gressibus vici feram
radiante clarum fronte gestantem caput?
1240 his fracta Calpe manibus elisit fretum?
his tot ferae, tot scelera, tot reges iacent?
his mundus umeris sedit? haec moles mei est,
haecne illa cervix? has ego opposui manus
caelo ruenti? quis mea custos manu
1245 trahetur ultra Stygius? ubi vires, pater,
in me sepultae?—quid patrem appello Iovem?
quid per Tonantem vindico caelum mihi?
iam, iam meus credetur Amphitryon pater.

Quaecumque pestis viscere in nostro lates,
1250 procede: quid me vulnere occulto petis?
quis te sub axe frigido Pontus Scythes,
quae pigra Tethys genuit aut Maurum premens
Hibera Calpe litus? o dirum malum!
utrumne serpens squalidum crista caput
1255 vibrans, an aliquod et mihi ignotum es malum?
numquid cruore es genita Lernaeae ferae,
an te reliquit Stygius in terris canis?
omne es malum nullumque! quis vultus tibi est?
concede saltem scire quo peream malo;
1260 quaecumque pestis sive quaecumque es fera,

1245f. pater / in me (or parens / in me) Fitch: prius / in me EA:
prius / memet Gronovius   1247 mihi A: miser E
1255 es Fitch: est A: line omitted by E

438

Behold, you nations, behold what now remains of that great Hercules. Do you recognise Hercules, father? Was it with these arms that I crushed and choked the neck of the Nemean menace? Did this hand draw the bow that brought down the Stymphalian birds from the very stars? Was it with these feet that I vanquished the swift beast that displayed a bright head with radiant brows?[76] Was it with these hands that Calpe was cleft, so the sea was forced through it? With these hands that so many beasts, so many crimes, so many kings were felled? On these shoulders that the sky rested? Is this my massive build, this that great neck? Are these the hands I set against heaven's fall? What guardian of Styx will be hauled any more by my hand? Where is my strength, father, now buried within me? But why do I call Jove father? Why lay claim to the heavens by right of the Thunderer? Now truly people will believe Amphitryon my father.

Whatever you are, you scourge hiding in my guts, come forth! Why strike me with a concealed wound? What Scythian Pontus engendered you beneath the chill pole, what sluggish ocean, or Spanish Calpe crowding the Moorish coast? Oh terrible evil! Are you a snake darting its coarse-crested head, or some evil unknown even to me? Were you bred from the blood of the Lernean beast, or left behind on earth by the Stygian hound? You are all evils, and none! What do you look like? At least allow me to know what evil is killing me! Whatever scourge, whatever beast

---

[76] The Arcadian hind had golden antlers.

palam timere! quis tibi in medias locum
fecit medullas? ecce direpta cute
viscera manus detexit, ulterior tamen
inventa latebra est—o malum simile Herculi!

1265   Unde iste fletus? unde in has lacrimae genas?
invictus olim vultus et numquam malis
lacrimas suis praebere consuetus (pudet)
iam flere didicit. quis dies fletum Herculis,
quae terra vidit? siccus aerumnas tuli.

1270 tibi illa virtus, quae tot elisit mala,
tibi cessit uni; prima et ante omnes mihi
fletum abstulisti. durior saxo horrido
et chalybe vultus et vaga Symplegade
victus minas infregit et lacrimam expulit.

1275 flentem, gementem, summe pro rector poli,
me terra vidit, quodque me torquet magis,
noverca vidit. urit ecce iterum fibras,
incaluit ardor: unde nunc fulmen mihi?

CHORUS

Quid non possit superare dolor?
1280 quondam Getico durior Haemo
nec Parrhasio lentior axe
saevo cessit membra dolori,
fessumque movens per colla caput
latus alterno pondere flectit.
1285 fletum virtus saepe resorbet:
sic arctoas laxare nives
quamvis tepido sidere Titan

1261 timere *Wilamowitz*: timeri *E*: timeres *A*
1274 victus minas *Axelson*: rictus meos *EA*

440

you are, be feared in the open! Who made you a place in the very marrow of my bones? See, my hand tore away the skin and uncovered my guts—yet you found some remoter hiding place. Oh evil resembling Hercules![77]

But why this weeping? Why tears on these cheeks? This face, once invincible and never given to bestowing tears on its troubles, has now learnt—shame on me!—to cry. What day, what land has seen Hercules in tears? I bore my hardships dry-eyed. To you that valour that crushed so many evils has yielded—to you alone.[78] You first, and in front of all, have drawn weeping from me. This face, harder than rugged rock or steel or the shifting Symplegades, has been overcome, abated its threats and forced out tears. By the high ruler of heaven! The earth has seen me crying and groaning, and what torments me more, my stepmother has seen it. Ah! The heat has intensified and burns my tissues again. Where is the thunderbolt to strike me?

CHORUS

Could anything *not* be conquered by pain?
Formerly harder than Getic Haemus,
no softer than the Parrhasian pole,
he has yielded his limbs to the cruel pain.
His neck tosses his weary head
and he shifts his weight from side to side.
Yet his valour repeatedly chokes back tears:
just so, however hot his orb,
the Titan does not make bold to melt

[77] In finding a way to the remotest places (cf. 33, 1197, 1765).
[78] I.e. the poison.

non tamen audet,
vincitque faces solis adulti
glaciale iubar.

HERCULES

1290 Converte vultus ad meas clades, pater.
numquam ad tuas confugit Alcides manus,
non cum per artus hydra fecundum meos
caput explicaret; inter infernos lacus
possessus atra nocte cum Fato steti
1295 nec invocavi; tot feras vici horridas,
reges, tyrannos, non tamen vultus meos
in astra torsi. semper haec nobis manus
votum spopondit; nulla propter me sacro
micuere caelo fulmina. hic aliquid dies
1300 optare iussit; primus audierit preces
idemque summus. unicum fulmen peto;
giganta crede! non minus caelum mihi
asserere potui; dum patrem verum puto,
caelo peperci. sive crudelis, pater,
1305 sive es misericors, commoda nato manum
properante morte et occupa hanc laudem tibi.

Vel si piget manusque detrectat nefas,
emitte Siculo vertice ardentes, pater,
Titanas, in me qui manu Pindum ferant
1310 Ossaque qui me monte proiecto opprimant.
abrumpat Erebi claustra, me stricto petat
Bellona ferro; mitte Gradivum trucem,
armetur in me dirus: est frater quidem,

1289 faces *E*: nefas *A*   adulti *Zintzerling*: adusti *EA*
1310 Ossaque *Housman*: aut ossa *E*: aut te ossa *A*

the arctic snows;
the sun's full blaze is overpowered
by the radiance of the ice.

HERCULES

Turn your eyes on my destruction, father! Alcides has never fled to your hands: not when the hydra stretched its fertile heads over my body; amidst the infernal pools in the grip of black night I stood with Fate, and did not call upon you; I conquered so many beasts, kings, tyrants, without turning my eyes up to the stars. Always this right hand has guaranteed what I prayed for; no thunderbolts have flashed out of the holy heavens on my account. But this day has bidden me request something. It will be the first to have heard my prayers, and the last. I ask for just one thunderbolt; consider me a giant![79] I could have laid claim to heaven no less than they; but believing you my true father, I spared the heavens. Whether in callousness or in mercy, father, lend your hand to your son in a speedy death, and appropriate this glory as your own.[80]

Or if that is repellent, if your hand recoils from such outrage, release the burning Titans from the Sicilian height,[81] father, so they can bear Pindus against me, fling Mt Ossa down on me and crush me. Let Bellona break the bonds of Erebus and attack me with sword drawn; send grim Gradivus, let him put on his dread armour against

---

[79] Jupiter had used his thunderbolts against the giants who attacked heaven.

[80] The "glory" of killing Hercules, which would otherwise accrue to Deianira or Juno.

[81] Etna.

443

sed ex noverca. Tu quoque, Alcidae soror

1315 tantum ex parente, cuspidem in fratrem tuum
iaculare, Pallas. Supplices tendo manus
ad te, noverca: sparge tu saltem, precor,
telum; perire feminae possum manu.
iam fracta, iam satiata quid pascis minas?

1320 quid quaeris ultra? supplicem Alciden vides,
et nulla tellus, nulla me vidit fera
te deprecantem. nunc mihi irata quidem
opus est noverca: nunc tuus cessat dolor?
nunc odia ponis? parcis ubi votum est mori!

1325   O terra et urbes, non facem quisquam Herculi,
non arma tradet? tela subtrahitis mihi?
ita nulla saevas terra concipiat feras
post me sepultum, nec meas umquam manus
imploret orbis, si qua nascentur mala

1330 nascatur ultor: undique infelix caput
mactate saxis, vincite aerumnas meas.
ingrate cessas orbis? excidimus tibi?
adhuc malis ferisque suppositus fores,
ni me tulisses. vindicem vestrum malis

1335 eripite, populi. tempus hoc vobis datur
pensare merita; mors erit pretium omnium.

ALCMENE

Quas misera terras mater Alcidae petam?
ubi natus, ubinam est? certa si visus notat,
reclinis ecce corde anhelante aestuat;

1340 gemit: peractum est. membra complecti ultimum,
o nate, liceat; spiritus fugiens meo

1322 quidem *A*: pater *E*

me; he is my brother, true, but by my stepmother. You too, sister to Alcides by his father only: hurl your sharp spear, Pallas, against your brother. I stretch out my hands in supplication to you, stepmother, I pray you: *you* at least must fire a thunderbolt; I can accept death at a female's hand. When already assuaged and satiated, why continue to feed your hostility? What more do you want? You see Alcides as a suppliant, and no land, no beast, has yet seen me begging you for mercy. Now I need an *angry* stepmother. *Now* your rage quits? *Now* you put aside hatred? You spare me when my prayer is to die!

O earth and its peoples: will no one hand Hercules a torch or arms? Do you keep weapons from me? I pray that no land may breed savage beasts after I am buried, that the world may never appeal to my hands, and that if evils *are* born, an avenger may be born—on this condition: surround me and stone my ill-fated self to death, vanquish my sufferings. Do you fail me, ungrateful world? Have you forgotten me? You would still be subject to troubles and wild beasts, if you had not borne me. Rescue your champion from his troubles, you nations. You are given this chance to repay my services; death will requite them all.

ALCMENE

[*Entering*] What lands must Alcides' wretched mother seek out? Where is my son, where in the world? If my sight is sure, see he lies there, panting and tossing feverishly; he groans: he is finished. Let me embrace your limbs for the last time, my son, and gather your fleeting life-breath

---

1330 ultor *Peiper*: alius *A*: odium *E*
1340 ultimum *Bothe*: ultima *EA*

[SENECA]

legatur ore: bracchia amplexu cape.
ubi membra sunt? ubi illa quae mundum tulit
stelligera cervix? quis tibi exiguam tui
1345   partem reliquit?

HERCULES

        Herculem spectas quidem,
mater, sed umbram et vile nescioquid mei.
agnosce, mater—ora quid flectis retro
vultumque mergis? Herculem dici tuum
partum erubescis?

ALCMENE

        Quis feram mundus novam,
1350   quae terra genuit? quodve tam dirum nefas
de te triumphat? victor Herculeus quis est?

HERCULES

Nuptae iacentem cernis Alciden dolis.

ALCMENE

Quis tantus est qui vincat Alciden dolus?

HERCULES

Quicumque, mater, feminae iratae sat est.

ALCMENE

1355   Et unde in artus pestis aut ossa incidit?

HERCULES

Aditum venenis palla femineis dedit.

ALCMENE

Ubinam ista palla est? membra nudata intuor.

HERCULES

Consumpta mecum est.

446

with my lips; accept my embracing arms. Where are those limbs? Where that star-bearing neck that supported heaven? Who has left you so small a remnant of yourself?

HERCULES

It is indeed Hercules you behold, mother, but a shadow and paltry *whatever* of myself. Recognise me, mother— why do you turn your eyes away and cover your face? Do you blush that Hercules is called your offspring?

ALCMENE

What world, what land has engendered some new beast? What terrible evil can triumph over you? Who is Hercules' conqueror?

HERCULES

It is through my wife's deceit that you see Alcides laid low.

ALCMENE

What deceit is great enough to conquer Alcides?

HERCULES

Any, mother, that suffices a woman's anger.

ALCMENE

And how did the bane invade your flesh and bones?

HERCULES

A robe gave access to the woman's poisons.

ALCMENE

Wherever is this robe? I see bare limbs.

HERCULES

It was devoured together with me.

1342 amplexu *Grotius*: et amplexus *E*: in amplexus *A*

ALCMENE

Tantane inventa est lues?

HERCULES

Errare mediis crede visceribus meis,
1360   o mater, hydram et mille cum Lerna feras.
quae tanta nubes flamma Sicanias secat,
quae Lemnos ardens, quae plaga igniferi poli
vetans flagranti currere in zona diem?
in ipsa me iactate, pro comites, freta
1365   mediosque in amnes!—quis sat est Hister mihi?
non ipse terris maior Oceanus meos
franget vapores; omnis in nostris malis
deficiet umor, omnis arescet latex.
    Quid, rector Erebi, me remittebas Iovi?
1370   decuit tenere. redde me tenebris tuis,
talem subactis Herculem ostende inferis.
nil inde ducam; quid times iterum Herculem?
invade, Mors, non trepida: iam possum mori.

ALCMENE

Compesce lacrimas saltem et aerumnas doma,
1375   malisque tantis Herculem indomitum refer,
mortemque differ: quos soles vince inferos.

HERCULES

Si me catenis horridus vinctum suis
praeberet avidae Caucasus volucri dapem,
Scythia gemente flebilis gemitus mihi
1380   non excidisset. si vagae Symplegades

---

[82] I.e. the fire of Mt Etna.   [83] A hyperbolic suggestion
that the equatorial zone in the heavens is too hot even for the sun,
whose path (ecliptic) lies outside that zone in summer.

ALCMENE

Has such a potent scourge been devised?

HERCULES

Believe me, mother, in my very guts there roams the hydra—and a thousand beasts along with Lerna. Is the flame as hot that pierces the clouds of Sicily,[82] or the blaze of Lemnos, or the tract of the fiery sky that bars the sun from coursing in its burning zone?[83] My comrades, hurl me far into the sea, into the midst of rivers! Yet what Hister can suffice me? Not even Ocean, though vaster than all lands, can quell my fever; against this torment of mine all moisture will fail, all water dry up.

O ruler of Erebus, why did you try to return me to Jove? You should have kept me. Take me back to your darkness, show Hercules in this state to the underworld he conquered! I shall take nothing thence; why do you fear Hercules once more? Attack me, Death, without fear: now I am capable of dying.

ALCMENE

At least control your tears and master your suffering! Once more show Hercules unconquered by such ordeals. And postpone your death: as is your custom, vanquish the powers below.

HERCULES

If the jagged Caucasus offered me, bound in chains, to the greedy vulture to feast on,[84] though Scythia might have groaned, no tearful groan would have escaped *me*. If the wandering Symplegades crushed me between their two

[84] He thinks of the torment from which he freed Prometheus.

utraque premerent rupe, redeuntis minas
ferrem ruinae. Pindus incumbat mihi
atque Haemus et qui Thracios fluctus Athos
frangit Iovisque fulmen excipiens Mimas.
1385   non ipse si in me, mater, hic mundus ruat
superque nostros flagret incensus toros
Phoebeus axis, degener mentem Herculis
clamor domaret. mille decurrant ferae
pariterque lacerent, hinc feris clangoribus
1390   aetheria me Stymphalis, hinc taurus minax
cervice tota pulset, et quidquid fuit
solum quoque ingens; surgat hinc illinc nemus
artusque nostros dirus immittat Sinis:
sparsus silebo. non ferae excutient mihi,
1395   non arma gemitus, nil quod impelli potest.

ALCMENE

Non virus artus, nate, femineum coquit,
sed dura series operis et longus tibi
pavit cruentos forsitan morbos labor.

HERCULES

Ubi morbus, ubinam est? estne adhuc aliquid mali
1400   in orbe mecum? veniat huc! aliquis mihi
intendat arcus—nuda sufficiet manus.
procedat agedum!

ALCMENE

        Vae mihi, sensus quoque
excussit illi nimius impulsos dolor.
1407   dolor iste furor est; Herculem solus domat.
1404   Removete quaeso tela et infestas, precor,

    1402 vae *Fitch*: ei *E*: et *A*

450

crags, I would endure the menace of their returning on-slaught. Pindus could bear down on me, and Haemus, and Athos that breaks the waves of Thrace, and Mimas that receives Jove's thunderbolts. Not even if the very heavens should fall upon me, mother, and Phoebus' burning chariot blaze above my couch, would unworthy cries master the spirit of Hercules. Let a thousand beasts together run at me and rend me; let the airborne Stymphalians strike me on this side with their wild cries, and on that side a menacing bull with all the force of his neck—and whatever was prodigious just in itself. On each side let trees spring up, and dread Sinis shoot my limbs skyward; though torn apart, I shall remain silent. No beasts, no weapons, nothing *assailable* will draw groans from me.

ALCMENE

It is no woman's poison, my son, that scorches your body, but the arduous round of labours and lengthy toil has perhaps bred bloody diseases in you.

HERCULES

Where is disease, where in the world? Is there still some evil on earth with me? Let it approach! Reach me my bow, someone. No, my bare hand will suffice. Let it come on, now!

ALCMENE

Alas, even his senses have been overthrown and driven out by excessive pain. Pain causes this madness; it alone can master Hercules. [*To attendants*] Please remove his weap-

---

1403 illi *Bentley*: ille *EA*
1407 *placed after* 1403 *by Zwierlein*

[SENECA]

1405 rapite hinc sagittas: igne suffuso genae
scelus minantur. quas petam latebras anus?—
1408 cur deinde latebras aut fugam vecors petam?
obire forti meruit Alcmene manu.
1410 vel scelere pereat, antequam letum mihi
ignavus aliquis mandat ac turpis manus
de me triumphat. Ecce lassatus malis
sopore fessas alligat venas dolor,
gravique anhelum pectus impulsu quatit.
1415 Favete, superi! si mihi natum inclitum
miserae negastis, vindicem saltem, precor,
servate terris. abeat excussus dolor,
corpusque vires reparet Herculeum novas.

HYLLUS

Pro lux acerba, pro capax scelerum dies!
1420 nurus Tonantis occidit, natus iacet,
nepos supersum; scelere materno hic perit,
fraude illa capta est. quis per annorum vices
totoque in aevo poterit aerumnas senex
referre tantas? unus eripuit dies
1425 parentem utrumque. cetera ut sileam mala
parcamque fatis, Herculem amitto patrem.

ALCMENE

Compesce voces, inclitum Alcidae genus
miseraeque fato similis Alcmenae nepos:
longus dolorem forsitan vincet sopor.
1430 —sed ecce, lassam deserit mentem quies
redditque morbo corpus et luctum mihi.

1418 novas *Axelson*: nefas *E*: suas *A*

452

ons, quickly carry those menacing arrows away from here, I pray you: his blazing eyes threaten some crime. What refuge shall an old woman look for? But then, why look for refuge or escape? Folly! Alcmene deserves to die by a valiant hand. Let her even perish by crime, before some coward assigns me death, or some dishonorable hand triumphs over me.

But see, the exhaustion of suffering and pain is binding his weary frame in sleep; his chest heaves and shakes in a laboured rhythm. Show him favour, you gods! If you have denied me my famous son to my sorrow, at least save the world its champion, I pray. Let his pain be driven away, and the body of Hercules regain strength anew.

HYLLUS

[*Entering*] O bitter light, o day disposed to crimes! The Thunderer's daughter-in-law is dead, and his son laid low, while I his grandson survive; *he* is dying through my mother's crime, *she* was taken in by deceit. What old man could tell of such sorrows through the passing years, through the whole of his life? One day has stolen both my parents. To say nothing of my other troubles, and not to reproach the fates, I am losing Hercules as my father.

ALCMENE

Curb your words, glorious son of Alcides, and grandson of unhappy Alcmene with a fate like hers! Perhaps a lengthy sleep will subdue his pain. But see, rest is forsaking his weary mind, returning his body to sickness, and heartache to me.

HERCULES

Quid hoc? rigenti cernitur Trachin iugo?
an inter astra positus evasi genus
mortale tandem? quis mihi caelum parat?
1435   te te, pater, iam video; placatam quoque
specto novercam. quis sonus nostras ferit
caelestis aures? Iuno me generum vocat.
video nitentem regiam clari aetheris
Phoebique tritam flammea zonam rota.
1440   —cubile video noctis; hinc tenebrae vocant.
quid hoc? quis axem claudit et ab ipsis, pater,
deducit astris? ora Phoebeus modo
afflabat axis, tam prope a caelo fui—
Trachina video; quis mihi terras dedit?
1445   Oete modo infra steterat ac totus fuit
suppositus orbis; tam bene excideras, dolor!
cogis fateri—parce et hanc vocem occupa.
     Haec, Hylle, dona matris; hoc munus parat!
utinam liceret stipite ingesto impiam
1450   effringere animam, quale Amazonium malum
circa nivalis Caucasi domui latus.
o clara Megara, tune cum furerem mihi
coniunx fuisti? stipitem atque arcus date;
dextra inquinetur, laudibus maculam imprimam,
1455   summus legatur femina Herculeus labor.

HYLLUS

Compesce diras, genitor, irarum minas:
habet, peractum est, quas petis poenas dedit;

1440 tenebrae vocant *E*: tenebras vocat *A*
1452 clara *EA*: cara *Heinsius*

454

HERCULES

What is this? Is it Trachis I see with its rugged mountains?
Or have I finally escaped the human race and been set
among the stars? Who is giving me access to heaven? *You*,
father, I see you now; my stepmother too, in a reconciled
mood. What is this heavenly sound that strikes my ears?
Juno calls me son-in-law![85] I can see bright heaven's glittering palace, and the circling track worn by Phoebus' fiery
wheels. But now I see the couch of night; darkness calls me
away. What is this? Who is closing the firmament, father,
and pulling me down from among the stars? Just now
Phoebus' horses were breathing on my face, I was so close
to heaven! It *is* Trachis I see. Who has given me the earth?
Just now Oeta stood below me, the whole world lay beneath my feet. It was so good to forget you, my pain! You
force me to admit—stop, forestall those words![86]

Hyllus, this is your mother's gift, this the boon she be-
stows! If only I could crush out her life with blows of my
club, just as I tamed the Amazon menace around the flanks
of snowy Caucasus. O renowned Megara, were *you* my
wife at the time of my madness?[87] [*To attendants*] Give
here my club and my bow. I must stain my right hand and
sully my glory, and a woman must be chosen as Hercules'
final labour.

HYLLUS

Stop these terrible threats arising from your anger, father.
It's done, all over![88] She has paid the penalty you demand.

---

[85] He is to become so through marriage to Hebe.
[86] He was about to admit that the pain is too strong for him.
[87] It should have been Deianira.
[88] The gladiatorial formula, used also at 1472 and *Ag* 901.

sua perempta dextera mater iacet.

HERCULES

Caecus dolore es! manibus irati Herculis
1460 occidere meruit; perdidit comitem Lichas.
saevire in ipsum corpus exanime impetus
atque ira cogit. cur minis nostris caret
ipsum cadaver? pabulum accipiant ferae.

HYLLUS

Plus misera laeso doluit; hinc aliquid quoque
1465 detrahere velles. occidit dextra sua,
tuo dolore; plura quam poscis tulit.
sed non cruentae sceleribus nuptae iaces
nec fraude matris: Nessus hos struxit dolos
ictus sagittis qui tuis vitam expulit.
1470 cruore tincta est palla semiferi, pater,
Nessusque nunc has exigit poenas sibi.

HERCULES

Habet, peractum est! fata se nostra explicant;
lux ista summa est. quercus hanc sortem mihi
fatidica quondam dederat et Parnassio
1475 Cirrhaea quatiens templa mugitu nemus:
"Dextra perempti victor, Alcide, viri
olim iacebis; hic tibi emenso freta
terrasque et umbras finis extremus datur."
nil querimur ultra: decuit hunc finem dari,
1480 ne quis superstes Herculis victor foret.

1459 caecus dolore es *Fitch*: caeci* dolores *A*: recte dolor es *E*:
cecidit dolose *Richter*

456

Mother lies dead, slain by her own hand.

HERCULES

You are blinded by grief! She deserved to perish at the hands of Hercules in his rage. Lichas has lost a counterpart. Impulse and anger drive me beserk, even against her lifeless body. Why should she be spared my violence even as a corpse? Let wild beasts have her to feed on!

HYLLUS

The poor woman suffered more pain than the one she harmed; you might even have wanted to lighten it. She died by her own hand, but by reason of your pain. She endured more than you are demanding. But it was no crime of a murderous wife that brought you down, no treachery of my mother's. Nessus was the one that devised this trick, when he was hit by your arrows and breathed his last. The robe was smeared with the blood of that half-beast, father; now Nessus is exacting his recompense.

HERCULES

It's done, all over! My fate unfolds; this is my final day. This destiny was foretold me long ago by the prophetic oak, the tree that shakes Cirrha's shrine as it resounds on Parnassus:[89] "By the hand of a dead man, Alcides, you will one day be laid low, though his victor. This final end is assigned you, following your travels across seas and lands and the world of shadows." I make no further protest. This end was rightly assigned me, so no one should conquer Hercules and live.

---

[89] The "speaking oak" of Chaonia may here be identified with Apollo's laurel at Delphi (*Oed* 228); or two separate prophecies may be meant.

Nunc mors legatur clara memoranda inclita,
me digna prorsus: nobilem hunc faciam diem.
caedatur omnis silva et Oetaeum nemus
concipiat ignes; Herculem accipiat rogus,
1485   sed ante mortem. Tu, genus Poeantium,
hoc triste nobis, iuvenis, officium appara:
Herculea totum flamma succendat diem.

    Ad te preces nunc, Hylle, supremas fero.
est clara captas inter, in vultu genus
1490   regnumque referens, Euryto virgo edita
Iole: tuis hanc facibus et thalamis para.
victor cruentus abstuli patriam lares
nihilque miserae praeter Alciden dedi—
et ipse rapitur. penset aerumnas suas,
1495   Iovis nepotem foveat et natum Herculis;
tibi illa pariat quidquid ex nobis habet.

    Tuque ipsa planctus pone funereos, precor,
o clara genetrix: vivet Alcides tibi.
virtute nostra paelicem feci tuam
1500   credi novercam, sive nascenti Herculi
nox illa certa est sive mortalis meus
pater est. licet sit falsa progenies mei,
materna culpa cesset et crimen Iovis,
merui parentem: contuli caelo decus,
1505   natura me concepit in laudes Iovis.
quin ipse, quamquam maximus, credi meus
pater esse gaudet. parce iam lacrimis, parens:
superba matres inter Argolicas eris.

    1498 vivet *A*: vivit *E*   1500 nascenti Herculi *Viansino*:
nascente hercule *A*: nascentē herculē *E*
    1506 maximus *Fitch*: iuppiter* *EA*

Now I must choose a death that will be glorious, memorable, renowned, and thoroughly worthy of me. I must make this day famous. Let all the woodland be cut, and Oeta's forest be set on fire; let a pyre receive Hercules—but *before* his death. Son of Poeas:[90] you must undertake this sad duty for me, young man. Let the flames of Hercules' pyre light up the whole day!

To you I direct my final request now, Hyllus. Among the captives is an illustrious girl, whose face attests her royal birth—the daughter of Eurytus, Iole. Make her your bride in torchlit nuptials. As a bloody conqueror I robbed her of fatherland and home, and gave the poor woman nothing save Alcides. Now he too is taken from her. Let her have some recompense for her sorrows in cherishing Jove's grandson, Hercules' son. If she has conceived a child by me, let her bring it to birth for you.

You too, my famous mother, must put aside laments over my death, I pray you. For you Alcides will be alive. My valour has resulted in my stepmother being thought a mere rival of yours, whether that celebrated night is beyond doubt for Hercules' conception, or whether my father is mortal. My pedigree may be false, an end may be put to my mother's shame and Jove's discredit,[91] yet I have come to deserve his parentage. I have brought heaven renown, nature conceived me for Jove's greater glory. Even he, though almighty, is glad to be thought my father. Stop your tears now, mother: you will be proud among the

[90] Philoctetes: he could have arrived with Hercules' bearers at the beginning of the Act.

[91] Both are entailed by the story that Jupiter fathered Hercules on Alcmene.

quid tale Iuno genuit aetherium gerens
1510   sceptrum et Tonanti nupta? mortali tamen
caelum tenens invidit, Alciden suum
dici esse voluit.
                  Perage nunc, Titan, vices
solus relictus: ille qui vester comes
ubique fueram, Tartara et manes peto.
1515   hanc tamen ad imos perferam laudem inclitam,
quod nulla pestis fudit Alciden palam,
omnemque pestem vicit Alcides palam.

CHORUS

O decus mundi, radiate Titan,
cuius ad primos Hecate vapores
1520   lassa nocturnae levat ora bigae:
dic sub Aurora positis Sabaeis,
dic sub occasu positis Hiberis,
quique ferventi quatiuntur axe,
quique sub plaustro patiuntur Ursae,
1525   dic ad aeternos properare manes
Herculem et regnum canis inquieti,
unde non umquam remeabit ille.
sume quos nubes radios sequantur,
pallidus maestas speculare terras
1530   et caput turpes nebulae pererrent.
quando, pro Titan, ubi, quo sub axe

1527 remeabit *Leo*: remeavit *EA*   ille *Schenkl*: ullus *A*: inde *E*

92 This cosmic announcement is adapted by Chapman, *Bussy D'Ambois* V.4.99–107: "haste thee where the grey-eyed morn per-

mothers of Greece. Has Juno, wife of the Thunderer and wielder of the heavenly sceptre, given birth to anything comparable? Ruling the heavens, she still envied a mortal, and wished Alcides was called her own.

Now you are left, Titan, to carry out your rounds alone; I, who accompanied you everywhere, am making for the shades of Tartarus. Yet I shall bear this glorious renown into the depths, that no scourge openly slew Alcides, and every scourge was openly defeated by Alcides. [*Exeunt omnes, Hercules carried on the litter*]

CHORUS

Glory of heaven, radiant Titan,
at whose first warming daylight Hecate
looses her weary team of night:
tell the Sabaeans beside the dawn,
tell the Spaniards beside the sunset,
and those who are shaken by your blazing chariot
or suffer beneath the Bear's own Wain:
Hercules is passing quickly to eternal
shades, to the kingdom of the unquiet hound,
from which he will never return again.[92]
Choose such rays as clouds attend,
look wanly on the gloomy earth,
let bleak fogs drift across your face.
When, Titan, where under heaven will you have

---

fumes / Her Rosy chariot with Sabaean spices; / Fly where the evening from the Iberian vales / Takes on her swarthy shoulders Hecate / Crowned with a grove of oaks; fly where men feel / The burning axletree, and those that suffer / Beneath the chariot of the Snowy Bear; / And tell them all that D'Ambois now is hasting / To the eternal dwellers."

Herculem in terris alium sequeris?
quas manus orbis miser invocabit,
si qua sub Lerna numerosa pestis
1535 sparget in centum rabiem dracones,
Arcadum si quis, populi vetusti,
fecerit silvas aper inquietas,
Thraciae si quis Rhodopes alumnus
durior terris Helices nivosae
1540 sparget humano stabulum cruore?
quis dabit pacem populo timenti,
si quid irati superi per urbes
iusserint nasci? iacet omnibus par,
quem parem tellus genuit Tonanti.
1545 planctus immensas resonet per urbes,
et comas nullo cohibente nodo
femina exertos feriat lacertos;
solaque obductis foribus deorum
templa securae pateant novercae.
1550   Vadis ad Lethen Stygiumque litus,
unde te nullae referent carinae;
vadis ad manes miserandus, unde
Morte devicta tuleras triumphum.
umbra nudatis venies lacertis
1555 languido vultu tenuique collo,
teque non solum feret illa puppis.
non tamen viles eris inter umbras:
Aeacon iuxta geminosque Cretas

1558 iuxta *Axelson*: inter *EA*

---

93 These allusions are respectively to the Lernean hydra, the
Erymanthian boar, and Diomedes.

462

another Hercules to escort on earth?
Whose hands will the hapless world invoke
if some prolific scourge near Lerna
deploys its rage in a hundred snakes,
or if some boar disquiets the forests
of Arcadians, that olden folk,
or a scion of Rhodope in Thrace,
harsher than Helice's snowy land,
spatters his stables with human blood?[93]
Who will bring peace to fearful folk
if amidst their cities the gods in anger
command some birth? He whom Earth produced
as the Thunderer's equal, lies everyone's equal.
Through countless cities let blows of grief
resound: with hair fully unfastened
let women bare and strike their arms.
Let the doors of the gods be closed, and only
his carefree stepmother's shrines be open.

    You fare to Lethe and the Stygian shore,
from which no boat will bring you back.
Pitiful! You fare to the shades from which
you returned in triumph, having conquered Death.
You will walk as a ghost with arms stripped bare,
with listless face and wasted neck,
and that ship will not bear you alone.[94]
Yet you will not join the common shades:
at Aeacus' side, with the Cretan pair,[95]

[94] Though it once carried Hercules as its sole passenger, and almost sank beneath his living weight (*Herc* 775–777).

[95] Minos and Rhadamanthus, like Aeacus judges of the dead.

facta discernes feriens tyrannos.
1560 Parcite, o dites, inhibete dextras:
laudis est purum tenuisse ferrum,
dumque regnabas, minimum cruentis
in tuas urbes licuisse factis.

Sed locum virtus habet inter astra.
1565 sedis arctoae spatium tenebis
an graves Titan ubi promit aestus?
an sub occasu tepido nitebis,
unde commisso resonare ponto
audies Calpen? loca quae sereni
1570 deprimes caeli? quis erit recepto
tutus Alcide locus inter astra?
horrido tantum procul a leone
det pater sedes calidoque cancro,
ne tuo vultu tremefacta leges
1575 astra conturbent trepidetque Titan.
Vere dum flores venient tepenti
1578 et comam silvis revocabit aestas
1579 pomaque autumno fugiente cedent
1577 et comam silvis hiemes recident,
1581 tu comes Phoebo, comes ibis astris.
1580 nulla te terris rapiet vetustas:
ante nascetur seges in profundo
vel fretum dulci resonabit unda,
ante descendet glacialis Ursae
1585 sidus et ponto vetito fruetur,
quam tuas laudes populi quiescant.

1562 minimum (nimium *PT*) cruentis *A*: minus in procellis *E*
1563 factis *Fitch*: fatis *EA*

you will sift men's deeds, chastising tyrants.
Forbear, you magnates, stay your hands!
Fame lies in keeping the sword unstained,
and in curtailing bloody deeds
against your peoples throughout your reign.

But valour has place among the stars.
Will you take a station in the northern sky
or where Titan's torrid heat arises?
Or shine far in the balmy west,
and listen from there as Calpe resounds
to its warring seas? What place will you burden
in the cloudless heaven? With Alcides admitted
among the stars, what place will be safe?
Just let the father seat you far
from the fearsome Lion and scorching Crab,
lest the stars in terror at your demeanour
confound their laws, and the Titan tremble.
    While flowers appear in springtime's warmth
and summer calls back forest leaves
and apples fall as autumn wanes
and winter pares back forest leaves,
you will be there with the stars and Phoebus.
Time will never efface you on earth.
Crops will sooner sprout on the deep
or seas resound with freshwater waves,
sooner the stars of the icy Bear
will descend and enjoy the forbidden waters,
than the nations will cease to tell your praises.

1577 *placed after* 1579 *by Spika
Richter*   1580 *placed after* 1581 *by*

465

Te, pater rerum, miseri precamur:
nulla nascatur fera, nulla pestis,
non duces saevos miseranda tellus
1590   horreat, nulla dominetur aula
qui putet solum decus esse regni
semper intensum tenuisse ferrum;
si quid in terris iterum timetur,
vindicem terrae petimus relictae.

1595   Heu quid hoc? mundus sonat ecce vastum.
maeret Alciden pater? an deorum
clamor, an vox est timidae novercae,
Hercule ac viso fugit astra Iuno?
passus an pondus titubavit Atlas?
1600   an magis diri tremuere manes,
Herculem et visum canis inferorum
fugit abruptis trepidus catenis?
fallimur: laeto venit ecce vultu
quem tulit Poeans umerisque tela
1605   gestat et notas populis pharetras,
         Herculis heres.

Effare casus, iuvenis, Herculeos precor,
vultuve quonam tulerit Alcides necem.

PHILOCTETES

Quo nemo vitam.

1595 vastum *Fitch*: maestum *Watt*: *word omitted by* A *(except*
mundus *P)*: 1564–1606 *omitted by* E

---

96 Accordingly his approach is as thunderous as Hercules' own
(*Herc* 520–523, *HO* 1128–30).

466

Father of the world, in distress we pray:
let no wild beast, no scourge be born;
no sorry land fear cruel lords,
no palace hold a potentate
who thinks the splendour of a throne lies solely
in holding the sword ever outstretched;
if terror comes again to the earth,
we crave a champion for the friendless earth.

What's this? A mighty sound through the world!
The father mourning Alcides? Or cries
from the gods? Or the voice of the frightened
    stepmother—
has Juno seen Hercules and fled from the stars?
Or Atlas staggering under his weight?
Or rather the dread shades trembling in terror
and the underworld hound breaking his chains
and running in fear at sight of Hercules?
We are wrong: Poeas' son is approaching, look,
with joyful face, his shoulders bearing
the weapons and quiver famed through the world:
    he is Hercules' heir.[96]

ACT 5

Pray tell us, young man: what befell Hercules? With what
demeanour did Alcides bear death?

PHILOCTETES
Better than anyone ever bore life!

467

CHORUS

Laetus adeone ultimos

1610 invasit ignes?

PHILOCTETES

Esse iam flammas nihil
ostendit ille. quid sub hoc mundo Hercules
immune vinci liquit? en domita omnia.

CHORUS

Inter vapores quis fuit forti locus?

PHILOCTETES

Quod unum in orbe vicerat nondum malum,
1615 et flamma victa est; haec quoque accessit feris:
inter labores ignis Herculeos abît.

CHORUS

Edissere agedum, flamma quo victa est modo?

PHILOCTETES

Ut omnis Oeten maesta corripuit manus,
huic fagus umbras perdit et toto iacet
1620 succisa trunco, flectit hic pinum ferox
astris minantem et nube de media vocat;
ruitura cautem movit et silvam tulit
secum minorem. Chaonis quondam loquax
stat vasta late quercus et Phoebum vetat,
1625 ultraque totum porrigit ramos nemus:
gemit illa multo vulnere impresso minax
frangitque cuneos; resilit incussus chalybs
vulnusque ferrum patitur et rigidum est parum.
commota tandem cum cadens latam sui
1630 duxit ruinam, protinus radios locus
admisit omnis. sedibus pulsae suis

CHORUS LEADER

Was he so joyful in confronting the final fire?

PHILOCTETES

He showed that even flames are nothing. What has Hercules left immune to conquest under heaven? See, everything has been vanquished!

CHORUS LEADER

In the midst of burning, what room was there for bravery?

PHILOCTETES

The one evil he had not yet conquered in the world, fire, is now conquered too. It has been added to the wild beasts; fire has ended up among the labours of Hercules.

CHORUS LEADER

Come now, explain how the flames were conquered.

PHILOCTETES

The whole sorrowful band set to work on Mt Oeta. At one man's blows a beech tree ceased to give shade, its long trunk lying felled. Another man ferociously overturned a pine tree that towered towards the stars; he called it down out of the clouds. As it began to topple it shook the mountainside and brought lesser timber down with it. A Chaonian oak, prophetic long ago, stood huge and wide, blocking Phoebus' rays and reaching its branches out beyond the entire copse. Battered by many wounds it groaned menacingly, and broke the wedges; steel rebounded when driven against it, iron was damaged and proved too soft. Finally dislodged, it spread its devastation far and wide as it fell. Straightway the whole place was

---

1625 totum *Raphelengius*: totos *EA*
1631 omnis *E*: omnes *A*

volucres pererrant nemore succiso diem
quaeruntque lassis garrulae pinnis domus.
iamque omnis arbor sonuit et sacrae quoque
1635   sensere quercus horridam ferro manum,
nullique priscus profuit luco metus.
aggeritur omnis silva et alternae trabes
in astra tollunt Herculi angustum rogum—
raptura flammas pinus et robur tenax
1640   et brevior ilex; summa sed complet rogum
populea silva, frondis Herculeae nemus.

At ille, ut ingens nemore sub Nasamonio
aegro reclinis pectore immugit leo,
fertur. quis illum credat ad flammas rapi?
1645   vultus petentis astra, non ignes erat.
ut pressit Oeten ac suis oculis rogum
lustravit omnem, fregit impositus trabes.
arcus poposcit. "Accipe haec" inquit, "sate
Poeante, dona, et munus Alcidae cape.
⟨has en sagittas Dardani sensit domus,⟩
1650   has hydra sensit, his iacent Stymphalides
et quidquid aliud eminus vici manu
victrice. felix iuvenis has numquam irritas
mittes in hostem; sive de media voles
auferre volucres nube, descendent aves
1655   et certa praedae tela de caelo fluent,
nec fallet umquam dexteram hic arcus tuam.

1636 priscus . . . metus *Jortin*: priscum . . . nemus *EA*
1640 summa *Bentley*: silva *EA*
1648 arcus poposcit *E*: arcumque poscit *A*
Lacuna before 1650 *suggested by* Zwierlein; *supplement by*
Zwierlein (has en sagittas) *and Fitch*

470

opened to the sun's rays. Driven from their perches, birds
flew haphazardly through the brightness left by the tree's
felling, chattering and searching for their homes on tired
wings. Now every tree resounded; even sacred oaks felt
hands that wielded the iron, and no grove was protected by
the reverence long accorded it. As every kind of wood was
piled up, the alternating layers of trunks raised the pyre
skyward—still a meagre pyre for Hercules. There was pine
to catch fire, firm-holding oak and the shorter holm oak;
but on top, crowning the pyre, were trunks of poplar, the
tree that bears Hercules' leaves.[97]

But he was borne along, like some great lion lying sick
and roaring with pain in a Nasamonian forest. Yet who
would have believed him hurried towards the flames? His
expression was that of one heading to the stars, not the fire.
Once Oeta bore him, and he had surveyed the whole pyre
with his gaze, he was placed upon it—and fractured its
beams. Then he called for his bow and arrows. "Receive
this gift," he said, "son of Poeas, accept this boon from
Alcides. ⟨These arrows were felt by the house of Dardanus,⟩ and felt by the hydra; they felled the Stymphalian
birds, and all the other foes I conquered from afar with my
victorious hand. Fortunate young man! You will never fire
them at an enemy without success. Or, if you would take
winged creatures from the very clouds, the birds will fall,
for the arrows will secure their prey before gliding from
the sky. This bow will never fail your hand. It is practiced in

[97] Hercules favoured poplar leaves for his victory wreaths.

1651 manu *Rossbach*: malum *EA*

librare telum didicit et certam dare
fugam sagittis; ipsa non fallunt iter
emissa nervo tela. tu tantum, precor,
1660 accommoda ignes et facem extremam mihi.
hic nodus," inquit, "nulla quem cepit manus,
mecum per ignes flagret; hoc telum Herculem
tantum sequetur. hoc quoque acciperes," ait,
"si ferre posses. adiuvet domini rogum."
1665 tum rigida secum spolia Nemeaei mali
arsura poscit; latuit in spolio rogus.
      Ingemuit omnis turba, nec lacrimas dolor
cuiquam remisit. mater in luctum furens
diduxit avidum pectus, atque utero tenus
1670 exerta vastos ubera in planctus ferit;
superosque et ipsum questibus pulsans Iovem
implevit omnem voce feminea locum.
"Deforme letum, mater, Herculeum facis;
compesce lacrimas," inquit, "introrsus dolor
1675 femineus abeat. Iuno cur laetum diem
te flente ducat? paelicis gaudet suae
spectare lacrimas. comprime infirmum iecur,
mater: nefas est ubera atque uterum tibi
laniare, qui me genuit." et dirum fremens,
1680 qualis per urbes duxit Argolicas canem,
cum victor Erebi Dite contempto redît
tremente Fato, talis incubuit rogo.
quis sic triumphans laetus in curru stetit
victor? quis illo gentibus vultu dedit
1685 leges tyrannus? quanta pax habitum tulit!
haesere lacrimae, cecidit impulsus dolor
nobis quoque ipsis, nemo periturum ingemit;
iam flere pudor est. ipsa quam sexus iubet

472

aiming a shaft, in flighting arrows accurately; the shafts
fired from this string do not miss their path. All I ask of you
is to furnish me with fire, with the final torch. This knotty
club," he said, "that no other hand has held, must burn in
the fire with me; it will be the one weapon to accompany
Hercules. You would receive it too," he said, "if you could
carry it. But let it contribute to its master's pyre." Then he
called for the Nemean monster's stiff pelt to be burnt with
him; that trophy covered and hid the pyre.

There were groans of sorrow from the whole company;
grief spared no one tears. His mother, passionate to
mourn, opened her eager bosom, stripped down to the
womb and struck ringing blows on her breasts. Assailing
the gods and Jove himself with her laments, she filled the
whole place with womanish cries. "You are disfiguring the
death of Hercules, mother! Control your tears," he said,
"hold in your womanish grief. Why should your weeping
gladden this day for Juno? She enjoys watching her rival's
tears. Restrain your emotional heart, mother. It is an outrage for you to wound those breasts and that womb that
bore me." And with an awesome roar he sank down on the
pyre, as forceful as when he led the hound through Argive
cities, returning as conqueror of Erebus, in defiance of
Dis, while Death trembled. What triumphant conqueror
ever stood as joyfully in his chariot? What sovereign ever
gave laws to the nations with such an expression? What
peace pervaded his demeanour! Tears ceased, grief ebbed
and died away in us too, no one lamented his coming
death; it seemed shameful now to weep. Even Alcmene

1661 cepit *E*: capiet *A*
1671 questibus *Axelson*: vocibus *EA*

maerere, siccis haesit Alcmene genis,
1690 stetitque nato paene iam similis parens.

CHORUS

Nullasne in astra misit ad superos preces
arsurus, aut in vota respexit Iovem?

PHILOCTETES

Iacuit sui securus et caelum intuens
quaesivit oculis, arce an ex aliqua pater
1695 despiceret illum. tum manus tendens ait:
"Quacumque parte prospicis natum, pater,
te te precor, cui nocte commissa dies
quievit unus: si meas laudes canit
utrumque Phoebi litus et Scythiae genus
1700 et omnis ardens ora quam torret dies,
si pace tellus plena, si nullae gemunt
urbes nec aras impias quisquam inquinat,
si scelera desunt, spiritum admitte hunc, precor,
in astra. non me noctis infernae locus
1705 nec maesta nigri regna conterrent Iovis,
sed ire ad illos umbra, quos vici, deos,
pater, erubesco. nube discussa diem
pande, ut deorum vultus ardentem Herculem
spectet: licet tu sidera et mundum neges
1710 ultro, pater, cogere. si voces dolor
abstulerit ullas, pande tunc Stygios lacus
et redde fatis. approba natum prius:
1716 noverca cernat quo feram flammas modo.
ut dignus astris videar, hic faciet dies.

1697 te te precor *Richter*: te te pater *E*: iste est pater *A*
1704 noctis *Heinsius*: mortis *EA*

474

herself, though her sex bade her mourn, broke off and stood dry-eyed, a mother who now almost resembled her son.

CHORUS LEADER

Did he not direct prayers to the heavenly gods before the flames, or look to Jove in appeal?

PHILOCTETES

He lay there with no concern for himself. But gazing at heaven he scanned to see whether his father was looking down on him from some height. Then, stretching out his hands, he spoke. "Father, for whom one day slept while night was joined to night: from whatever quarter you look upon your son, I pray to you. If my praises are sung by both of Phoebus' coasts and the Scythian race and the whole region scorched by blazing daylight; if peace fills the earth, if no cities groan and no one defiles altars with sacrilege, if there are no crimes, I pray you admit this spirit of mine to the stars. It is not that I fear the place of infernal night, the gloomy realm of dark Jove, but I feel it shameful, father, to go as a shade to those gods I conquered. Disperse the clouds and unfold the day, so the gazing gods can watch the burning of Hercules. Then, though you deny me heaven's stars, you will be compelled, father, against your will. If pain wrests any cries from me, then show me the Stygian lakes and return me to death. Yes, demonstrate your son's qualities first! Let my stepmother see how I endure the flames. This day will ensure that I am recognised as deserv-

---

1708 vultus* *EA*: coetus *Heinsius*
1716 *placed after* 1712 *by Fitch, after* 1718 *by Gronovius*

475

leve est quod actum est; Herculem hic, genitor, dies
1715 inveniet aut damnabit."

                                   Haec postquam edidit,
1717 flammas poposcit. "Hoc age, Alcidae comes,
non segnis" inquit "corripe Oetaeam facem.
quid dextra tremuit? num manus pavida impium
1720 scelus refugit? redde iam pharetras mihi,
ignave iners enervis! en nostros manus
quae tendat arcus! quid sedet pallor genis?
animo faces invade quo Alciden vides
vultu iacere. respice arsurum, miser!
1725 vocat ecce iam me genitor et pandit polos;
venio, pater"—vultusque non idem fuit.
tremente pinum dextera ardentem intuli.
refugit ignis et reluctantur faces
et membra vitant, sed recedentem Hercules
1730 insequitur ignem. Caucasum aut Pindum aut Athon
ardere credas: nullus erumpit sonus,
tantum ingemescit ignis. o durum iecur!
Typhon in illo positus immanis rogo
gemuisset ipse, quique convulsam solo
1735 imposuit umeris Ossan Enceladus ferox.
     Ast ille medias inter exsurgens faces,
semustus ac laniatus, intrepidum tuens,
"Nunc es parens Herculea: sic stare ad rogum
te, mater" inquit, "sic decet fleri Herculem."
1740 inter vapores positus et flammae minas
immotus, inconcussus, in neutrum latus
correpta torquens membra adhortatur, monet,
gerit aliquid ardens. omnibus fortem addidit

       1721 enervis *Bentley*: inermis *EA*

ing the stars. What I have achieved is slight; this day, father, will reveal Hercules—or else condemn him."

After uttering these words he called for the fire. "Do it, comrade of Alcides! Grasp the Oetean torch without hesitation. Why does your hand tremble? Can it be shunning the task in fear, as an unholy crime? Return my quiver to me, idle, inert, impotent man! Look at the hand that is to bend my bow! Why has pallor settled on your cheeks? You see Alcides' countenance as he lies here: grasp the torch with the same spirit! Wretched man, think of the one who is about to burn! See, my father is summoning me now, and opening heaven. I come, father!" And his countenance was transformed. With my hand trembling I thrust in the burning pinewood. The flames recoiled, the brands resisted and avoided his limbs, but Hercules pursued the fire when it retreated. You would have thought it was the Caucasus or Pindus or Athos that was blazing. No sound burst from him, only the fire groaned. O tough heart! If placed on that pyre, even monstrous Typhon would have groaned, or the one who tore Ossa from the earth and set it on his shoulders, ferocious Enceladus.

Then, rising up amidst the brands, though half-burnt and lacerated, he looked out fearlessly and spoke: "*Now* you are Hercules' parent: this is how you should stand at my pyre, mother, and how Hercules should be mourned!" Enveloped by the heat and the menacing flames, yet unmoved, unshaken, not twisting onto either side with his burning limbs, he gave encouragement and counsel, and remained active, all ablaze. He strengthened the courage

animum ministris: urere ardentem putes.
1745 stupet omne vulgus, vix habent flammae fidem:
tam placida frons est, tanta maiestas viro.
nec properat uri; cumque iam forti datum
leto satis pensavit, igniferas trabes
hinc inde traxit: minima quas flamma occupat
1750 totas in ignes vertit, et quîs plurimus
exundat ignis repetit intrepidus ferox.
tunc ora flammis implet: ast illi graves
luxere barbae; cumque iam vultum minax
appeteret ignis, lamberent flammae caput,
1755 non pressit oculos.
                        Sed quid hoc? maestam intuor
sinu gerentem reliquias magni Herculis,
crinemque iactans squalidum Alcmene gemit.

ALCMENE
Timete, superi, fata: tam parvus cinis
Herculeus, huc huc ille decrevit gigas!
1760 o quanta, Titan, in nihil moles abît!
anilis, heu me, recipit Alciden sinus.
hic tumulus illi est: ecce vix totam Hercules
complevit urnam. quam leve est pondus mihi,
cui totus aether pondus incubuit leve!
1765   Ad Tartara olim regnaque, o nate, ultima
rediturus ibas: quando ab inferna Styge

1750 totas *Gronovius*: totasque *EA*
1762 tumulus *EA*: cumulus *Axelson*   illi *A*: ille *E*

478

of all his attendants: you would think him burning while being burnt![98] The whole crowd stood in amazement, and the flames were scarcely thought real, so calm was his brow, so great the hero's majesty. He did not hasten the burning, but when he judged that the demands of a courageous death had been fulfilled, he dragged together the fiery beams: the ones least caught by the flames he moved fully into the fire, and then, fierce and unafraid, gathered those from which the fire poured most strongly. Then he thrust his face full into the flames. His heavy beard blazed up; but as the menacing fire attacked his face and the flames licked around his head, he did not close his eyes.

[*Alcmene approaches carrying Hercules' funerary urn*] But what is this? I see a woman of sorrows bearing in her bosom the remains of Hercules; Alcmene tosses her ash-filled hair[99] and laments.

ALCMENE

Fear doom, you gods! The ashes of Hercules are so small, that giant is diminished to this! O Titan, what vastness has vanished into nothing! An old woman's bosom, alas, has room enough for Alcides. *This* is that great one's tomb: see, Hercules has scarcely filled the urn full. How light a weight he is for me, though the whole heaven rested as a light weight on him!

Once you would go to Tartarus' distant realm, son, with the prospect of return. When will you come once more

[98] This phrase plays on *urere* to burn (transitive) and *ardere* to burn (intransitive). It could be glossed in several ways, e.g. "you would think he created the fire while suffering it," or (taking *ardentem* metaphorically) "you would think him afire to burn."

[99] Mourners poured dust and ashes over their heads.

remeabis iterum? non ut et solitum trahas
rursusque Theseus debeat lucem tibi—
sed quando solus? mundus impositus tuas
1770 compescet umbras, teque Tartareus canis
inhibere poterit? quando Taenarias fores
pulsabis? aut quas mater ad fauces agar
qua mors aditur? vadis ad manes iter
habiturus unum.
               Quid diem questu tero?
1775 quid misera duras vita? quid lucem hanc tenes?
quem parere rursus Herculem possum Iovi?
quis te parentem natus, Alcmene, suam
tantus vocabit? o nimis felix, nimis,
Thebane coniunx: Tartari intrasti loca
1780 florente nato, teque venientem inferi
timuere forsan, quod pater tanti Herculis,
vel falsus, aderas. quas petam terras anus,
invisa saevis regibus (si quis tamen
rex est relictus saevus)? ei miserae mihi!
1785 quicumque caesos ingemunt nati patres,
a me petent supplicia, me cuncti obruent:
si quis minor Busiris aut si quis minor
Antaeus urbes fervidae terret plagae,
ego praeda ducar; si quis Ismarios greges
1790 Thracis cruenti vindicat, carpent greges
mea membra diri. forsitan poenas petet
irata Iuno, totus exsurget dolor;
secura victo tandem ab Alcide vacat,

1767 solitum *E*: spolium *A*   1777 te . . . Alcmene *Bentley*:
me . . . alcmenen (*or* -am) *EA*   1789 ismarios *A*: ismarius *E*
1792 exsurget *Bentley*: uretur *EA*

from the Stygian world below? Not so as to drag the usual trophy[100] with you, or so Theseus may owe the daylight to you a second time; but when will you come by yourself? Shall the overburden of the cosmos confine your shade,[101] will the hound of Tartarus be able to detain you? When will you pound at the gates of Taenarus? Or what yawning tunnel must your mother approach that gives access to death? You fare to the shades, with the propect of a single journey.

But why waste the day in lament? Why does my wretched life endure? Why cling to the light? What second Hercules can I bear to Jove? What son of such might, Alcmene, will call you his mother? Oh so fortunate, so fortunate, my Theban husband:[102] you entered the domain of Tartarus while our son thrived, and those below perhaps trembled at your arrival, at the presence of mighty Hercules' father, even if falsely so called. What country shall I head for, an old woman hated by cruel kings—if indeed any cruel king survives? What wretchedness! Every son that mourns his slain father[103] will seek satisfaction from me, they will all overwhelm me. If some young Busiris or young Antaeus is terrorizing the peoples of the torrid region, I shall be led away as his plunder; if someone avenges the Ismarian herds of the bloodthirsty Thracian,[104] his monstrous herds will tear at my limbs. Perhaps angry Juno will seek revenge, with her rage arising in full force. Alcides' defeat leaves her confident and unpreoccupied at

---

[100] Cerberus.   [101] Since *mundus* can also mean "the heavens," the phrase glances at their being "imposed" on Hercules formerly without overwhelming him.

[102] Amphitryon.   [103] I.e. slain by Hercules.

[104] Diomedes.

paelex supersum. quanta supplicia expetet
1795 ne parere possim! fecit hic natus mihi
uterum timendum.
                Quae petam Alcmene loca?
quis me locus, quae regio, quae mundi plaga
defendet aut quas mater in latebras agar,
ubique per te nota? si patriam petam
1800 laresque miseros, Argos Eurystheus tenet.
marita Thebas regna et Ismenon petam,
thalamosque nostros, in quibus quondam Iovem
dilecta vidi? pro nimis felix, nimis,
si fulminantem et ipsa sensissem Iovem!
1805 utinam meis visceribus Alcides foret
exsectus infans! nunc datum est tempus, datum est
videre natum laude certantem Iovi,
ut hoc daretur, scire quid fatum mihi
eripere posset.
             Quis memor vivit tui,
1810 o nate, populus? omne iam ingratum est genus.
petam Cleonas? Arcadum an populos petam,
meritisque terram nobilem quaeram tuis?
hic dira serpens cecidit, hic ales fera,
hic sus cruentus, hic tua fractus manu
1815 qui te sepulto possidet caelum leo:
si grata terra est, populus Alcmenen tuam
defendat omnis. Thracias gentes petam

1794 quanta *Axelson*: magna *Courtney*: a qua *E*: de qua *A*
1809 vivit *Koetschau*: vivet *A*: 1807–10 *omitted by E*
1814 sus *Zwierlein*: rex *EA*

last, while I her rival survive. What punishments she will demand to prevent my bearing children! This son has made my womb a source of danger for me.

What country shall Alcmene make for? What place, what region, what tract of the earth will protect me? What hiding place can your mother find, now she is known everywhere through you? If I make for my native land and my unhappy home—Eurystheus holds Argos. Shall I make for Thebes and the Ismenos, my husband's realm, and that marriage chamber in which I once beheld Jove as my lover? Oh fortunate, so fortunate, if I too had felt the lightning of Jove! I wish that Alcides had been cut from my womb as an infant![105] But as it is, time was granted me, granted to see my son vying with Jove in glory—so that this too could be granted, to know what fate could steal from me.

What nation still remembers its debt to you, my son? The whole race is already lacking in gratitude. Shall I make for Cleonae? Or make for the communities of Arcadia, seek out the land made famous by your beneficial deeds? Here the monstrous serpent fell, here the fierce birds, here the bloodied boar; here your hands crushed the lion that now occupies heaven while you are buried below.[106] If the land is grateful, all its people should protect your Alcmene. Shall I make for the tribes of Thrace, the peoples

[105] "I too" like Semele, another mortal woman impregnated by Jupiter; when she was killed later by the lightning, the infant Bacchus was rescued from her womb.   [106] These references are to the hydra of Lerna, the birds of Stymphalus, the boar of Erymanthus and the lion of Nemea, near Cleonae. Stymphalus and Erymanthus are in Arcadia, the other places in the Argolid.

Hebrique populos? haec quoque est meritis tuis
defensa tellus; stabula cum regno iacent.
1820 hic pax cruento rege prostrato data est—
ubi enim negata est?
                 Quod tibi infelix anus
quaeram sepulcrum? de tuis totus rogis
contendat orbis. reliquias magni Herculis
quis populus aut quae templa, quae gentes rogant?
1825 quis, quis petit, quis poscit Alcmenes onus?
quae tibi sepulcra, nate, quis tumulus sat est?
hic totus orbis; fama erit titulus tibi.
    Quid, anime, trepidas? Herculis cineres tenes!
complectere ossa; reliquiae auxilium dabunt,
1830 erunt satis praesidia, terrebunt tuae
reges vel umbrae.

PHILOCTETES

           Debitos nato quidem
compesce fletus, mater Alcidae incliti.
non est gemendus nec gravi urgendus nece,
virtute quisquis abstulit fatis iter.
1835 aeterna virtus Herculem fleri vetat;
fortes vetant maerere, degeneres iubent.

ALCMENE

Sedabo questus vindice amisso parens
terrae atque pelagi, quaque purpureus dies
utrumque clara spectat Oceanum rota?

1831b-1836 *attributed to Philoctetes by A, to Hyllus by E, to the*
Chorus tentatively by Herrmann   1837–1839 *There may be a*
lacuna in this sentence; Zwierlein suggests loss of two half-lines
beginning qua *between* pelagi *and* quaque *in* 1838.

of the Hebrus? This land too was defended by your worthy deeds; the stables lie overthrown with the ruler.[107] Here peace was bestowed by the downfall of the bloodstained king—indeed, when was it ever withheld?

What tomb shall an ill-starred old woman try to find for you? The whole world should compete for your ashes. What nation, what temples, what tribes desire the remains of great Hercules? Who asks for, who demands Alcmene's burden?[108] What tomb, my son, what burial mound is sufficient for you? This whole world! And fame will be your epitaph.

Why are you anxious, my spirit? You hold the ashes of Hercules! Clasp his bones; his remains will give aid, they will be protection enough; even your shade will frighten kings.

PHILOCTETES

Mother of glorious Alcides; hold back your tears, deserved as they are by your son. One who by his valour has denied doom access is not to be mourned nor weighed down with the heaviness of death. His deathless valour forbids weeping for Hercules; the brave forbid mourning, the ignoble require it.

ALCMENE

Shall I quiet my laments as a mother, after losing the one who protected land and sea, where the gleaming sunlight looks on both oceans[109] from its bright chariot? How many

---

[107] Diomedes.

[108] I.e. the urn containing her son's ashes.

[109] I.e. in the far east and far west, implying "and everywhere in between" (cf. line 2).

1840   quot misera in uno condidi natos parens!
       regno carebam, regna sed poteram dare.
       una inter omnes terra quas matres gerit
       votis peperci, nil ego a superis petî
       incolume nato: quid dare Herculeus mihi
1845   non poterat ardor, quod deus quisquam mihi
       negare poterat? vota in hac fuerant manu;
       quidquid negaret Iuppiter, daret Hercules.
       quid tale genetrix ulla mortalis tulit?
       deriguit aliqua mater, ut toto stetit
1850   succisa fetu, bisque septenos greges
       deplanxit una: gregibus aequari meus
       quot ille poterat! matribus miseris adhuc
       exemplar ingens derat: Alcmene dabo.
       cessate, matres, pertinax si quas dolor
1855   adhuc iubet lugere, quas luctus gravis
       in saxa vertit: cedite his cunctae malis.
           Agedum senile pectus, o miserae manus,
       pulsate.—et una funeri tanto sat est
       grandaeva anus defecta, quod totus brevi
1860   iam quaeret orbis? expedi in planctus tamen
       defessa quamquam bracchia. invidiam ut deis
       lugendo facias, advoca in planctus genus.
           Flete, Alcmenae magnique Iovis
           plangite natum,
1865   cui concepto lux una perît
           noctesque duas contulit Eos;
           ipsa quiddam plus luce perît.

      1845 quod deus quisquam *Axelson*: quis deus quicquam *A*: quisquam *E*

sons have I, his wretched mother, laid to rest in this one
son? I held no throne, but had power to grant thrones.
Alone of all mothers on earth I refrained from prayers,
asked nothing of the gods, while my son lived. Could not
Alcides' ardour grant me anything that any god could deny
me? The answer to my prayers lay in this hand; whatever
Jove would deny me, Hercules would grant me. Has any
mortal mother ever given birth to anything like him?
There was a mother that grew rigid with grief,[110] when she
stood with her whole brood cut away, one mother mourning a twice sevenfold flock. But that son of mine could
equal so many such flocks! For sorrowful mothers there
was no great exemplar as yet: I Alcmene shall provide one.
Cease, you mothers still compelled to grieve by persistent
pain, or turned to stone by your weight of grief: all must
yield place to these sorrows of mine.

Come sad hands, pound this old breast. And can a single, ancient, failing old woman suffice for so great a death,
which the whole world will soon be mourning? Yet free
your arms, however weary, for blows of sorrow. To arouse
rancour against the gods through your grieving, summon
the whole race to join your lament.[111]

Weep, rain blows
for the son of Alcmene and great Jove,
for whose conception one day perished
and dawn's deferment merged two nights;
something more than even the day has perished.

[110] Niobe.
[111] Alcmene now shifts into anapaests, a metre associated with
keening.

totae pariter plangite gentes,
quarum saevos ille tyrannos
1870   iussit Stygias penetrare domos
populisque madens ponere ferrum.
fletum meritis reddite tantis;
totus, totus personet orbis.
fleat Alciden caerula Crete,
1875   magno tellus cara Tonanti;
centum populi bracchia pulsent.
nunc Curetes, nunc Corybantes
arma Idaea quassate manu:
armis illum lugere decet.
1880   nunc, nunc funus plangite verum:
iacet Alcides
non minor ipso, Creta, Tonante.
flete Herculeos, Arcades, obitus,
nondum Phoebe nascente genus;
1885   iuga Parthenii Nomiaeque sonent
feriatque gravis Maenala planctus:
magno Alcidae poscit gemitum
stratus vestris saetiger agris
alesque sequi iussa sagittas
1890   totum pinnis furata diem.
flete, Argolicae, flete, Cleonae:
hic terrentem
moenia quondam vestra leonem

1885 Nomiaeque *Fitch*: Nemeaeque* *EA*   1890 pinnis
furata *Birt*: pinnis velata *EA*: pinna velante *Heinsius*

---

112 "Idaean" refers to two mountains called Ida, one on Crete

Rain blows together, all you nations
whose cruel tyrants he commanded
to enter the house of Styx, and drop
the swords soaked in their peoples' blood.
Pay tears as tribute to his great service;
let all, yes all the world resound.
Weep for Alcides, Crete, you sea-blue
land beloved of the mighty Thunderer,
let your hundred peoples beat their arms.
Now, Curetes, now, Corybantes,
brandish weapons in Idaean hands:
weapons are suited for mourning *him*.
Now strike blows for a genuine death.[112]
Alcides is dead,
who matched, o Crete, the very Thunderer.
Weep for Hercules' death, you Arcadians,
a lineage from before the birth of Phoebe;
let the heights of Nomia and Parthenius resound,
and heavy blows strike Maenalus.
You owe mourning to great Alcides,
since he slew the bristling boar in your fields,
and made the birds, whose wings entirely
stole the daylight, yield to his arrows.
Weep, Argive Cleonae, weep:
the lion that here
once terrorized your city walls

where Jupiter was brought up, the other in the Troad, the region
from which the Corybantes came. The Curetes were famous for
clashing their shields, particularly at the birth of Jupiter on Crete.
Cretans claimed that Jupiter also died on the island—falsely, according to others: hence "a genuine death" here.

fregit nostri dextera nati.
date, Bistoniae, verbera, matres,
1895 gelidusque sonet planctibus Hebrus;
flete Alciden,
quod non stabulis nascitur infans
nec vestra greges viscera carpunt.
fleat Antaeo libera tellus
1900 et rapta fero plaga Geryonae.
mecum miserae plangite, gentes:
audiat ictus utraque Tethys.
        Vos quoque, mundi turba citati,
flete Herculeos, numina, casus:
1905 vestrum Alcides cervice meus
mundum, superi, caelumque tulit,
cum stelligeri vector Olympi
pondere liber spiravit Atlas.
ubi nunc vestrae, Iuppiter, arces?
1910 ubi promissi regia mundi?
nempe Alcides mortalis obît,
nempe sepultus.
totiens telis facibusque tuis
ille pepercit,
1915 quotiens ignis spargendus erat.
in me saltem iaculare facem
Semelenque puta!
        Iamne Elysias, o nate, domos,
iam litus habes,
ad quod populos Natura vocat?
1920 an post raptum Styx atra canem
praeclusit iter,

1913 totiens *Richter*: quotiens *EA*

490

was crushed by the right hand of my son.
Scourge yourselves, Bistonian mothers,
let cold Hebrus resound with blows;
weep for Alcides,
since now no infant is born for the stables
and no beasts tear flesh of your flesh.[113]
The land freed from Antaeus must weep,
and the region saved from wild Geryon.
Rain blows of sorrow with me, you nations:
let either Ocean hear their beat.

    You too, you host of the whirling heavens,
must weep for the fall of Hercules:
your celestial world, you gods on high,
was borne on the neck of my Alcides,
when the usual bearer of starry Olympus,
Atlas, breathed easy, freed of his burden.
Where are your lofty heights now, Jove?
Where is the promised palace in heaven?
Clearly Alcides is dead and buried,
clearly a mortal.
And yet, whenever you would have needed
to shower fire,
he saved you from using your lightning bolts.
Hurl the lightning at me, at least,
and think me Semele!

    Have you reached Elysium, my son,
have you reached the shore
to which whole throngs are summoned by Nature?
Or has the black Styx barred your way
since you stole the hound—

---

[113] Again a reference to Diomedes' man-eating horses.

teque in primo limine Ditis
fata morantur?
quis nunc umbras, nate, tumultus
manesque tenet?
fugit abducta navita cumba
1925   et Centauris Thessala motis
ferit attonitos ungula manes
anguesque suos hydra sub undas
territa mersit
teque labores, o nate, timent?
1930   fallor, fallor vesana furens,
nec te manes umbraeque timent:
non Argolico rapta leoni
fulva pellis contecta iuba
laevos operit dira lacertos
1935   vallantque feri tempora dentes;
donum pharetrae cessere tuae
telaque mittet iam dextra minor.
vadis inermis, nate, per umbras,
ad quas semper mansurus eris.

HERCULES

1940   Quid me tenentem regna siderei poli
caeloque tandem redditum planctu iubes
sentire fatum? parce: iam virtus mihi
in astra et ipsos fecit ad superos iter.

ALCMENE

Unde sonus trepidas aures ferit?
1945   unde meas inhibet lacrimas fragor?
agnosco agnosco, victum est chaos.
a Styge, nate, redis iterum mihi

do the Fates detain you
at the outer threshold of the realm of Dis?
What kind of commotion grips the shades
now, my son?
Has the oarsman taken his boat and fled?
Are the Centaurs of Thessaly bolting away,
trampling the panicked shades with their hooves?
Has the hydra plunged its snaky heads
underwater in fright?
Are your labours in fear of you, my son?
—I am wrong, wrong, crazy, insane!
The shades and ghosts do not fear you now.
No more does the pelt you stripped from the Argive
lion, with its mantle of a tawny mane,
make a fearsome shield for your left arm,
nor its savage fangs fence round your brows.
Your quiver now has gone as a gift,
and a lesser hand will shoot your arrows.
You walk unarmed among the ghosts,
my son, where you will stay forever.

HERCULES

[*Appearing above, unseen at first by Alcmene*] Now I have
reached the realms of the starry sky and have finally been
granted my place in heaven, why do you force me by your
mourning to taste death? Refrain! My valour has paved a
way for me now to the stars and the very gods.

ALCMENE

Whence is that sound that strikes my affrighted
ears—that shout that forbids my weeping?
Now I recognise: he has conquered chaos!
Son, you return from the Styx once more to me,

fractaque non semel est mors horrida;
vicisti rursus noctis loca
1950 puppis et infernae vada tristia.
pervius est Acheron iam languidus,
an remeare licet soli tibi,
nec te fata tenent post funera?
an tibi praeclusit Pluton iter
1955 et pavidus regni metuit sibi?
certe ego te vidi flagrantibus
impositum silvis, cum plurimus
in caelum fureret flammae metus;
arsisti certe: cur ultima
1960 non tenuere tuas umbras loca?
quid timuere tui manes, precor?
umbra quoque es Diti nimis horrida?

HERCULES

Non me gementis stagna Cocyti tenent,
nec puppis umbras furva transvexit meas;
1965 iam parce, mater, questibus: manes semel
umbrasque vidi. quidquid in nobis tui
mortale fuerat, ignis evictum tulit;
paterna caelo, pars data est flammis tua.
proinde planctus pone, quos nato paret
1970 genetrix inerti; luctus in turpes eat;
virtus in astra tendit, in mortem timor.
praesens ab astris, mater, Alcides cano:
poenas cruentus iam tibi Eurystheus dabit;
curru superbum vecta transcendes caput.

1949 noctis *A*: mortis *E*   1951 an *Fitch*: et *EA*
1967 evictum *Heinsius*: evictus *E*: invictus *A*

494

crushing grim death for a second time;
again you have conquered the region of darkness
and the gloomy waters of the underworld vessel.
Is Acheron sluggish and crossable now,[114]
or is return possible only for you—
even after death can the fates not hold you?
Or was it that Pluto barred your way in,
fearing for his realm, scared for himself?
Surely with these very eyes I saw you
laid on the blazing timber, as fiery
terror raged powerfully towards the heavens;
surely you burnt there: why could the final
dwelling not hold your ghost? I pray you,
what was it about you that frightened the shades?
Is even your ghost too daunting for Dis?

HERCULES

The pools of wailing Cocytus do not hold me, nor did the
dark vessel ferry me across. Refrain now from lamenting,
mother: it was only once that I saw the shades and ghosts.
All that was yours and mortal in me has been mastered and
taken by the fire; my father's part has been assigned to
heaven, your part to the flames. So put aside mourning,
such as a mother would undertake for a lacklustre son;
grief should be spent on the ignoble; valour heads to the
stars, cowardice to death. Coming from the stars in very
presence, mother, I Alcides prophesy: the bloodthirsty
Eurystheus will soon be punished to your satisfaction; you
will ride in triumph above his proud head. Now I must

---

[114] Normally Acheron's violent current prevents the shades
from escaping over it (*Herc* 714).

1975   me iam decet subire caelestem plagam:
       inferna vici rursus Alcides loca.

ALCMENE

  Mane parumper—cessit ex oculis, abît,
  in astra fertur. fallor, an vultus putat
  vidisse natum? misera mens incredula est.
1980   es numen et te mundus aeternum tenet:
       credo triumphis. regna Thebarum petam
       novumque templis additum numen canam.

CHORUS

      Numquam Stygias fertur ad umbras
      inclita virtus.
      vivite fortes,
1985   nec Lethaeos saeva per amnes
      vos fata trahent;
      sed cum summas exiget horas
      consumpta dies,
      iter ad superos gloria pandet.
         Sed tu, domitor magne ferarum
1990   orbisque simul pacator, ades!
      nunc quoque nostras aspice terras,
      et si qua novo belua vultu
      quatiet populos terrore gravi,
      tu fulminibus frange trisulcis;
1995   fortius ipso genitore tuo
      fulmina mitte.

<hr>

1984 vivite *A*: vivunt *E*

ascend to the heavenly regions. Alcides has once more conquered the underworld.

ALCMENE

Stay a little while! He has vanished from my sight, left me, set out for the stars. Am I deceived, or do my eyes reckon they saw my son? My poor mind cannot believe it. You *are* a god, the heavens hold you forever. I believe in your triumph. I shall make for the kingdom of Thebes, and proclaim this new god that joins their temples.

CHORUS

Never does glorious valour pass
to the Stygian shades.
Live, all, with courage,
and the cruel fates will then not haul you
over Lethe River.
No: when the final hour is imposed
at the end of your days,
glory will open a path to heaven.
    But you, great conqueror of beasts
and bringer of peace to the world, be with us!
Continue to show regard for our earth,
and if some new and strange-faced monster
shakes the nations with grievous fear,
crush it with the three-forked lightning bolts;
hurl the lightning
more valiantly than your very father.

OCTAVIA

INTRODUCTION

Background

Octavia and her younger sibling Britannicus were the children of the emperor Claudius by his wife Messalina. Promiscuous and increasingly unstable, Messalina was executed in A.D. 48 (when Octavia was perhaps 9) for going through a public marriage ceremony with one of her lovers, Gaius Silius, though married to the emperor. Soon thereafter Claudius took to wife his niece Agrippina, who persuaded him to adopt her son from a previous marriage and give him the Claudian name Nero; being three years older than Britannicus, Nero now took precedence over him. Agrippina had already arranged the recall of the leading man of letters, Seneca (exiled in 41 through Messalina's intrigues), to take on the thankless role of tutor to her son. Also through Agrippina's influence, Octavia was betrothed to Nero, and married to him in 53, when she was perhaps 14 and he 15.

The following year Claudius died: it was generally believed that Agrippina had poisoned him with a dish of mushrooms, in order to bring Nero to the throne. Britannicus died in 55, almost certainly poisoned on Nero's orders. Agrippina initially exercised power through her son, but he became increasingly resentful of her attempts to control him, and had her murdered in dramatic fashion in 59 (see *Octavia* 309–376).

Hated with good reason by his wife Octavia, Nero took the ex-slave Acte as his mistress in 55. Later she was gradually displaced in his affections by the noblewoman Poppaea Sabina. In 62, as this play narrates, Nero divorced Octavia and married Poppaea; shortly afterwards, on trumped-up charges of adultery and treason, Octavia was exiled to the island of Pandataria and put to death.

Poppaea herself was to die in 65, allegedly as a result of a kick from Nero while she was pregnant. In the same year Seneca was ordered by the emperor to commit suicide for supposed involvement in the Pisonian conspiracy. Three years later, with the legions and the praetorian guard in revolt, Nero fled from his palace and died ignominiously.

Summary

Scene. Octavia and her Nurse lament her plight and the destruction of her family. The Nurse urges submissiveness toward Nero for safety's sake, but Octavia cannot overcome her repugnance toward him.

Ode. The chorus of citizens recalls how the Roman people long ago deposed tyrants; as a parallel to those tyrants' crimes, they recount how Agrippina was murdered on Nero's orders.

Scene. Seneca regrets his recall from peaceful exile, and charts the increase in human wickedness, which has now reached a zenith. On cue, Nero appears, ordering two executions. Seneca argues that Nero would be more secure by showing mercy and thereby gaining popularity, but Nero insists that power must be maintained by terror and ruth-lessness. Seneca warns that the people will not tolerate Nero's plan to divorce Octavia and marry Poppaea; Nero spurns the advice and sets the morrow as the wedding day.

Scene. Agrippina's ghost appears early on the wedding day to blight the marriage and prophesy Nero's downfall.

Scene. Octavia leaves the palace, hoping but doubting that she can survive the divorce.

Ode. The chorus decides to protest violently against Poppaea's preferment.

Scene. Next morning, Poppaea recounts an ill-omened dream she has just had; her Nurse attempts to interpret it favourably.

Ode. A secondary chorus of Poppaea's supporters likens her beauty to that of mythical paragons.

Scene. A messenger reports that the people are overthrowing statues of Poppaea and planning to attack the palace.

Ode. The secondary chorus warns that the rioters cannot hope to overcome the power of the Love god.

Scene. An enraged Nero determines to punish the riot by burning the city and beggaring the masses. He upbraids the Prefect for merely quelling the uprising, and orders him to deport and execute Octavia as its supposed instigator.

Ode. The people's support can doom those it favours.

Scene. A lyric interchange between Octavia, who resigns herself to death, and the chorus, which recall the fates of other women of her family, and comments on Rome's destruction of its own.

Comment

Octavia has great intrinsic interest as the only play surviving from antiquity on a Roman historical subject. We know that other plays on Roman subjects (legendary or historical) were composed from roughly 200 B.C. to A.D. 100, but because information about them is scanty, we cannot say how closely *Octavia* resembles any of them in ethos, style, or structure. It seems likely, however, that such plays often dealt with Roman identity and nationhood in the context of defining events, as *Octavia* does. The term *praetexta* is sometimes used in antiquity as a label for such an historical play, and it will be used so here for convenience. But the label should not be taken to conjure up a well-defined distinct genre of drama: it denotes that the chief characters of the play wore the *toga praetexta* of leading Roman citizens (as distinct e.g. from the Greek-style dress of mythological plays), but it specifies nothing about the form of such plays.

In fact drama in antiquity was too vigorous and manifold to fit into a system of well-separated types. To illustrate this point, there is some overlap between the terms *praetexta* and *tragoedia* (tragedy), and *tragoedia* in turn can have the general sense of "a high-style play on serious themes" or the more specific sense of "a play embodying a fall into disaster." *Octavia* is clearly a tragedy in the latter sense. Octavia's story is tragic in itself: deprived of her mother, father, and brother by violence, married while young to a brute, she paradoxically loses her life because of

503

the people's love and support, which enrages her husband against her. So there is nothing artificial, as has been alleged, about this casting of historical material in the form of tragic drama. Historical figures as well as mythical ones fall into tragic paradigms: witness Aeschylus' *Persians*, Shakespeare's *Richard II,* and (more controversially) Marlowe's *Edward II*. Consequently the echoes in *Octavia* of Sophocles' plays about young, childless tragic heroines—Electra in the opening scene, Antigone in the closing scene—are natural and unforced.[1] Such echoes deepen the archetypal tragic pattern of life and its constituents (here specifically daylight and marriage) becoming inverted and death-oriented.

Octavia's tragedy is presented as the outcome not just of Nero's brutality but of a long series of transgressions (recounted in the first scene) going back to Messalina's disastrous folly. In this respect too Octavia resembles Antigone, whose tragic family history is similarly recalled in her prologue and orients her inevitably towards death. The tragic viewpoint of *Octavia* is broadened still further by Seneca's soliloquy (377–434), which sees human evil as growing

[1] Compare *Oct* 929–946 with Soph. *Antig.* 806–882 and 944–987. Nor would it have seemed artificial that Octavia should explicitly compare her situation with Electra's, as she does at lines 57–71. Contemporary audiences were keenly aware of the relevance of Greek myths to Rome, and especially to the imperial family (see introduction to *Thyestes*). Indeed a blurring of the division between Greece and Rome, stage and reality, can be seen in the fact that Nero acted many tragic roles onstage, sometimes in a mask made to resemble his own features. After his matricide he spoke of himself as hounded Orestes-like by the Furies.

from a primal violation of humans' relationship with the original mother, Earth herself.

Octavia dramatises not only the individual tragedy of the young empress but also its impact on the people of Rome; Nero's tyranny effectively links the two topics. The play's primary chorus represents ordinary Roman citizens. Already appalled at the murders of Britannicus and Agrippina, the citizens rise up in a futile attempt to reinstate the discarded Octavia, upon which Nero decides to burn the city to punish them. This gives the chorus a much more active, participatory role than it has in any Senecan tragedy, or indeed in most Greek tragedies. Such a role is in keeping with republican Roman traditions. Roman national consciousness was indelibly republican, taking as its defining event the expulsion of the kings in 510 B.C. and the establishment of a constitution designed to avoid absolutism. These very events had been dramatised in Accius' praetexta *Brutus*, named for the leader of the uprising against the Tarquins: at least one scene of that play is echoed in *Octavia*, while the expulsion of the Tarquins is recalled in the first choral ode, and serves as a paradigm for the uprising against Nero.

Republican traditions, however, had been eroded as Rome grew into an empire in which military might was all-important and lay in the hands of an emperor. Indeed, the ineffectiveness of the people as a political force had become evident in the second century B.C. in the events surrounding the Gracchi, which are recalled at the end of *Octavia* (882–886) as a parallel to the present failure. Because the citizens are so closely involved in the play's plot, *Octavia* could be seen in part as a tragedy of the Roman people. Its final line, "Rome revels in her citizens' blood," links the empress' fall with that of ordinary citizens.

But despite the failure of the uprising, the strong presence of a witnessing, reacting, participating community means that the overall impression left by the play is less bleak—at least to this reader, though others may respond differently—than that of the authentic Senecan tragedies. The people, like Octavia herself, represent something like moral normalcy; there still exists a fund of decency, loyalty, and traditional values. For this reason, and because Nero is presented as an aberration, a monster, destined soon to fall, there is a sense (absent from the Senecan plays) that right order could conceivably restore itself. That order would include the ideal described in the play by Seneca: a benign emperor, concerned for the interests and wellbeing of the people, and in turn deserving their loyalty.

In connection with the issue of the emperor's proper role it is intriguing to observe how the play represents the historical relationship between Seneca and Nero.[2] At the beginning of Nero's reign Seneca, as his chief advisor and minister, had published an essay *On Clemency* (*De Clementia*), which was intended to commit the new emperor to a benign use of his unlimited power: the essay is an important intertext for much of the Seneca–Nero scene in

[2] Did such a meeting as that dramatised by the play ever take place? Tacitus recounts that early in 62 Seneca asked Nero for permission to retire (*Annals* 14.53–56). Permission was denied, but Seneca thereafter spent little time in Rome, pleading ill health or philosophical studies. If Tacitus is right, Seneca is unlikely to have spoken to Nero either about the exiles' execution or about Octavia's divorce.

Octavia. In the essay Seneca holds up Augustus as an exemplar of mercy, but with strong qualifications about his early career. By transferring these qualifications from Seneca to Nero in his major speech (492–532), *Octavia* makes it appear that Nero has a better grasp of the practicalities of power, while Seneca's speech (472–491) seems impractically idealistic by comparison. Nevertheless the scene as a whole clearly presents Seneca's views in a highly favourable light, and condemns the ruthlessness which it attributes to Nero.

The essay *On Clemency* envisages an ideal of political harmony, with citizens grateful for the peace granted by the emperor, and reciprocally granting him their loyal support. But it has no room for even the most modified libertarianism; all initiative is the the hands of the omnipotent emperor. This position is hardly compatible with the suggestion made by "Seneca" in *Oct* 572–587 that the emperor should be prepared to accommodate the people's wishes. It looks as if the author, though basically aligned with Seneca, saw the essay's emphasis on the emperor's unlimited power as dangerous. He therefore rewrote history by modifying the philosopher's position. His purpose was perhaps to distance the memory of Seneca from absolutism, and at the same time to attach his great prestige to a more balanced political position.

What of the play's portrayal of Nero? According to the historian Tacitus, Nero was manipulated by his praetorian prefect into executing Plautus and Sulla, and by Poppaea into exiling Octavia after her divorce (*Annals* 14.57–63). The dramatist, by contrast, makes Nero solely responsible for these decisions. He also removes the feyness of character that appears in Tacitus' account, and portrays Nero as a standard tyrant. Some critics see him as the play's dominant character, and view the play as really Nero's play. But this Nero lacks the dark fascination of some of Seneca's criminals; he is neither a force of nature like Medea, nor a connoisseur of power and cruelty like Atreus. The play's sympathies are fully aligned with Octavia and the Roman people, and against the emperor whom it portrays as their oppressor.

Dramaturgy

For dramatic purposes the author compresses the historical events, which must have occupied several weeks, into three days: Day 1 dawns as Octavia wakes and the play begins, Day 2 (the day of the wedding) starts before dawn with the appearance of Agrippina's ghost (593), and Day 3 begins as Poppaea wakes from her nightmare (690). This is the sole surviving play from antiquity that diverges so overtly from the "unity of time." It seems likely, however, that there were precedents in earlier *praetextae*: Accius' *Brutus*, for example, covered a sequence of events that could not plausibly be represented as occupying a single day.

The author fashions the play's three days into a triptych in which the day of the wedding is at the centre while Day 3 mirrors Day 1, with the Poppaea–Nurse scene on Day 3 matching the Octavia–Nurse scene of Day 1, and Nero–Prefect matching Nero–Seneca.[3] These mirror scenes

[3] In this interest in symmetrical structural design, the play differs from the Senecan dramas. The author's liking for symme-

could be dramatically effective if staged in such a way as to bring out the parallels and differences.

The scenes of Day 3 are much shorter than their counterparts of Day 1—appropriately so, since Poppaea and the Prefect are not as significant for the play as Octavia and Seneca. From the beginning of Day 2, in fact, the drama proceeds by a sequence of short, intercut scenes which give the impression of a crisis developing and breaking. This dramaturgy is different from that of Seneca's plays, and could not be fitted into their five-act structure. It may have had precedents in *praetextae*, for it provides an effective means of dramatising highly charged and swiftly moving events: for a roughly similar effect one might compare the battlefield scenes of Euripides' *Rhesus* or Shakespeare's *Henry V*.

Despite the author's obvious debts to Seneca (see under "Sources"), it is noteworthy that he takes care to avoid post-classical (i.e. post-fifth-century) dramatic techniques found in Seneca. He has no asides, no entrance monologues with other characters "frozen" onstage, no entrances of new characters without preparatory announcement. No more than two speakers take part in any one conversation. There are no spectacular scenes like the murders of *Hercules*, the sacrifices of *Oedipus,* or the conjuration of *Medea*. Remarkably, Poppaea's wedding is entirely absent from the scenes of Day 2, and covered only by the Nurse's description of it the following day (697–

try extends into the details of composition: for example, the anapaestic sequence 57–99 is almost concentric in its distribution of lines, while the following speeches of Octavia and the Nurse are of equal length (37 lines each).

709):[4] contrast the wedding procession onstage in *Medea*. Though the scenes of Octavia's departure, first from the palace and later from Rome, could have provided opportunities for spectacle or for dramatic confrontations, their focus is rather on Octavia's state of mind. All this suggests a deliberate pursuit of classical restraint and decorum, in conscious divergence from Senecan dramaturgy.

Setting

The opening scenes of Day 1 and Day 3 are specified as set inside and outside the imperial bedchamber. Other scenes can be inferred from their content to take place elsewhere in the palace, others again in front of the palace. The final scene of Octavia's departure is set at a dock: since the citizens of the chorus are still present, the Roman audience might think of the Tiber dock just a few hundred yards from the palace, though this is not specified.[5]

Such fluidity of setting, combined with a lack of specificity (or at least consistent specificity) about the location, is comparable with the treatment of dramatic space in several of Seneca's dramas (*Tro, Phoen, Med, Pha*).

Authorship

Octavia is transmitted among Seneca's plays, but in the A manuscripts only, not in E. For a variety of reasons most

[4] It has been suggested that the wedding was represented by a processional scene after line 646 or 668. One wonders, however, whether the magnificence of such a procession would not have counteracted the play's consistent alignment of sympathy with Octavia.

[5] In fact Octavia was first sent to live in Campania under house arrest, then taken from there to Pandataria some days later.

scholars now believe that it was not written by Seneca, though some maintain Senecan authorship.

Despite obvious similarities to the first eight plays of the corpus, the style of *Octavia* is plain in comparison, lacking in rhetorical vigour, in bite and verbal pyrotechnics. This plainness is due in part to the subject matter: it would not do to put high-style compound adjectives such as *incestificus* and *luctificus* (*Phoen* 223, *Med* 577) into the mouths of near contemporaries. Yet the real Nero, at least according to Suetonius, had a piquant verbal style (Last Words: *qualis artifex pereo*, "What an artist is lost here!"); except for the good pun on *clementia/dementia* (496) there is little indication of it here, and indeed little sense of the connection between power over words and power over people. The play's language, in fact, is somewhat impoverished. The author overworks obviously "tragic" adjectives such as *saevus, dirus, ferus, miserandus*; he also courts monotony by repeatedly ending trimeters with disyllabic personal adjectives and pronouns such as *meus, tuus, suus, mihi, tibi*. In metre there are small but significant idiosyncracies: final -*o* is shortened scarcely at all, and the frequency of hiatus and double spondee in the second metra of anapaestic dimeters is much higher than in the Senecan plays.[6]

Another argument against Senecan authorship is that

Here as elsewhere the play simplifies and foreshortens historical events.

[6] On the relative frequency of long and shortened final -*o* see *AJPhil* 102 (1981) 303. In anapaests *Oct* allows double spondee in the second metron twice as frequently as Seneca; and there are more instances of second-metron hiatus in *Oct* (9) than in all the Senecan plays together (7).

the play appears to allude to events subsequent to Seneca's death in A.D. 65. Agrippina's ghost prophesies a series of events, seemingly in correct chronological order, from the construction of Nero's Golden House after the Great Fire of 64 to the death of Nero in 68 (lines 624–631). Poppaea's dream (lines 718–733), though less explicit, appears designed to foreshadow, for an audience with knowledge of the events of 62–68, the deaths of Poppaea herself, her former husband and their son, and Nero, in that order. Naturally the prophecy and dream do not go into great detail: otherwise they would have looked too much like hindsight from 68 or later, rather than foresight from 62 (the play's dramatic date). Because of this vagueness, supporters of Senecan authorship argue that the prophecy and dream represent good guesswork on Seneca's part.

Date

Probably, then, the play was written after Nero's death in June 68. It is unlikely to have been written later than the 90's A.D., when the vogue for Seneca's work was diminishing and memories of Octavia fading. It is also unlikely to have been written in the reign of the dictatorial Domitian (emperor 81–96); although *praetextae* and other dramas were occasionally vehicles for political protest against tyranny at Rome, the tone of *Octavia* seems more elegiac than defiant or militant.

Indeed, considerations of relevance and interest suggest that the play was composed while the memory of Nero's reign and partisan feelings about it were still strong. It has been argued that the play's popularism, albeit qualified, may echo the slogans and ideology of the rebellion against Nero, the short reign of Galba, and the start of

512

Vespasian's reign, which would point to composition between mid-68 and 70. Likewise the condemnation of extravagant expenditure (*luxuria*, lines 426–428, 433–434, 624–628), irrelevant to the plot, may reflect the policy of parsimony instituted by Galba and Vespasian.

Sources

The author borrows freely from Seneca's phrasing and thought, both in the tragedies and in the prose works. No less than three of his scenes (Octavia–Nurse, and the two scenes involving Nero) use elements from Senecan passion-restraint scenes (see vol. 1 p. 17): the Nero–Prefect scene is particularly reminiscent of the Atreus–Assistant scene in *Thyestes*, while the debate between Nero and Seneca on the uses of power has much in common with Act 2 of *Trojan Women*, as well as with *On Clemency*. Like Seneca himself, the writer models much of his phrasing on Ovid, and to a lesser extent on Vergil.

How much the author owes to tragedies or *praetextae* by other authors we cannot say, because of the loss of almost all that material. We can, however, glimpse an allusion in the Poppaea–Nurse scene to a scene in Accius' *Brutus*, in which an ominous dream was recounted and interpreted.

The play's account of historical events bears similarities to that of the historian Tacitus in Book 14 of his *Annals*, written early in the second century A.D. If the suggested date of *Octavia* is correct, the dramatist cannot have drawn on Tacitus. Indeed the opposite may be the case: Tacitus' account of Octavia's exile (14.64), with its tragic tone and its anonymous group of sympathetic onlookers recalling

513

the similar fates of other imperial women, may well be indebted to our play (see particularly lines 932–957). No
doubt there was a spate of partisan accounts of Nero's
reign soon after his death; probably the author himself also
had a good knowledge of the events as a contemporary.

BIBLIOGRAPHY

Commentary

R. Ferri, *Pseudo-Seneca, Octavia; Edited with Introduction and Commentary* (Cambridge, 2004).

Criticism

T. D. Barnes, "The Date of the *Octavia*," *MH* 39 (1982),
215–217.

M. Carbone, "The *Octavia*: Structure, Date and Authen-
ticity," *Phoenix* 31 (1977), 48–67.

R. Ferri, "Octavia's Heroines," *HSCPh* 98 (1998), 339–356.

C. J. Herington, "*Octavia Praetexta*: a Survey," *CQ* 11
(1961), 18–30.

P. Kragelund, *Prophecy, Populism, and Propaganda in the
'Octavia'* (Copenhagen 1982).

———"Historical Drama in Ancient Rome: Republican
Flourishing and Imperial Decline?" *Symb.Osl.* 77
(2002), 5–105 (including comments by other critics).

D. Sutton, *The Dramaturgy of the Octavia* (Königstein
1983).

M. Wilson (ed.), *The Tragedy of Nero's Wife: Studies on the
Octavia Praetexta* (Auckland, 2003) (= *Prudentia* 35.1.
A collection of papers by Wilson and other critics).

DRAMATIS PERSONAE

OCTAVIA, *daughter of the emperor Claudius, wife of Nero*
NURSE *of Octavia*
SENECA, *philosopher, advisor to Nero*
NERO, *emperor of Rome*
PREFECT *of the Guard*
Ghost of AGRIPPINA, *mother of Nero*
NURSE *of Poppaea*
POPPAEA, *mistress then wife of Nero*
MESSENGER
CHORUS *of Roman citizens*
Secondary CHORUS *of Poppaea's supporters*

Scene

Inside and outside the imperial palace at Rome; later at a nearby dock (see Introduction).

OCTAVIA

OCTAVIA

Iam vaga caelo sidera fulgens
Aurora fugat;
surgit Titan radiante coma
mundoque diem reddit clarum.
5   age, tot tantis onerata malis,
repete assuetos iam tibi questus,
atque aequoreas vince Alcyonas,
vince et volucres Pandionias:
gravior namque his fortuna tua est.
10   Semper genetrix deflenda mihi,
prima meorum causa malorum,
tristes questus natae exaudi,
si quis remanet sensus in umbris.
utinam ante manu grandaeva sua
15   mea rupisset stamina Clotho,
tua quam maerens vulnera vidi
oraque foedo sparsa cruore!
o lux semper funesta mihi!
tempore ab illo

This play is found in A but not in E.

OCTAVIA

OCTAVIA

[*Alone in her bedchamber*]

Now Dawn's brilliance
sweeps the wandering stars from the sky;
Titan arises radiance-crowned
and returns bright daylight to the world.
Come then, with so many weighty troubles,
renew the laments that are now your habit;
outdo the halcyons of the sea,[1]
outdo Pandion's winged daughters,
for your fortune is more grievous than theirs.
   O mother for whom I must always weep,
starting point and source of my troubles,
hear your daughter's sad laments,
if any perception is left in the shades.
I wish the age-old spinner Clotho
had snapped my life thread with her hand
before I saw through tears your wounds,
your face horribly sprayed with blood.
O daylight that always means death to me!
Ever since that time

[1] See Index under Alcyone.

20   lux est tenebris invisa magis.
           tulimus saevae iussa novercae,
           hostilem animum vultusque truces.
           illa, illa meis tristis Erinys
           thalamis Stygios praetulit ignes.
25   teque extinxit, miserande pater,
           modo cui totus paruit orbis,
           ultra Oceanum cuique Britanni
           terga dedere,
           ducibus nostris ante ignoti
30   iurisque sui.
           coniugis, heu me, pater, insidiis
           oppresse iaces,
           servitque domus cum prole tua
           capta tyranno.

NUTRIX

    Fulgore primo captus et fragili bono
35 fallacis aulae quisquis attonitus stupet,
    subito latentis ecce Fortunae impetu
    modo praepotentem cernat eversam domum
    stirpemque Claudi, cuius imperio fuit
    subiectus orbis, paruit liber diu
40 Oceanus et recepit invitus rates.
    en qui Britannis primus imposuit iugum,
    ignota tantis classibus texit freta,
    interque gentes barbaras tutus fuit
    et saeva maria, coniugis scelere occidit;
45 mox illa nati: cuius extinctus iacet

the daylight has been more hateful than darkness.
I have borne my cruel stepmother's commands,
her hostile spirit and grim looks.
She was the dismal Erinys that lit
my marriage chamber with Stygian torches;
and she quenched your light, piteous father,
by whom the whole world had been ruled,
and before whom Britons across the ocean
had turned and fled,
though previously beyond the control or ken
of our armies' leaders.
By your own wife's treachery, poor father,
you lie destroyed,
and your house and offspring are enslaved
and captive to a tyrant.

NURSE

[*Alone, outside the bedchamber*] Are people captivated
and awestruck by the glittering first impression, the unstable boon, of a beguiling throne? They should look at the
results of lurking Fortune's sudden onslaught—behold the
overthrow of Claudius' house, just now supremely powerful, and of his offspring! The whole world was subject to his
sway; Ocean, free for so long, obeyed him and reluctantly
received his ships. See, the man who first imposed the yoke
on the Britons, who covered unknown straits with vast
fleets and passed safely through barbaric tribes and savage
seas, fell through his own wife's wickedness! Then *she* fell
through her son's; poisoned by him, his brother[2] lies dead,

---

[2] Britannicus, both stepbrother and brother by adoption to
Nero. The use of terms of relationship here underlines the destruction of the Claudian house and the *impietas* involved.

frater venenis, maeret infelix soror
eademque coniunx nec graves luctus valet
ira coacta tegere crudelis viri.
secreta repetit semper, atque odio pari
50   ardent mariti, mutua flagrant face.
animum dolentis nostra solatur fides
pietasque frustra: vincit immitis dolor
consilia nostra nec regi mentis potest
generosus ardor, sed malis vires capit.
55   heu quam nefandum prospicit noster timor
scelus, quod utinam numen avertat deum.

OCTAVIA

O mea nullis aequanda malis
fortuna, licet
repetam luctus, Electra, tuos!
60   tibi maerenti
caesum licuit flere parentem,
scelus ulcisci vindice fratre,
tua quem pietas hosti rapuit
texitque fides;
65   me crudeli sorte parentes
raptos prohibet lugere timor
fratrisque necem deflere vetat,
in quo fuerat spes una mihi
totque malorum breve solamen.
70   nunc in luctus servata meos
magni resto nominis umbra.

---

49 secreta repetit *Fitch*: secreta refugit *recc.*: quem secreta
refugit *A, unmetrically*
50 ardent *Peiper*: ardens *A*   flagrant *Peiper*: flagrat *A*
52 vincit *Bücheler*: mittit *A*

while his ill-starred sister-wife mourns and cannot conceal her deep grief, though obliged to do so by her cruel husband's anger. She always hurries back into seclusion; wife and husband equally burn strongly with a fire of mutual hatred. Out of loyalty and devotion I try to console her grieving spirit, but in vain; her bitter pain prevails over my advice, and the noble ardour of her mind cannot be ruled, but draws strength from her troubles. Oh, what an unspeakable crime my fear foresees! May the power of the gods avert it!

OCTAVIA

No other troubles can match this fate
of mine, not though
I call to mind your griefs, Electra.
In your time of sorrow
you were able to weep for your slain father
and avenge that crime, championed by your brother,
who was rescued and hidden from the foe
by your loyal devotion.
But I am prevented by fear from mourning
the loss of my parents, cruelly taken,
forbidden to weep for my murdered brother,
in whom had lain my only hope,
my short-lived solace in so many woes.
Now, surviving solely to mourn,
I am left, the shadow of a mighty name.

[SENECA]

NUTRIX

Vox en nostras perculit aures
tristis alumnae:
cesset thalamis inferre gradus
tarda senectus?

OCTAVIA

75 Excipe nostras lacrimas, nutrix,
testis nostri fida doloris.

NUTRIX

Quis te tantis solvet curis,
miseranda, dies?

OCTAVIA

Qui me Stygias mittet ad umbras.

NUTRIX

80 Omina quaeso sint ista procul.

OCTAVIA

Non vota meos tua nunc casus,
sed fata regunt.

NUTRIX

Dabit afflictae meliora deus
tempora mitis;
tu modo blando vince obsequio
85 placata virum.

OCTAVIA

Vincam saevos ante leones
tigresque truces
fera quam saevi corda tyranni!

NURSE

Ah! The voice of my sorrowing child
strikes my ears.
Must I be slow to enter her room
through tardy old age?

[*She enters the bedchamber*]

OCTAVIA

Oh nurse, be receptive to my tears,
you faithful witness to all my pain.

NURSE

Pitiful one,
what day will free you from such sorrows?

OCTAVIA

The day that sends me to the Stygian shades.

NURSE

I pray that omen will be turned aside!

OCTAVIA

It is not your prayers any more, but doom
that rules my lot.

NURSE

After affliction
a kindly god will grant better times.
You must just calmly win your husband
by sweet submission.

OCTAVIA

I shall sooner win cruel lions over
and brutal tigers
than the fierce heart of this cruel tyrant!

odit genitos sanguine claro,
spernit superos hominesque simul,
90　nec fortunam capit ipse suam,
quam dedit illi per scelus ingens
infanda parens.
licet ingratum
dirae pudeat munere matris
hoc imperium cepisse, licet
95　tantum munus morte rependat,
feret hunc titulum post fata tamen
femina longo semper in aevo.

NUTRIX

Animi retine verba furentis,
temere emissam comprime vocem.

OCTAVIA

100　Toleranda quamvis patiar, haud umquam queant
nisi morte tristi nostra finiri mala.
genetrice caesa, per scelus rapto patre,
orbata fratre, miseriis luctu obruta,
maerore pressa, coniugi invisa ac meae
105　subiecta famulae, luce non grata fruor,
trepidante semper corde—non mortis metu,
sed sceleris: absit crimen a fatis meis,
mori iuvabit. poena nam gravior nece est
videre tumidos et truces miserae mihi
110　vultus tyranni, iungere atque hosti oscula,
timere nutus cuius obsequium meus
haud ferre posset fata post fratris dolor

---

3 Acte, Nero's former mistress.

He hates those born of noble blood,
sneers at gods and humans alike,
and cannot cope with his own good fortune,
bestowed upon him through dreadful crime
by his monstrous parent.
Despite the ingrate's
shame at receiving imperial power
as the gift of his dire mother, despite
his repaying so great a gift with death,
yet she, a woman, will always bear
that posthumous claim to fame through the ages.

NURSE

Do not give your angry spirit voice;
stifle such rashly uttered words.

OCTAVIA

However much I might put up with what must be endured,
my troubles could never end except in my unhappy death.
With my mother killed and my father wickedly taken, bereft of my brother, overwhelmed with misery and grief,
burdened with sorrow, hated by my husband, and subordinate to my own slavewoman,[3] I take no pleasure in the light
of day. My heart trembles always—with fear not of death,
but of villainy. As long as no evil is involved[4] in my doom, to
die will be welcome. For it is suffering worse than death to
see this tyrant's haughty black looks against my poor self, to
share kisses with my enemy, to fear his very nod. I could
not have endured submitting to him in my pain after the

---

[4] The phrase could have a second meaning, perhaps unintended by Octavia, viz. a reference to the trumped-up *crimen* or
charge of adultery that was used to justify her banishment.

scelere interempti, cuius imperium tenet
et sorte gaudet auctor infandae necis.

115   Quam saepe tristis umbra germani meis
offertur oculis, membra cum solvit quies
et fessa fletu lumina oppressit sopor!
modo facibus atris armat infirmas manus
oculosque et ora fratris infestus petit,
120   modo trepidus idem refugit in thalamos meos;
persequitur hostis atque inhaerenti mihi
violentus ensem per latus nostrum rapit.
tunc tremor et ingens excutit somnos pavor
renovatque luctus et metus miserae mihi.

125   Adice his superbam paelicem, nostrae domus
spoliis nitentem, cuius in munus suam
Stygiae parentem natus imposuit rati;
quam, dira post naufragia, superato mari,
ferro interemit saevior pelagi fretis.
130   quae spes salutis, post nefas tantum, mihi?
inimica victrix imminet thalamis meis
odioque nostri flagrat et pretium stupri
iustae maritum coniugis captat caput.
Emergere umbris et fer auxilium tuae
135   natae invocanti, genitor, aut Stygios sinus
tellure rupta pande, quo praeceps ferar.

NUTRIX

Frustra parentis invocas manes tui,
miseranda, frustra, nulla cui prolis suae

<hr>

133 captat *A*: poscit *Gronovius*

criminal slaying of my brother; for he holds *his* power and enjoys *his* position, while responsible for his unspeakable murder!

How often my real brother's sad shade appears to my sight, when my body relaxes in rest and sleep subdues my eyes, wearied with weeping! Sometimes he arms his feeble hands with black torches, and furiously attacks his brother's face and eyes. Sometimes in terror he takes refuge in my bedroom; his enemy pursues him and stabs him violently, thrusting the sword through my side as he clings tightly to me. Then trembling and panic drive off sleep, and renew the grief and fear in my sad heart.

Add to all this his arrogant mistress,[5] glittering with spoils taken from my house. As a favour to her, the mother was set on a Stygian ship by her own son, and then, after the dreadful shipwreck, after surviving the sea, she was assassinated by that son, crueller than the sea's waves.[6] After such an outrage, what hope of safety is there for me? My victorious enemy has designs on my marriage; she burns with hatred for me, and as the price of adultery she keeps asking my husband for the head of his lawfully wedded wife. Come forth from the shades and bring help in response to your daughter's appeal, father! Or else rend the earth and open the Stygian depths, so I can plunge headlong into them.

NURSE

It is futile to invoke your father's spirit, poor girl, futile! No concern for his offspring remains with him among

[5] Poppaea.
[6] These events are described more fully in lines 310–376.

manet inter umbras cura: qui nato suo
140 praeferre potuit sanguine alieno satum,
natamque fratris coniugem pactus sibi
toris nefandis flebili iunxit face.
hinc orta series facinorum: caedes, doli,
regni cupido, sanguinis diri sitis;
145 mactata soceri concidit thalamis gener
victima, tuis ne fieret hymenaeis potens.
pro facinus ingens! feminae est munus datus
Silanus et cruore foedavit suo
patrios penates, criminis ficti reus.
150 intravit hostis, ei mihi, captam domum
dolis novercae, principis factus gener
idemque natus, iuvenis infandi ingeni,
capaxque scelerum, dira cui genetrix facem
accendit et te iunxit invitam metu.
155   Tantoque victrix facta successu ferox
ausa imminere est orbis imperio sacri.
quis tot referre facinorum formas potest
et spes nefandas feminae et blandos dolos
regnum petentis per gradus scelerum omnium?
160 tunc sancta Pietas extulit trepidos gradus,
vacuamque Erinys saeva funesto pede
intravit aulam, polluit Stygia face
sacros penates, iura naturae furens
fasque omne rupit. miscuit coniunx viro

---

141 gnatamque *Heinsius*: genitamque *A*   pactus *Peiper*:
captus *A*   156 sacri *A*: sacro *Gronovius*

---

7 By adopting Nero, who then took precedence over Britannicus by age.   8 Agrippina was the daughter of Claudius'

the shades. He was even capable of setting another's seed above his own son![7] And he betrothed his brother's daughter to himself and took her to bride[8]—an illicit union, a disastrous marriage. That began a series of crimes: murder, treachery, lust for the throne, thirst for sacrilegious blood. The son-in-law fell as a victim sacrificed to his father-in-law's bridal bed, to prevent his gaining power through marriage to you. What a monstrous crime! A present was made of Silanus to a woman; accused on a trumped-up charge, he stained the house gods of his fathers with his own blood.[9] Then, alas, the foe entered the captured house; through your stepmother's schemes he became both son-in-law and son to the emperor—a young man of unspeakable character and aptitude for crime, whose dire mother lit the torch and made you his reluctant, fearful bride.

In triumph, and truculent as a result of such success, she dared to pursue the dominion of the hallowed world. Who could recount the many forms of evil, the woman's criminal ambition and fawning treachery, as she sought the throne through a series of crimes of every kind? That was when holy Righteousness departed with trembling steps; once the palace was empty, cruel Erinys entered on deadly feet, defiled the sacred house gods with her Stygian torch, and frantically broke nature's laws and all standards of right. The wife mixed deadly potions for her husband, and

brother Germanicus. Marriage between an uncle and niece had previously been forbidden as incestuous. [9] Silanus had been betrothed to Octavia, and thus was Claudius' prospective son-in-law. The betrothal was broken off, and Silanus disgraced, through the machinations of Agrippina. Silanus committed suicide on the very day of Agrippina's marriage to Claudius.

165 venena saeva, cecidit atque eadem sui
    mox scelere nati. tu quoque extinctus iaces,
    deflende nobis semper, infelix puer,
    modo sidus orbis, columen Augustae domus,
    Britannice, heu me, nunc levis tantum cinis
170 et tristis umbra; saeva cui lacrimas dedit
    etiam noverca, cum rogis artus tuos
    dedit cremandos, membraque et vultus deo
    similes volanti saeviens flamma abstulit.

     *   *   *   *   *

OCTAVIA

Extinguat et me, ne manu nostra cadat!

NUTRIX

175 Natura vires non dedit tantas tibi.

OCTAVIA

Dolor ira maeror miseriae luctus dabunt.

NUTRIX

Vince obsequendo potius immitem virum.

OCTAVIA

Ut fratrem ademptum scelere restituat mihi?

NUTRIX

Incolumis ut sis ipsa, labentem ut domum
180 genitoris olim subole restituas tua.

OCTAVIA

Expectat aliam principis subolem domus;
me dira miseri fata germani trahunt.

---

173 saeviens *Baehrens*: fervens *A, unmetrically*
After 173 CS *leave a space of* 30 *lines,* P *of* 26 *lines*

530

then she herself fell by her own son's crime. You too lie dead, ill-fated boy for whom we must ever weep, once the world's bright star and bulwark of the Augustan house, Britannicus, but now, alas, no more than light ash and a sorrowful shade. Even your cruel stepmother bestowed tears on you, when she gave your body to the pyre for cremation, and those limbs and face that resembled the winged god[10] were consumed by the raging flames.[11]

*   *   *   *   *

OCTAVIA

He must destroy me too, or he will fall by my hand.

NURSE

Nature has not given you such strength.

OCTAVIA

Pain, anger, sorrow, misery, grief will give it.

NURSE

Instead you should use submissiveness to win over your unkind husband.

OCTAVIA

So he can restore the brother he wickedly stole from me?

NURSE

So you yourself can be safe, and so you can one day restore your father's failing house with children of your own.

OCTAVIA

The emperor's house awaits other children.[12] I am dragged down by my poor brother's terrible doom.

---

[10] Cupid.   [11] Between 173 and 174 some lines have been lost, in which the topic turned back to Nero.

[12] Poppaea was now pregnant by Nero.

NUTRIX

Confirmet animum civium tantus favor.

OCTAVIA

Solatur iste nostra, non relevat mala.

NUTRIX

185 Vis magna populi est.

OCTAVIA

Principis maior tamen.

NUTRIX

Respiciet ipse coniugem.

OCTAVIA

Paelex vetat.

NUTRIX

Invisa cunctis nempe.

OCTAVIA

Sed cara est viro.

NUTRIX

Nondum uxor est.

OCTAVIA

Iam fiet, et genetrix simul.

NUTRIX

Iuvenilis ardor impetu primo furit,
190 languescit idem facile nec durat diu
in Venere turpi, ceu levis flammae vapor;
amor perennis coniugis castae manet.
violare prima quae toros ausa est tuos
animumque domini famula possedit diu,

NURSE

The citizens' firm support for you should strengthen your heart.

OCTAVIA

It consoles me in my troubles, but it does not lessen them.

NURSE

The people's power is great.

OCTAVIA

But the emperor's greater.

NURSE

He himself will show regard for his wife.

OCTAVIA

His mistress forbids it.

NURSE

She is hated by all, you see.

OCTAVIA

But dear to her husband.

NURSE

She is not yet a wife.

OCTAVIA

Soon she will be, and a mother too.

NURSE

Young men's ardour is wild in its first onset, but it readily wanes, and does not persist long in an illicit affair, like the heat of a feeble flame; whereas love for a chaste wife remains and endures. The very woman who first dared to dishonour your marriage bed—the servant who long commanded her master's heart—is now fearful, you see, of

195 iam metuit eadem nempe praelatam sibi
subiecta et humilis, atque monumenta extruit
quibus timorem falsa testatur suum.
et hanc levis fallaxque destituet deus
volucer Cupido; sit licet forma eminens,
200 opibus superba, gaudium capiet breve.
    Passa est similes ipsa dolores
    regina deum,
    cum se formas vertit in omnes
    dominus caeli divumque pater,
205   et modo pinnas sumpsit oloris,
    modo Sidonii cornua tauri,
    aureus idem fluxit in imbri.
    fulgent caelo sidera Ledae,
    patrio residet Bacchus Olympo,
210   deus Alcides possidet Heben
    nec Iunonis iam timet iras,
    cuius gener est qui fuit hostis.
    vicit sapiens tamen obsequium
    coniugis altae pressusque dolor:
215   sola Tonantem
    tenet aetherio secura toro
    maxima Iuno,
    nec mortali captus forma
    deserit altam Iuppiter aulam.

195b nempe praelatam sibi *assigned to Octavia by Ritter: part of Nurse's speech in A*   197 falsa δη: fassa C

---

13 The reference is to Acte. A surviving inscription (*CIL* XI 1414) records the dedication of a monument to the goddess Ceres

the woman favoured above her, subdued and humble; and she is building monuments that testify to her fear now she is disappointed.[13] This one too will be deserted by that fickle, untrustworthy god, the winged Cupid; though outstanding in beauty and arrogant in her wealth, the delight she enjoys will be brief.

>Similar pains were borne by the very
>queen of the gods,
>when the lord of heaven, the father divine,
>changed himself into manifold shapes—
>put on once the wings of a swan,
>once the horns of a bull at Sidon,
>once poured down in a shower of gold.[14]
>Leda's stars now shine in the sky,
>Bacchus has a place on his father's Olympus,
>and Alcides is a god with Hebe to wife,
>no longer the target of Juno's anger,
>now son-in-law, though once her foe.
>Yet wise compliance, suppression of pain,
>brought victory for the wife on high:
>the sole, unchallenged
>mate of the Thunderer on his heavenly couch
>is mighty Juno;
>mortal beauty no longer entices
>Jove to abandon his palace on high.

by a freedwoman of the imperial household named Acte—perhaps the selfsame woman.   [14] As a swan Jove mated with Leda, two of whose offspring (Castor and Pollux) are now "Leda's stars" (208), i.e. Gemini; as a bull with Europa, as a golden shower with Danae. He fathered Bacchus and Alcides/Hercules (209–210) on other mortal women, Semele and Alcmene.

tu quoque, terris altera Iuno,
220   soror Augusti
coniunxque, graves vince dolores.

OCTAVIA

Iungentur ante saeva sideribus freta
et ignis undae, Tartaro tristi polus,
lux alma tenebris, roscidae nocti dies,
225   quam cum scelesti coniugis mente impia
mens nostra, semper fratris extincti memor.
utinam nefandi principis dirum caput
obruere flammis caelitum rector paret,
qui saepe terras fulmine infesto quatit
230   mentesque nostras ignibus terret sacris
novisque monstris; vidimus caelo iubar
ardens cometen pandere infesta face,
qua plaustra tardus noctis alterna vice
regit Bootes, frigore Arctoo rigens.
235   en ipse diro spiritu saevi ducis
polluitur aether: gentibus clades novas
minantur astra, quas regit dux impius.
non tam ferum Typhona neglecto Iove
irata Tellus edidit quondam parens;
240   haec gravior illo pestis, hic hostis deum
hominumque templis expulit superos suis
civesque patria, spiritum fratri abstulit,
hausit cruorem matris—et lucem videt
fruiturque vita noxiam atque animam trahit!
245   Pro summe genitor, tela cur frustra iacis
invicta totiens temere regali manu?

232 infesta face *Fitch*: infestam facem *A*

536

You too, a second Juno on earth,
Augustus' sister[15]
and wife, must conquer your grievous pain.

OCTAVIA

Cruel seas will unite with stars, fire with water, heaven with gloomy Tartarus, kindly light with darkness, day with dewy night, before my mind, with its constant memory of my dead brother, will unite with my wicked husband's unrighteous mind. If only heaven's ruler, who often shakes the earth with storming thunderbolts, and frightens our minds with supernatural fires and strange portents, would plan to heap fire on the monstrous head of this evil emperor! We have seen a comet's menacing flames spread their blazing radiance through the heavens, where each successive night the Wain is driven by slow Bootes, stiff with arctic cold. Look, how the very sky is tainted with the menace breathed by this savage leader: the stars threaten new disasters for the nations ruled by his unrighteousness. Not such a savage was Typhon, born once in anger by mother Earth in Jove's despite; this scourge is graver than that, this foe of gods and men has expelled divinities from their temples and citizens from their fatherland, robbed his brother of life, drained his mother's blood—and he still sees the light of day, is blessed with life and draws his pestilential breath! O father on high, why does your royal hand so often hurl your invincible bolts uselessly, at random?

---

[15] Augustus was a title of successive emperors, here Nero.

---

233 alterna *Heinsius*: aeterna *Avantius*: aeternae* *A*

in tam nocentem dextra cur cessat tua?
utinam suorum facinorum poenas luat
Nero insitivus, Domitio genitus patre,
250 orbis tyrannus, quem premit turpi iugo
morumque vitiis nomen Augustum inquinat!

NUTRIX

Indignus ille, fateor, est thalamis tuis;
sed cede fatis atque fortunae tuae,
alumna, quaeso, neve violenti move
255 iram mariti. forsitan vindex deus
existet aliquis, laetus et veniet dies.

OCTAVIA

Gravi deorum nostra iam pridem domus
urgetur ira, prima quam pressit Venus
furore miserae dura genetricis meae,
260 quae nupta demens nupsit incesta face,
oblita iusti coniugis, legum immemor.
usto soluta crine, succincta anguibus
ultrix Erinys venit ad Stygios toros,
raptasque thalamis sanguine extinxit faces;
265 incendit ira principis pectus truci
caedem in nefandam: cecidit infelix parens,
heu, nostra ferro meque perpetuo obruit
extincta luctu; coniugem traxit suum
natumque ad umbras, prodidit lapsam domum.

NUTRIX

270 Renovare luctus parce cum fletu pios,

261 iusti *recc.*: nostri A
262 usto *Fitch*: illo A

538

Why does your right hand not act against one who is so guilty? If only he might be punished for his crimes, this spurious Nero,[16] really Domitius' son, tyrant of the world, which he oppresses and degrades, as he tarnishes the name Augustus with his depravity!

NURSE

I admit he is not worthy to share your marriage bed. But I beg you, dear child, submit to your fate and fortune; do not stir up your violent husband's anger. Perhaps some god will appear to take vengeance, and a day of joy will come.

OCTAVIA

Our house has long been burdened with the gods' heavy anger. The first to afflict it was cruel Venus, using the madness of my poor mother, who made an insane, unholy marriage while already married, oblivious to her rightful husband and heedless of the law. With her scorched hair loosened, girded with snakes, the vengeful Erinys attended those Stygian nuptials, stole the torches from the marriage chamber and quenched them in blood. She fired the emperor's heart to commit sacrilegious murder in his fierce anger.[17] My unhappy mother fell, alas, to the sword, and by her death she engulfed me in everlasting grief. She dragged down her husband and son to the shades; she put our fallen house into jeopardy.

NURSE

Forbear from renewing your laments, your tears of devo-

[16] Nero was a name of the Claudian *gens*, received by the future emperor when he was adopted by Claudius.

[17] I.e. to execute Messalina (actually put to death on the orders of Claudius' freedman secretary Narcissus).

manes parentis neve sollicita tuae,
graves furoris quae sui poenas dedit.

CHORUS

Quae fama modo venit ad aures!
utinam falso credita perdat
275 frustra totiens iactata fidem,
nec nova coniunx
nostri thalamos principis intret,
teneatque suos
nupta penates Claudia proles;
edat partu pignora pacis,
280 qua tranquillus gaudeat orbis
servetque decus Roma aeternum.
fratris thalamos sortita tenet
maxima Iuno:
soror Augusti sociata toris
285 cur a patria pellitur aula?
sancta quid illi prodest pietas
divusque pater?
quid virginitas castusque pudor?
    Nos quoque nostri sumus immemores
post fata ducis,
cuius stirpem prodimus aevo
290 suadente metum.
vera priorum
virtus quondam Romana fuit
verumque genus Martis in illis
sanguisque viris.
illi reges

290 metum *Wilamowitz*: metu *A*

540

tion—and do not disturb the spirit of your mother, who has
paid a heavy penalty for her madness.

CHORUS

What a rumour has just now reached our ears!
I pray it prove baseless, lose all credence,
though idly bandied about so often.
May no new wife
enter our emperor's marriage chamber;
may Claudius' daughter
keep her own hearth and home and marriage,
and bear in childbed pledges of peace,
so the world can enjoy untroubled times,
and Rome maintain her undying glory.
Mighty Juno
is her brother's appointed, established spouse:
then why is the sister and marriage partner
of Augustus driven from her father's palace?
What help to her is her unstained goodness,
her deified father,
her maidenhood, her chastity?
    Even we are disloyal to the memory
of our dead leader:
our age encourages fear, and so
we betray his offspring.
True Roman manliness was found
in our ancestors once;
the true heredity and blood of Mars
was in those men.
It was they who drove

hac expulerant urbe superbos,
295   ultique tuos sunt bene manes,
virgo dextra caesa parentis,
ne servitium paterere grave et
improba ferret praemia victrix
dira libido.
300   te quoque bellum triste secutum est,
mactata tua, miseranda, manu,
nata Lucreti,
stuprum saevi passa tyranni.
dedit infandi sceleris poenas
305   cum Tarquinio Tullia coniunx,
quae per caesi membra parentis
egit saevos impia currus
laceroque seni
violenta rogos nata negavit.
    Haec quoque nati videre nefas
310   saecula magnum,
cum Tyrrhenum rate ferali
princeps captam fraude parentem
misit in aequor.
properant placidos linquere portus
iussi nautae,
315   resonant remis pulsata freta;

300 *and* 296–299 *placed, in that order, after* 303 *by Baehrens*:
296–300 *deleted by Richter*

---

18 Virginia: the tradition says she was killed by her own father
to save her from the designs of the tyrannical decemvir Appius
Claudius. The scandal led ultimately to the overthrow of the
decemvirate (board of ten with supreme power).

proud kings out of this city, and later
avenged *your* spirit well and truly,
maiden slain by your father's hand[18]
to prevent you from suffering grievous slavery,
and monstrous lust
from gaining its shameless prize in triumph.
Civil war ensued from your death too,
daughter of Lucretius,
when you died by your own hand, pitiful woman,
after suffering the brutal tyrant's lust.[19]
Along with Tarquin, Tullia his wife
was punished for unspeakable crime:
cruelly, unnaturally, she drove her chariot
over her slaughtered father's body,
and refused the torn old man (savage daughter)
a funeral pyre.[20]

    This epoch has likewise seen an enormous
outrage by a son,
when the emperor deceived his mother
and sent her out on the Tyrrhene Sea
in a death-bound ship.
On command, the sailors
hasten to leave the calm of the harbour.
The sea resounds to the slap of oars,

[19] Lucretia was raped by Sextus Tarquinius, son of Tarquin
"the Proud," Rome's last king. Her subsequent suicide led to the
expulsion of the Tarquins from Rome.
[20] Tullia had encouraged Tarquin the Proud to murder the
reigning king, her father Servius Tullius, and take the throne.

fertur in altum provecta ratis,
quae resoluto robore labens
pressa dehiscit sorbetque mare.
tollitur ingens clamor ad astra
320   cum femineo mixtus planctu.
mors ante oculos dira vagatur;
quaerit leti sibi quisque fugam:
alii lacerae puppis tabulis
haerent nudi fluctusque secant,
325   repetunt alii litora nantes;
multos mergunt fata profundo.
    Scindit vestes Augusta suas
laceratque comas
rigat et maestis fletibus ora.
330   postquam spes est nulla salutis,
ardens ira, iam victa malis,
"Haec" exclamat
"mihi pro tanto munere reddis
praemia, nate?
hac sum, fateor, digna carina,
335   quae te genui, quae tibi lucem
atque imperium nomenque dedi
Caesaris amens.
Exere vultus Acheronte tuos
poenisque meis pascere, coniunx:
340   ego causa tuae, miserande, necis
natoque tuo funeris auctor
en, ut merui,
ferar ad manes inhumata tuos,
obruta saevis aequoris undis."
345   feriunt fluctus ora loquentis,

the vessel stands out into the deep.
Then the ship's timbers open, it collapses,
splits under pressure and drinks the sea in.
A deafening outcry mounts to heaven,
mingled with women's lamentation.
Before their eyes prowls fearsome death,
everyone for himself looks to escape:
some, stripped of everything, cling to planks
from the broken ship and face the waves;
others try to swim back to shore;
many are fated to drown in the deep.
    The lady Augusta[21] rends her clothes,
tears her hair
and drenches her face with tears of anguish.
After all hope of safety is gone,
burning with anger, undone by disaster,
she cries, "Is this the reward you pay me
for my great service to you, my son?
I admit I have earned such a vessel as this,
I who bore you, who gave you the light,
and, in my folly,
imperial power and the name of Caesar.
Raise your eyes from Acheron
and feast them on my punishment, husband!
I, the cause of your pitiful murder
and source of death for your son—behold,
as I deserve,
shall fare unburied to face your shade,
overwhelmed by the cruel waves of the sea."
The surf buffets her mouth as she speaks,

[21] Agrippina had been given this title as wife of the emperor.

ruit in pelagus
rursusque salo pressa resurgit;
pellit palmis cogente metu
freta, sed cedit fessa labori.
350 mansit tacitis in pectoribus
spreta tristi iam morte fides:
multi dominae ferre auxilium
pelago fractis viribus audent;
bracchia quamvis lenta trahentem
355 voce hortantur manibusque levant.
      Quid tibi saevi fugisse maris
profuit undas?
ferro es nati moritura tui,
cuius facinus vix posteritas,
360 tarde semper saecula credent.
furit ereptam
pelagoque dolet vivere matrem
impius ingens geminatque nefas,
ruit in miserae fata parentis
365 patiturque moram sceleris nullam.
missus peragit iussa satelles:
reserat dominae pectora ferro.
caedis moriens illa ministrum
rogat infelix,
370 utero dirum condat ut ensem:
"Hic est, hic est fodiendus" ait
"ferro, monstrum qui tale tulit."
post hanc vocem
cum supremo mixtam gemitu

349 freta set *Bücheler*: fata et A

she is plunged in the sea;
although engulfed, she rises again
and flails the surface with her arms, impelled
by fear—but the effort tires and defeats her.
Still there remains in people's hearts
an unspoken allegiance that scorns grim death.
Many make bold to render help
to their lady, despite being weakened by the sea;
although she drags her leaden arms,
they rally her with cries, support her with their hands.
    But what was the good of making your escape
from the cruel sea's waves?
You are doomed to die by the sword of your son,
whose deed posterity will scarcely believe
and every age will be slow to credit.
He is furious and troubled that his mother still lives,
saved from the sea,
and renews his unnatural villainy,
spurs on with his wretched mother's death,
tolerates no delay in the crime.
An attendant is sent and carries out orders:
he opens the lady's breast with the sword.
Dying, the ill-starred woman asks
the agent of her murder
to bury that heinous sword in her womb.
"*This* is what you must stab," she said,
"with the steel: it brought forth such a monster."
After these words,
mixed with a final groan,

375   animam tandem per fera tristem
        vulnera reddit.

SENECA

    Quid, impotens Fortuna, fallaci mihi
    blandita vultu, sorte contentum mea
    alte extulisti, gravius ut ruerem edita

380   receptus arce totque prospicerem metus?
    melius latebam procul ab invidiae malis
    remotus inter Corsici rupes maris,
    ubi liber animus et sui iuris mihi
    semper vacabat studia recolenti mea.

385   o quam iuvabat, quo nihil maius parens
    Natura genuit, operis immensi artifex,
    caelum intueri, solis et cursus sacros
    mundique motus, noctis alternas vices
    orbemque Phoebes, astra quem cingunt vaga,

390   lateque fulgens aetheris magni decus!
        Qui si senescit, tantus in caecum chaos
    casurus iterum, nunc adest mundo dies
    supremus ille, qui premat genus impium
    caeli ruina, rursus ut stirpem novam

395   generet renascens melior, ut quondam tulit
    iuvenis, tenente regna Saturno poli.
    tunc illa virgo, numinis magni dea,
    Iustitia, caelo missa cum sancta Fide,
    terra regebat mitis humanum genus.

400   non bella norant, non tubae fremitus truces,
    non arma gentes, cingere assuerant suas
    muris nec urbes; pervium cunctis iter,
    communis usus omnium rerum fuit;

she yielded her sorrowing spirit at last
through her cruel wounds.

Why, wilful Fortune, smiling on me with your deceiving
face—why, when I was content with my lot, did you raise
me on high, so that once admitted to this lofty eminence I
could fall more heavily, and look out on so many terrors? I
was better off when hidden far from envy's mischief, out of
the way amidst Corsica's sea crags, where my mind was
free and sovereign and always at liberty for me to pursue
my studies. Oh what a delight it was to gaze at the greatest
creation of Mother Nature, architect of this measureless
fabric—the heavens, the holy paths of the sun, the movements of the cosmos, the recurrence of night and the circuit traced by Phoebe, with the wandering stars around
her, and the far-shining glory of the great firmament!

If the heavens are growing old, doomed despite their
immensity to fall back into blind chaos, we are now approaching that final day which will crush this sacrilegious
race beneath the collapsing sky. That will allow a reborn
and better cosmos to bring forth once again a new progeny,
such as it bore in youth when Saturn held the throne of
heaven. In those days that virgin goddess of great power,
Justice, descended with holy Faithfulness from heaven,
and ruled the human race mildly on earth. The nations
knew no wars, no grim trumpet's blare, no weapons, nor
the practice of surrounding cities with walls; travel was
open to all, everything was held in common; and the glad

---

377 impotens *Siegmund*: me potens *A*
387 cursus *recc.*: currus *A*

et ipsa Tellus laeta fecundos sinus
405 pandebat ultro, tam piis felix parens
et tuta alumnis.
                    Alia sed suboles minus
conspecta mitis. tertium sollers genus
novas ad artes extitit, sanctum tamen;
mox inquietum, quod sequi cursu feras
410 auderet acres, fluctibus tectos gravi
extrahere pisces rete vel calamo levi,
decipere volucres crate vel ‹posito vagas›
412bis tenere laqueo, premere subiectos iugo
tauros feroces, vomere immunem prius
sulcare terram, laesa quae fruges suas
‹summisit aegre, quasque habet largas opes›
415 interior alte condidit sacro sinu.
Sed in parentis viscera intravit suae
deterior aetas: eruit ferrum grave
aurumque, saevas mox et armavit manus.
partita fines regna constituit, novas
420 extruxit urbes, tecta defendit sua
aliena telis aut petît praedae imminens.
neglecta terras fugit et mores feros
hominum, cruenta caede pollutas manus,
Astraea virgo, siderum magnum decus.
425 cupido belli crevit atque auri fames
totum per orbem; maximum exortum est malum
luxuria, pestis blanda, cui vires dedit
roburque longum tempus atque error gravis.
Collecta vitia per tot aetates diu
430 in nos redundant; saeculo premimur gravi,

---

407 *lacuna between* mitis *and* tertium *suspected by Richter*

earth opened her fertile bosom without coercion, a mother blessed and unharmed by nurslings who so revered her.

But a second breed appeared, of less gentle character. A third race arose, inventive of new arts, yet reverent; but then a restless race, that ventured to pursue wild beasts in the chase, to draw fish from their shelter in the waves with heavy nets or light rods, to trick birds into wickerwork traps or set snares to hold the vagrants fast, to subject fierce bulls to the weight of the yoke, and to furrow with the plough the previously unscathed earth; when injured she ⟨put forth⟩ her crops ⟨grudgingly, and the lavish resources⟩ within her she hid deep in her sacred bosom.

But a worse generation delved into the body of its own parent, rooted out heavy iron and gold, and soon made weapons for its cruel hands. It assigned boundaries and established kingdoms, built cities for the first time, defended its homes or attacked others', bent on plunder. Away from the earth where she was scorned, from the savagery of humans, from hands polluted with bloody slaughter, fled the virgin Astraea, great glory of the stars. Lust for war and hunger for gold grew throughout the world; and the great evil arose of extravagant excess, a seductive curse, given strength and force by the lengthening years and grave moral blindness.

The vices accumulated over time, over so many ages, are flooding out over *us*; we are burdened by an oppres-

412 ⟨posito vagas⟩ *Peiper*: calamo aut levi *(from* 411) *A*

413 vomere *G (in margin), recc.*: vulnere *A*

414 *lacuna identified and supplement proposed by Zwierlein*

420 sua *Bücheler*: suis *A*

quo scelera regnant, saevit impietas furens,
turpi libido Venere dominatur potens,
luxuria victrix orbis immensas opes
iam pridem avaris manibus, ut perdat, rapit.
435   Sed ecce, gressu fertur attonito Nero
trucique vultu. quid ferat mente horreo.

NERO
Perage imperata: mitte, qui Plauti mihi
Sullaeque caesi referat abscisum caput.

PRAEFECTUS
Iussa haud morabor: castra confestim petam.

SENECA
440   Nihil in propinquos temere constitui decet.

NERO
Iusto esse facile est cui vacat pectus metu.

SENECA
Magnum timoris remedium clementia est.

NERO
Extinguere hostem maxima est virtus ducis.

SENECA
Servare cives maior est patriae patri.

NERO
445   Praecipere mitem convenit pueris senem.

---

22 Sulla was Nero's brother-in-law as husband of Antonia, Claudius' daughter by his second wife; Plautus was more distantly related through Augustus. Both had been exiled as alleged threats to Nero's position.

23 The title *Pater patriae* had been taken by Nero, as by previ-

sive era in which crime reigns, unrighteousness runs mad, lust rules, gaining power through sexual degradation, and triumphant extravagance has long been plundering the world's immense resources with greedy hands, in order to squander them.

But see, Nero is approaching with agitated steps and a grim expression. I shudder to think of his intentions.

NERO

Discharge your orders! Send someone to kill Plautus and Sulla and bring me their severed heads.

PREFECT

I shall not delay your orders, but head for the camp forthwith. [*Exit*]

SENECA

No decision against one's kin[22] should be taken hastily.

NERO

It is easy to be just when your heart is free of fear.

SENECA

Mercy is a great antidote to fear.

NERO

The greatest virtue in a leader is to destroy an enemy.

SENECA

A greater virtue for the Father of the Country is to safeguard citizens' lives.[23]

NERO

A soft old man should be teaching boys.

ous emperors except Tiberius: for the implication read into it here cf. Seneca's *On Clemency* 1.14.

SENECA

Regenda magis est fervida adulescentia.

NERO

Aetate in hac satis esse consilii reor.

SENECA

Ut facta superi comprobent semper tua?

NERO

Stulte verebor, ipse cum faciam, deos.

SENECA

450 Hoc plus verere quod licet tantum tibi.

NERO

Fortuna nostra cuncta permittit mihi.

SENECA

Crede obsequenti parcius: levis est dea.

NERO

Inertis est nescire quid liceat sibi.

SENECA

Id facere laus est quod decet, non quod licet.

NERO

455 Calcat iacentem vulgus.

SENECA

Invisum opprimit.

NERO

Ferrum tuetur principem.

---

24 He had deified his predecessor Claudius.

SENECA

Guidance is needed even more for a young man's vehemence.

NERO

I think my time of life has judgment enough.

SENECA

Enough that the gods always approve of your deeds?

NERO

I should be foolish to fear the gods, when I myself create them![24]

SENECA

You should fear all the more because you have so much power.

NERO

My good fortune gives me licence to do anything.

SENECA

Do not put such trust in her compliance: she is a fickle goddess.

NERO

It is spineless not to understand what one can do.

SENECA

Praise lies in doing what one should, not what one can.

NERO

The mob tramples on a supine ruler.

SENECA

But overthrows a hated one.

NERO

Steel is the emperor's protection.

[SENECA]

SENECA
Melius fides.

NERO
Decet timeri Caesarem.

SENECA
At plus diligi.

NERO
Laudent necesse est . . .

SENECA
Quidquid exprimitur grave est.

NERO
iussisque nostris pareant.

SENECA
Iusta impera.

NERO
460   Statuam ipse.

SENECA
Quae consensus efficiat rata.

NERO
Destrictus ensis faciet.

SENECA
Hoc absit nefas!

NERO
An patiar ultra sanguinem nostrum peti,
inultus et contemptus ut subito opprimar?
exilia non fregere summotos procul

---

458 laudent *Ferri*: metuant *A*

556

SENECA

Loyalty a better one.

NERO

It befits Caesar to be feared.

SENECA

But more to be loved.

NERO

They have to praise me—

SENECA

Anything compelled is irksome.

NERO

—and obey my orders.

SENECA

Then give just commands.

NERO

I shall determine what they are.

SENECA

In such a way that general approval will ratify them.

NERO

The drawn sword will ratify them!

SENECA

No to such outrage!

NERO

Am I to go on tolerating attempts to shed my blood, and in consequence suffer a sudden overthrow, unavenged and despised? Exile in far-off places has not broken Plautus

465 Plautum atque Sullam, pertinax quorum furor
armat ministros sceleris in caedem meam,
absentium cum maneat etiam ingens favor
in urbe nostra, qui fovet spes exulum.
tollantur hostes ense suspecti mihi,
470 invisa coniunx pereat et carum sibi
fratrem sequatur. quidquid excelsum est cadat!

SENECA

Pulchrum eminere est inter illustres viros,
consulere patriae, parcere afflictis, fera
caede abstinere, tempus atque irae dare,
475 orbi quietem, saeculo pacem suo.
haec summa virtus, petitur hac caelum via.
sic ille patriae primus Augustus parens
complexus astra est, colitur et templis deus.
illum tamen Fortuna iactavit diu
480 terra marique per graves belli vices,
hostes parentis donec oppressit sui.
tibi numen incruenta summisit suum
et dedit habenas imperi facili manu
nutuque terras maria subiecit tuo.
485 invidia tristis, victa consensu pio,
cessit; senatus, equitis accensus favor;
plebisque votis atque iudicio patrum
489 electus orbem spiritu sacrum regis.
488 tu pacis auctor, generis humani arbiter,
490 patriae parens: quod nomen ut serves petit
suosque cives Roma commendat tibi.

489 *placed before* 488 *by Frassinetti*   sacrum *Leo:* sacra *A*

and Sulla: with fanatical persistence they are arming their henchmen to murder me, since despite their absence they still have great popularity in our city—that is what nurtures their hopes in exile. These suspected enemies of mine must be removed by the sword; my hated wife must die, and follow the brother she holds dear. Everything that stands high must fall!

SENECA

It is a glorious thing to be preeminent among illustrious men, to watch over the fatherland, spare the downtrodden, refrain from savage slaughter, give anger time to cool, and grant tranquillity to the world and peace to one's own time. This is the highest virtue, this is the path to heaven. This was how that first August[25] Father of the Country gained the stars, and is worshipped in shrines as a god. Yet Fortune had long tossed him about over land and sea through the grievous chances of war, until he crushed his father's enemies. To you she provided her divine support without bloodshed, accommodatingly handed you the reins of empire, and made land and sea subject to the nod of your head. Sour ill-will vanished, overpowered by a collective sense of devotion; there was an outburst of enthusiasm from senators and equestrians. Chosen by the wishes of the common people and the judgment of the Fathers,[26] you rule the hallowed world by your spirit; you are provider of peace, arbiter of the human race, Father of the Country. Rome asks you to maintain that title, and she entrusts her citizens to your care.

25 Augustus is both a title and an adjective.
26 The Senate.

NERO

Munus deorum est, ipsa quod servit mihi
Roma et senatus, quodque ab invitis preces
humilesque voces exprimit nostri metus.
495 servare cives principi et patriae graves,
claro tumentes genere, quae dementia est,
cum liceat una voce suspectos sibi
mori iubere? Brutus in caedem ducis,
a quo salutem tulerat, armavit manus;
500 invictus acie, gentium domitor, Iovi
aequatus altos saepe per honorum gradus,
Caesar nefando civium scelere occidit.
    Quantum cruoris Roma tunc vidit sui,
lacerata totiens! ille qui meruit pia
505 virtute caelum, divus Augustus, viros
quot interemit nobiles, iuvenes senes,
sparsos per orbem, cum suos mortis metu
fugerent penates et trium ferrum ducum,
tabula notante deditos tristi neci!
510 exposita rostris capita caesorum patres
videre maesti, flere nec licuit suos,
non gemere dira tabe polluto foro,
stillante sanie per putres vultus gravi.
    Nec finis hic cruoris aut caedis stetit.
515 pavere volucres et feras saevas diu
tristes Philippi, sorpsit et Siculum mare

501 altos *A*: alto *Zwierlein*
516 sorbsit *Heinsius*: hausit *A*

NERO

It is through the generosity of the gods that Rome herself and the Senate are at my service, and that prayers and humble words are wrung from the unwilling by fear of me. To safeguard citizens who are troublesome to emperor and country, puffed up by noble ancestry—what madness is that, when one can order the death of suspects with a single word? Brutus armed himself to slay the very leader who had granted him life;[27] undefeated in battle, conqueror of nations, raised to the level of Jove through a continual series of high honours, Caesar fell through an unspeakable crime committed by citizens.

Then what quantities of her own blood Rome saw, being wounded so often! He who earned a place in heaven by his virtues and sense of duty, the deified Augustus— how many noblemen *he* killed, young and old! They had scattered throughout the world in fear for their lives, in flight from their own homes and from the swords of the three leaders;[28] a notice board listed those consigned to the horror of death! Sorrowing fathers saw the heads of the slain exposed on the Rostra, yet they could not weep for their own kin, nor lament in a forum polluted with horrible gore, as foul putrescence trickled down the rotting faces.

And this was not the end of blood and slaughter. Grim Philippi long feasted birds and savage beasts, and the seas around Sicily often swallowed fleets and men as they

[27] Brutus was pardoned by Julius Caesar after the battle of Pharsalus (48 B.C.), but was one of his assassins in 44 B.C.

[28] The Triumvirate of Octavian, Antony, and Lepidus; they published proscription lists of those to be killed.

[SENECA]

classes virosque saepe caedentes suos;
concussus orbis viribus magnis ducum.
superatus acie puppibus Nilum petit
520 fugae paratis, ipse periturus brevi.
hausit cruorem incesta Romani ducis
Aegyptus iterum; non leves umbras tegit.
illic sepultum est impie gestum diu
civile bellum. condidit tandem suos
525 iam fessus enses victor hebetatos feris
vulneribus, et continuit imperium metus.
armis fideque militis tutus fuit,
pietate nati factus eximia deus,
post fata consecratus et templis datus.
530   Nos quoque manebunt astra, si saevo prior
ense occuparo quidquid infestum est mihi,
dignaque nostram subole fundaro domum.

SENECA

Implebit aulam stirpe caelesti tuam
generata divo, Claudiae gentis decus,
535 sortita fratris more Iunonis toros.

NERO

Incesta genetrix detrahit generi fidem,

522 non *M. Müller*: nunc *A*

---

29 Philippi is used by the poets to designate both the battle of
Pharsalus (48 B.C., Caesar vs. Pompey) and that of Philippi proper
(42 B.C., Octavian and Antony vs. Brutus and Cassius): hence
"long." Between 43 and 36 B.C. Sicily was used as a base by
Pompey's son Sextus, who fought several naval battles around its
coasts against the forces of Octavian.

butchered their own people.[29] The warlords' mighty forces shook the world. The one defeated in battle made for the Nile with ships he had readied for flight, himself soon doomed to perish. Incestuous Egypt drank the blood of a Roman leader a second time;[30] they are no insubstantial ghosts she shrouds! There was buried the civil war whose fighting had been so long and inhuman. At last the weary victor cached his swords, blunted by dealing savage wounds; what maintained his power was fear. It was his soldiers' arms and loyalty that kept him safe, and his son's[31] exceptional devotion that made him a god, hallowed him after death and set him in our shrines.

The stars will be my destiny too, if I use the cruel sword to strike preemptively at all that is hostile to me, and make my house secure through worthy offspring.

SENECA
Your house will be filled with children of heavenly descent by one who is the daughter of a god, the glory of the Claudian clan, who like Juno has been granted her brother's marriage bed.

NERO
But the line is uncertain as a result of her mother's promis-

[30] The second is Antony, who when defeated at Actium fled to Egypt and committed suicide there; the first was Pompey the Great. "Incestuous" alludes to the sister-brother marriages of the Egyptian royal house, including Cleopatra's successive marriages to her brothers Ptolemy XIII and XIV.

[31] Viz. Tiberius, his adopted son.

[SENECA]

animusque numquam coniugis iunctus mihi.

SENECA

Teneris in annis haud satis clara est fides,
pudore victus cum tegit flammas amor.

NERO

540   Hoc equidem et ipse credidi frustra diu,
manifesta quamvis pectore insociabili
vultuque signa proderent odium mei,
tandem quod ardens statuit ulcisci dolor.
dignamque thalamis coniugem inveni meis
545   genere atque forma, victa cui cedet Venus
Iovisque coniunx et ferox armis dea.

SENECA

Probitas fidesque coniugis, mores pudor
placeant marito. sola perpetuo manent
subiecta nulli mentis atque animi bona;
550   florem decoris singuli carpunt dies.

NERO

Omnes in unam contulit laudes deus,
talemque nasci fata voluerunt mihi.

SENECA

Recedet a te (temere ne credas) amor.

553 recedet *Bothe*: recedat *A*

---

32 According to the historian Tacitus, the justification given by
Nero for his divorce of Octavia was her alleged sterility. But the
play strongly hints that Octavia had refused sexual relations with
Nero (e.g. line 287).

cuity; and my wife's heart has never been one with mine.[32]

SENECA

Allegiance is not really evident in the tender years, when love is quelled by modesty and hides its warmth.

NERO

Indeed, for a long time I too held that futile belief, though her face and her uncongenial heart gave clear signs revealing her hatred for me—for which my burning resentment has finally decide to retaliate. And I have found a wife whose ancestry and beauty make her worthy of marriage to me—one to whom Venus would concede victory, and Jove's wife, and the fierce warrior goddess.[33]

SENECA

A wife's probity and fidelity, character and modesty should be what pleases her husband. The only enduring qualities are those of mind and spirit, which are under no external control; the flower of beauty is diminished by each passing day.

NERO

God has brought together every distinction in this one woman; the Fates willed that such a paragon should be born for me.

SENECA

Love will forsake you; do not have blind faith!

---

[33] Pallas. These three goddesses competed for beauty in the Judgment of Paris.

NERO

Quem summovere fulminis dominus nequit,
555 caeli tyrannum, saeva qui penetrat freta
Ditisque regna, detrahit superos polo?

SENECA

Volucrem esse Amorem fingit immitem deum
mortalis error, armat et telis manus
arcuque sacras, instruit saeva face
560 genitumque credit Venere, Vulcano satum.
vis magna mentis blandus atque animi calor
Amor est; iuventa gignitur, luxu otio
nutritur inter laeta Fortunae bona.
quem si fovere atque alere desistas, cadit
565 brevique vires perdit extinctus suas.

NERO

Hanc esse vitae maximam causam reor,
per quam voluptas oritur; interitu caret
cum procreetur semper humanum genus
Amore grato, qui truces mulcet feras.
570 hic mihi iugales praeferat taedas deus
iungatque nostris igne Poppaeam toris!

SENECA

Vix sustinere possit hos thalamos dolor
videre populi, sancta nec pietas sinat.

NERO

Prohibebor unus facere quod cunctis licet?

SENECA

575 Maiora populus semper a summo exigit.

NERO

You mean the tyrant of heaven, who cannot be banished by the lord of the thunderbolt, who penetrates the cruel seas and the realm of Dis, and draws down gods from the sky?[34]

SENECA

It is human wrongheadedness that fancies winged Love as an implacable god, arms his holy hands with bow and arrows, equips him with a cruel torch, and believes him to be Venus' son by Vulcan. A powerful impulse in the mind, a seductive warmth in the heart—that is what Love is. It is generated by youth, and fostered by leisure and high living amidst Fortune's genial bounty. If you stop cherishing and nurturing it, it fades, and is soon quenched and loses its strength.

NERO

I think it the chief source of life, the fount of pleasure. The human race is preserved from extinction by being constantly engendered through enchanting Love, who charms even wild beasts. May this god carry torches to herald my marriage, and his fire bring Poppaea to share my bed!

SENECA

The people's displeasure could scarcely bear to see such a marriage; their reverence and devotion would not allow it.

NERO

Shall I alone be forbidden to do what all may do?

SENECA

The people always demand more from the greatest.

---

[34] I.e. to visit human loves; the "tyrant" is Amor/Cupid.

NERO

Libet experiri, viribus fractus meis
an cedat animis temere conceptus furor.

SENECA

Obsequere potius civibus placidus tuis.

NERO

Male imperatur, cum regit vulgus duces.

SENECA

580   Nihil impetrare cum valet, iuste dolet.

NERO

Exprimere ius est, ferre quod nequeunt preces?

SENECA

Negare durum est.

NERO

Principem cogi nefas.

SENECA

Remittat ipse.

NERO

Fama sed victum feret.

SENECA

Levis atque vana.

NERO

Sit licet, multos notat.

SENECA

585   Excelsa metuit.

577 furor *Avantius*: favor *A*

568

NERO

I should like to discover whether this rashly conceived madness will be forgotten, once it is broken by my power.

SENECA

Better defer graciously to your citizens.

NERO

Poor governance, when the commons rule their leaders!

SENECA

When they cannot win any concessions, they are justly aggrieved.

NERO

Is it just to extort what they cannot gain by appeals?

SENECA

To say no is harsh.

NERO

To coerce the emperor is outrageous.

SENECA

Let him yield of his own accord.

NERO

But rumour will say he was beaten.

SENECA

It is idle and empty.

NERO

Maybe, but it stigmatizes many.

SENECA

It fears the great.

[SENECA]

NERO

Non minus carpit tamen.

SENECA

Facile opprimetur. merita te divi patris
aetasque frangat coniugis, probitas pudor.

NERO

Desiste tandem, iam gravis nimium mihi,
instare! liceat facere quod Seneca improbat.
590   et ipse populi vota iam pridem moror

*   *   *   *   *

cum portet utero pignus et partem mei.
quin destinamus proximum thalamis diem.

AGRIPPINA

Tellure rupta Tartaro gressum extuli,
Stygiam cruenta praeferens dextra facem
595   thalamis scelestis: nubat his flammis meo
Poppaea nato iuncta, quas vindex manus
dolorque matris vertet ad tristes rogos.
manet inter umbras impiae caedis mihi
semper memoria, manibus nostris gravis
600   adhuc inultis: reddita est meritis meis
funesta merces puppis et pretium imperi
nox illa qua naufragia deflevi mea.
comitum necem natique crudelis nefas
deflere votum fuerat: haud tempus datum est
605   lacrimis, sed ingens scelere geminavit nefas.

After 590 *Lacuna recognised by Zwierlein*
600 est *Bücheler*: et A

35 The gist of the missing line(s) was presumably that the

NERO

But carps nonetheless.

SENECA

It will easily be crushed. You should be swayed by your obligations to your deified father, by your wife's youth, her probity and modesty.

NERO

Enough, stop pressing the point! You are trying my patience now. Let me act in a way that Seneca disapproves. Indeed *I* have been delaying the people's wishes for some time . . . [35] since she is carrying in her womb a token and portion of myself. Come, let us set tomorrow as the day for the wedding. [*Exeunt*]

[*Time: towards dawn of the next day*]

GHOST OF AGRIPPINA

Bursting through the earth I have made my way from Tartarus, bearing a Stygian torch in my bloody hand to herald this iniquitous wedding. Let Poppaea marry my son by the light of these flames, which my hand of vengeance, my anger as a mother, will turn to funeral fires. Even amidst the dead the memory of that unnatural murder remains with me always, and burdens my still unavenged shade: the payment rendered for my services was that lethal ship; the reward for imperial power, that night on which I wept over my shipwreck. I would have wished to weep over my companions' deaths and my cruel son's villainy, but no time was given for tears: he renewed his great villainy with more

people are eager for an heir to the throne, and will therefore support Nero's marriage to Poppaea.

perempta ferro, foeda vulneribus sacros
intra penates spiritum effudi gravem
erepta pelago—sanguine extinxi meo
nec odia nati: saevit in nomen ferus
610   matris tyrannus, obrui meritum cupit,
simulacra, titulos destruit memores mei
totum per orbem, quem dedit poenam in meam
puero regendum noster infelix amor.

    Extinctus umbras agitat infestus meas
615   flammisque vultus noxios coniunx petit,
instat, minatur, imputat fatum mihi
tumulumque nati, poscit auctorem necis.
iam parce: dabitur, tempus haud longum peto.
ultrix Erinys impio dignum parat
620   letum tyranno, verbera et turpem fugam
poenasque quîs et Tantali vincat sitim,
dirum laborem Sisyphi, Tityi alitem
Ixionisque membra rapientem rotam.
licet extruat marmoribus atque auro tegat
625   superbus aulam, limen armatae ducis
servent cohortes, mittat immensas opes
exhaustus orbis, supplices dextram petant
Parthi cruentam, regna divitias ferant,
veniet dies tempusque quo reddat suis
630   animam nocentem sceleribus, iugulum hostibus,
desertus ac destructus et cunctis egens.

    Heu, quo labor, quo vota ceciderunt mea!

607 intra β: inter δ
611 memores mei *Grotius*: mortis metu̧ *A*

crime. Dispatched by the sword, befouled by wounds, amidst the sanctities of my home I gave up my labouring spirit, just rescued from the sea. Yet my blood did not quench my son's hatred. The fierce tyrant rages against his mother's name, wants my services obliterated, throws down the statues and inscriptions that bear my memory throughout the world—the world that my ill-starred love gave him as a boy to rule, to my own harm.

My spirit is hounded fiercely by my dead husband; he thrusts burning brands at my guilty face, looms over me, threatens me, blames me for his death and his son's grave, and demands his murderer.[36] Wait—he will be provided, I need only a little time! The avenging Erinys is planning a worthy death for that unnatural tyrant: lashes, and shameful flight, and torments to surpass the thirst of Tantalus, Sisyphus' dreadful labour, the vulture of Tityos, and the wheel that spins Ixion's limbs. Though he may pile up a palace of marble and cover it with gold[37] in his arrogance, though armed squadrons guard their commander's door, though the depleted world sends him its immense resources, though Parthians seek to kiss his bloody hand in supplication, though kingdoms bring him their riches, there will come a day and time when he will pay for his crimes with his guilty spirit and pay his enemies with his throat, deserted and thrown down and utterly destitute.

Oh, how far my labours and prayers have fallen! How

---

[36] The son is Britannicus, his murderer Nero. Probably Agrippina sees or imagines Claudius' ghost before her (cf. Medea's vision at *Med* 958–966); or she may mean that Claudius attacks her in the underworld.   [37] A prophetic reference to Nero's lavish Golden House, begun in A.D. 64.

quo te furor provexit attonitum tuus
et fata, nate, cedat ut tantis malis
635 genetricis ira, quae tuo scelere occidit!
utinam, antequam te parvulum in lucem edidi
aluique, saevae nostra lacerassent ferae
viscera: sine ullo scelere, sine sensu innocens
meus occidisses; iunctus atque haerens mihi
640 semper quieta cerneres sede inferum
proavos patremque, nominis magni viros—
quos nunc pudor luctusque perpetuus manet
ex te, nefande, meque quae talem tuli.
    Quid tegere cesso Tartaro vultus meos,
645 noverca coniunx mater infelix meis?

OCTAVIA

Parcite lacrimis
urbis festo laetoque die,
ne tantus amor nostrique favor
principis acres suscitet iras,
650 vobisque ego sim causa malorum.
non hoc primum pectora vulnus
mea senserunt;
graviora tuli.
dabit hic nostris finem curis
vel morte dies.
non ego saevi cernere cogar
655 coniugis ora,

640 quieta . . . sede *recc.*: quietam . . . sedem *A*

far your wild madness and your destiny have brought
you, son—to a point where your mother's anger fades before such disasters, though she died by your crime. I wish
that before I brought you into the light as a tiny baby and
suckled you, wild beasts had ripped apart my womb! You
would have died my innocent child, free of crime and consciousness; clinging close to me in a peaceful corner of the
underworld, you would have gazed forever on your father
and forefathers, men of great name—but now doomed to
everlasting shame and grief by you (so evil!) and by me who
bore such a son.

Why am I slow to hide my face in Tartarus, I who blight
my kin as stepmother, wife, and mother?

[*Time: later that morning*]

OCTAVIA

Weep no more[38]
on this festive, joyful day for the city,
lest so much love and support for me
arouse the emperor's bitter anger
and bring you trouble for my sake.
This wound is not the first my heart
has felt: I have born
worse things before.
This day will grant an end to my cares,
be it by death.
I shall not be forced to look at the face
of my brutal husband,

---

[38] She is addressing her attendants, or (less probably) the citizens who speak at 669.

non invisos intrare mihi
thalamos famulae;
soror Augusti, non uxor ero.
absint tantum tristes poenae
660   letique metus.
—scelerum diri, miseranda, viri
potes hoc demens sperare memor?
hos ad thalamos servata diu
victima tandem funesta cades.
665   Sed quid patrios saepe penates
respicis udis confusa genis?
propera tectis efferre gradus,
linque cruentam principis aulam.

CHORUS

En illuxit suspecta diu
670   fama totiens iactata dies:
cessit thalamis
Claudia diri pulsa Neronis,
quos iam victrix Poppaea tenet,
cessat pietas
dum nostra gravi compressa metu
675   segnisque dolor.
ubi Romani vis est populi,
fregit claros quae saepe duces,
dedit invictae leges patriae,
fasces dignis civibus olim,
680   iussit bellum pacemque, feras
gentes domuit,
captos reges carcere clausit?

677 claros *A*: diros *M. Müller*

nor enter the hateful chamber of that
slavewoman;[39] I shall be
Augustus' sister, but not his wife.
Just let me be spared forbidding torments
and the terror of death.
Poor woman, knowing your monstrous husband's
crimes, can you hope for this? Insane!
Long set aside for this wedding, you will die
at last as a sinister sacrifice.
    But why look back at your father's home
so often, with eyes that are blurred by tears?
Hurry, make your escape from this house,
quit the emperor's bloodstained palace. [*Exit*]

CHORUS

See, the day has dawned whose coming
was long suspected, often rumoured:
Claudia[40] is banished
from monstrous Nero's married quarters,
where now Poppaea presides in triumph,
while our devotion
holds back, subdued by the weight of fear,
and our anger is inert.
Where is the might of the Roman people
which often crushed renowned commanders,
safeguarded our country and gave it laws,
gave power to *worthy* citizens once,
commanded war or peace, subdued
ferocious tribes,
shut away captured kings in prison?

---

[39] Acte (cf. 105).   [40] Octavia.

gravis en oculis undique nostris
iam Poppaeae fulget imago,
iuncta Neroni!
685   affligat humo violenta manus
similes nimium vultus dominae
ipsamque toris detrahat altis,
petat infestis mox et flammis
telisque feri principis aulam.

NUTRIX

690   Quo trepida gressum coniugis thalamis tui
effers, alumna, quodve secretum petis
turbata vultu? cur genae fletu madent?
certe petitus precibus et votis dies
nostris refulsit: Caesari iuncta es tuo
695   taeda iugali, quem tuus cepit decor
et culta sancte tradidit vinctum tibi
genetrix Amoris, maximum numen, Venus.
o qualis altos quanta pressisti toros
residens in aula! vidit attonitus tuam
700   formam senatus, tura cum superis dares
sacrasque grato spargeres aras mero,
velata summum flammeo tenui caput;
et ipse lateri iunctus atque haerens tuo
sublimis inter civium laeta omina
705   incessit habitu atque ore laetitiam gerens
princeps superbo. talis emersam freto
spumante Peleus coniugem accepit Thetin,
quorum toros celebrasse caelestes ferunt

689 feri δ: feris β
696 culta sancte *Birt*: culpa senece *A*

578

Everywhere now our eyes are affronted,
look, by Poppaea's gleaming image,
paired with Nero's!
Let us dash to the ground with violent hands
these too-real images of her highness' face,
drag *her* from her exalted bed,
and then storm on with flames and weapons
to attack this cruel emperor's palace. [*Exeunt*]

[*Time: next morning*]

POPPAEA'S NURSE

Where are you hurrying fearfully from your husband's
bedchamber, my child? Are you looking for privacy, with
such disquiet in your face? Why are your cheeks wet with
tears? Surely the day we prayed and hoped for has dawned!
By the light of marriage torches you were united with your
dear Caesar, who had been captivated by your beauty, and
delivered as your prisoner by the goddess you had worshipped devoutly, the mother of Love, Venus, greatest of
divinities. How fine, how grand you looked as you reclined
on your high couch in the palace! The Senate was spell-
bound at the sight of your beauty, as you offered incense
to the gods and sprinkled the holy altars with thanksgiving wine, with the light bridal veil covering your upper
face; and pressing close to your side, walking tall amidst
words of glad omen from the citizens, his face and bearing
proudly revealing his joy, was the emperor himself. Peleus
looked so as he received his bride Thetis rising from the
foaming sea; their nuptials were celebrated, as the story

pelagique numen omne consensu pari.
710 quae subita vultus causa mutavit tuos?
quid pallor iste, quid ferant lacrimae doce.

POPPAEA

Confusa tristi proximae noctis metu
visuque, nutrix, mente turbata feror,
defecta sensu. laeta nam postquam dies
715 sideribus, atrae cessit et nocti polus,
inter Neronis vincta complexus mei
somno resolvor; nec diu placida frui
quiete licuit. visa nam thalamos meos
celebrare turba est maesta: resolutis comis
720 matres Latinae flebiles planctus dabant.
inter tubarum saepe terribilem sonum
sparsam cruore coniugis genetrix mei
vultu minaci saeva quatiebat facem.
quam dum sequor coacta praesenti metu,
725 diducta subito patuit ingenti mihi
tellus hiatu; lata quo praeceps toros
cerno iugales pariter et miror meos,
in quîs resedi fessa. venientem intuor
comitante turba coniugem quondam meum
730 natumque. properat petere complexus meos
Crispinus, intermissa libare oscula,
irrupit intra tecta cum trepidus mea
ensemque iugulo condidit saevum Nero.
tandem quietem magnus excussit timor;

715 atrae *Peiper*: atris *A*

---

41 Both were named Rufrius Crispinus. The ex-husband was

tells, with equal approval by the gods of heaven and every divinity of the sea. What has caused your sudden change of countenance? Tell me the meaning of this pallor and these tears.

POPPAEA

I am disturbed by a grim, fearful vision from last night, nurse—restless, troubled in my mind, bereft of my senses. After the joyful day had given way to the stars, and the heavens to black night, I relaxed and slept, held fast in my Nero's embrace. But I was not allowed to enjoy peaceful rest for long. For it seemed that my marriage chamber was thronged by a sorrowful crowd: with hair unbound, Latin mothers were beating themselves in mourning. Amidst the frequent, terrifying sounds of trumpets, my husband's mother was fiercely wielding a bloodstained torch, while gazing menacingly. As I followed her, impelled by an urgent fear, suddenly the earth split apart, and a huge crevasse opened beneath me. Cast into its depths, I discerned, to my amazement, my marriage bed, on which I sank down exhausted. Coming towards me I saw my former husband and my son,[41] accompanied by a crowd of people. Crispinus was eagerly trying to embrace me and kiss me as before, when Nero burst into my house in fright and buried the cruel sword in his throat.[42] Then finally terror roused me from sleep. My face and body shook

put to death shortly after Poppaea died in 65; the son too did not survive Nero's reign.

[42] The Latin does not specify *whose* throat here or at 752, nor *which* husband is meant at 739. Consequently the dream could mean, with the ambiguity of prophecy, that the frightened Nero stabs his own throat—as happened in his suicide in A.D. 68.

735 quatit ora et artus horridus nostros tremor
  pulsatque pectus; continet vocem timor,
  quam nunc fides pietasque produxit tua.
  heu quid minantur inferum manes mihi
  aut quem cruorem coniugis vidi mei?

NUTRIX

740 Quaecumque mentis agitat intentus vigor,
  ea per quietem sacer et arcanus refert
  veloxque sensus. coniugem thalamos toros
  vidisse te miraris amplexu novi
  haerens mariti? sed movent laeto die
745 pulsata palmis pectora et fusae comae?
  Octaviae discidia planxerunt sacros
  intra penates fratris et patrium larem.
  fax illa, quam secuta es, Augustae manu
  praelata clarum nomen invidia tibi
750 partum ominatur; inferum sedes toros
  stabiles futuros spondet aeternae domus.
  iugulo quod ensem condidit princeps tuus,
  bella haud movebit, pace sed ferrum teget.
  recollige animum, recipe laetitiam, precor,
755 timore pulso redde te thalamis tuis.

POPPAEA

  Delubra et aras petere constitui sacras,
  caesis litare victimis numen deum,
  ut expientur noctis et somni minae,
  terrorque in hostes redeat attonitus meos.
760 tu vota pro me suscipe et precibus piis
  superos adora, maneat ut praesens status.

---

740 intentus *Gronovius*: infestus *A*

with violent tremors, my heart pounded; fear stopped my words, but now your faithful love has drawn them from me. Oh! What threatening meaning do the underworld shades have for me? What is this vision of my husband's blood?

NURSE

There is a sacred faculty, swift and mysterious, that brings back to the mind in sleep those matters that busied it when active and engaged. You wonder that you saw your husband, bedroom, and bed? You were deep in the embrace of your new husband! But you are troubled that women beat their breasts on a day of joy, and untied their hair? It was Octavia's divorce they mourned, there in her brother's house, her father's home. That torch you followed, held aloft in the Augusta's hand, is an omen of bright fame born for you out of ill will; the underworld abode promises a stable marriage in an abiding home. Since your emperor buried his sword in a throat, he will not embark on wars, but hide the sword in peace. Take heart again, regain your joyfulness, I beg you; banish your fears and take your place again in the marriage chamber.

POPPAEA

I have decided to visit the sacred shrines and altars, and appease the sovereign gods with animal sacrifices, so as to avert the menace of night and the dream, and deflect this shock and terror onto my enemies. You, make vows on my behalf, and appeal to the gods with devout prayers not to allow any change of circumstances.

---

[747] intra *Avantius*: inter *A*
[761] status *Bücheler*: metus *A*

[SENECA]

CHORUS

Si vera loquax fama Tonantis
furta et gratos narrat amores
(quem modo Ledae pressisse sinum
765   tectum plumis pinnisque ferunt,
modo per fluctus raptam Europen
taurum tergo portasse trucem),
quae regit et nunc deseret astra;
petet amplexus, Poppaea, tuos,
770   quos et Ledae praeferre potest
et tibi, quondam cui miranti
fulvo, Danae, fluxit in auro.
formam Sparte iactet alumnae
licet et Phrygius praemia pastor,
775   vincet vultus haec Tyndaridos,
qui moverunt horrida bella
Phrygiaeque solo regna dedere.
     Sed quis gressu ruit attonito
aut quid portat pectore anhelo?

NUNTIUS

780 Quicumque tectis miles exultat ducis,
defendat aulam, cui furor populi imminet.
trepidi cohortes ecce praefecti trahunt
praesidia ad urbis, victa nec cedit metu
concepta rabies temere, sed vires capit.

---

780 miles exultat *A*: excubat miles *Bothe* (miles excubat *Raphelengius*)

584

OCTAVIA

CHORUS[43]

Is it true what chattering hearsay tells
of the Thunderer's sweet stolen loves?
They say he once clasped Leda's breast
to his own, disguised in feathered plumage,
and another time bore off Europa
through the waves on his back as a grim-faced bull.
Then he will abandon the stars he rules
once more, and seek your embrace, Poppaea,
which he might well prefer to Leda's,
or yours, Danae, to whose amazement
he once flowed down in tawny gold.
Sparta may boast her daughter's beauty,
and the Phrygian shepherd boast of his prize:
one here surpasses the Tyndarid's looks,[44]
that face which launched the horrors of war
and razed the realm of Phrygia to the ground.
        But who rushes here, alarm in his steps?
What news does he bring with labouring breath?

MESSENGER

Those soldiers who are celebrating beneath the emperor's
roof must defend the palace! It is threatened by the people's fury. The Prefects, look, are alarmed and are bringing up cohorts to protect the city. This frenzy, that started
so recklessly, is not caving in to fear, but rather gaining
strength.

---

[43] Here and in 806–819 we have a secondary chorus consisting
of Poppaea's supporters, perhaps her attendants.
[44] The Tyndarid is Spartan Helen, awarded by Venus to the
shepherd Paris.

CHORUS

785 Quis iste mentes agitat attonitus furor?

NUNTIUS

Octaviae favore percussa agmina
et efferata per nefas ingens ruunt.

CHORUS

Quid ausa facere quove consilio doce.

NUNTIUS

Reddere penates Claudiae divi parant
790 torosque fratris, debitam partem imperi.

CHORUS

Quos iam tenet Poppaea concordi fide?

NUNTIUS

Hinc urit animos pertinax nimium favor
et in furorem temere praecipites agit.
quaecumque claro marmore effigies stetit
795 aut aere fulgens, ora Poppaeae gerens,
afflicta vulgi manibus et saevo iacet
eversa ferro; membra per partes trahunt
diducta laqueis, obruunt turpi diu
calcata caeno. verba conveniunt feris
800 immixta factis, quae timor reticet meus.
saepire flammis principis sedem parant,
populi nisi irae coniugem reddat novam,
reddat penates Claudiae victus suos.
ut noscat ipse civium motus mea
805 voce, haud morabor iussa praefecti exequi.

792 hinc *M. Müller*: hic *A*
800 reticet *Delrius*: recipit *A*

OCTAVIA

CHORUS LEADER
What is this insane fury affecting their minds?

MESSENGER
Partisanship for Octavia has stirred the mob up, and made them run wild, committing great outrage.

CHORUS LEADER
What are they making bold to do, what is their aim? Tell us!

MESSENGER
They plan to give Claudia back her deified father's home and marriage with her brother—her rightful share of the throne.

CHORUS LEADER
But now Poppaea holds these things, with pledges given on both sides.

MESSENGER
That is why they are inflamed with an all too stubborn sense of partisanship, and driven pell-mell into mindless rage. Every statue of bright marble or gleaming bronze that carries Poppaea's features lies dashed down by the hands of the rabble, toppled with the merciless steel; they are pulling off the limbs with rope nooses, dragging them away piecemeal, trampling them at length and driving them into the filthy mud. Their wild actions are accompanied and matched by words—which I am afraid to utter. They are preparing to ring the emperor's house with flames, unless he hands over his new wife to the people's anger, admits defeat, and gives Claudia back her own home. He himself is to learn of these civil disturbances from my lips; so I shall carry out the Prefect's orders without delay.

587

CHORUS

Quid fera frustra bella movetis?
invicta gerit tela Cupido.
flammis vestros obruet ignes
quîs extinxit fulmina saepe
810   captumque Iovem caelo traxit.
laeso tristes dabitis poenas
sanguine vestro;
non est patiens fervidus irae
facilisque regi.
ille ferocem iussit Achillem
815   pulsare lyram,
fregit Danaos, fregit Atriden,
regna evertit
Priami, claras diruit urbes.
et nunc animus quid ferat horret
vis immitis violenta dei.

NERO

820 O lenta nimium militis nostri manus
et ira patiens post nefas tantum mea,
quod non cruor civilis accensas faces
extinguit in nos, caede nec populi madet
funerea Roma, quae viros tales tulit!
825 admissa sed iam morte puniri parum est;
graviora meruit impium plebis scelus.
et illa, cui me civium subicit furor,

811 laeso *Bothe*: laesi* A

---

[45] This is apostrophe, i.e. address to people who are not present (in this case the rioters).   [46] Love for Briseis led Achil-

OCTAVIA

CHORUS

Why start a fierce battle to no avail?[45]
Cupid wields invincible weapons!
His flames will overwhelm your fires:
he has often quenched the lightning with them,
and hauled Jove prisoner down from heaven.
For offending him you will pay a grim price
in your own blood;
the ardent god is not slow to anger
or easily ruled.
It was he that commanded fierce Achilles
to strike the lyre,
broke the Danaans, broke Atrides,[46]
overturned Priam's kingdom, and laid
bright cities low.
This time what will stem—I shudder to think—
from the pitiless god's aggressive might?

NERO

Oh, my soldiers' hands are too slow, my own anger too tolerant after such an outrage as this! Witness the fact that the torches the citizens lit against me are not being quenched in their own blood, and that Rome, which bore such men, has not been left desolate and soaked by a massacre of the people. But now death is too slight a penalty for their offences; the rabble's sacrilegious crimes have deserved something weightier. And that woman to whom the citizen's fury would subject me, that wife and sister whom I

les to turn from fighting to music after she was taken from him by Agamemnon. His absence broke the Greeks (Danaans), who could not withstand Hector without him, and broke Agamemnon (Atrides) by forcing him to return Briseis.

suspecta coniunx et soror semper mihi,
tandem dolori spiritum reddat meo
830 iramque nostram sanguine extinguat suo.
mox tecta flammis concidant urbis meis,
ignes ruinae noxium populum premant
turpisque egestas, saeva cum luctu fames.
    Exultat ingens saeculi nostri bonis
835 corrupta turba, nec capit clementiam
ingrata nostram, ferre nec pacem potest,
sed inquieta rapitur hinc audacia,
hinc temeritate fertur in praeceps sua.
malis domanda est et gravi semper iugo
840 premenda, ne quid simile temptare audeat
contraque sanctos coniugis vultus meae
attollere oculos. fracta per poenas metu
parere discet principis nutu sui.
    Sed adesse cerno rara quem pietas virum
845 fidesque castris nota praeposuit meis.

PRAEFECTUS

Populi furorem caede paucorum, diu
qui restiterunt temere, compressum affero.

NERO

Et hoc sat est? sic miles audisti ducem?
compescis? haec vindicta debetur mihi?

PRAEFECTUS

850 Cecidere motus impii ferro duces.

After 848 lacuna postulated by Leo

have always suspected, must finally forfeit her life to my wrath and quench my anger with her blood. Next the city's buildings must fall to flames set by me.[47] Fire, ruined homes, sordid poverty, cruel starvation along with grief must crush this criminal populace.

The masses have grown unruly, spoiled by the blessings of my reign. They cannot appreciate my policy of mercy or feel grateful or endure peace. No, they are seized with a restless daring, and in addition carried to extremes by their own recklessness. They must be tamed by hardships and crushed continuously with a heavy yoke, so they will not dare to try anything similar or to raise their eyes to meet my wife's exalted gaze. Broken by fear through suffering, they will learn to obey when their emperor nods his head.

But here I see the man whose rare duty and signal loyalty have set him in command of my garrison.

PREFECT
I come to report that by killing a few who recklessly made a stand we have controlled the rage of the people.

NERO
And is this sufficient? Is this your soldierly duty to your commander? You *restrain* them? Is this the vengeance I am owed?

PREFECT
The leaders of this sacrilegious revolt *have* fallen to the sword.

---

[47] The author alludes to the Great Fire of A.D. 64, which Nero was widely thought to have set.

NERO

Quid illa turba, petere quae flammis meos
ausa est penates, principi legem dare,
abstrahere nostris coniugem caram toris,
violare quantum licuit incesta manu
855 et voce dira? debita poena vacat?

PRAEFECTUS

Poenam dolor constituet in cives tuos?

NERO

Constituet, aetas nulla quam famae eximat.

PRAEFECTUS

Tua temperetur ira, non noster timor.

NERO

Iram expiabit prima quae meruit meam.

PRAEFECTUS

860 Quam poscat ede, nostra ne parcat manus.

NERO

Caedem sororis poscit et dirum caput.

PRAEFECTUS

Horrore vinctum trepidus astrinxit rigor.

NERO

Parere dubitas?

PRAEFECTUS
Cur meam damnas fidem?

858 tua *Bücheler*: qua *A*   temperetur *Fitch*: temperet nos *A*

NERO

What of that mob that made bold to attack my house with flames, legislate for their emperor, tear my dear wife from my bed, and outrage anything they could with their filthy hands and hideous cries? Are they without due punishment?

PREFECT

Is your wrath going to decree punishment against your own citizens?

NERO

Punishment whose fame no age will efface.

PREFECT

There should be some moderation of your anger—though not of our fear.

NERO

She who first earned my anger shall expiate it.

PREFECT

Tell me whom it demands: my hand will not spare her.

NERO

It demands the execution of my sister, demands her loathsome head.

PREFECT

I am seized with horror, benumbed with fear.

NERO

You hesitate to obey?

PREFECT

Why do you censure my loyalty?

NERO

Quod parcis hosti.

PRAEFECTUS

Femina hoc nomen capit?

NERO

865   Si scelera cepit.

PRAEFECTUS

Estne qui sontem arguat?

NERO

Populi furor.

PRAEFECTUS

Quis regere dementes valet?

NERO

Qui concitare potuit.

PRAEFECTUS

Haud quemquam reor—

NERO

Mulier, dedit natura cui pronum malo
animum, ad nocendum pectus instruxit dolis.

PRAEFECTUS

870   Sed vim negavit.

NERO

Ut ne inexpugnabilis
esset, sed aegras frangeret vires timor
vel poena; quae iam sera damnatam premet
diu nocentem. tolle consilium ac preces

---

868 mulier *attributed to Nero by* A: *to Prefect by Zwierlein*

NERO

Because you would spare my enemy.

PREFECT

Can a woman take that name?

NERO

Yes, if she has taken on crimes.

PREFECT

Would anyone accuse her of guilt?

NERO

The people's frenzy does.

PREFECT

Who can govern their madness?

NERO

The one who could incite it.

PREFECT

I do not think anyone could—

NERO

A *woman* could! Nature has given her a spirit prone to evil, and furnished her heart with trickery for use in wrong-doing.

PREFECT

But denied her strength.

NERO

Yes, so she should not be invincible, since her feeble strength would be broken by fear or punishment. And punishment, now overdue, shall crush this condemned criminal of long standing. No more advice or appeals!

et imperata perage: devectam rate
875 procul in remotum litus interimi iube,
tandem ut residat pectoris nostri tumor.

CHORUS

O funestus multis populi
dirusque favor!
qui cum flatu vela secundo
ratis implevit vexitque procul,
880 languidus idem
deserit alto saevoque mari.
flevit Gracchos miseranda parens,
perdidit ingens quos plebis amor
nimiusque favor,
genere illustres,
885 pietate fide lingua claros,
pectore fortes, legibus acres.
te quoque, Livi,
simili leto Fortuna dedit,
quem neque fasces texere sui
nec tecta domus.
890 plura referre
prohibet praesens exempla dolor.
modo cui patriam reddere cives
aulam et fratris voluere toros,
nunc ad poenam letumque trahi

889 sui *A*: suae *(sc.* domus) *Wilamowitz*

---

48 Tiberius and Gaius Gracchus and Livius Drusus each used
the office of tribune of the people (133, 123–122, 91 B.C. respec-

Carry out your orders. Have her transported by ship to
some distant remote shore, and killed, so that the ferment
of anger in my heart can finally subside.

CHORUS

How dire and deadly
the people's backing proves to many!
It fills the sails of your ship with favouring
winds and carries you far from land,
then fades away
and leaves you on the deep and dangerous sea.
A weeping mother mourned the Gracchi—
destroyed by the people's fervent love
and immoderate backing,
though nobly born,
famed for loyalty, eloquence, duty,
courageous of heart, forceful in the laws.
You too, Livius,
were assigned a similar death by Fortune;
behind your fasces, under your own roof
you were not secure.[48]
More instances
could be told, but the present grief forbids.
Just now the citizens planned to restore her
to her father's palace, her brother's bed,
but now they can watch her dragged away

tively) to introduce reforms which would *inter alia* ameliorate the
condition of the common people in Rome and Italy. Each man
quickly lost influence and met a violent death. Cornelia, mother of
the Gracchi, was an exemplar both of bereavement and of cultured nobility.

895   flentem miseram cernere possunt.
bene paupertas
humili tecto contenta latet;
quatiunt altas saepe procellae
aut evertit Fortuna domos.

OCTAVIA

Quo me trahitis, quodve tyrannus
900   aut exilium regina iubet—
si mihi vitam fracta remittit,
tot iam nostris evicta malis?
sin caede mea
cumulare parat luctus nostros,
invidet etiam
905   cur in patria mihi saeva mori?
—sed iam spes est nulla salutis:
fratris cerno miseranda ratem.
hac est cuius vecta carina
quondam genetrix;
nunc et thalamis expulsa soror
910   miseranda vehar.
nullum Pietas nunc numen habet,
nec sunt superi;
regnat mundo tristis Erinys.

    Quis mea digne deflere potest
915   mala? quae lacrimis nostris questus
reddere aedon?
cuius pinnas
utinam miserae mihi fata darent!
fugerem luctus ablata meos

895 possunt Σ: possit *A*: possis *recc.*

598

in tears and sorrow to suffering and death.
How wise to live simply,
content and hidden in a lowly home!
Towering houses are often shaken
by storms or overturned by Fortune.

Where do you drag me? What place of exile
is decreed by the tyrant or his queen?—
assuming she grants me my life, won over
and softened at last by my many sorrows.
But if she plans to crown my ordeals
with murder, why does she cruelly grudge me
even to die in my native land?
But now I see my brother's boat:
piteous, no hope of safety left!
This is the vessel on which his mother
was passenger once;
now its piteous passenger will be his sister,
the wife he divorced.
There is no god of Righteousness now,
no gods exist;
the grim Erinys rules the world.
    Who could make a fitting lament
for my troubles? What plaintive nightingale
could express my sorrows?
I sadly wish
that fate had granted me her wings!
With swift wings I could get away

---

908 hac *A*: haec *recc*.

pinna volucri
procul et coetus hominum tristes
920   caedemque feram.
sola in vacuo
nemore et tenui ramo pendens
querulo possem gutture maestum
fundere murmur.

CHORUS

Regitur fatis mortale genus,
925   nec sibi quisquam spondere potest
firmum et stabile⟨m vitae cursum⟩,
per quem casus volvit varios
semper nobis metuenda dies.
    Animum firment exempla tuum,
930   iam multa domus quae vestra tulit.
quid saevior est Fortuna tibi?
tu mihi primum
tot natorum memoranda parens,
nata Agrippae,
nurus Augusti, Caesaris uxor,
935   cuius nomen clarum toto
fulsit in orbe—
utero totiens enixa gravi
pignora pacis,
mox exilium,

925 quisquam *A*: quicquam *recc*.
926 *lacuna recognised by Peiper; supplement by Richter*
927 per quem *A*: quem per *Herington*

49 Agrippina "the elder," who married Germanicus Caesar,

to escape my griefs,
far from the dismal haunts of men
and bestial slaughter.
Alone in the empty
woods, and perched on a slender bough,
I could utter a stream of plaintive notes,
my song of sorrow.

CHORUS

Mortal folk are ruled by fate.
No one can guarantee himself
a sure and stable ‹course of life›:
along its path the passing days,
each perilous to us, throw varied chances.

Strengthen your heart with past examples,
of which your house has borne many now;
was Fortune crueller at all to them?
You are the first
I must mention, mother of so many children,
daughter of Agrippa,
Augustus' daughter-in-law, wife of a Caesar,[49]
you whose name shone bright throughout the world,
whose teeming womb so often bore
pledges of peace,
but who then suffered
exile, lashes, cruel chains,

adoptive son of the emperor Tiberius (here given his title Augustus), and bore him nine children including the future emperor Gaius (Caligula) and the Agrippina (the younger) of this play. At odds with Tiberius after her husband's death, she was exiled to the island of Pandataria (like Octavia after her), and died there of starvation.

verbera, saevas passa catenas,
funera, luctus,
940   tandem letum cruciata diu.
felix thalamis Livia Drusi
natisque ferum ruit in facinus
poenamque suam.
Iulia matris fata secuta est:
945   post longa tamen tempora ferro
caesa est, quamvis crimine nullo.
quid non potuit quondam genetrix
tua quae rexit principis aulam
cara marito partuque potens?
950   eadem famulo subiecta suo
cecidit diri militis ense.
quid cui licuit regnum et caelum
sperare, parens tanta Neronis?
non funesta violata manu
955   remigis ante,
mox et ferro lacerata diu
saevi iacuit victima nati?

OCTAVIA

Me quoque tristes mittet ad umbras
ferus et manes ecce tyrannus.
960   quid iam frustra miseranda moror?
rapite ad letum

952 et *Watt*: in *A*
958 mittet *A*: mittit *recc*.

---

50 Livia Julia, often called Livilla, married Tiberius' son
Drusus and had children by him. She became the mistress of
Sejanus, Tiberius' scheming Praetorian Prefect, and on his fall in

grief, bereavement,
and death at the last, after long torment.
Livia, blessed in marriage to Drusus
and in children, rushed into callous crime
and the punishment due.[50]
Julia[51] followed her mother's fate:
though many years later, she was put
to the sword, despite being charged with nothing.
What power was in your mother's hands
earlier, when she ruled the emperor's court
through her husband's affection and her status as a
    mother!
Yet even she became subject to her slave[52]
and fell to a brutal soldier's sword.
What of her who could once aspire to the throne
and heaven,[53] Nero's exalted mother?
Did she not suffer outrage at the murderous hands
of sailors first,
then a lengthy mangling by the sword,
dying as a sacrifice to her savage son?

OCTAVIA

I too shall be sent, as you see, to join
the gloomy shades by this cruel tyrant.
Why make pitiful, pointless delays?
[*To soldiers*] Haul me to my death,

A.D. 31 was executed on a charge of having poisoned Drusus eight
years earlier.   [51] Daughter of Livilla and Drusus, executed
in the reign of Claudius.

[52] The ex-slave Narcissus, who ordered Messalina's execution.

[53] I.e. official deification after death, such as had been granted
previously to Augustus' wife Livia.

quîs ius in nos Fortuna dedit.
testor superos—quid agis, demens?
parce precari
quîs invisa es numina divum.
Tartara testor
965   Erebique deas scelerum ultrices
et te, genitor,
dignum tali morte et poena
‹esse tyrannum qui me extinxit.›

      *   *   *   *   *

non invisa est mors ista mihi.
Armate ratem, date vela fretis,
970   ventisque petat puppis rector
Pandatariae litora terrae.

CHORUS

Lenes aurae zephyrique leves,
tectam quondam nube aetheria
qui vexistis raptam saevae
975   virginis aris Iphigeniam,
hanc quoque tristi procul a poena
portate, precor, templa ad Triviae.
urbe est nostra mitior Aulis

After 967 *lacuna of at least two lines recognised, and partial supplement supplied, by Fitch*
971 Pandatariae *Lipsius*: tandem Phariae* *A*

since Fortune has given me into your power.
Witness, heaven—what madness is that?
Spare your prayers
to those divinities that hate you.
Witness Tartarus
and goddesses of Erebus, avengers of crimes,[54]
and you, father,
that suffering and death like mine
are deserved ‹by the tyrant who has quenched my
    life›.[55]

   * * * * *

death on these terms is not hateful to me.
[*To sailors*] Rig your boat, set sail on the seas,
and let the helmsman steer with the winds
for the shores of Pandataria.

CHORUS

Gentle breezes and light zephyrs:
once you wafted a girl rescued
from the altar of the cruel virgin,[56] cloaked
in heaven-sent cloud, Iphigenia.
Bear this one too, we pray you, far
from bitter suffering to Trivia's temple.
Compared with our city, Aulis is kinder

[54] The Furies.
[55] The gist of the following line(s) may have been, "As long as Nero will receive due punishment . . . "
[56] Diana, to whom Iphigenia was about to be sacrificed when (in this version) she was miraculously removed and conveyed to Diana's (=Trivia's) temple in the Taurian land.

et Taurorum barbara tellus:
980   hospitis illic caede litatur
numen superum;
civis gaudet Roma cruore.

and the barbaric land of the Tauri:
there they appease the gods of heaven
by slaying strangers;[57]
Rome revels in her citizens' blood.

[57] "There" refers to the Taurian land, where strangers were
sacrificed (see Euripides' *Iphigenia among the Taurians*); Aulis is
"kinder" because Iphigenia was replaced as sacrificial victim by a
deer.

INDEX

References are to the line numbers of the plays (for abbreviations of titles see page viii); only the first line of each passage is cited. Passages of special importance to the subject are starred (*). An arrow (→) following a name indicates that references are given under that name. Names of individual dramatis personae *are distinguished by small capitals. Parenthetic "cj" denotes a reference based on textual conjecture.*

Absyrtus, brother of Medea→ killed by her.

Abydos, town on Hellespont, *Phoen* 611.

Acastus, king of Thessaly. Seeks to punish Jason and Medea for death of his father Pelias, *Med* 257, 415, 521, 526.

Achaean = Peloponnesian, *Thy* 122; approximately = Greek, *Tro* 853, 1119, *Med* 227. See also Greek.

Acharnian, inhabitant of Acharnae, deme north of Athens, *Pha* 21.

Acheloüs, river of Aetolia, *HO* 586. Its god defeated by Hercules in fight over Deianira, 299, *495.

Acheron, river of underworld, *Herc* *714, *Ag* 606, *HO* 1951; = underworld, *Pha* 98, 1200,

Oed 578, *Thy* 17, 1016, *Oct* 338.

Achilles, son of Peleus and Thetis. Taught by Chiron, *Tro* *832. Disguised as a girl on Scyros, 213, 569; there seduced Deidamia, fathering Pyrrhus, 342. Conquests en route to Troy, *215. Slew Memnon and Penthesilea, 239, and Cycnus, 183, and Troilus, *Ag* 748; deprived of Briseis, *Tro* 305, *Ag* 186, he almost attacked Agamemnon, 208, and withdrew from fighting, *Tro* 194, *318, *Oct* 814. Loved Patroclus and avenged him, *Ag* 617; slew Hector and dragged his body around the walls, *Tro* 188, 235, 238, 413; returned his body for gold, 664. Killed by

609

611

INDEX

Althaea, mother of Meleager. When he killed her brothers in a quarrel, she avenged them by burning the brand on which his life depended, *Med* 644, 780, *HO* 954.

Amazons, unwed female warriors near Black Sea, *Med* 214, *Pha* 399, *Ag* 736, *HO* 1185. Conquered by Bacchus, *Oed* 479. See also Antiope, Hippolyte, Penthesilea; Maeotis, Tanais, Thermodon.

Amphion, son of Jupiter, brother of Zethus. Built Thebes' walls by moving stones with his music, *Herc* 262, *Phoen* *566, *Oed* 178, 612.

AMPHITRYON (*Herc*), Theban prince, husband of Alcmene and so quasi-father to Hercules, *Herc* passim, *HO* 1248, 1781. Encourages Megara and defies Lycus, *Herc* 275; welcomes Hercules' return but witnesses his killing of his family, 618, 918; urges him not to commit suicide, 1186. Died before Hercules, *HO* 1778.

Amyclae, town near Sparta, *Tro* 70.

Ancaeus, Arcadian, killed by Calydonian boar, *Med* 643.

ANDROMACHE (*Tro*), wife of Hector, mother of Astyanax. Attempts to hide her son

from Ulysses, *Tro* 430; confronts Helen, 888; assigned by lot, 59, to Pyrrhus, 976.

Antaeus, Libyan giant killed by Hercules, *Herc* 482, 1171, *HO* 24, 1788, 1899.

Antenor, leading Trojan, husband of Theano, *Tro* 60.

ANTIGONE (*Phoen*), daughter of Oedipus, 1, 536, 551.

Antiope, Amazon wife of Theseus. Mother of Hippolytus, *Pha* 232, 398, 575, 658, 928; killed by Theseus, 226, 927, 1167.

Antony, Roman general, *Oct* 519 and fn.

Aönian = Boeotian, *Med* 80.

Aphidnae, territory in northern Attica, *Pha* 24.

Apollo, see Phoebus.

Aquarius, zodiacal sign, *Thy* 864 fn.

Aquilo, the north wind, *Med* 634, *Ag* 479, *HO* 778. More usually called Boreas→.

Arabs. Their wealth from spices, *Herc* 910, *Pha* 67, *Oed* 117, *Ag* 807, *HO* 793; use poisoned arrows, *Med* 711.

Araxes, mod. Aras, cold river in Armenia, *Med* 373, *Pha* 58, *Oed* 428.

Arcadia, region of central Peloponnese. Home of Callisto (see Bears); of Auge, *HO* 367; of the Erymanthian boar→ and of the hind with golden horns pursued and

ferring to Pentheus' killers *Herc* 134, *Oed* 617.

Bacchus, divine son of Jupiter and Semele. His deeds and attributes hymned *Oed* 402. Born prematurely when Semele was consumed by lightning, *Herc* 457, *Med* 84, *Oed* 502, *HO* 1804; disguised to escape Juno's jealousy, *Oed* *418; kidnapped by pirates whom he then transformed, *Oed* *449. His victorious progress through the East, *Herc* 903, *Pha* 753, *Oed* *114, 424, *HO* 95, including Lydia, *Phoen* 602, *Oed* 467; demonstrated his power among northern peoples, *Oed* *471, including Amazons, *Oed* 479; punished Lycurgus→ and Pentheus→ for resisting him; won recognition in Argos, *Oed* 486. Helped Jupiter against Giants, *Herc* 458. Father of Hymen, *Med* 110. Found Ariadne abandoned, *Oed* *488, cf. *Pha* 760 fn.; made her his divine bride, *Oed* 497; won a place in heaven, *Herc* 16, 66, *HO* 94, *Oct* 209.

God of wine, *Oed* 157, *Thy* 687, and synonymous with wine, *Herc* 697, *Pha* 445, *Oed* 324, 566, *Ag* 886, *Thy* 65, 467, 701, 900, 915, 973, 983, 987. Inspires maenads *Tro* 673, *Med* 383, *Oed* 439, *Ag*

244, *HO* 243. Effeminate style, *Herc* 472, *Oed* 412. Favours Phocis, *Oed* 279, and Tmolus, *Phoen* 602; his groves, *Herc* 1286. Biennial festival, *HO* 594. Also called Bromius, Iacchus, Liber, Lyaeus, Nyctelian→ (all).

Baetis, river in province of Baetica in Spain, *Med* 726.

Bassarid, Thracian term for Maenad→, *Oed* 432.

Bears, Great and Lesser, northern constellations. Never set in Ocean, *Med* 405, *Oed* 507, *Thy* 477, *HO* 281, 1584, except by magic, *Med* 758; Greeks steer by Great Bear, Phoenicians by Lesser, *Herc* 7, *Med* 697; associated with cold of North Pole, *Herc* 129, 1139, *Pha* 288, *HO* 40, 1523; separated by Snake, *Thy* 869. Great Bear has 7 stars, *Herc* 130, *Tro* 439; is catasterised form of Callisto→, *Herc* 6, hence "Arcadian" *Pha* 288, *Oed* 477. See also Cynosura, Wain.

Bear-Ward (Arctophylax), constellation (= Bootes), *Thy* 874.

Beliad, "granddaughter of Belus" = Danaid→, *HO* 960.

Bellona, Roman goddess of war, *Ag* 82, *HO* 1312.

Bessa, town in east-central Greece, *Tro* 848.

Bistonia = Thrace→, *HO* 1042,

615

INDEX

Calliope, Muse, mother of Orpheus, *Med* 625, *HO* 1034.

Callisto, Arcadian nymph loved by Jupiter, transformed into Ursa Major (see Bears), *Herc* 6.

Calpe, mod. Gibraltar, one of two mountains separated by Hercules to create an entrance to the Mediterranean, *Herc* *237, *HO* 1240, 1253, 1569.

Calydnae, group of islands in the Aegean, *Tro* 839.

Calydon, town in Aetolia. Home of Deianira's attendants, *HO* 582, and vicinity of boar killed by Meleager, *Tro* 845.

Cancer, see Crab.

Caphereus, cape at southeast end of Euboea, *HO* 776, 804. Here Nauplius lured the Greek fleet to destruction, *Ag* *560.

Capricorn, see Goat's Horn.

Carthage, city of North Africa, *Pha* 348.

Carystos, town on south coast of Euboea, *Tro* 836.

Caspian Sea, *Tro* 1105; Caspian used of nearby Caucasus mountains, *Herc* 1206, *Thy* 374, and beasts, *HO* 145.

CASSANDRA (*Ag*), daughter of Priam and Hecuba. Prophet of Phoebus, *Tro* 978, *Ag* 255, 710, 722, who however caused her warnings of Troy's fall not to be believed, *Tro*

34, *Ag* 725. Allotted as slave, *Tro* 61, to Agamemnon, 968, 977. Seen as future rival to Clytemnestra, *Ag* 188, 194, 253; reaches Argos with other Trojan women, 586; "sees" Agamemnon's murder, 720, 867; takes sanctuary, 951; her death ordered by Clytemnestra, 1001.

Castalia, sacred spring near Delphic Oracle, *Oed* 229, 276, 712.

Castor and Pollux, twin sons of Jupiter and Leda, wife of Tyndareus. Hence Spartans, *Phoen* 128, *Thy* 627, and Tyndarids→. Castor a horseman, *Pha* 810, Pollux a boxer, *Med* 88. Sailed on *Argo*, *Med* 230. Catasterised as Gemini: see Twins.

Caucasus mountains, *Pha* 1135, *HO* 1451, 1730. Wild, *Med* 43, *Thy* 1048; place of Prometheus' punishment, *Herc* 1209, *Med* 709, *HO* 1378. See also Caspian.

Caÿcus, river in Mysia, *Tro* 228.

Cecropian = Athenian or Attic, from Cecrops the first king, *Med* 76, *Pha* 2, *Thy* 1049.

Cenaean, title of Jupiter in reference to his temple on Cenaeum, a promontory of Euboea, *HO* 102, 783.

Centaurs, half human, half horse. Mountain-dwellers in northern Greece, *Herc* 969,

617

Danaë, mother of Perseus by
Jupiter, who came to her in a
shower of gold, *Oct* 207, 772.
Danaïds, 50 daughters of
Danaus, forcibly married to
50 sons of Aegyptus; all save
one (Hypermnestra) slew
their husbands on their wed-
ding night, and are punished
in underworld, *Herc* 498,
757, *Med* 748, *HO* 948, 960.
See also Beliad.
Danube river, *Med* 724, *Thy*
376; also called Hister→.
Dardanus, ancestor of Trojan
royal family, *Tro* 871, *Ag* 223,
774, 863, *HO* 363, 1649 (cj.);
Dardan = Trojan, *Tro* 27,
135, *Ag* 358, 612; = Asiatic,
Herc 1165.
Daulian refers to Procne and
Philomela (sometimes associated with Daulis in Phocis),
Thy 275, *HO* 192.
Dawn, see Aurora, Eos.
Dawn Star, see Lucifer.
Death personified *Herc* 56, 555,
872, 1069, *Tro* 1171, *Med*
742, *Pha* 1188, *Oed* 126, 164,
652, *HO* 766, 1116, 1373,
1553.
Deianira (*HO*), an Aetolian,
daughter of Oeneus, 319,
581, 583, and of Althaea, 954;
sister of Meleager, 388.
Famed as wife of Hercules,
397; mother of Hyllus.
Achelous and Hercules
fought over her, 495. The epi-

sode of Nessus, 500, who
gave her an alleged love
charm, 523. Jealous of Iole,
237, she uses it, 535; her suspicion of its deadly effect,
706, is confirmed, 742; she
kills herself, 1024, 1456.
Deïdamia, see Achilles.
Deïphobus, son of Priam.
Married Helen in last year of
war; betrayed by her and mutilated by Menelaus in revenge, *Ag* 749.
Delia = Diana (born on Delos)
= moon, *HO* 150.
Delos, Aegean island, birthplace of Apollo and Diana,
Herc 451, *HO* 150; previously
floating, but fixed after their
birth, *Herc* 14, 453, *Ag* *369.
Delphi, site of Apollo's oracle,
which foretold Oedipus' fate,
Phoen 259, *Oed* 16, 800, and
Hercules', *HO* 1474. Laius
was travelling there when
killed, *Oed* 276. Consulted by
Oedipus through Creon
about the plague, *Oed* 214,
*223. See also Phoebus.
Deucalion, see Pyrrha.
Diana, goddess of hunt, *Pha* 72.
See Phoebe.
Dictaean = Cretan (from Mt
Dicte), *Ag* 833.
Dictynna, Cretan goddess iden-
tified with Phoebe qua moon,
Med 795.
Diomedes (1), Thracian king.
Fed his horses human flesh,

INDEX

Elean, adjective of Elis→.

ELECTRA (*Ag*), daughter of Agamemnon and Clytemnestra, 195. Sends her brother Orestes into safekeeping after their father's murder, 924; defies the murderers, 953. Her situation compared to Octavia's, *Oct* 59.

Eleusis, town near Athens, and its Eleusinian Mysteries, *Herc* 302, *842, *Tro* 843, *Pha* 106, 838, *HO* 598.

Elis, town and region in western Peloponnese, *Phoen* 129; refers to Olympic Games, *Herc* 840, *Tro* 849, *Ag* 918.

Elysium, setting of blessed afterlife for favoured spirits, *Herc* 744, *Tro* 158, 944, *HO* 956, 1917.

Enceladus, a Giant. Capable of uprooting mountains, as in the Giants' assault on Olympus; now buried beneath Mt Etna. *HO* 1140, 1145, 1159, 1735.

Endymion, herdsman loved by Diana, *Pha* 309, 422.

Enispe, town in Arcadia called "windy" by Homer, *Tro* 841.

Eös, the dawn, *HO* 614, 1866; see also Aurora.

Epidaurus, town in northeast Peloponnese, *Pha* 1022.

Erasinus, river south of Argos, *Ag* 316.

Erebus, the Underworld→, *Herc* 54, 1224, *Tro* 179, *Oed* 160, 394, 410, 521, *HO* 1065, 1311, 1369, 1681, *Oct* 965.

Eridanus, river in north Italy (mod. Po) where Phaethon fell, *HO* 186.

Erinys = Fury, infernal spirit of vengeance, discord, madness, *Herc* 982, *Med* 953, *Oed* 590, 644, *Ag* 83, *Thy* 251, *HO* 609, 671, *Oct* 23, 161, 263, 619, 913.

Erymanthus, mountain in Arcadia. Home of wild boar killed by Hercules, *Herc* 228, *Ag* 832, *HO* 17, 980, 1536, 1814, 1888.

Eryx (1), mountain in Sicily, *Med* 707, *Oed* 600, sacred to Venus, *Pha* 199.

Eryx (2) challenged strangers to deadly boxing matches; worsted by Hercules, *Herc* 482.

ETEÖCLES (*Phoen*), son of Oedipus and Jocasta. He and his brother Polynices agreed to rule alternately, but Eteocles would not give up the throne, causing Polynices to raise an army against him, *Herc* 389, *Phoen* 56, 280, 483, 651. The brothers' enmity fated, *Phoen* 277, 338, *Oed* 237, 360, 646, 750.

Etesians, northerly summer winds, *Thy* 129.

Etna, fiery volcano in Sicily, *Herc* 106, *Phoen* 314, *Pha* 102, *HO* 285, 1361. It contains Vulcan's forges, *Pha*

623

190, worked by the Cyclopes, *Thy* 582, where Jove's bolts are forged, *Pha* 156, *HO* 542; beneath it is buried a Giant or Titan(s), *Herc* 80, *Med* 409, *HO* 1157, 1308.

Euboea, large island off east coast of Greece, *Herc* 378, *HO* 103, *775, 839. See also Caphereus, Cenaean, Chalcis, Euripus.

Eumenides = Furies, *Herc* 87, 577, *HO* 1002.

Euripus, fast-flowing strait between Euboea and mainland Greece, *Herc* 378, *Tro* 838, *HO* 103, *779.

Europa, daughter of Agenor king of Tyre. Abducted by Jupiter in form of a bull, *Pha* *303, *HO* 551, *Oct* 206, 766, later catasterised as Taurus, *Herc* 9. Cadmus' fruitless search for her, *Oed* 716.

Europe, used expansively for Greece in contrast to Asiatic Troy, *Tro* 896, *Ag* 205, 274.

Eurotas, river on which Sparta stands, *Phoen* 127, *Ag* 281, 317.

Eurus, the east wind, *Pha* 1129, *Ag* 476, 482, *Thy* 360, *HO* 114, 729.

EURYBATES (*Ag*), herald. Announces Agamemnon's imminent arrival in Argos, 391, and the wreck of the Greek fleet, 406.

Eurydice, wife of Orpheus. His unsuccessful rescue of her from the underworld, *Herc* *571, *HO* 1083.

Eurystheus, king of Argos, *Herc* 1180, *HO* 1800. By accelerating his birth and delaying Hercules', Juno ensured him the throne and power over Hercules, *Herc* 830, whose labours he prescribes, *Herc* 43, 78, 398, 432, 479, 526, *HO* 59, 403; his punishment prophesied, *HO* 1973.

Eurytus, king of Oechalia, father of Iole, *HO* 1490. Refused her to Hercules, who sacked his town and killed him, *Herc* 477, *HO* 100, *207, 221, 354.

Euxine, the Black Sea, *Ag* 66. See Pontus, Scythian.

Evenus, river of Aetolia, *Oed* 285 (cj.), *HO* 501.

Fate personified, *Pha* 467, *Oed* 125, 1059, *HO* 1198, 1294, 1985, *Oct* 552. For the three Fates, see Parcae.

Favonius, the west wind, *Herc* 550. See also Zephyr.

Fescennine verses, characterised by banter and ribaldry, associated with weddings, *Med* 113.

Fish (Pisces), constellation, *Thy* 866, *HO* 596.

Fortune personified, *Herc* 326, *524, 1272, *Tro* 259, 269, 275, 697, 711, 735, *Phoen* 82,

bles; (6) Stymphalian birds; (7) Cretan bull; (8) Diomedes' horses; (9) Hippolyte's baldric; (10) cattle of Geryon; (11) golden apples of Hesperides; (12) Cerberus.

Cheated by Laomedon, king of Troy, he took the city, with arrows used again later against Troy (see Philoctetes), *Tro* 136, 825, *Ag* 614, 862, and installed young Priam as king, *Tro* *718. In the west he relieved Atlas temporarily of the burden of the heavens, and sundered Mt Calpe to make an entrance to the Mediterranean. He escaped from the Syrtes on foot. In Thessaly he sundered mountains to create the Vale of Tempe. He killed Cycnus son of Mars, Eryx, Periclymenus, Centaurs, and the tyrants Antaeus, Busiris, and Lycus. He freed Prometheus in the Caucasus, and Theseus in the underworld. On the Argonautic expedition he lost Hylas, and killed Zetes and Calais; his eventual violent death resembled other Argonauts', *Med* 637. He wounded Dis at Pylos, and aided Jupiter in battle against the Giants, *Herc* 445, *HO* 1215.

Fetching of Cerberus seen as opening of the underworld, *Herc* 47, 610, 890, *Tro* 723, *Med* 638, *HO* 1553. Deeds on earth seen as a pacification of land and sea, *Herc* 442, 882, *Med* 637, *HO* 3, 283, 794, 1838, 1990. He has no equal, *Herc* 84, *HO* 838, 1848. Extent of his travels, *HO* 744, comparable to the sun's, *Herc* 1057, *HO* 42, 1512, 1531. Renown worldwide, *Herc* 1331, *HO* 38, 315, 414, 1586, 1698, 1799, 1827. Jupiter's proxy on earth, *HO* 750, 850, 1143, 1544; his renown vies with Jupiter's, *HO* 417, 1807, 1881, and reflects credit on Jupiter as father, *HO* 8, 1505. Promised deification, *Herc* 23, 959, *HO* 1910.

Women he desired include Auge, Hesione, Iole, Thespius' daughters. He was a slave of love to Omphale. In Thebes he married Megara; killed her and their sons in a bout of madness; he was purified either in Athens, *Herc* 1341, or in the river Cinyps, *HO* 907. Later he wooed Deianira, defeating his rival Achelous. Travelling with his bride, he shot Nessus, who attempted to abduct her. By her he had a son Hyllus. Refused Iole by her father Eurytus, he killed him and sacked his city Oechalia. Journeyed to Euboea, *HO*

INDEX

Jove, see Jupiter.
Judges of dead, *Herc* 579, *731, *HO* 1007, 1558. See Aeacus, Minos, Rhadamanthus.
Julia, daughter of Livilla and Drusus, *Oct* 944.
JUNO (*Herc*), sister and wife of Jupiter. Her anger over his infidelities, *Herc* 5, *Oct* 202. Her enmity towards his bastard Hercules, *Herc* 30, 214, 447, 456, 479, 606, 615, *HO* 9, 38, 63, 66, 75, 257, 297, 313, 843, 883, 940, 1182, 1186, 1598. Decides to use him against himself, *Herc* 85. Blamed for his madness, 1201, 1297; thought to triumph in his death, *HO* 746, 1675. Outdone as a mother by Alcmene, *HO* 1509; might persecute her, 1792. Eventually reconciled to Hercules, *Oct* 211, cf. *HO* 1437. Hostile to young Bacchus, *Oed* 418; reconciled, 487. Now secure as Jupiter's wife, *Oct* 216. Patron of Argos–Mycenae, *Ag* *341, 805, 809. In Judgment of Paris, *Oct* 546. See Octavia.
Jupiter or Jove, king of gods, brother and spouse of Juno. Ruler of Olympus/heaven, *Herc* 597, *Pha* 960, *Oed* 249. His infancy on Crete, *Herc* 459, *HO* 1875; alleged death there, *HO* 1880. Sacrifices etc. to him, *Herc* 923, *Tro* 140, *Ag* 802, *Thy* 463; prayers

etc., *Herc* 927, *Ag* 793, *HO* 87, 1671, 1692. Controls thunder and lightning, *Herc* 517, 598, 932, 1202, *Phoen* 59, *Med* 531, *Pha* 155, 673, 1134, *Oed* 501, 1029, *Ag* 382, 528, 802, *Thy* 290, 1080, *HO* 2, 324, 551, 847, 881, 1384, *Oct* 228, 245 hence called Thunderer→; his thunderbolts forged on Etna→. Stands for upper world, *HO* 1369. Dethroned Saturn→; fought Giants→ and their allies. Chief deity of Olympic Games, *Tro* 849, *Ag* 938.

Unfaithful to Juno, *Herc* *2; henpecked by her, *Herc* 1019. Susceptible to passion, *Pha* 187, *HO* 551, 558, *Oct* *203, 218, *763, 810. His amours (references under individual names) included Callisto, Europa, and three of Atlas' daughters (Pleiades); he fathered Apollo and Diana on Latona; Hercules on Alcmene in a double night; Bacchus on Semele; Perseus on Danae; Castor, Pollux, and Helen on Leda. Father of Pallas by no mother. Father of Amphion and Zethus; also of Minos, hence grandfather of Phaedra, *Pha* 129, 158; progenitor of Argive dynasty as father of Tantalus, *Ag* 385; ancestor of Achilles, *Tro* 346. Titles include Cenaean,

Son of Cn. Domitius, 249,
641, and Agrippina (2).
Adopted by Claudius, 139,
150, 249; married to Octavia,
156. Murdered Britannicus→
and Agrippina→. His mistress
first Acte, 105, 194, 657, then
Poppaea→. Orders execution
of exiles, 437; divorces Octavia and marries Poppaea, 530,
671, 703. Enraged at popular
support for Octavia, 820, orders her death, 861, 875. His
death prophesied, 620, 733.

Nessus, centaur, offspring of
Ixion and Nephele, *HO* 492.
Attempts to abduct Deianira,
HO *503; shot by Hercules,
516, 921. Dying, he gives his
blood mingled with hydra
venom to Deianira, allegedly
as a love charm, 520, but actually for revenge, 966, 1468;
its effect toxic, *716, *Med*
775, and fatal, *Med* 641, *HO*
1476.

Nestor, king of Pylos, *Herc* 561;
proverbial for old age, *Tro*
848.

Night personified, *Thy* 1071.

Nile river, *Herc* 1323, *Oed* 606,
Oct 519.

Niobe, daughter of Tantalus;
wife of Amphion of Thebes,
Herc 390, *Oed* 613. With 7
sons and 7 daughters, *Med*
954, boasted of outdoing
Latona; punished by Diana
and Apollo, who killed all her

children, *Ag* 375; changed to
weeping rock, *Herc* 390, *Ag*
376, *HO* 185, 1849; her shade
still arrogant, *Oed* 613.

Nomia, mountain in western
Arcadia, *HO* 1885 (cj.).

Notus, the south wind, *Herc*
550, 1090, *Med* 323, *Pha*
1129, *Ag* 90, 476, [481], *HO*
382, 729.

NURSE (1) of Medea, *Med* 150,
380, 568, 670, 817, 891; (2) of
Phaedra, *Pha* 129, 358, 406,
719, 854; (3) of Deianira, *HO*
233, 884; (4) of Octavia, *Oct*
34; (5) of Poppaea, *Oct* 690.

Nyctelian, epithet of Bacchus,
Oed 492.

Nysa, legendary eastern mountain where Bacchus was born,
Med 384, *Oed* 404.

Ocean, flows around known
world, *Tro* 383, *Med* 376,
755, *Pha* 717, 931, 958, 1029,
1162, *Oed* 504, *Ag* 484, *HO*
49, 743, 1366, *Oct* 37, 40, especially far east and west,
Herc 26, 234, 238, 1141, *HO*
489, 781, 1839.

OCTAVIA (*Oct*), daughter of
Claudius and Messalina, wife
of Nero. Compared to Juno
as sister-wife of a ruler, *Oct*
201, 219, 282, 535. Mourns
her parents, 10, and brother
Britannicus, 67, and her own
loveless marriage. Popular
support for her 183, 276, 572,

639

lifethreads, *Herc* 181, 188, 559, *HO* 1098. See also Clotho, Lachesis.

Parian marble famed for whiteness, *Pha* 797.

Paris, son of Priam and Hecuba, but raised on Ida as shepherd. Judges three goddesses' beauty, *Tro* 66, *Ag* 730, *Oct* 545; abducts Helen, *Tro* 70, 867, 908, *Ag* 188, as his prize from Venus, *Tro* 921. An archer, *Ag* 212, who shoots Achilles fatally, *Tro* 347, 956.

Parnassus, mountain above Delphi, *Phoen* 129, *Oed* 227, 281, *Ag* 721, *HO* 1474.

Parnethus = Parnes, mountain in Attica, *Pha* 4.

Parrhasian = Arcadian, *Ag* 315 (cj.); of Hercules' hind, *Ag* 831; of Great Bear, *Pha* 288, and hence of North Pole, *HO* 1281.

Parthenius, mountain in east Arcadia, *HO* 1885.

Parthians, dominant power east of Euphrates, *Thy* 462, 603, *Oct* 628; archers, *Med* 710, *HO* 161, who fire volleys into air, *Phoen* 428, *Pha* 816, and shoot while feigning retreat, *Oed* 119, *Thy* 384.

Pasiphaë, daughter of Sun; wife of Minos. Mated with bull and bore Minotaur, *Pha* *113, 143, 688. Mother also of Ariadne and Phaedra.

Patroclus, loved by Achilles, *Ag*

616; dressed in his armour to rout Trojans, 617; Hector killed him and took the armour as spoil, *Tro* 447.

Peace as goddess, *Med* 63.

Pegasus, winged horse, *Tro* 385.

Pelasgian = Greek, *Tro* 353, 597, 628, 737, 753, 876, 1007, *Med* 127, 178, 240, 528, 697, 870, *Ag* 632; = Argive *Ag* 9. See also Greek.

Peleus, Thessalian, son of Aeacus. Husband of Thetis, father of Achilles, *Tro* 247, 882, *Ag* 615, *Oct* 707; Argonaut, later exiled from Thessaly, *Med* 657.

Pelias usurped Thessalian throne from Jason's father, and sent Jason on Argonaut expedition, *Med* 664; killed through wiles of Medea→.

Pelion, mountain in Thessaly, home of Chiron; piled up with Ossa and Olympus by Giants to scale heaven, *Herc* 971, *Tro* 415, 829, *Ag* 338, *Thy* 812, *HO* 1152.

Pelopia, daughter of Thyestes, mother by him of Aegisthus, *Ag* 30, 52.

Pelops, son of Tantalus→, butchered by him and resuscitated by gods. Coming from Asia to Greece, defeated Oenomaus in race by bribing his charioteer Myrtilus, *Tro* 855, *Thy* 140, 660. Gave name to Peloponnese, *Med*

attack his food, *Herc* 759,
Phoen 425, *Thy* 154.

Phlegethon, "burning" river of
underworld, *Pha* 1180, 1227,
Thy 73, 1018; = underworld,
Pha 848, *Oed* 162, *Ag* 753.

Phlegra, site of Giants' battle
with gods in Thrace, *Herc*
444, *Thy* 811.

Phocis, region of central
Greece, *Herc* 334, *Oed* 279,
772, *Ag* 918.

Phoebe, daughter of Latona,
twin sister of Phoebus, *Herc*
136, 905, *Med* 86, *Pha* 311,
Oed 44, *Ag* 321, 381. She
commanded their birthplace,
Delos→, to cease moving, *Ag*
*369. Identified with moon,
Herc 136, *Pha* 410, *Oed* 44,
Thy 838, *HO* 150; called
Phoebe (shining one) particularly qua moon, *Med* 97, *Pha*
747, *Oed* 253, *Ag* 818, *HO*
1884, *Oct* 389. Goddess of
wilderness, *Pha* 55, 406;
Hippolytus' patron in hunt-
ing, 654, invoked to help him,
*54, and soften him, 405; de-
stroyed Actaeon→, *Oed* 762.
Triumphant over Niobe→,
Ag 375. Vulnerable to magic
spells, *Med* 791, *Pha* 421,
790, *HO* 468, 526. Susceptible to handsome youths, *Pha*
*785; loved Endymion, 309,
422, cf. 785. Identical with
Diana, 654; Dictynna, *Med*

795; Hecate, *Med* 770;
Lucina, *Ag* 369; Trivia→.
See also Cynthian, Delia,
Lucina.

Phoebus, "shining," title of
Apollo, especially as Sun god,
Herc 25, 595, 607, 844, 940,
Tro 1140, *Phoen* 87, *Med* 298,
728, [768], 874, *Pha* 889, *Oed*
122, 250, 540, 545, *Ag* 42, 56,
463, 577, 816, *Thy* 602, 838,
HO 2, 41, 337, 666, 680, 688,
727, 792, 1022, 1387, 1439,
1442, 1581, 1624, 1699. Twin
brother of Phoebe→. His two
homes, east and west, *Herc*
1062, *HO* 2. As sun, revealed
amour of Venus, who hates
his offspring, *Pha* 124.
Turned back after Thyestes'
feast, *Ag* 296, 909, *Thy* 121,
776, 789, 822, 1035, 1095, cf.
Med 31, *HO* 1131. Father of
Phaethon→; father of
Pasiphae, so grandfather of
Phaedra→; grandfather of
Medea through Aeetes, *Med*
28, 210, 512, 572. See also
Sun, Titan.

  Gives oracles at Delphi,
Med 86, *Oed* 20, 34, 109,
214, 222, 235, 252, 269, 288,
296, 718, 1046, *Ag* 294. His
cult at Cilla, *Tro* 227; hymned
at Argos, *Pha* *310. His priest
at Thebes: Tiresias, *Oed* 291,
296; at Troy: Chryses, *Ag*
176; his prophet: Cassan -

INDEX

Pluto = Dis→, *Pha* 628, *HO* 935, 1142, 1954.

Poeas, father of Philoctetes, *HO* 1485, 1604, 1649.

Pollux, see Castor.

Polybus, king of Corinth, believed by Oedipus to be his father, *Oed* 12, 81, 272, 662, 785.

POLYNICES (*Phoen*), exiled by brother Eteocles→, 372, 484, 502, 586, 652, 662; married Adrastus' daughter, 374, *505, 595; raised army of allies, the Seven against Thebes, *Herc* 389, *Phoen* 58, 282, 391, 483, 543.

POLYXENA (*Tro*), daughter of Priam and Hecuba. Betrothed to Achilles, *Tro* 195, *Ag* 641; her death demanded by his ghost, *Tro* 195, by Pyrrhus→ and Calchas→; sacrificed, 861, 1118.

Pompey the Great, assassinated on coast of Egypt, *Oct* 522.

Pontus = Black Sea, *Tro* 13, *Med* 44, 212, 231, 454, *Pha* 399, 716, or its hinterland, *HO* 465. See also Euxine.

POPPAEA (*Oct*), mistress of Nero. Pregnant by him, 181, 188, 591; marries him, 592, 693; her foreboding dream, 712. Former husband Crispinus, 729.

PREFECT of Guard (*Oct*), 846.

Priam, king of Troy, husband of Hecuba, *Tro* 134, 270, *718,

[996], 1068, 1103, *Ag* 709, 880, *HO* 363, *Oct* 817. His offspring and their fates, *Tro* 57, 247, 369, 875, 934, 1090, *Ag* 191. Ransomed Hector's body, *Tro* 314, 326, 486, *Ag* 447. His death, *Tro* 29, *44, 139, 309, 312, 572, 1002, 1177, *Ag* 448, 656, 793, 1177; called fortunate, *Tro* 143, 156, *Ag* 514; mourning for him, *Tro* 131, 908, *Ag* 655.

Procne, daughter of Pandion. Wife of Tereus; served him the flesh of their son Itys to avenge Philomela→, *Thy* 56, 273, *HO* 953; transformed into mourning bird, *HO* 200, *Oct* 8, swallow, *Ag* 673, or nightingale, *HO* 192.

Procrustes, Attic bandit, *Pha* 1170, *Thy* 1050.

Proetides, *Oed* 486 and fn.

Prometheus stole fire from heaven, punished by birds feeding on his innards, *Med* 709, 824, *HO* 1378; freed by Hercules, *Herc* 1207.

Proserpine, queen of underworld, *Herc* 549, 805, 1105. Kidnapped in Sicily by Dis, *Med* 12; her mother Ceres searched for her, *Herc* 660; Pirithous→ tried to abduct her.

Proteus, sea god who tends beasts of sea, *Pha* 1205.

Prothoüs, Thessalian ruler, *Tro* 829.

Titans tried to dethrone Jupiter,
were buried under Etna,
Herc 79, 967, *Med* 410, *Ag*
334, *HO* 144, 1212, 1308.

Titaressos, Thessalian stream,
flows under sea back to its
underworld source, *Tro* 847.

Tityos, giant who attempted to
rape Latona. Tormented in
underworld by vulture(s),
Herc 756, 977, *Pha* 1233, *Ag*
18, *Thy* 9, 807, *HO* 947,
1070, *Oct* 622.

Tmolus, viniferous mountain in
Lydia, *Phoen* 602, *HO* 371.

Toxeus, brother of Iole, *HO*
214.

Trachis ("rough"), town in
Thessaly near Mt Oeta, setting of most of *HO*. Hercules'
home at time of his death,
HO 135, 195, 1432, 1444; in
reference to Philoctetes too,
Tro 818.

Tricce, town in Thessaly, *Tro*
821.

Triptolemus, king of Eleusis, in-
troduced cereal crops, *Pha*
838.

Tritons, marine musicians, *Tro*
202.

Triumvirate of 43 B.C., *Oct*
508.

Trivia, goddess of crossroads.
Identified with Phoebe qua
moon, *Med* 787, and on
earth, *Ag* 367, *Oct* 977.

Troezen, town on bay of Saronic
Gulf, *Tro* 828.

Troilus, young Trojan killed by
Achilles, *Ag* 748.

TROJAN WOMEN (*Tro*, *Ag*), captives after Troy's fall. Mourn
Hector and Priam, *Tro* 67;
speculate about death, 371,
and about their destinations
in Greece, 814; anticipate
pain of separation, 1009. One
group, reaching Argos, recalls
events leading to Troy's fall,
Ag 589, and responds to Cassandra, 664. See also Troy.

Troy, Trojans. Walls built by
gods, *Tro* 7, *Ag* 651. Twice attacked by arrows of Hercu-
les→. Its might, *Tro* 6, 875.
The ten-year siege, *Tro* 23,
Ag 42, 206, 249, 615, 624,
866, 921; Troy's human and
divine allies, *Tro* *8, *Ag* 212,
*546; Hector→ its vital de-
fender; Greek and Trojan
dead there, *Tro* 893, *Ag* 514;
blamed on Helen→. Its capture, *Ag* *611, 791, 876, and
destruction, *Tro* *14, 30, 43,
56, 86, 103, 478, 744, 889,
900, 1051, 1068, *Ag* 190, 421,
435, 459, 709, 725, 743, 1011;
Polyxena and Astyanax its
shortlived hope, *Tro* 286, 428,
454, 462, 471, 529, 550, 734,
740–1, 767, 790, 1131. Troy
an exemplar of the fragility of
power, *Tro* 4, 264, *Ag* 794;
mourned, *Tro* 65, 111, *Ag*
649; avenged, *Ag* 577, 870,
1008.